Jewels, Jewelry, and Other Shiny Things in the Buddhist Imaginary

Jewels, Jewelry, and Other Shiny Things in the Buddhist Imaginary

Edited by Vanessa R. Sasson

University of Hawai‘i Press
Honolulu

Paperback edition 2022

Printed in the United States of America

Library of Congress Cataloging-in-Publication Data

Names: Sasson, Vanessa R., editor.
Title: Jewels, jewelry, and other shiny things in the Buddhist imaginary / edited by Vanessa R. Sasson.
Description: Honolulu : University of Hawai'i Press, 2021. | Includes bibliographical references and index.
Identifiers: LCCN 2021030658 | ISBN 9780824887858 (cloth) | ISBN 9780824889524 (pdf) | ISBN 9780824889548 (epub) | ISBN 9780824889531 (kindle edition)
Subjects: LCSH: Gems—Religious aspects—Buddhism. | Buddhist relics.
Classification: LCC BQ4570.G46 J49 2021 | DDC 294.3/437—dc23
LC record available at https://lccn.loc.gov/2021030658

ISBN: 9780824889555 (paperback)

Cover art: Chenrezig from the Royal Bhutan Monastery, Bodhgaya, India. Photo by Vanessa R. Sasson.

University of Hawai'i Press books are printed on acid-free paper and meet the guidelines for permanence and durability of the Council on Library Resources.

"Nothing succeeds like excess. . . ."

Dowager Countess of Grantham, Downton Abbey

(Also Oscar Wilde)

Contents

Jewels, Jewelry, and Other Shiny Things in the Buddhist Imaginary

Chapter 1

Introduction

The Emerald Buddha as a Map

Vanessa R. Sasson

A few years ago, I gave a lecture on the Buddha's hagiography in one of my classes. I showered the students with descriptions of the Bodhisatta's palace life, pools filled with different colored lotus flowers, and mansions many stories high. I told them about the moment, as described in the *Lalitavistara,* when the Bodhisatta climbs up to the roof of one of his mansions to contemplate his Great Departure, only to be met with a host of glittery deities, each one of whom removes their crown to bow at his bejeweled feet.[1] I described the road leading up to the Mahabodhi tree that shimmers with crystals and precious gems and told them about the jeweled walkway the Buddha later conjured in the sky at Śrāvastī. I spent the entire class on Buddhist splendor. I was convinced the students were spellbound, but then a hand shot into the air with determination: "I don't understand how you can be saying all this," the student complained. "I thought Buddhism was supposed to be austere."

It was at that moment that I knew this book needed to come into being.[2] My student's expectation was to be expected. The Buddha's narrative highlights his decision to renounce, but as we shall see in this volume, renunciation is not necessarily austere. Renunciation remains a central feature of the tradition, but renunciation can certainly be met with splendor. Indeed, renunciation very often is.

Introducing a topic as vast as "jewels" has caused me many months of consternation. The more I think about jewels, the more I have come to appreciate how omnipresent they actually are. A review of the literature could, in fact, become a review of the entire tradition because jewels are everywhere. Phyllis Granoff was probably the first to put her finger on this point with her seminal article, "Maitreya's Jewelled World: Some Remarks on Gems and Visions in Buddhist Texts." Although her focus is the *Gaṇḍavyūha,* she opens her article with a similar sentiment to the experience I noted above: despite what we may have come to expect of the tradition, "diamonds and rubies, sapphires and crystal, gold and silver, virtually glitter from the pages of many a Buddhist text."[3] Since her contribution, no overarching study of jewels in the Buddhist tradition has been attempted. Many specialized studies that touch on jewels have emerged but nothing quite like what this book is attempting to offer. An important contribution to note is the recent collection entitled *Soulless Matter, Seats of Energy: Metals, Gems and Minerals in South Asian Traditions.*[4] It offers what is perhaps the most global discussion on the role jewels can play in the religions of South Asia, but it is not exclusively focused on Buddhism. It does, however, bring the theme of "jewels" to the forefront with examples from multiple perspectives.

For the most part, however, "jewels" appears to be too wide a category for any useful review of the literature to attempt to capture. We may, for example, consider the burgeoning field of material culture as the direction this introduction might take, following research by scholars such as Fabio Rambelli and his book, *Buddhist Materiality: A Cultural History of Objects in Japanese Buddhism,* John Kieschnick's *The Impact of Buddhism on Chinese Material Culture,* and James Duncan Gentry's *Power Objects in Tibetan Buddhism: The Life, Writings, and Legacy of Sokdokpa Lodrö Gyeltsen.*[5] Renunciation is undoubtedly one of the key doctrinal principles of the Buddhist tradition, and monastics—*as* monastics—are instructed by the Vinaya to keep very few articles in their possession. But if we leave behind "the world of recondite doctrines and statements of principle and look instead at the way Buddhism has been practiced, we find material goods everywhere."[6] The lived tradition can certainly reflect its principle of non-attachment, but it can also be glamorous, with jewels showering the material culture of the Buddhist world. These jewels are not always dismissed by Buddhist rhetoric but can be used as expressions of merit, of karma accrued and exchanged.

Art history has much to say about visual representations of jewels, particularly when it comes to a variety of crowned and bejeweled Buddha images that appear throughout South and Southeast Asia. Scholars have long debated these representations. (Are they even Buddhas? Or are they Bodhisattvas? Is a crowned Buddha a contradiction in terms, or is it a natural expression of devotion?) This discussion in the academy begins with Alfred Foucher and Paul Mus almost one hundred years ago.[7] Today, scholars, such as Claudine Bautze-Picron, have offered new insights that bring the question of jeweled Buddhas into much clearer focus.[8] This material could also function as an introduction to the theme of this book.

We might look at specific jewels. Wendy Doniger's book *The Ring of Truth: And Other Myths of Sex and Jewelry* explores a variety of myths and stories about South Asian jewels, while Brian Ruppert and Bernard Faure have each examined the role of the Wish-Fulfilling Jewel specifically.[9] There are also famous historical jewels worth considering, such as the fabulous Koh-i-Noor that was "gifted" by a young Mahārāja to the Queen of England under suspicious circumstances.[10] Although not a Buddhist story, it is difficult to resist the drama this Indian jewel has generated.[11] Scholars of Buddhism might have been slow to recognize the glittery materiality of the Buddhist tradition, but looters and conquerors have never been so blind.

All of these trajectories (along with many others) could serve as introductions to this book, but none of them alone would do the subject justice. I have therefore chosen to do something different. Instead of attempting to artificially gather all the jewels into one basket and identify a constructed history, I will follow one jewel in particular and allow it to outline some of the themes on which this volume touches. One of the most famous jewels in the Buddhist world is the Emerald Buddha, which currently resides in the Thai Grand Palace in Wat Phra Si Rattana Satsadaram.[12] The story of this Buddhist jewel embodies every theme that arises in this volume (and then some). This introduction will use the Emerald Buddha as a map, following its story as a way of engaging with the material this book hopes to explore.

The Emerald Buddha Story

The story of the Emerald Buddha begins, in many accounts, with Nāgasena, who is best known for his role in the *Milindapañha,* where he calmly catches a king's curiosities and shapes them into brilliant dialogue. One question after another is launched at the venerable being, but Nāgasena does not flinch. Whether he is addressing the theoretical complexities of rebirth or explaining the ethical dilemma presented by the *Vessantara Jātaka,* Nāgasena has an answer for everything.

But Nāgasena is not limited to the role he plays in the *Milindapañha:* he is also the man behind the Emerald Buddha.[13] According to the

Jinakālamālī, Nāgasena wanted to make an image of the Buddha to ensure the continuity of the tradition, and the first question Nāgasena has to contend with is what material would be most suitable for the task.[14] He considers gold and silver but decides against those because people of the future might be overcome by greed and harm the image.[15] Nāgasena therefore decides that the image should be fashioned from a gem of miraculous power—something that would, in other words, be capable of staving off future generations' proclivities for theft.

Sakka and Vissakamma now jump into the narrative and offer to help Nāgasena with his contribution. Sakka suggests the Cakkavatti's Jewel of the Radiant Gem (*maṇijotiratana*), which sits on Mount Vipulla, and asks Vissakamma to fetch it, but Vissakamma is all too aware of how heavily guarded it is and declines. As the more audacious character of the two, Sakka feels compelled to give the famous jewel a try. He flies off to the fabulous mountain to ask the guardians for it; predictably, they refuse, citing its exclusive association with a Wheel-Turning Emperor as their reason why. They do, however, offer an alternative: "Within this same walled enclosure where the Jewel of the Radiant Gem (*maṇijotiratana*) is, amidst more than 50 gems of the seven varieties, there is the Immortal Unmade Jewel (*amarakaṭa*), which measures two hands and three finger-breadths," they say.[16] "Please take it Mahārāja." Sakka accepts the alternative and returns to Nāgasena with it in hand.

One might find this negotiation a bit surprising. The Cakkavatti's jewel obviously belongs with the Cakkavatti, but why would the text make reference to a more coveted jewel only to sidestep it and use something less impressive instead? The gem that will produce the Emerald Buddha seems diminished as a result—better not to reference the Cakkavatti's jewel at all than to compare it in this way. But as Frank Reynolds notes, the Cakkavatti's jewel would have been familiar to a Thai audience.[17] It would have been one of the first jewels in the community's collective repertoire (second only to the Wish Fulfilling Jewel); some literary accountability for its not being used to shape the Emerald Buddha may have been required. In the *Trai Phum Phra Ruang* (The three worlds according to King Ruang), a few pages are dedicated exclusively to the description of this magical gem. According to this source, the Jewel of the Radiant Gem is as large as the hub of a large cart wheel; it has many strings of pearls attached to a central pearl, which is attached to two golden lotuses at the top. It is the king of all the other eighty-four thousand kinds of gems, and it follows the Cakkavatti wherever he goes. It resides on the top of Mount Vipulla, but when the Cakkavatti summons it, this gem "is enticed and persuaded to come; the gem is unable to stay in its dwelling" and soars through the air to join him.[18] Whenever the Cakkavatti thinks of this gem, it emits rays that compete with the moon, and follower gems soar through the sky alongside it. When the Cakkavatti wants to test the gem's power, he has it hoisted onto a golden staff and has someone carry the staff with the jewel in front. This creates a light so radiating and bright that people mistake the night for the day. It is then, the text tells us, that people know "the splendor, the sacred power, and the influence of the gem king, which results from the accumulation of the merit of the great Cakkavatti king.[19] It is this powerful and fantastical jewel that is indelibly tied to the Wheel-Turning Emperor. It cannot possibly be used by anyone else, nor indeed could it ever be melted down to create something new—not even if Sakka, Vissakamma, or Nāgasena request it.

The surprise in this story is, therefore, not that the guardians declined the request but that Sakka suggested it in the first place. This Radiant Gem Jewel is a jewel with a life of its own, similar to the Wish-Fulfilling Jewel, which materializes and rematerializes throughout the Buddhist world. Both of these jewels are associated with the Wheel-Turning Emperor, and both are therefore strictly off limits.

The Wish-Fulfilling Jewel, however, stands apart. No jewel sparks the Buddhist imagination quite like the Wish-Fulfilling Jewel, which also belongs to the Cakkavatti and is connected to Avalokiteśvara, cupped between his (/her) hands, serving as a symbol of protection. Richard Payne's contribution to this volume offers a detailed study of the ritual engagement with the deity known as Wish-Fulfilling Jewel Avalokiteśvara, and he argues that far from being an isolated phenomenon of esoteric Shingon, the practice "spans an historical and cultural arc from India through China to Japan."[20] Indeed, it is in the image of this jewel-offering deity that the paradox of this topic is perhaps most beautifully expressed: the compassionate Bodhisattva holds out a jewel that promises to heal suffering. Payne notes that the jewel is often associated with material prosperity, and as Andy Rotman argues in this volume, material prosperity is not a forbidden Buddhist goal. "Buddhism is like a convenient currency exchange," Rotman argues. "It allows one to convert money and moral action into merit, and merit into money and moral attainment. And it offers excellent rates of return. One can accrue merit by giving to Buddhist saints and shrines, and merit can be transformed into roots of virtue for fervent aspirations that promise future wealth, be it economic or spiritual."[21] The Wish-Fulfilling Jewel is a perfect case in point: it is a jewel about wishes fulfilled, and in the material world, material needs beg to be met.[22]

Casey Collins in this volume provides a fascinating example of the Wish-Fulfilling Jewel's continuity in the new religious movement, Shinnyo-en. The founders of this movement combined *homa* ashes with spring water from the Shinnyo-en headquarters to create a gem that they then placed in Jizō images. They distributed these jeweled images to the community, thereby successfully connecting themselves with the power of the Wish-Fulfilling Jewel, ritually sealing their identity as Buddhist leaders. The Wish-Fulfilling Jewel is a pan-Buddhist icon, a living mythology that connects spiritual aspirations with worldly needs. Second to this extraordinary object is the Jewel of the Radiant Gem, and together these jewels follow the Cakkavatti wherever he needs them. Under no circumstances can either become the material out of which other jewels are made, but the mountain that carries these gems is also home to other magical stones, and the future Emerald Buddha would be fashioned from one of those.

Jeweled Buddha Images

The *Jinakālamālī* tells a wonderful story, threading a variety of Buddhist principles together with ease. One of the more interesting features of this narrative is the fact that it is claiming to record a story about an image of the Buddha that was produced without precedent. The story describes the image being produced magically, without reliance on a previous image for inspiration. The gods fashion a magical gem into the shape of a Buddha without studying a model or following a traditional pattern.

Visual accuracy (where the Buddha's image is concerned) would be an unrealistic expectation under most circumstances. Regardless of how one interprets early Buddhist art (whether it was initially an "aniconic" tradition or not),[23] the first images of the Buddha's physical form only appear centuries after his (assumed) death.[24] Any image of the Buddha is therefore necessarily inaccurate. Some Buddhist texts attempt to bridge this gap with stories of Buddha images produced in the presence of the Buddha,[25] but the narrative of the Emerald Buddha does not make that claim. It is described in the *Jinakālamālī* as having been produced five centuries after the Buddha's *parinibbāna*.[26] The first historical images of the Buddha (once they finally begin taking shape), along with magical images like the Emerald Buddha, are therefore all generated in the Buddha's absence.[27]

The Emerald Buddha, however, has the advantage of supernatural intervention (something our earliest images in Gandhāra and Mathura probably do not share). Despite the Buddha's physical absence, the Emerald Buddha is created by magical beings who have the skills to produce the Buddha's likeness.[28] Although this may seem unusual, supernatural Buddha-image-making narratives appear repeatedly in Buddhist literature. Indeed, the *Jinakālamālī* preserves a story of another magically produced Buddha image that is almost equally as famous: the Sīhaḷa Buddha. The story here is of a king who yearns to see a likeness of the Buddha and goes to the monastery in Lanka to inquire about his options. Ceylonese chronicles describe the Buddha visiting Lanka on a few occasions, and the king wonders if any of the elders might remember what he looked like during that time. The problem, of course, is that this story is described as taking place seven centuries after the Buddha's visit to Lanka,[29] so most living beings will prove unhelpful in this regard. The king, however, will not be disappointed: the king of the Nāgas rises out of the earth, disguised as a young man. He remembers what the Buddha looked like all those centuries ago, and he creates an image in the Buddha's likeness. This image is then diligently copied by the king's artisans until a perfect and resplendent replica is produced.[30]

Nāgas have a long history with the Buddha's hagiography, making regular appearances throughout his narrative, serving to protect his person and his relics.[31] As magical beings that belong to the netherworlds, Nāgas can boast of long memories too. It is therefore appropriate that the king of the Nāgas enables the production of the Sīhaḷa Buddha for the king of Lanka. As with the Emerald Buddha, magical beings play key roles in narratives about Buddha images. Not only does this supernatural intervention allow for the possibility of the Buddha's actual physical likeness, but more important, it also allows for magically powerful productions. As Robert DeCaroli argues, the issue with making a Buddha image has to do with "the potency, power, and danger attributed to figural art."[32] Imaging the Buddha is not simply about creating a physical reflection; it is also about manifesting the Buddha's power.

It is therefore fitting that important images of the Buddha be fashioned from powerful materials. In the case of the Emerald Buddha, the image is created out of a magical jewel retrieved from the mythical Mount Vipulla. Just as the Buddha is the best jewel of the

Buddhist tradition, the jewel is transformed into the Buddha—the material and spiritual acting as one. Maria Heim's chapter in this volume highlights this point particularly well. Focusing on Buddhaghosa's commentary to the Jewel Sutta, she notes the many ways a jewel can act as a metaphor for the Buddha and yet at the same time how limited the metaphor ultimately becomes when one places the Buddha in relationship to material jewels. The Buddha is the ultimate jewel, the most rare and most precious being in the universe, and all material jewels necessarily pale by comparison. The result of the metaphor (of the Buddha as a jewel) therefore eventually "reorients one's understanding whereby the original jewels stop being jewels at all, once one grasps the maximal greatness of the "'true' Jewels."[33] When material and spiritual worlds collide, as they so often do when jewels are at stake, one of the outcomes is a clearer understanding of the tradition's priorities. Material jewels help one see spiritual jewels with greater clarity. Without the material jewels, this would be much more difficult to accomplish.

Jewel Power

The jewel that is to become the Emerald Buddha is a magical jewel, specifically chosen for its task by supernatural beings, with its own independent value, comparable to other magical jewels like the extraordinary Jewel of the Radiant Gem. The jewel is, therefore, just as significant as the image out of which it will be carved. This leads us to another theme in this volume—namely, that a jewel, *as a jewel,* has its own properties and, by extension, its own power. The jewel that is to become the Emerald Buddha is magical by virtue of the fact that it comes from Mount Vipulla (or the nāga realm). But as a specific jewel, it has its own properties that provide it with its own power to act on the world.[34] Frank Reynolds suggests that the green-bluish color of emeralds (and emerald-type stones) is regularly associated with vegetation and fertility and, by extension, the power to protect and regenerate.[35] This association works well with the Emerald Buddha's personal history, as it is described as having protective powers on those communities that legitimately host it. For instance, the inhabitants in Lanka are said to have had their wishes fulfilled during the Emerald Buddha's stay in the country,[36] and in 1820, when a cholera epidemic swept through Bangkok, the Emerald Buddha was paraded through the city to bless the inhabitants and ward off the evil forces that were causing harm.[37] According to Lingat, the Emerald Buddha also has the power to reflect people's true intentions: when the image was rediscovered (after a period during which it was apparently lost), the king of Chiang Mai invited his subjects to participate in a ritual bathing of the image. It is said that when someone with a pure heart approached the image and poured oil over it, the oil spread all over the image, dripped into the lamp, and caused the light to shine beautifully. But when someone with an evil heart tried to anoint the image, the oil would not spread or drip into the lamp, and no light would shine. Although the Emerald Buddha is an object, one might say that it is nonetheless alive, "rejecting the sins of those who do evil, and welcoming the merits of those who do good."[38]

The Emerald Buddha's power to ward off cholera, reflect people's intentions, or even stall an elephant in its tracks (yet another wonderful story), is not the exclusive result of its material substance.[39] The Emerald Buddha is powerful—and even alive—because it is a Buddha image, because it is consecrated (which we will discuss below), *and* because it is made of a powerful jewel. All of these features work in tandem to create the image's agency. But here, I would like to add a few words about its *jewellness* because it is its jewellness that is in part responsible for this great image's power.

Throughout this volume, we will see that jewels—*as* jewels—have particular attributes. This belief may be as old as time, but it is also at least in part linked to an ancient puranic narrative in which jewels are formed out of a deity's body. According to the *Garuḍapurāṇa,* the gods were humiliated by the demon Bala when he managed to conquer Indra and overtake the god realm, becoming supreme in the universe. In their quest to reclaim their status, the gods trick Bala into submission (a ploy they use often when demons become unruly) by planning an animal sacrifice and jokingly suggesting that Bala play the sacrificial part. Since Bala had earlier vowed to support any sacrifice performed by the gods, he agrees, but the gods quickly turn their joke into the real deal, with the demon as the central victim. Bala is duly slaughtered and dismembered in the course of the ritual act.

It is, however, what happens with Bala's body parts that interests us here. As his limbs plummet toward the ground, each one turns into a seed gem. The gods swoop down in the hopes of catching them, unleashing a wonderful mid-air wrestling match. Some of the gods manage to catch seed gems, but most of them land on the earth. Wherever a seed gem lands, "whether in oceans, rivers, mountains or wildernesses, there origined mines of those gems through the celestial potency of their respective seeds."[40] Bala's bones become diamonds, his teeth become pearls, and his blood becomes rubies.[41] Each part of his body produces the seed of a separate gem that lodges itself inside the earth. Gems are therefore not just material objects, but also the products of a powerful celestial body, each type with its own attributes and healing properties.

Christoph Emmrich examines some of these types of attributes in this volume. As with the Bala narrative in the *Garuḍapurāṇa,* Newar gemmology outlines clear associations between gems and celestial deities. Metals are likewise classified, with gold ranking at the top and bronze near the bottom. Emmrich explains that an internal caste hierarchy is affiliated with the ranks of metals, as each metallurgist is associated with the metal they work with (high castes working with gold, lower castes working with bronze and tin). Each metal, moreover, has its allocated position on the body so that gold is placed at the head, while silver is relegated to the feet. When a jeweler is asked to produce a jewel for a particular client, all of these associations are taken into consideration so that its properties can act on the client in the most effective way.

To relegate jewels to the superficial category of "decoration" in such a context would therefore be a terrible injustice. Just as the jewel that became the Emerald Buddha was significant in its own right, so too are the jewels used to fashion the ritual jewelry of the Newar community. Although they may be beautiful and may act as ornaments, this volume also highlights the fact that ornamentation is not to be misunderstood as mere embellishment. In her study of the Fifth Dalai Lama's reliquary in this volume—known as the Sole Ornament of the World—Nancy Lin explains that "ornament" has unfortunately become a pejorative term used to identify something as useless and often associated with excessive luxury. But just because something is beautiful does not mean it is useless. The Fifth Dalai Lama's reliquary is hailed as the "sole ornament of the world" and functions as an extension of the Dalai Lama's person. It is the best of all possible things, which is why it is beautiful (and not the other way around). The ornaments that cover a young Newari bride or the ritual ornamentation of the Bodhisattva prior to his Great Departure—a scene I describe in my chapter in this volume—do much more than decorate. They enhance and complete. In my chapter, I argue that "adornment" (*alaṃkāra*) has to do with making someone ready and fit for a specific purpose. It also serves to protect (like an amulet). When the Bodhisattva prepares for his departure, the gods descend from the heavens and ritually adorn him with a jewel-studded turban of ten thousand layers. This turban completes him, protects him, and makes him ready for the next step in his extraordinary journey. Like the Newari bride covered in gold bangles, the Bodhisattva leaves the palace adorned by the gods. He is like a celestial monarch, just as she is a living goddess for a day. The jewels do more than bedazzle; they have powers, play roles, and are active participants in the stories into which they are invited.

Jeweled Intimacies

The Emerald Buddha can be quite forbidding. It sits on its golden pedestal in a temple glistening with jewels, heavily protected by watchful guards. It is Thailand's national treasure. "Intimacy" is not the first word that comes to mind when thinking about this extraordinary image.

And yet, intimate it may be. Not only is it a very personal image for the members of the community to which it belongs, but it is also treated with affectionate reverence on specific occasions: three times a year, Thailand hosts a profoundly intimate moment with this image in a public way, when the king changes the Emerald Buddha's clothes in accordance with the seasons (fig. 1). As with the Buddha's story, when the gods rush down from the heavens to adorn the Bodhisattva before his Great Departure, so too does the king acknowledge cosmic hierarchies by attending to the Buddha's ritual adornment himself.[42] The intimacy with which he cares for the image, first by dusting it with his royal hands and then by supplying the jeweled ornaments that will prepare the image for the incoming season, speaks beautifully to the types of relationships people often have with special objects.[43]

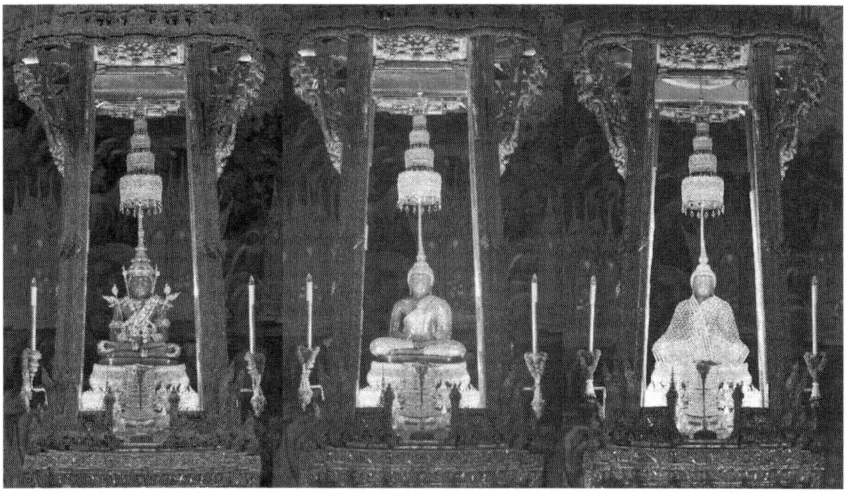

Fig. 1. A photograph of the Emerald Buddha dressed in seasonal attire. Left to right: summer, rains, winter. Public domain.

Wendy Doniger recounts a number of stories about jewels in her chapter in this volume, noting how often jewels function as personal identifiers when nothing else will do. Focusing on rings, Doniger provides a number of wonderful examples where rings do more than just adorn the wearer. Rings serve as identifiers, signifiers, and messengers, whether they are summoning a beloved or acting as proof of paternity. Jewels can play these parts because, perhaps more than anything else, jewels are profoundly personal items. Be they wedding rings or magical amulets, jewels are worn directly on the human body. Jewels are, moreover, often the material representatives of who we are, what stage of life we are in (widows, for example, removing the jewels they once received as brides), and how financially viable we might be. They might not always be the most reliable markers of our deepest truths, particularly when it comes to proofs of paternity ("a piece of jewelry is a stupid way to identify someone," as Doniger says),[44] but jewels can be counted among the most personal items we have.

In his chapter in this volume, Emmrich echoes this point with his example of the Newari goldsmith who not only produces traditional Newari jewelry for important ritual occasions, but is also the one to place these jewels directly onto his clients' bodies: "What he has wrought with his own hands is what makes his clients look their best, represents their status, celebrates their bodies and their auspiciousness and prestige on key occasions in their life. His work is in constant contact with their bodies most of their waking time (and much of their sleeping time) and has become one with their skin and flesh more than almost any other service or artefact in the Newar world."[45] The intimacy with which he works as a ritual specialist is unparalleled.

Even more revealing is the fact that jewels sometimes replace the wearer when the wearer is not available. John Strong's contribution in this volume describes the fascinating journey of the relic jewels that were removed from the Piprahwa stūpa in the late nineteenth century. Some of these traveled all the way to London, where they still reside today in personal collections (including the basement of the Royal Asiatic Society). Although jewels have been found amid relics elsewhere, the number of individual pieces in this case (more than one thousand!) is unprecedented. Moreover, the variety of jewels is remarkable: gold, silver, glass, topaz, amethyst, coral, crystal, and much more. Beautiful stones of every type were buried with the relics, and some of these were not just simple stones: they were fashioned and set as individual pieces before they were buried into the mound. Strong lists ornaments of gold leaf stamped with images of lions or elephants, gold figurines, a variety of different-sized pearls, leaves with serrated veins, and more. It is certainly possible that these ornaments were commissioned for disposal inside the reliquary, but as Strong submits, it is more likely that they belonged to individuals before they were deposited.

Following Rienjang's work on Gandhāran relic-jewels,[46] Strong argues that these jewels may have been deposited among the relics as a way of representing the individual owners: rather than place themselves personally inside the mound to remain close to the relics, these gems may have been an alternative way for devotees to get close—indeed very close—to the holy relics. By placing their own personal jewelry in the reliquaries themselves, the owners of these ornaments could "have their 'extended bodies' close to the . . . corporeal remains of the venerated entity, as in the case of *burial ad sanctos*."[47] Since, moreover, gems are hard and durable, they provide a much more permanent extension of the self. Nancy Lin, in her chapter, notes a similar phenomenon: the Fifth Dalai Lama's reliquary is covered in jewels. Included among these are items of personal jewelry. What is fascinating about Lin's research is that these items are all carefully catalogued: Desi's mother, Magen Butri Gyelmo, gave her forehead turquoise; Gyaltsen Tönpo gave pearl *mālā*(s); the Lamo state oracle offered his "lotus petal" earrings, etc. Each item is identified with the donor's name so that there is no doubt: jewels that were once worn by the owner now cover the Sole Ornament of the World. Jewels can be our most personal and most durable representatives, long after we ourselves have dissolved.

Jewel Relics

There are many more themes I could discuss here. The topic of "jewels" is an intellectual treasure house, with no limit as to where it may lead, but a number of contributions in this volume followed jewels to the reliquaries, where jewels often reside in abundance. It is therefore to the reliquaries that the last piece of our discussion will go.[48]

The Emerald Buddha is no stranger where relics are concerned. Like most important Buddhist images, it has a consecration narrative that serves to bring it to life. According to the *Jinakālamālī,* after his adventure on Mount Vipulla, Sakka returns to Nāgasena with the retrieved jewel in his arms, prepared to tackle the last obstacle in their Buddha-image-making process: how to carve it. Obviously, no mere mortal could qualify for the task. Thankfully, Vissakamma suddenly appears, disguised as a master sculptor, to offer his services. He then spends the next seven days and seven nights transforming the gem into an image of the Buddha. When his work is done, seven relics fly into the image simultaneously, "one at the head, one in the forehead, one at the heart, two in the two hands and two in the two knees."[49] The image consecrates itself, bringing itself to life without human intervention.

Much has been written on consecration rituals and the empowerment produced as a result. Although still a material object, once an image is ritually consecrated, the line between the materiality of the object-world and the immateriality of the subject-world is necessarily blurred, enabling "a controlled fluidity of power between human and non-human domains."[50] Consecrated images of the Buddha in many ways become extensions of the Buddha's person; they have an aliveness that is precisely what the biblical commandment is warning its adherents against.[51] The Emerald Buddha is a particularly dramatic example of this phenomenon since it is not simply consecrated. It consecrates itself, expressing independence even before it is supposed to have any. Its power is therefore not only the result of its consecration. It is also the product, as we have been discussing, of the magical material out of which it is produced, thereby making its *jewelness* particularly significant.

Not only do relics help bring sacred objects to life, *enlivening* them as Tarocco explains in her contribution in this volume, but they can also have a life of their own, transforming themselves over time into precious substances. Ellen Huang's chapter in this volume is a study of the Nanjing Porcelain Pagoda, which is connected to a third-century legend of the Buddha's relics. In the fabled stories she cites, the relics rattle inside their vase and emit five colors, leading monks directly to them. Huang highlights the miraculous agency of these relics: "Rather than waiting to be discovered, described, and identified, the holy remains revealed themselves as agential forces rather than static objects. They moved, glowed, resisted decay, and made sounds. By rattling, the relics seemed sentient, almost as if they spoke through a language of material impact."[52] The relics, which include a wide array of jewels (which were then buried beneath a pagoda of porcelain *jewelness*), have a life of their own, identifying them as clear social agents.[53]

This relationship between relics and jewels is often so close as to become interchangeable. In John Strong's study of the Piprahwa relics (discussed above), he notes an interesting detail: when Willie Peppé separated the jewels from the relics and retained them in glass cases, he labeled the jewels "relics of the Buddha."[54] Even without the bones, the jewels were identified as relics, Peppé showing them to devotional pilgrims who were passing through. This association between relics and jewels is not necessarily metaphorical but is the product of a complex Buddhist cosmology whereby an awakened being's presence acts on the world even after death. Relics can even multiply themselves, created as they sometimes are "through monastic ritual, prayer, and meditation, thus continually increasing in quantity," as Tarocco explains. Relics may be described as jewels, may replace jewels, may be encased with jewels, and sometimes can even *become* jewels.[55] Just as the Buddha is described as a jewel, just as the Emerald Buddha is made from a jewel, so too are Buddhist relics connected with jewels—pointing us to the perpetual loop in which we find ourselves throughout this volume, where metaphor becomes reality and reality transcends metaphor.

Notes

I am grateful to Martin Seeger and Susan Kerekes, who both generously read earlier drafts of this introduction and offered helpful feedback.

1. *Lalitavistara* 1.316. I relied on Gwendolyn Bays's translation for this chapter. See Bays, *The Lalitavistara Sūtra, Voice of the Buddha: The Beauty of Compassion,* 2 vols. (Berkeley: Dharma Publishing, 1983); Tibetan Translation Series. See my chapter in this volume for discussion of this scene.
2. I wrote about this classroom moment in a piece for BuddhistDoor Global. See Sasson, "Tales of the Emerald Buddha: Simplicity and Splendor," June 18, 2019. https://www.buddhistdoor.net/features/tales-of-the-emerald-buddha-simplicity-and-splendor.
3. Phyllis Granoff, "Maitreya's Jewelled World: Some Remarks on Gems and Visions in Buddhist Texts," *Journal of Indian Philosophy* 26, no. 4 (1998): 347.
4. Fabrizio M. Ferrari and Thomas W. P. Dähnhardt, eds., *Soulless Matter, Seats of Energy: Metals, Gems and Minerals in South Asia* (Sheffield: Equinox, 2016).
5. Fabio Rambelli, *Buddhist Materiality: A Cultural History of Objects in Japanese Buddhism* (Stanford: Stanford University Press, 2007); John Kieschnick, *The Impact of Buddhism on Chinese Material Culture* (Princeton, NJ: Princeton University Press, 2003); James Duncan Gentry, *Power Objects in Tibetan Buddhism: The Life, Writings, and Legacy of Sokdokpa Lodrö Gyeltsen* (Leiden: Brill, 2017). The studies referenced here are obviously just the tip of a much larger iceberg. When discussing material culture, we may also include archaeology (with *stūpas* functioning as particularly relevant material). See for example, work by Gregory Schopen, such as his article, "Burial *Ad Sanctos* and the Physical Presence of the Buddha," in *Bones, Stones and Buddhist Monks: Collected Papers on the Archaeology, Epigraphy, and Texts of Monastic Buddhism in India* (Honolulu: University of Hawai'i Press, 1997), 114–147. Another venue would be the role amulets play throughout the Buddhist world. For an example, see Justin McDaniel's wonderful book, *The Lovelorn Ghost and the Magical Monk: Practicing Buddhism in Modern Thailand* (New York: Columbia University Press, 2014).
6. Kieschnick, *The Impact of Buddhism on Chinese Material Culture,* 5.
7. Alfred Foucher, *L'art greco-bouddhique du Gandhāra: Étude sur les origines de l'influence classique dans l'art bouddhique de l'Inde et de l'Extrême-Orient* (Paris: Imprimerie Nationale, 1922). See Mus's article, "Le Buddha paré, son origine indienne, Çākyamuni dans le

Mahāyānisme moyen," *Bulletin de l'École Française d'Extrême-Orient* 28, no. 1 (1928): 153–278.

8. Claudine Bautze-Picron has written extensively on this subject. See in particular her book, *The Bejewelled Buddha: From India to Burma, New Considerations* (New Delhi: Sanctum Books, 2010).
9. Wendy Doniger, *The Ring of Truth: And Other Myths of Sex and Jewelry* (New York: Oxford University Press, 2017). See, for example, Brian Ruppert, "Pearl in the Shrine: A Genealogy of the Buddhist Jewel of the Japanese Sovereign," *Japanese Journal of Religious Studies* 29, nos. 1–2 (2002): 1–33. See also, Ruppert, *Jewel in the Ashes: Buddha Relics and Power in Early Medieval Japan* (Cambridge, MA: Harvard University Press, 2000); Harvard East Asian Monographs 188. While Bernard Faure makes reference to the wish-fulfilling jewel in many of his writings, he devotes the two closing chapters of his book to it specifically in *Gods of Medieval Japan*, vol. 1: *Fluid Pantheon* (Honolulu: University of Hawai'i Press, 2016).
10. Danielle C. Kinsey, "Koh-i-Noor: Empire, Diamonds, and the Performance of British Material Culture," *Journal of British Studies* 48, no. 2 (2009): 391–419. See also William Dalrymple and Anita Anand, *Koh-i-Noor: The Story of the World's Most Famous Diamond* (New York: Bloomsbury, 2017).
11. Another fabulous jewel-story worth noting here is the story of the Imperial Diamond. It became so inextricably bound to its zany and enigmatic merchant, Mr. Jacob, that it has come to be known as the Jacob Diamond. For a riveting account of this piece of history, see John Zubrzycki, *The Mysterious Mr. Jacob: Diamond Merchant, Magician, and Spy* (Gurgaon: Penguin India, 2012).
12. This collection was initially conceived with the idea of at least one chapter on Southeast Asian Buddhism; unfortunately, it was not meant to be. Plans developed and fell apart, as often happens with collections like this. I am grateful to those who tried to contribute but were unable to, and I find myself especially glad to have decided to follow the Emerald Buddha in this introduction, as a small offering to the region that has been unintentionally left out.
13. The story of the Emerald Buddha appears in a variety of sources throughout Southeast Asian literature. According to Lingat, three Thai chronicles in particular focus on the history of the Emerald Buddha: the *Ratanabimbavaṃsa,* the *Jinakālamālī,* and the *Amarakaṭabuddharūpanidāna.* See Robert Lingat, "Le culte du Bouddha d'Émeraude." *Journal of the Siam Society* 27, no. 1 (1934): 9–38. The

story of the Emerald Buddha also makes appearances in Javanese, Cambodian, Laotian, and Burmese sources. See Eric Roeder, "The Origin and Significance of the Emerald Buddha." *Explorations in Southeast Asian Studies* 3 (1999): 1–24; Louis Finot, "Recherches sur la littérature Laotienne." *Bulletin de l'École Française d'Extrême-Orient* 17 (1917): 151.

14. The *Jinakālamālī* is a sixteenth-century Thai text composed in Pali. For a discussion, see Georges Coedès, "Notes sur les ouvrages Pālis composés en pays Thai." *Bulletin de l'École Française d'Extrême-Orient* 15 (1915): 44ff.
15. Frank Reynolds describes this as a concern about a future "degenerate humanity." See "The Holy Emerald Jewel: Some Aspects of Buddhist Symbolism and Political Legitimation in Thailand and Laos," in *Religion and Legitimation of Power in Thailand, Laos and Burma,* edited by Bardwell L. Smith (Chambursburgh: Anima Books, 1978), 176. The Pali reads: *manussā lobhavasikā balavapāpajjhāsasayasampannā;* Pali text taken from Coedès, "Documents sur l'histoire politique et religieuse du Laos occidental," 54. A similar concern is noted in a tale discussed by Brian Ruppert: in the *Konjaku monogatari shū,* the Japanese are described as not being trustworthy enough to receive the Wish-Fulfilling Jewel and are thus offered a magical gold-producing stone instead. See Ruppert, "Pearl in the Shrine," 6–7.
16. *pariṇāhato tiyaṅguluttaraṃ dvihatthaparimānaṃ amarakataratanaṃ idaṃ pannāsādhikasattaratanasataparivāraṃ manijotiratanapākāre thitaṃ taṃ gaṇhatha Maharaja.* Coedès and Jayawickrama provide slightly different translations of this passage (Coedès reads this as there being more than 750 gems in the enclosure, while Jayawickrama reads this as there being more than 5,000 gems). See Coedès, "Documents sur l'histoire politique et religieuse du Laos occidental," 112; N. A. Jayawickrama, trans. *The Sheaf of Garlands of the Epochs of the Conqueror: Being a Translation of the Jīnakālamālīpakaraṇaṃ* (London: Pali Text Society, 1978), 141.
17. Reynolds, "The Holy Emerald Jewel," 183.
18. Frank E. Reynolds and Mani B. Reynolds, trans. *Three Worlds According to King Ruang: A Thai Buddhist Cosmology* (Berkeley: Asian Humanities Press, 1982), 164.
19. Reynolds and Reynolds, trans. *Three Worlds According to King Ruang,* 165.
20. Richard K. Payne in this volume.
21. Andy Rotman in this volume.

22. In a discussion about the role of the Wish-Fulfilling Jewel, Brian Ruppert makes a brilliant comparison to the Holy Grail: "Like the wish-fulfilling jewel and the Buddha relics tradition, the grail is the ultimate gift, which offers satisfaction in the form of an object that is both a material and a spiritual cornucopia" (Ruppert, *Jewel in the Ashes*, 270).
23. I am here referring to the now well-recognized debate that began with Foucher's work in the early twentieth century. See *Beginnings of Buddhist Art, and Other Essays in Indian and Central Asian Archaeology*, trans. L. A. Thomas and F. W. Thomas (Paris: Paul Geuthner, 1917). Foucher's reading of early Buddhist art (and the Buddha's physical absence therein) led him to the conclusion that Buddhism was initially aniconic where imaging the Buddha was concerned (in his words, "If they did not do it, it was because it was not custom to do it" [7]). This interpretation was the accepted conclusion for decades, but Susan L. Huntington eventually challenged the position, and it has led to an ongoing debate about whether or not Buddhist visual culture was predominantly aniconic at first. Huntington's challenge to Foucher begins with her article "Early Buddhist Art and the Theory of Aniconism." *Art Journal* 49 (1990): 401–408; Vidya Dehejia's response to Huntington: "Aniconism and the Multivalence of Symbols," *Ars Orientalis* 21 (1991): 45–66. And Susan L. Huntington's response to Dehejia's response: "Aniconism and the Multivalence of Emblems: Another Look." *Ars Orientalis* 22 (1992): 111–156.
24. I say "assumed" death because there is obviously no hard evidence that the "historical" Buddha existed.
25. For a discussion of some of these narrative accounts, see Donald K. Swearer, *Becoming the Buddha: The Ritual of Image Consecration in Thailand* (Princeton, NJ: Princeton University Press, 2004), 14–24.
26. Jayawickrama, *The Sheaf of Garlands of the Epochs of the Conqueror*, 141.
27. Another dispute among art historians has to do with the question of the first production of Buddha images. Images of the Buddha arise in both Gandhāra (with Greek influence) and Mathura around the same time, and it is unclear which of the two came first in the running. Once again, Foucher's influence proves significant, with his argument that the Gandhāran images are earlier in "The Greek Origin of the Buddha Image" (an essay in his *The Beginnings of Buddhist Art*), while A. K. Coomaraswamy makes a case for a Mathuran (and therefore indigenous) start to the tradition. See Coomaraswamy, "The Origin of the Buddha Image." *Art Bulletin* 9 (1927): 287–328.

28. As noted above, the *Jinakālamālī* is not the only text to discuss the Emerald Buddha (see footnote 15), and in alternative renditions, the gem does not always come from Mount Vipulla, but it does remain magical. In one case, it is discovered inside a melon! This may not sound as spectacular, but the story maintains its link with the supernatural just as effectively, because a nāga is the one to place the magical gem inside the melon for a devoted laywoman to discover. For a discussion of this narrative, see Angela S. Chiu, *The Buddha in Lanna: Art, Lineage, and Power in Northern Thailand* (Honolulu: University of Hawaii Press, 2017), 78–84.
29. The claim is that the story takes place seven centuries after his death; presumably, the Buddha visited Lanka before even that.
30. Jayawickrama, *The Sheaf of Garlands of the Epochs of the Conqueror,* 120.
31. For a discussion of the magical power of nāgas, see Robert DeCaroli, *Haunting the Buddha: Indian Popular Religions and the Formation of Buddhism* (New York: Oxford University Press, 2004); for a discussion of their role in the preservation of the Buddha's relics, see John S. Strong, *Relics of the Buddha* (Princeton, NJ: Princeton University Press, 2004).
32. Robert DeCaroli, *Image Problems: The Origin and Development of the Buddha's Image in Early South Asia* (Seattle: University of Washington Press, 2015), 28.
33. Maria Heim in this volume.
34. Many have noted that the Emerald Buddha is probably not actually an emerald, but more likely jade or jasper. In the *Jinakālamālī,* as elsewhere, the gem is called the *amarakaṭa.* See for example, Eric Roeder, "The Origin and Significance of the Emerald Buddha," 2; Angela S. Chiu, *The Buddha in Lanna,* 46.
35. Frank Reynolds, "The Holy Emerald Jewel," 179. This interpretation of emeralds is not universally consistent. Jewels obviously mean different things to different communities. For example, in his study of emeralds in the 17th century, Lane argues that emeralds were valued by the shahs because the green color represented "the visions and journeys of the Prophet in the form of the green pastures and palms of paradise." See Lane, *Colour of Paradise: The Emerald in the Age of Gunpowder Empires* (New Haven, CT: Yale University Press, 2010), 208.
36. Chiu, *The Buddha in Lanna,* 46.
37. Lingat, "Le culte du Bouddha d'Émeraude," 24.
38. "*Repoussant les péchés de ceux qui font le mal, acceuillant les mérites de ceux qui font le bien*"; Lingat, "Le culte du Bouddha d'Émeraude," 22.

39. Lingat, "Le culte du Bouddha d'Émeraude," 19.
40. *Garuḍapurāṇa* 68. For a translation of this text, see Ernst Wood and S. V. Subrahmanyam, *Garuḍa Purāṇa (Sāroddhāra)* (Allahabad: Sudhindra Nath Vasu, 1911).
41. For a brief description and discussion of this legend, see Anthony Cerulli and Caterina Guenzi, "Mineral Healing: Gemstone Remedies in Astrological and Medical Traditions," in Ferrari and Dähnhardt, *Soulless Matter, Seats of Energy,* 80.
42. For a description of this ceremony, see Roeder, "The Origin and Significance of the Emerald Buddha," 18–19; see also Karen Schur Narula, *Voyage of the Emerald Buddha* (Kuala Lumpur: Oxford University Press, 1994), 1–6, 85–86.
43. Martin Seeger reminded me that the intimacy of the Emerald Buddha in fact goes further than this royal ritual. The Emerald Buddha is probably the most reproduced image in Thailand. People throughout the country carry (or wear) a replica of the image. It is therefore intimately cared for by the larger public and not just by the king.
44. Wendy Doniger in this volume.
45. Christoph Emmrich in this volume.
46. Rienjang began this work with her PhD dissertation. A portion was recently published in Wannaporn Kay Rienjang, Jonathan Mark Kenoyer, and Margaret Sax, "Stone Beads from the Relic Deposits: A Preliminary Morphological and Technological Analysis," in *Charles Masson and the Buddhist Sites of Afghanistan: Explorations, Excavations, Collections 1833–1835,* edited by Elizabeth Errington (London: British Museum, 2017), 52–57.
47. John Strong in this volume.
48. A thorough overview of the literature would be impossible in a short footnote, but certainly worth noting here is John Strong's *Relics of the Buddha.* Likewise worth noting is Kevin Trainor's *Relics, Ritual, and Representation in Buddhism: Rematerializing the Sri Lankan Theravāda Tradition* (Cambridge: Cambridge University Press, 1997), and Brian Ruppert, *Jewel in the Ashes.*
49. *ekā moliyaṃ, ekā naḷāṭe, ekā hadaye, dve dvīsu hatthesu, dve dvīsu jaṇṇukesu pavisiṃsu* (Coedès, "Documents sur l'histoire politique et religieuse du Laos occidental," 54).
50. Gentry, *Power Objects in Tibetan Buddhism,* 7.
51. For discussion, see in particular Donald K. Swearer, "Hypostasizing the Buddha: Buddha Image Consecration in Northern Thailand," *History of Religions* 34, no. 3 (1995): 263–280; see also Swearer, *Becoming the*

Buddha. Statements against idolatry appear throughout the Hebrew Bible, but the most famous iteration is found among the Ten Commandments (Exodus 20:3–4). Western scholarship has long struggled with difference where images are concerned. For a thoughtful discussion, see Robert H. Sharf, "On the Allure of Buddhist Relics," *Representations* 66 (Spring 1999): 75–99.

52. Ellen Huang in this volume.
53. There are many ways to understand "agency" in the context of material culture. I am here following Alfred Gell's broad view of agency. See his book, *Art and Agency: An Anthropological Theory* (Oxford: Clarendon Press, 1998), 16ff.
54. Strong in this volume.
55. For the argument that jewels were encased inside the heads of Gandhāran Buddha statues, see Juhyung Rhi, "Images, Relics, and Jewels: The Assimilation of Images in the Buddhist Relic Cult of Gandhāra: Or Vice Versa," *Artibus Asiae* 65, no. 2 (2005): 169–211. A fascinating question raised by Tarocco in this volume is whether glass rosaries are cremated along with the body to produce gemlike substances. See also Dan Martin, "Pearls from Bones: Relics, Chortens, Tertons and the Signs of Saintly Death in Tibet." *Numen* 41 (1994): 273–323, and Martin Seeger, *Gender and the Path to Awakening: Hidden Histories of Nuns in Modern Thailand* (Chiang Mai: Silkworm, 2018).

Chapter 2

Jewels of Recognition and Paternity in Buddhist, Jain, and Hindu Traditions

Wendy Doniger

Buddhist stories about jewelry are part of a broader corpus of stories about women and their jewelry that is shared among the religions of South Asia. Its source is in the folk traditions that transcend—indeed in many cases precede and underlie—the various religious texts. In this essay, I will try to set the stage for the more specifically Buddhist essays in this volume by considering, after an introductory general discussion of rings in ancient India, a Buddhist story of a woman who boasted that she never lost anything (and found a ring in a deep pool); two Buddhist versions of the story of the ring that proves paternity and another about a ring that identifies an elusive woman; a Jain story of multigenerational incest exposed by a ring; a classical Sanskrit play about a woman identified by her necklace; and a set of Indian, primarily Hindu, folktales about clever wives who use jewelry to establish paternity. I will conclude with some general speculations about the tension between common sense and tradition in Indian stories about jewelry.[1]

Rings in Ancient India

Charles Edwards, in the nineteenth century, rather naïvely reported that "signets of lapis lazuli and emerald have been found with Sanscrit [*sic*] inscriptions, presumed to be of an antiquity beyond all record."[2] But in recorded history, signet rings appear in Indian texts only from the third century BCE, after the arrival of the Indo-Greeks in the wake of Alexander's aborted invasion of northwest India in 326 BCE.[3] A signet ring is used to forge a royal document in a quasi-historical political play, Viśakhadatta's *Mudrārākṣasa* (The minister's seal-ring), composed in south India probably during the seventh century CE.[4] Seal rings, of both men and women, played a part in romantic assignations, according to the *Kāmasūtra,* the third-century CE ancient Indian textbook of erotic love:

> When the king arises from his afternoon siesta, the women attendants who keep track of the roster come to him followed by the servants of the woman whose turn it is to spend the night with the king, of the woman who has been passed over on her night, and of the woman who is in her fertile season. And they present the king with scented oils, each marked with the stamp of the woman's seal ring, and tell him whose turn it is to sleep with him that night and who is in her fertile season. Whichever one among these oils the king takes, he announces that the woman who owns it will sleep with him that night.[5]

It's worth noting that the women as well as the king have seal rings, which here identify them as potential sexual partners. On the other side of the harem wall, a lover sending a message to a woman in the harem is advised to give her his seal ring marked with an impression.[6] (The commentator explains that he leaves a ring with his name on it, marked with traces of his nails and teeth.)

The cultural connections between women and circular jewelry in India are complex. In Śūdraka's play *The Little Clay Cart,* also from the third century CE, the courtesan and wife use jewelry in ways that challenge European stereotypes: the courtesan lends her casket of jewelry to a poor man whom she loves, and when it is stolen from him, his wife gives him her pearl necklace to pay back the courtesan. Eventually the stolen jewelry is found, and the courtesan returns the pearls to the wife. The usual roles are reversed here: the stereotypical courtesan milks a man of everything he has and is the bitter enemy of his wife, often usurping a wife's place or masquerading as a wife; but here the courtesan lends the man jewelry, and the wife's necklace redeems the courtesan's jewels.[7]

An anklet plays a key role in the ancient Tamil epic *The Tale of an Anklet* (*Cilappatikaram*), traditionally believed to have been composed in the fifth century CE by Ilanko Atikal, a Tamil prince.[8] It tells the tale of Kovalan, who, having squandered all his money on a courtesan, travels to Maturai, the capital of the Pandyan kingdom, to sell one of the gold anklets of his wife, Kannaki. Falsely accused of having stolen the anklet of the Pandyan queen, he is executed. When Kannaki learns of her husband's death, she rushes to the palace in a fury, accuses the king of murder, and proves that the anklet was hers by breaking it open and revealing rubies inside, where the queen's anklet contained nothing but pearls. (In this South Indian land of pearl fishers, rubies are less precious than pearls and lack their symbolic value.) The king acknowledges his guilt and dies; the queen follows him.[9] The circular jewelry in this story proves the innocence not of the woman (as it does in most of the tales we will consider) but of her husband.

A Buddhist Variant of the Story of the Ring in the Belly of a Fish

The many stories in which a magic ring is found in the belly of a fish are the mythical exaggeration of a perfectly banal happening: fishermen fish things up out of the deep. The ring stories are counterfactual, promising a happy ending that could seldom have been the case in real life: the lost ring is miraculously regained, to the owner's relief and delight. But the point of the story, and the reason for its extraordinary popularity, must be found elsewhere than in the actual habits of gold rings and fish. These stories generally regard as a benevolent miracle the return of the ring from the ocean, a place from which everything eventually returns but from which one cannot expect any particular thing to return. This sort of ring is the key to the great lost-and-found of the narrative world, driven by a hopeful attitude that marks this Chinese translation of a Tibetan translation of an Indian text (Skt. *Mahāsammata-rāja*) recorded by Édouard Chavannes:

> There was once a married woman who used to say all the time, "I never lose anything." Her son took his mother's ring and threw it into the water; then he went to ask his mother where her gold ring was. She said to him: "I never lose anything." The next day, his mother invited three Buddhist sages to dinner; she sent a man to the market to buy a fish. When the man returned, they prepared the fish and in its stomach they found the gold ring. The mother said to her son, "I never lose anything." Her son, delighted, went to the spot where the Buddha was staying and asked him: "What is the cause of my mother's good fortune in never losing anything?" The Buddha explained that, in an earlier birth, his mother had lived alone in the northern mountains, and when, in winter, all the inhabitants went south, she was so poor that she was not able to leave; she stayed there all alone and kept in order all the utensils and goods of the tribe; in spring, all the men came back and the mother gave each object, without exception, back to its owner. Because of that, she attained this good fortune of never losing anything.[10]

The return of the objects each spring after the hard winter is analogized, superficially, to the miraculous return of the ring and, more profoundly, to the return of the woman's good fortune in a better rebirth.

Two Buddhist Versions of the Ring of Śakuntalā

A famous Indian version of the tale of the ring swallowed by a fish is the story of Śakuntalā, best known from a Sanskrit play by the poet Kālidāsa, in the fourth century CE, but based upon a story in the *Mahābhārata* (the great Sanskrit epic, composed between about 300 BCE and 300 CE). The *Mahābhārata* tells us that King Duṣyanta seduced Śakuntalā, who bore him a child, but when she brought the child to court, the king lied, saying that he had never seen her before. She left, and a disembodied voice from the sky told the king, "Support your son, and do not reject Śakuntalā." Then Duṣyanta accepted his son.[11] There is no ring in this earliest recorded version, where the proof of Śakuntalā's honesty is provided supernaturally, but a ring soon enters the story in two of the Buddhist jātakas. Although the woman in both Buddhist versions of this story has no name, the son is named; indeed, both of the Buddhist texts are named after the child. Śakuntalā has lost both her name and her voice, both of which have been transferred to her son. Here is a summary of the version in the Pali *Kaṭṭhahāri Jātaka*, which introduces not only the ring, but also common sense:

> King Brahmadatta of Benares was wandering in his pleasure groves when he saw a woman and fell in love with her. He seduced her and she conceived a child who was the future Buddha, the Bodhisatta. He gave her the signet ring from his finger and dismissed her with these words: "If it is a girl, spend this ring on her nurture; but if it is a boy, bring ring and child to me." She gave birth to a boy, and the children teased him, calling him "No-father." He asked his mother about his father, and she told him. At his request, she took her son to the palace and said to the king, "This is your son, sire." The king knew well enough that this was the truth, but shame before all his court made him reply, "He is no son of mine." "But here is your signet-ring, sire; you will recognize that." "Nor is this my signet-ring." Then said the woman, "Sire, I have now no witness to prove my words, except to appeal to truth. Wherefore, if you be the father of my child, I pray that he may stay in mid-air; but if not, may he fall to earth and be killed." So saying, she seized the Bodhisatta by the foot and threw him up in the

> air. The child, suspended in the air, told the king he was his son. The king stretched out his hands and cried, "Come to me, my boy! None, none but me shall rear and nurture you!" A thousand hands were stretched out to receive the Bodhisatta; but it was into the arms of the king and of no other that he descended, seating himself in the king's lap. The king made him viceroy and made his mother queen-consort. At the death of the king his father, he came to the throne by the title of King Kaṭṭhavāhana, and after ruling his realm righteously, passed away to fare according to his deserts.[12]

This text invokes the commonsense fact that jewelry doesn't actually prove anything at all unless other people acknowledge it. The story also recognizes the hardheaded value of a precious ring, a very early instance of the argument that diamonds are a girl's best friend. But it also introduces a gender bias: if the child is a boy, it's all well and good to use the ring to secure his patrimony, but if it's a girl, it might as well be used for her dowry. Thus the ring serves both as a proof of identity and as a kind of child support. These rational considerations lead back into irrational religion, an act of truth reminiscent of the voice from the sky in the *Mahābhārata* tale of Śakuntalā: a miracle, a suspension of the law of gravity, which proves the identity of the child and epitomizes, like the judgment of Solomon, the liminality of the child torn between two parents.[13] But where Solomon's proposed solution to split the child, which would kill it, smoked out the true mother in protest, the father here quite blithely accepts the possibility that his son may crash and die. (The mother has faith that since the child really is the king's, he will be safe.) This text spells out, as the *Mahābhārata* does not, the king's total disregard for the child as well as the mother.

Another Pali jātaka story, the *Uddālaka Jātaka,* reverts to the more conventional assumption that the ring is an incontrovertible proof. Again, I will summarize:

> Once upon a time, when Brahmadatta was king in Benares, the Bodhisatta was his chaplain. He fell in love with a woman and lived with her, and when she became pregnant he gave her a seal-ring, and said, "If you give birth to a girl, use this to help bring her up; but if it is a boy, name him Uddālaka and bring him to me when he grows up." In due time she brought forth a son, and named him Uddālaka. When he grew up, he asked his mother, "Mother, who is my father?"—"The chaplain, my boy."—"If that is so, I will learn the holy books."

> So, receiving the ring from his mother, and a teacher's fee, he journeyed to Taxila and studied with the ascetics there. At last he came to Benares with the ascetics, and stayed in the king's park and gave sermons there. The king learned that a wise man, a great ascetic, was living in the park and went there with his chaplain. Uddālaka greeted him graciously. Then he and the chaplain recited four stanzas and responsory stanzas to one another, until Uddālaka thought, "I must not be on bad terms with this man. If I tell him I am his son, he will have to love me. I will tell him I am his son." He recited a fifth stanza, in which he declared that he was Uddālaka, the chaplain's son. "Are you indeed Uddālaka?" the chaplain asked. "Yes," said the boy.
>
> Then the chaplain said, "I gave your mother a token; where is it?" Uddālaka replied, "Here it is, Brahmin," and handed him the ring. The Brahmin recognized the ring and said, "Without doubt you are a Brahmin; but do you know the duties of a Brahmin?" He questioned him about these duties in several stanzas, as well as about the path to Nirvana and the irrelevance of caste. Uddālaka answered him each time, until the chaplain had the last word and Uddālaka fell silent. Finally, the chaplain persuaded Uddālaka to abandon his asceticism and to be the chaplain under him, to which the king consented.[14]

In this version, the chaplain accepts the boy not merely as his son (which he had already done on the basis of the ring) but also as a Brahmin worthy to succeed him as royal chaplain (which he decides on the basis of the boy's knowledge). The child must use his achievements as well as his ancestry to ensure his recognition by his father, who now is not a king, who rules by power, but a chaplain, who rules by knowledge. And so the test of his paternity is no longer a royal miracle but the ability to understand Buddhist doctrine.

Another Jātaka

Another jātaka, this one from the *Mahāvastu,* again introduces rational changes into an inherited narrative pattern. Here is the story as it appears in the *Kinnarī Jātaka:*

> Prince Sudhanu of Hastināpura saved a Kinnarī named Manoharā from being sacrificed by his father the king. They fell in love, but the

> king insisted on sending Manoharā back to her home in the Himalayan mountains. As she left, she met two hunters, and gave them a finger-ring which she wore, worth a hundred-thousand pieces, and a garland, saying, "If Prince Sudhanu comes after me looking for me, give him these tokens and greet him in my name. You are to say to him, 'Return hence, you are on a difficult road beyond the haunts of men.' For it is my destiny to live apart from men."
>
> The prince went to seek her, and found the two hunters, who told him: "She forewarned us, saying, 'If a man, named Sudhanu, should come after me, hunters, give him this token. Give him this finger-ring of mine and this garland. . . . He is my husband, lord and master. Hunters, greet my lord in my name. Bid him return to Hastināpura. For it is my destiny to live in continence apart from him.' " Joyfully he seized the garland and took hold of the ring and said, "I'll go to my death or to reunion with Manoharā."
>
> He went on and eventually found her kingdom, on the top of Mount Kailāsa, where he saw several Kinnarīs carrying water in golden pitchers. They told him, "Manoharā is going to have a bath so that the smell of men shall be removed from her." The prince put the finger-ring in the last pitcher, in such a way that it was not seen by the Kinnarīs. Manoharā had her bath, and as she bathed the finger-ring fell out of the pitcher on to her lap. When she saw the finger-ring she recognized it. She thought to herself, "Prince Sudhanu has come to seek me." She begged her parents to let him live with her. Her father asked, "Did you see him yourself, or did you hear of him from another?" She replied, "I have neither seen him myself nor have I heard of him from another. But as I was bathing, Sudhanu's finger-ring dropped into my lap."
>
> They were united and lived together for many years. Eventually, he wanted to return to his home. He and Manoharā went back to Hastināpura, where they were joyously received.[15]

Kinnarīs are supernatural women of great beauty. In India they are said to be half-horse, and in Southeast Asia, half-bird. Often, they are regarded as dangerously seductive; here, apparently just seductive (though still dangerous in the eyes of the prince's father). This story follows a line familiar from many folktales but twists it in creative ways. At first it stays within the conventional story's boundaries, according to which the prince finds a woman from another world who gives him a magic ring that protects him and helps him to find her when they are parted. Here, however, the ring ostensibly warns him *not* to find her, though he ignores the warning. In many tellings of the story, the human prince eventually longs to visit his old world but intends to return to the woman from the other world; he makes a fatal error, however, and is eternally parted from her (or dies or suddenly grows old, having broken the spell that kept him young for hundreds of years).[16] Here, however, when he falls prey to that usually disastrous longing, he sensibly takes her with him, and they stay in the human world forever after. The Buddhist text has Euhemerized the story, scaling it down to purely human concerns; the Kinnarī lives not in another world but simply on a particularly high mountain, and her animal associations (equine or avian) are never mentioned. The ring does not have the magic ability to speak but becomes articulate through the hunters, who repeat the Kinnarī's warning (with minor variations). Thus the text makes everyone reasonable and gives them a happy ending.

A Jain Story of Multigenerational Incest Exposed by a Ring

A ring is the key to a Jain didactic text that depicts a horrendously convoluted incest scenario, told in the service of religious renunciation. It involves two signet rings belonging to identical twins with identical names (though the "ā" at the end of the feminine name will distinguish it from the masculine):

> A courtesan named Kuberasenā bore a son and daughter, twins, and nursed them for eleven days, but her madam insisted that she abandon them. She made a signet ring for the boy inscribed with the name Kuberadatta, and a similar ring for the girl, marked with the name Kuberadattā. And then, terrified of the madam, she placed the two children in a casket studded with jewels and set the casket afloat in the waters of the Yamuna River.
>
> A pair of merchants found them, and each took one of the children home, naming them after the names on the rings. When the children were grown, the two merchants married the boy and girl to one another, "even though they seemed indeed to be twin brother and sister." One day Kuberadatta placed his own ring in his wife's hand; astonished, Kuberadattā said to him, "How is it that these rings are so like

> each other, just as our names are so similar? I fear that we are in truth brother and sister, and that we are not the two children of those merchants at all." They asked the merchants, and heard the story, and "they deeply regretted their marriage."
>
> Both of them were filled with the desire to renounce life. Kuberadattā became a Jain nun and hid her jeweled signet ring. Kuberadatta became a trader and went to the city of Mathura, where he met Kuberasenā, his mother, but neither recognized the other. He became her lover and she bore him a son, named Kubera.
>
> Kuberadattā had developed supernatural knowledge and knew "the terribly improper things" that her brother was doing. She showed her signet ring to her superior and told her about herself and went to Mathura. She met Kuberadatta's son, Kubera, and told him everything; he realized that Kuberasenā was both his grandmother and his mother, and that Kuberadattā was both his sister and his aunt. Then she gave him the jeweled signet ring, and "by that signet ring, . . . Kubera became enlightened and became a monk." Kuberadatta also renounced the householder's life and went into the forest. He meditated and went to heaven. "Even Kuberasenā saw how topsy-turvy the world of sense objects is, and she became disgusted with life in this world and took on herself the vows of the Jain householder."[17]

The incest here spans two generations, doubling back to involve both siblings and parents. But what is most significant for our central theme is that neither the fact that the children are found together, nor the fact that they look alike, nor the fact that they have the same names (but for a gendering a/ā variation) is sufficient to identify them as people who must not wed. Only the signet rings are taken as hard evidence of the incest that has already taken place, and the ring is what enlightens the final child in this twisted lineage.

Ratnāvalī, the Lady with the Necklace

The association between fine jewelry and women of a certain class underlies the plot of a Sanskrit drama, *The Lady of the Jeweled Necklace,* attributed to King Harṣa, who ruled much of North India in the seventh century CE.[18] Here is a summary of the plot: The princess Ratnāvalī ("[Woman with a] Jeweled Necklace"), on her voyage to become one of King Udāyana's wives, was shipwrecked and fished out by a merchant. He brought her to Udāyana's minister, who recognized her by the jeweled necklace that she always wore. Not wishing to anger the chief queen, he put her in the queen's service as a handmaid named Sāgarikā ("Ocean Woman"). She met the king and they fell in love. But she would not agree to keep meeting him, and the king said, "My beloved, who is like a jeweled necklace found by chance, slipped out of my hand before I could hang her around my neck." The queen imprisoned Sāgarikā, who gave her jeweled necklace to the Brahmin jester; the jester realized from its value that Sāgarikā must be of noble birth. Then the chief councilor of Ratnāvalī's father arrived; when he saw the necklace on the jester, he thought he recognized it as Ratnāvalī's but decided that this might be sheer coincidence. Then Sāgarikā appeared, still in chains. The councilor, looking at Sāgarikā, said, "She looks just like the princess." And, recalling the necklace, he decided that this must in fact be Ratnāvalī. The jester said, "As soon as I saw the jeweled necklace I knew that this was the property of no common person." The queen had Ratnāvalī's chains taken off, embraced her, and adorned her with her own ornaments.

Sāgarikā, the Ocean Woman, is rescued out of the ocean—like a ring or a fish. Her jeweled necklace suggests, if it does not prove, that she is Ratnāvalī, and it brings with it, as it surfaces, the usual submerged recognition. Like a signet ring, the necklace is here associated with a hidden name: Ratnāvalī at first is *like* a necklace (which the king fears he has lost), then is known to *have* a necklace (by which the king's minister recognizes her before the play begins, and her father's councilor half-recognizes her at the end), and finally is recognized as being *named* a necklace.

The necklace is at first taken as evidence but is then ruled inadmissible. When the chief councilor of Ratnāvalī's father arrives and sees the jeweled necklace, he remarks, "I know that necklace! It's the very one that the king gave the princess at the time of her departure." But then he decides that this might be sheer coincidence, thinking, "There are so many jewels in a royal family that it is not hard to find a 'speaking resemblance' of ornaments."[19] The word he uses is *saṃ-vāda,* literally a conversation, a form that "talks together." The commentator glosses it as "resemblance" (*sādṛśyam*) and says that the councilor means that it might be another, similar jewel. Thus the councilor invokes coincidence to explain away the striking resemblance between the necklace last seen on Ratnāvalī and the necklace now seen on the jester: princesses have so many jewels.

The argument about the "speaking resemblance" deflects the power of the jewelry so that it isn't the essential clue, the single clue by which all stands or falls, after all, but merely one piece in a more complex puzzle of mistaken identity. The text simultaneously presents the traditional, formulaic symbol of identity (the piece of jewelry that identifies the person in disguise) and mocks it: a piece of jewelry is a stupid way to identify someone. Thus common sense intrudes, momentarily, into the romanticism of the myth, and a reasonable, rather flat-footed realization challenges the equally flat-footed assumption that if she's wearing the same ring or necklace, she must be the same person. When Sāgarikā appears, the councilor says, "She looks just like the princess." And then, aside, "Since the necklace bears such a strong resemblance, and since this girl came from the ocean, it's clear that this is Ratnāvalī, the daughter of the King of Simhala."[20] The jewelry is a part of the cumulative weight of evidence. Though the hard evidence of the jewelry is undermined, the "soft" evidence of somatic memory is validated in the end. The truth that the necklace reveals from the start is not Ratnāvalī's identity (which is finally established by her face) but her class. (The connection is supported by the near-homonym of the Sanskrit words for noble birth [*abhijāna*] and recognition [*abhijñāna*].) As the jester remarks to himself at the end, "I knew that this was the property of no common person." She is the daughter of a foreign king, masquerading as someone of a lower class, the princess as the pauper—but wearing a necklace no pauper could afford.

Here the text suddenly plays the harsh light of reason on a traditional romantic theme: *anyone* who has a fabulous necklace of emeralds and rubies must be a princess, if not necessarily the particular princess one is looking for. And Sāgarikā's class is eventually the key to her individual identity. In the end, class reconciles the queen to her fate: the knowledge that the Ocean Woman is in fact the Lady of the Jeweled Necklace forces the queen to welcome her as a co-wife.

The Clever Wife in Indian Folklore

A number of stories of this genre are told and retold in oral variants in India, often without doctrinal markers that would locate them in any of the various religious traditions of India (Buddhist, Jain, or Hindu), so that the stories may serve as sources for religious discourses in any or all of them. One of these is the tale known to folklorists as "The Clever Wife" or "The Clever Wench," in which a husband challenges his wife to get a child (almost always a son) fathered by him, though he will never sleep with her.[21] She succeeds by tricking him into bed, where she masquerades as another woman (a maneuver known as a bedtrick).[22] Usually he also challenges her to get his ring, which he will never take off. Sometimes he does not mention the ring, but rather she insists on having it before she submits to him so that later she can prove that she was the woman in his bed (or he in hers, depending on one's point of view) and that her child is his. This myth has a very long shelf life indeed as it travels through Europe, Asia, and the Middle East, and there are many variants attested in India.

Three pieces of jewelry, though with only one child, appear in a South Indian oral tale retold by A. K. Ramanujan, who called it "The Wager":

> A king's son came upon a local man's rich daughter; she was utterly beautiful, and he stopped and posed a riddle, but she out-riddled him. He flew into a rage and said, "You don't know who you're talking to. You talked back to me. So I'll marry you and shut you up in my basement. If I don't, I wouldn't be my father's son." She countered, "King's son, I'll marry you then and I'll get your own son to tie you up to the post in the marketplace. If I don't, my breast is no breast." He told his father how she had insulted him, bandying wager for wager, and concluded, "So I must marry her and teach her a lesson." His father tried to reason with him, saying, "That's no good reason to marry anyone." Moreover, the king pointed out, she was not of their caste. But the prince insisted, and the king arranged the marriage. Meanwhile, the prince had an underground basement house built for his bride.
>
> When she came to the palace, the prince didn't even look at her. He sent her to the basement house and shut her up in it. Then he went to another country in search of a new bride, married again, and lived with his new wife quite happily; they had several children. Meanwhile, with the help of her father, the girl escaped from the basement, learned acrobatic dancing and black magic, performed for her husband (who did not recognize her, though again he was struck by her beauty), and allowed him to seduce her. She stayed with him for three nights, and made him give her the ring on his finger, his necklace, and his dagger.
>
> She returned home pregnant, gave birth to a son, and raised him, teaching him all the arts she had learned. One day she told him the story of the two wagers, and the boy asked the pivotal question: "If my father

never came here, how did I come about?" And she told him about the acrobatic dancing. The son managed to get into the palace and steal the silver legs off the king's golden bed, as well as every piece of jewelry the queen was wearing from all over her body. He disguised himself as the bailiff's son-in-law and slept with the bailiff's daughter. And then he tricked the king into letting him tie him up in a bundle of dirty clothes. When a crowd gathered, he untied the king, who looked at his captor, amazed, for the young man looked just like him. King and thief, thief and king, it was hard to tell who was who. Only their ages gave them away.

The young man sent for his mother, who told everyone about the wager and displayed the dagger, the necklace, and the signet ring that had once belonged to the king. The king admitted that she had won the wager. Everyone, needless to say, was happy.[23]

Where the prince swears by his resemblance to his father (a crucial point in many of these stories, as we will see), she swears by her secondary sexual characteristics and her beauty. But he marries her to punish her, as usual, despite his father's warning that this is a really bad idea. The boy brings off a literal bed-trick, but he also steals the queen's jewelry (which might have been expected to lead to yet another subplot of identification-by-jewelry but doesn't) and even throws in a sexual bed-trick (with the bailiff's daughter) to prove that he is not just a thief, but also a sexual trickster like his mom. And in this version, the boy himself asks the riddle that is usually stated only by the husband and the clever wife: How did you get pregnant—with *me*—if your husband "never came here?," as he delicately words it.

A contemporary Tamil folk telling is so truncated that it works only if the storyteller can assume that the listeners are familiar with the full version, evidence of its wide popularity:

A raja went to a village to find a bride. He asked a woman a riddle, and she asked him another in return; neither could answer the other's riddle. "So the prince said, 'I'm going to marry you and lock you up in prison until I find the answer to your riddle!' To which, she said, 'I'll marry you, but if I don't have your child, without you even knowing about it, then I'm not the woman I think I am.' She made this pledge, but he married her anyway." He locked her up in a stone prison, where he visited her, chewed betel nuts and enjoyed himself.

> But she dug a tunnel and escaped to her parents' house. "'This stupid raja won't recognise me,' she thought and disguised herself as a dancer, with her father as her teacher. Soon the raja called them to dance in his assembly, and when she danced he was infatuated." She spent one night with him, and in the morning she asked him for his ring and riding whip as souvenirs. She returned to the stone prison via the tunnel, and eventually gave birth to a son, who grew up in his father's house.
>
> One day the boy stole the raja's golden bed right out from under him, and tricked the raja into hiding in a sack. "When the raja's men . . . saw the raja's son, they thought he was the raja himself! He was sitting on the raja's horse. . . . Then the son beat the sack with his riding whip. . . . But when they opened the sack in the palace, they found the raja, and still they couldn't tell the difference between him and his son. 'Who are you?' they asked the raja's son. 'My mother's the woman in the prison; let her out, and she'll tell you the whole story.' When they brought her from the prison, the raja said, 'How did you give birth to a child?' And she said, 'Well, here's your ring and your riding whip. Remember now? Anyhow, I won the bet.' "[24]

Since neither the man nor the woman can answer the riddles at the start, she is no cleverer than he. And though the raja ostensibly imprisons her to find the answer to the riddle, he makes no effort to do so. It is she who makes the impossible vow, which she later refers to as a "bet." Unlike the prisons in other stories, this one does not isolate her at all; the raja visits her there and apparently sleeps with her, which is what seems to be implied by the chewing of betel (an essential part of loveplay in Indian literature, like the post-coital cigarette in Western erotic conventions) and the euphemism that he "enjoyed himself." Nevertheless, she disguises herself to get pregnant by him (remarking, cynically, that the raja is too stupid to see through any disguise), just as she does in stories where he has *not* already slept with her, and he is later surprised that she managed to get pregnant, apparently forgetting his own nights with her. It is as if the old pattern of the bed-trick hangs on even when a new twist has made it superfluous. She gets from him, along with his ring, not his horse (as often happens in other variants) but his whip, which her son has—and uses—when he tricks his father, though the son now also has, inexplicably, the horse. Though the raja did not notice that the dancing girl looked an awful lot like his wife, everyone does notice that the bed thief looks just like the raja. And when the raja finally demands an explanation, she merely shows him the ring (and the whip!) and assumes that he will now remember—what? The night they spent together or the well-known tale of the Clever Wife?

The core of the story, with the bed-trick and the vindicating ring, appears in a Hindu folktale about the god Śiva and his wife the goddess Pārvatī, whose marriage is celebrated in myth, literature, and ritual throughout the Hindu world. Annual festivals reenact every phase of the marriage, from the courtship through the wedding and even beyond, to the bride's annual return visits to her father's home, celebrated at the festival of Dūrgāpūjā in Bengal. But the solemn joy of these celebrations is frequently undercut by acknowledgment of the problems that bedevil even a marriage literally made in heaven. Pārvatī berates Śiva for his refusal to beget a son, as well as for his addiction to marijuana, his cheating at their dice games, his poverty, his infidelity, his refusal to get a job, and other marital shortcomings. Sometimes she deals with Śiva's habitual womanizing (or goddessizing) by masquerading as the object of his desire. In a Bengali story, Pārvatī disguises herself as a *dom* (low-caste) ferrywoman and gets a diamond ring from her husband, who fails to recognize her.[25]

A Tulu tale, recorded in Karnataka in 1970, begins when Śiva and Pārvatī quarrel and Pārvatī leaves in fury. This time she makes a paste of charcoal and water and smears it on her face to make herself black. Then she dresses as a woman of a forest tribe, a Korpalu, a person of very low caste. Śiva approaches her, but she protests:

> "Oh, my! What kind of a way is that to speak to a Korpalu?" "What difference does it make if you are a Korpalu? You are a human being, aren't you? I'm a human being too. Our blood is the same, is it not?" argued Śiva. "What you are saying is not right," answered the woman. "You are a god. I am a Korpalu." Then Śiva and the woman remained in the forest together for two days and three nights.
>
> On the third day, Śiva said, "I'm going now, Korpalu." "If you are going, go," she replied, "but just one thing. If I get pregnant, who will pay for my expenses?" "I will provide for your needs. Here is a golden knife, a silver case for lime, and a silver snuffbox. I also have a golden ring with my seal. Take these things. Use them for your expenses if you get pregnant!" said Śiva. "Now I am going back to my palace, Korpalu." Śiva ran home by one path, while Pārvatī ran home by another.

> When she reached her house, Pārvatī quickly took a bath and combed her hair. Before she even had a chance to put on her sari, however, Śiva arrived home. She said, "I have the feeling that you had a good time with a forest woman." "No, I didn't," said Śiva. "Didn't you have sex with a Korpalu?" asked Pārvatī. "When you left here you took your golden knife, your silver box for lime, and the silver snuff box. Didn't you give those things to the Korpalu?" "I didn't give them to her," said Śiva. "Don't say things like that about me. I didn't do it!" "Don't lie to me!" said Pārvatī. "A Korpalu came here and gave those things to me!"
>
> "Where did you see her?" asked Śiva. "She came here and gave them to me," repeated Pārvatī. Then Śiva said, "You have no defects. You were born from truth. Let us be on good terms together."[26]

Pārvatī gets Śiva's jewelry—including a golden ring with his seal—as a kind of prenatal medical insurance to defray her expenses if she gets pregnant, a practical use for the ring that we have already noted in a Buddhist jātaka story and that extends the role of jewelry beyond its classic function as identification into the realm of home economics. It is worth noting that Pārvatī does not mention the golden ring when she catches Śiva out in the end. The ring seems almost an atavism in this story, a convention that has no actual effect. When she masquerades as the Korpalu, she does not ask explicitly for the ring, but she asks for something, and what else would he give her? (In a Himalayan folktale the woman has hardheaded misgivings and explicitly asks for the ring as she says to her departing seducer, "The male of the species is very bad. You will forget me and marry again. Give me your token." And he gives her his ring, with all ten of his names inscribed on it.)[27] Equally down-to-earth is Pārvatī's inspired lie about how she knows that he gave away the jewelry: she implies that, good housekeeper that she is, she *misses* those items on his person and deduces that he must have given them to some woman. This tale was told by a woman, and a woman's eye for jewelry, and for household inventory, may have put that bit of sharp observation into the story.

Pārvatī appears to Śiva doubly disguised, as a human and as low-caste. Śiva dismisses both problems, lying by saying that he is a human (he is a god, as she immediately reminds him) and lying in the eyes of Hindu caste law by saying that all human beings are equal when it comes to sex. Pārvatī thus uses sex and jewelry to deconstruct the power of a husband, the power of a god, and the power of caste.

Jewelry versus Common Sense

Many of these tales were borrowed by one culture from another within India or diffused from a common source. But the very fact that these stories, and not others, were able to travel, like certain wines, and to be told again and again in such different contexts, often by storytellers from different religions, indicates that they are in a very real sense at home in several cultures, however much they may be differently inflected and take on different meanings in each new context.[28]

Why do so many people tell these same stories again and again? Why do these mythic structures have such a stranglehold on the human imagination? More particularly, why do people keep telling stories that fly so blatantly in the face of logic and reason, of the culture's construction of common sense, even when logical concerns are explicitly raised in the course of the stories themselves? Right at the start of the Indian tradition, the king in the *Kaṭṭhahāri Jātaka,* when presented with his signet ring, simply says, "That's not my ring." Why do so few of the husbands in the other stories tell this simple lie that would get them off the hook? The signet ring is the only kind of ring that is a certain sign of identity, with the bearer's name or emblem on it. And even the signet ring is not proof of what the bearer had *done;* someone else might have stolen it, sold it, and so forth, and worn it to commit the act in question, or indeed *not* to commit the act in question. That such arguments from reason were always available to storytellers and audiences is easily demonstrated by a number of stories we have seen in which someone does question how, after all, a ring can prove that someone did or did not commit an act of sexual infidelity. Common sense is explicitly brought into play when the "hard evidence" of Ratnāvalī's necklace is challenged. Reason often pipes up to argue against the "proof"; reason says, "Look for the ring where you lost it"; reason says, "Lots of people have rings like that" or "You stole the ring" or "That's not my ring"—in other words, "The ring lies."

The unreasonable recognition by means of rings is balanced by the equally unreasonable non-recognition of people in disguise. Sometimes a reasoned explanation is given for the success of such deceptions. In a fantastical story in the *Mahābhārata* (which does not involve a ring), this sort of non-recognition is justified by a boon that the god Dharma grants to his son, King Yudhiṣṭhira.[29] Yudhiṣṭhira tells Dharma that he and his brothers have been forced to go into exile in disguise and will lose their kingdom if they are recognized. He asks the god to promise that they will not be recognized, and the god agrees. This boon justifies the shallowness of the disguises that the king and his brothers subsequently adopt, parodies of their well-known characters. Magical though it is, the god's promise does interject a reasonable, if not realistic, explanation of how they got away with such obvious and playful masquerades. But the Hindu god's explicit boon is implicit in every recognition plot in every culture: no matter how poor your masquerade is, no one will recognize you. Similarly, the ring as evidence would never stand up in court, but it either jogs the forgetful husband's memory, if he really has forgotten, or jogs his conscience, if he is lying, so that he confesses. The clever wife is like a sharp courtroom lawyer, tap-dancing with material that she knows would not actually be admitted as evidence. Is it possible that all of the clever wife folktales are satires on the dumb idea that one could prove paternity with a ring?

One reasonable argument that challenges the "proof" of the ring is the argument from coincidence: maybe two unrelated people just happen to have the same ring (or the same name or the same face). But the idea of coincidence itself flies in the face of reason and can be challenged. In *The Lady of the Jeweled Necklace,* someone helpfully explains the "resemblance" of two people who are actually the same person by reference to coincidence, using a word (*ghuṇākṣara*) that literally designates an alphabet letter eaten into a page by a bookworm, rather like our quantum metaphor of a monkey randomly typing out the complete works of Shakespeare.[30] Yet this same text also remarks that a piece of jewelry is a stupid way to identify someone. The coincidences of resemblance point us toward another sort of coincidence, the coincidence of the masquerading self with the undisguised self, of the clever wife with the make-believe prostitute.[31] This high-wire act, the self flying through the masquerade to catch the outstretched hands of some other self, must be performed without any net but the narrative chain-mail made up of rings. And that chain-mail is what preserves these illogical stories even in cultures, such as India's, where the more logical likelihood has been acknowledged long ago.

Notes

1. Some of the material in this essay is reworked from several sections of my book, *The Ring of Truth: Myths of Sex and Jewelry* (New York: Oxford University Press, 2016).
2. Charles Edwards, *The History and Poetry of Finger Rings* (New York: John W. Lovell, 1855), 17.

3. Romila Thapar, *Sakuntala: Texts, Readings, Histories* (New Delhi: Kali for Women, 1999), 54.
4. Viśakhadatta, *Mudrārākṣasa,* translated by M. R. Kale (Delhi: Motilal Banarsidass, 2011).
5. Vātsyāyana, *Kāmasūtra* (with the commentary of Śrī Yaśodhara) (Bombay: Laksmivenkatesvara Steam Press, 1856); Vatsyayana, *Kamasutra,* translated by Wendy Doniger and Sudhir Kakar. (Oxford: Oxford University Press, 2002; Oxford's World Classics), 4.2.63.
6. Vātsyāyana, *Kāmasūtra,* 5.6.19, with Yaśodhara's commentary.
7. Vātsyāyana, *Kāmasūtra,* book 6.
8. R. Parthasarathy, trans. *The Tale of an Anklet: An Epic of South India (The Cilappatikaram of Ilanko Atikal)* (New York: Columbia University Press, 1993).
9. Kannaki then tears off her left breast, sets the city on fire with it, curses the city, dies, and becomes a great goddess. But that is another story.
10. Édouard Chavannes, *Cinq cents contes et apologues extraits du Tripitaka Chinois,* 4 vols. (Paris: E. Leroux, 1910), 1:389–390, Number 188. From *Tripitika* 191.7, p. 22. My translation from the French. The three sages are Maudgalyāyana, Aniruddha, and Mahākaśyapa.
11. *Mahābhārata* of Vyāsa (Poona: Bhandarkar Oriental Research Institute, 1933–1969), 1.64–69.
12. *Kaṭṭhahāri Jātaka* (no. 7), in E. B. Cowell, ed. *The Jātaka or Stories of the Buddha's Former Births,* 6 vols. (London: Pali Text Society, 1995), 1:27–28. The name *Kaṭṭhavāhana* means "bearer-of-fuel-sticks."
13. 1 *Kings* 3:16–27.
14. *Uddālaka Jātaka* (no. 487), in Cowell, *The Jātaka,* 4:188–191. The name *Uddalāka* is derived, according to this text, from an Uddāla tree that was growing in the park where he was conceived.
15. J. J. Jones, trans. *The Mahāvastu,* 3 vols. (London: Pali Text Society, 1976; Sacred Books of the Buddhists), 2:91–114.
16. Wendy Doniger, *The Bedtrick: Tales of Sex and Masquerade* (Chicago: University of Chicago Press, 2000), ch. 3; Doniger, *The Ring of Truth,* 39, 128–130.
17. Phyllis Granoff, trans. "The Story of Kuberadatta and Kuberadattā from the *Dharmābhyudāyamahākāvya,*" in *Religions of India in Practice,* edited by Donald S. Lopez Jr. (Princeton, NJ: Princeton University Press, 1995; Princeton Readings in Religion), 415–417. My paraphrase.
18. Harṣa: *Ratnāvalī,* edited by Ashokanath Bhattacharya and Maheshwar Das (Calcutta: Modern Book Agency, 1967), and *Priyādarśikā,* edited by V. D. Gadré (Bombay, 1884); Wendy Doniger, trans., *The Lady of*

the Jewel Necklace and The Lady Who Shows Her Love (New York: New York University Press, 2006; Clay Sanskrit Series).

19. Harṣa, *Ratnāvalī* 4.125.
20. Harṣa, *Ratnāvalī* 4.19ff. Here I follow the alternative reading (*āyuṣmaī ratnāvalī, tvam idṛṣīm avasthām gatāsī*).
21. The folklorist Stith Thompson called the theme "The Rejected Wife as Lover," while filing it under the evocative title of AT 891D. See Thompson, *Motif-Index of Folk Literature,* 6 vols. (Bloomington: Indiana University Press, 1955–1958).
22. Doniger, *The Bedtrick.*
23. A. K. Ramanujan, *A Flowering Tree, and Other Oral Tales from India* (Berkeley: University of California Press, 1997), 199–206. I have condensed Ramanujan's narration.
24. Stuart Blackburn, *Moral Fictions: Tamil Folktales in Oral Tradition* (Helsinki: Suomalainen Tiedeakatemia, 2001; Folklore Fellows' Communication, no. 278), 218–220; Tale 81: "A Clever Woman's Riddle." I have paraphrased Blackburn's telling except in passages where I quote him directly, indicating that with quotation marks.
25. *Manasabijay* of Bipradas, 1–235; cited by Pradyot Kumar Maity, *Historical Studies in the Cult of the Goddess Manasa: A Socio-Cultural Study* (Calcutta: Punthi Pustak, 1966), 79. Pārvatī also becomes a ferrywoman in the *Manasa-mangal* of Ketaka Das.
26. "Siva and Parvati," from Karnataka, #48, in Brenda E. F. Beck et al., eds. *Folktales of India* (Chicago: University of Chicago Press, 1987), 171–174. See also Peter Claus, "Playing *Cenne:* The Meanings of a Folk Game," in *Another Harmony: New Essays on the Folklore of India,* edited by Stuart Blackburn and A. K. Ramanujan (Berkeley: University of California Press, 1986), 290–293; David Shulman, *God Inside Out: Siva's Game of Dice* (New York: Oxford University Press, 1997), 108; Doniger, *The Bedtrick,* 17–20.
27. Translated by William Sax, *Dancing the Self: Personhood and Performance in the Pandav Lila of Garhwal* (New York: Oxford University Press, 2002), 69–70.
28. Claude Lévi-Strauss, "Split Representation in the Art of Asia and America," in Lévi-Strauss, *Structural Anthropology,* translated by Claire Jacobson and Brooke Grundfest Schoepf (Harmondsworth: Penguin, 1963), 245–268.
29. *Mahābhārata* 3.298.
30. The commentary on the very first verse of the *Kāmasūtra* says, "You can, of course, learn about pleasure from other teachings, just as you

can read meaning into a hole shaped like a letter of the alphabet that a bookworm has eaten out of a page, but you do not understand what you should do and what you should not do. And so people say: A man should not be congratulated if he happens to succeed at something without knowing its science, for it is pure chance, like a bookworm eating a hole in the shape of a letter of the alphabet."

31. Wendy Doniger, *The Woman Who Pretended to Be Who She Was* (New York: Oxford University Press, 2005), 229–232.

Chapter 3

Taking Refuge in Jewels

Maria Heim

Buddhists everywhere "take refuge" in the "Three Jewels"—that is, the Buddha, the Dhamma, and the Saṅgha. And students of Buddhism everywhere have wondered exactly what this might mean. What is it to take shelter in and seek protection from jewels? In what way are the Buddha, the Dhamma, and the Saṅgha *jewels?* And how did this formulation become central to Buddhist understandings of what it is to be Buddhist? In this chapter, I take up how the Theravāda commentarial tradition understood this complex of ideas by focusing on its treatment of the well-known and often recited Jewel Sutta.

The Jewel Sutta (Ratana Sutta) is a short *sutta* of seventeen stanzas that occurs in two anthologies in the Pali canon's "Miscellaneous Collection" (*Khuddaka Nikāya*): the *Suttanipāta* and the *Khuddakapāṭha*. It is much more widely circulated, however, in the later noncanonical collections of "protective texts" (*paritta*) in which it always appears, such as the *Catubhāṇāvarapāli* and its Sinhala version (the *Maha Pirit Pota* or *Pirit Pota* in Sri Lanka) and similar collections in Burma, Thailand, and Laos.[1] In these collections, *paritta suttas* like the Jewel Sutta are chanted regularly in ritual ceremonies, making them among the most widely known texts in the Theravāda world.

Paritta texts offer protection. The Jewel Sutta is said to protect people from natural catastrophes and meddlesome supernatural agents. From early on this *sutta* was considered to have potent protective powers. It was mentioned in the *Milindapañha* as a *paritta* against danger, and fifth-century Buddhaghosa lists it among other *suttas* as having protective powers. Specifically, he claims that the *sutta* can protect beings anywhere throughout "a hundred thousand million world-spheres" in the buddha-field in which the Buddha's authority reigns.[2] The *Mahāvaṃsa* describes its deployment in a public ceremony when Lanka was afflicted by drought and disease, recounting how monks processed through the streets sprinkling water and chanting the Jewel Sutta, effecting instant relief.[3]

Paritta texts belong to a widespread tradition in Indian religion in which scriptural texts and sacred sounds have potency, as we see with mantras, *dhāraṇīs,* and *rakṣā* texts in other Buddhist traditions. As far back as the Vedic traditions of sacred mantras and ritual chanting, there is a long-standing pan-Indic respect for the efficacy of powerful formulas and scriptures recited ritually. Justin McDaniel points out that the magical efficacy of *parittas* like the Jewel Sutta "lies in their sound and role in a protective ceremony, and less (or not at all) in their semantic meaning," a meaning that may "have nothing to do with their role and result in a ritual."[4] It is in the recitation of the sound, not a grasping of the sense, that the *paritta*'s power rests.

That the Jewel Sutta's meaning may not always be salient in its widespread ritual use does not entail, however, that no one was ever interested in what it means or how it works. In fact, the lengthy exegesis on the *sutta* in the commentaries on both canonical anthologies in which it appears suggests otherwise: the commentator (who the tradition considers to be Buddhaghosa) offers meticulous exposition on the form and the meaning of the *sutta.*[5] In it, he frames its efficacy in terms of an original narrative of the Buddha's visit to Vesālī, where the truth statements in each stanza of the *sutta* were first delivered. This commentary, fascinating for its narrative structure, its account of the workings of truth statements, and its unremitting insistence on the superlative greatness of the Buddha, the Dhamma, and the Saṅgha, lingers on the central metaphor of the tradition—the Three Jewels—and how they come to offer protection and refuge.

The Jewel Sutta commentary explains how the Jewel Sutta gets its ritual potency to provide protection and how the Buddha, Saṅgha, and Dhamma are the protective jewels at the core of Buddhist devotional practice. It represents a Theravāda (or more precisely a Mahāvihāra) sensibility and reasoning, yet the sumptuous jewels described intimate that not all the glam and glitter of early Buddhism belong to the Mahāyāna; nor are Mahāyāna *suttas* alone conceived to be powerful. How representative, known, or acceptable this reading would be to other Buddhist traditions is of course another question. Within its own terms, the text offers a subtle interpretation of the form and meaning of the Jewel Sutta and how to understand its central extended metaphor of the Three Jewels offering shelter. My exploration of this commentary submits how one articulate and thoughtful strand of the tradition understood the power and potency of the jewel imagery we find everywhere in Buddhist thought and practice.

The *Sutta*

The Jewel Sutta is just seventeen stanzas long. (Readers can find my translation of it as an appendix to this chapter.) Stanza 1 opens with an invocation to any and all beings present of the earth or in the sky to be happy and to listen carefully. These beings are then enjoined, in stanza 2, to "show lovingkindness" to the human population who bear them offerings and to protect them. The next eleven stanzas offer "truth statements," exemplified by stanza 3:

> Whatever treasure there is here or the other world, or whatever excellent jewel may be in the heavens,
> There is none on par with the Tathāgata. There is only an excellent jewel in the sense of the Buddha. By this truth may there be safety![6]

Each of the next ten stanzas repeats the last two lines, affirming that there is only an excellent jewel in the sense of the Buddha (and in turn, the Dhamma and the Saṅgha), which comprises the truth statement formula on the basis of which there is to be safety.

The final three stanzas of this short *sutta* again address the supernatural beings assembled and call on all to praise, in turn, the Buddha, the Dhamma, and the Sangha and to assure safety, starting with the Buddha:

> Whatever beings are gathered here, of the earth or in the sky,
> We honor the Buddha, the Tathāgata worshipped by gods and men. May there be safety![7]

The overall liturgy is a summoning of supernatural beings, a series of affirmations of the unequaled excellence of the Buddha, the Dhamma, and the Saṅgha, and then on the basis of the truth of their being, in fact, the *only* excellent jewels, an appeal to protection. The final three lines urge that the supernatural beings assembled respond to the Three Jewels in worship and in honoring them, assure safety to humans.

The general logic of the truth statements or acts of truth prevalent across Indic literature is that stating a deep and profound truth—particularly of some rare and sublime reality—requires submission.[8] By an irrefutable affirmation of a truth, beings are obliged to comply. Through this mechanism harassment can turn to protection, curses can become blessings (or at least can be softened), and boons can be granted. In this *sutta*, truth statements comprise most of the verses. By the *sutta*'s end, the supernatural beings are assimilated into the community of human and divine worshippers, securing their protection of humans.

The Story

In his commentary on the Jewel Sutta, Buddhaghosa situates it in a narrative context, for the commentarial tradition insists that every *sutta* be embedded in a narrative frame (a narrative framing that the commentators often must supply). All *suttas* must have stories that situate them in a particular place, time, audience, and purpose. These become the circumstances through which a *sutta* is to be interpreted. This context is referred to in the *Suttanipāta* commentary as its "origin" (*uppatti*).[9] The commentary on the *Khuddakapāṭha* lists the whys and wherefores of the *sutta* that are prerequisite to understanding its meaning: "having shed light on by whom, when, where, and why this matter was said, we will make an exegesis of the meaning."[10]

The context of the Jewel Sutta, according to Buddhaghosa, is a catastrophe in Vesālī at the time of the Buddha. The mention of Vesālī occasions an account of the founding of this ancient city ruled by the Licchavis. They trace their lineage to the queen of Bārāṇasī, who in a distant time gave birth to a "lump of flesh" and sent it down the Ganges, where it was retrieved by a kindly cowherd family and eventually developed into a healthy boy and girl. They became the progenitors of Vesālī, which grew to a large and prosperous kingdom. But at the time of our story Vesālī is afflicted with drought, famine, and pestilence, and piles of dead bodies have grown high. Nonhuman beings (*amanussa*), drawn to the smell of the corpses, enter the city and further harass its occupants.[11]

To address the crisis, the Licchavi king invites the Buddha, then residing at Rājagaha under the patronage of King Bimbasāra, to Vesālī. The Buddha agrees, foreseeing that he will offer the Jewel Sutta in Vesālī, where "its protection will pervade a hundred thousand *koṭis* of world systems, and at the end of the *sutta* 84,000 living creatures will fully grasp the Dhamma."[12] What follows is a friendly rivalry between King

Bimbasāra and the Licchavi princes as to who can honor the Buddha more lavishly. Bimbasāra adorns the path from Rājagaha to Vesālī with newly built monasteries, flags, banners, and knee-deep flowers. A jewel-encrusted boat is supplied to ferry the Buddha and his retinue across the Ganges, and a pavilion is erected (the jewel-encrusted boat furnishes yet another example of the gem-studded life the Buddha leads even [or perhaps *particularly*] after his renunciation and awakening, as Vanessa R. Sasson discusses in her chapter in this volume). Bimbasāra himself enters the water up to his neck to see the Buddha off and vows to remain waiting at the bank until the Buddha returns.

For their part, the Licchavi princes pledge to double this splendor, and they enter the water up to their necks to receive him. Thereupon a magnificent rain falls, ending the drought, washing away the corpses and pestilence, and purifying the region. The Buddha's presence in Vesālī prompts the god Sakka to visit with his retinue of *devas,* and their presence scatters many of the nonhuman beings afflicting the city. As he enters the city, the Buddha instructs Venerable Ānanda: "Having learned this Jewel Sutta, Ānanda, take the materials for food offerings around the three city walls of Vesālī along with the Licchavi princes, and do the protection [*paritta*]."[13] He then teaches the *sutta.* This narrative is thus considered the "where, when, why, and by whom" the *sutta* was given.[14]

The Ritual

The commentary then describes Ānanda mastering the Jewel Sutta (which had been "uttered for the sake of warding off affliction")[15] and processing around the city, sprinkling water taken from the Buddha's almsbowl while reciting it. As soon as he uttered "whatever treasure" (the first line of stanza 3 above), nonhuman beings still lurking in the city fled, trying to squeeze through the city gates but cramming them to such an extent that some had to break through the city walls to get out. As soon as they were gone, the plague lifted, and people emerged from their houses to pay homage to Ānanda and to adorn a seat for the Buddha and a hall for the Saṅgha. The Buddha then gives the Jewel Sutta to the entire community (although Buddhaghosa notes that some authorities hold that the Buddha gave only the first five verses at this time, and Ānanda supplied the rest).[16]

These ritual elements are echoed in the subsequent *Mahāvaṃsa* account of a royal ceremony in Lanka under King Upatissa, who, though righteous (like the Licchavis), found his kingdom suffering famine and plague. The chronicle describes the adorning of the city, the ritual sprinkling of water as monks circumambulate the city walls, and the reciting of the Jewel Sutta. This ceremony prompts a healing and purifying rain, ridding the island of plague and famine.[17]

Speech Acts

Buddhaghosa is attentive to the nature of the speech that the Buddha uses in the Jewel Sutta, and he draws several distinctions that illuminate how he understands its efficacy. For example, the first two stanzas invite the nonhuman beings to be present and enjoin them to show "lovingkindness" to humans. These verses act as a gentle appeal to these beings' better nature and their own prudential considerations. The Buddha's purport in these two verses of invitation is described in this way: "The intention here is: 'When I say "Show lovingkindness to human beings,'" I do not speak through the power of the supremacy of a Buddha, but rather for the sake of benefiting both you and human beings."[18] Buddhaghosa goes on to list the many benefits of lovingkindness. On his reading, these two stanzas are not grounded in an appeal to the Buddha's authority, nor is the Buddha issuing commands challenging the supernatural beings. Rather, he coaxes them. Buddhaghosa goes on to show how the Buddha tells the nonhuman beings that humans make many offerings to them, and they should be gracious and protect them.

When it comes to the truth statements uttered in stanzas 3–14, however, the Buddha is now uttering commands (*āṇā*). Buddhaghosa signals this when he begins to comment on stanza 3, in which the Buddha is "starting to employ a statement of truth," and that it is by "showing the qualities of the Buddha, etc." that truth statements are employed.[19] Later he is very forthright: these truth-statement stanzas constitute "commands that are accepted by the nonhuman beings in the 100,000 world-spheres."[20] In this account, the reason the truth statements work is that they are the Buddha's orders, not simply observations about a certain true state of affairs.

Further, these truth statements are metaphors, where the Buddha, the Dhamma, and the Saṅgha are said to be excellent jewels and in fact, once properly understood, the *only* jewels. It is these utterances recognizing that they are the supreme and unique jewels that become the truths by which safety is commanded.

The final three stanzas in the *sutta* are not the Buddha's words at all. Buddhaghosa reports that they are the words of Sakka, accepting the truth statements and offering worship on behalf of the deities. Sakka assents to the commands and thereby ensures the efficacy of the protection: "Now Sakka, the chief of the gods, thought 'by the Bhagavan's employing [these] truth statements based on the qualities of the Three Jewels, the welfare of the city is achieved, and so something should be said by me also, based on the qualities of the Three Jewels, for the welfare of the city.' "[21] Sakka goes on to describe the Buddha's qualities, and then he circumambulates the city. The Buddha then continues to recite the Jewel Sutta every day for seven days and then returns to King Bimbasāra in great splendor.

To sum up, we have three different kinds of speech acts in the *sutta*. The first two stanzas are *invitations* issued by the Buddha to nonhuman beings to listen and benefit. The bulk of the *sutta* contains truth statements that consist of metaphors that indicate the qualities of the Three Jewels and that act as *commands*. The final stanzas are the gods, represented by Sakka, responding in *assent* and *praise*.

"Based on the Qualities"

Essential to the logic of truth utterances in the commentarial understanding is that they work through showing the qualities (*guṇa*) of the Buddha, the Dhamma, and the Saṅgha. As Sakka puts it above, the Buddha employed these truth statements "*based on the qualities* of the Three Jewels." Truth statements work because they reveal or demonstrate the qualities of the Three Jewels, a claim echoed multiple times in the commentary.[22] It is not just any true statement that can have such efficacy. Rather, only truth statements that invoke extraordinary qualities of someone or something will be binding to those who hear them. And for Buddhaghosa this is quite specific, referring only to extraordinary qualities of a certain sort: the Buddha commands these truth statements based on the unequaled status of his morality and concentration practices and not his "birth, clan, good family, beauty of complexion, or anything else."[23]

The idea of *guṇa* (quality or attribute) has of course wide resonance in Indian thought. I think that in the Pali commentaries *guṇa* functions as a quality or excellent attribute of something that is known in a relational way. *Guṇas* are attributes of a thing or person to which others respond; in fact, to define those qualities is to discern their effects on those who observe them. This definition of *guṇa* later emerges in Daṇḍin's Sanskrit literary theory, which utilizes a fourfold distinction in analyzing poetic figures: act (*kriyā*), attribute (*guṇa*), genus (*jāti*), and substance (*dravya*). Daṇḍin's example of *guṇa* demonstrates its relational impact: "the touch of the beloved provokes a tingling in the limbs, happy release in the mind, a closing of the eyes."[24] The qualities of the beloved's touch are evident in the responses it elicits; these qualities are known relationally and contextually (unlike the agentive [*kriyā*], generic [*jāti*], and substantive [*dravya*] ways something may be described). Perhaps the paradigmatic example in the Pali commentaries is their treatment of the ninefold *guṇas* of the Buddha as elaborated in the *itipiso gāthā;* each quality is known through the way it evokes devotion and worship.[25] Mattia Salvini also notes the significance of the idea of *guṇa* in relational terms: the Three Jewels are "*ratanas* because their genuine good qualities are the basis of a supreme delight (*rati*) based on the unmistaken recognition of their worth"; similarly, the *guṇas* of jewels in general "in fact, are not exhausted by their physical traits, but they consist (primarily) in their ability to bring about beneficial results."[26]

As outlined below, the extended metaphor of the Buddha, the Dhamma, and the Saṅgha being jewels rests on comparing, point by point, the qualities of jewels with the qualities of the Buddha, the Dhamma, and the Saṅgha. There are many features of jewels that might be discussed: their size, price, class, characteristics, color, etc. (as, for example, these are detailed in the earliest text we have on gemology, Kauṭilya's *Arthaśāstra*).[27] But these are not the qualities in which Buddhaghosa is interested. Instead, he observes that jewels bring pleasure and are honored, greatly valued, used by high-status persons, inestimable in worth, and rare (as we will consider below). These qualities are all relational and highly evaluative, known by how they impact people. And it is on the basis of these qualities of jewels that the analogy with the Buddha, the Dhamma, and the Saṅgha is forged.

The Metaphor

We now have all the tools to turn to how Buddhaghosa understands the workings of the jewel metaphor. He takes the jewel metaphor to be semantically complex: the qualities of jewels structure how one is to understand the qualities of the Buddha. In this sense they are cognitively and pedagogically important for acquiring knowledge. The use of jewels—both actual stones and symbolic jewels—also has aesthetic impact; jewels are beautiful things and are connected to splendid realities that are delightful and pleasing.[28] But the comparison works only to a certain point; as we have seen in the *sutta* itself, once properly understood, the only real jewels are the Buddha, the Dhamma, and the Saṅgha. That is, if one comes to fully understand the qualities that make jewels jewels, then only the Three Jewels can truly be seen as jewels, as all others will fall far short. Implicit in this move appears to be a logic about jewels that is unstated in the *sutta* and its commentary but which seems to have been widely attested in both Sanskrit and Pali lexica. As shown by Salvini, one definition of jewel (*ratna/ratana*) is "what is best in its class."[29] Once the Buddha, the Dhamma, and the Sangha are placed in the class of jewels, they become the "best in their class," so other items in that class are no longer the best and thus, in some sense, no longer even jewels at all.

Let us turn to the lexical structuring of the analogy. Jewels have certain qualities that elicit responses in humans. We can start with definitions. "Treasure," as it occurs in the third stanza, is defined by Buddhaghosa as "anything humans use to engage in trade or for adornment and enjoyment, such as gold, silver, pearls, gemstones, beryl, coral, rubies, and emeralds, etc., as well as the wealth held by such beings as nāgas and Supaṇṇas born in realms many hundreds of *yojanas* wide in palaces made of jewels on lands strewn with sands of pearl and gemstone."[30]

Treasure is the broader category, and it refers to wealth adorning the abodes of supernatural but still earthly creatures like nāga serpents and Supaṇṇa birds and found more rarely in the human world to serve in trade or adornments for us. As for "jewels" more specifically: "A jewel [*ratana*] leads to, brings, begets, and increases pleasure [*rati*], and thus is a 'jewel.' It is a name for anything honored, of great value, inestimable, rarely seen, and used by high-status beings."[31] That is, the connection of jewels and the pleasure they bring us is implicit in the very word for jewel—*ratana* sounds like *rati,* pleasure. Further, these qualities of jewels—being *honored, of great value, inestimable, rarely seen,* and *used by high-status beings*—become the precise qualities for comparison with the jewels of the Buddha, Dhamma, and Saṅgha, and it is on these points that the commentary provides extensive development of the metaphor. It is noteworthy that while jewels have been widely prized in Indic culture for their healing and protective powers, Buddhaghosa makes no appeal to these attributes here.[32]

Let us take the example of "being honored": Buddhaghosa elaborates how the Wheel Jewel and the Gem Jewel of the Wheel-Turning

Emperor are among the most *honored* jewels known to humans. (These are two of the seven royal jewels bestowed on this great sovereign, with the others being the Horse Jewel, the Elephant Jewel, the Woman Jewel, the Treasurer Jewel, and the Minister Jewel.)[33] When the Wheel Jewel and the Gem Jewel are present, "people honor nothing else, do not bother offering flowers or incense, and do not go to *yakkhas,* or other such beings."[34] The seven royal jewels are incomparable in the sense of being *honored,* and yet, truly, even these "are not the equal of the Buddha." Indeed, "if something is a jewel in the sense of *being honored,* then really only the Tathāgata is a jewel."[35] The jewels of the emperor are not really jewels even by the criteria of their own qualities because the Tathāgata far surpasses them.

This is to say that the jewel metaphor works in two ways. First, it demonstrates likeness: the Buddha is *like* the world's most precious jewels in being honored, of great value, etc. (though none can equal him). The commentary works its way through this structural comparison parallel to what we just saw: when a Buddha is present, "powerful gods and humans do not honor anything else and do not worship anyone else" (and it elaborates from here the extravagant worship such gods and kings bestow on him). But then, at a second level, the metaphor points to the unique and maximal greatness of the Buddha: when considered properly, *only* the Tathāgata is a jewel; what is being said at this point is their inequality or dissimilarity.[36] Once we really know what a jewel is, we see that only the Buddha (and in later stanzas, the Dhamma and the Sangha) can be a jewel, the best in their class, and the comparison falls away.

This same structural logic is developed at all points of the comparison: as jewels are *of great value, inestimable, rarely seen, used by high-status beings,* and *generating pleasure,* so too is the Tathāgata. These are at first points of comparison, but then, finally, points of incomparability. They affirm, in the end, the Buddha's maximal greatness, where only he can be a jewel once a jewel is properly understood. For example, like silk from Varanasi, he is of "*great value,*" while of course surpassing its value. But "if something is a jewel in the sense of being of *great value,* then only the Tathāgata is a jewel."[37] Similarly, like the Wheel Jewel of the Wheel-Turning Emperor (with its "hub made of sapphire, its thousand spokes made of the seven jewels, its rim made of coral, its lynch pin of glittering gold"), the Buddha is *inestimable,* priceless.[38] And like the Gem Jewel ("a jewel of finest beryl, lustrous and well cut with eight facets, [in size] like the hub of a wheel, mined from Vepulla mountain") he is *inestimable.*[39] And yet, "If something is a jewel in the sense of being *inestimable* then really, only the Tathāgata is a jewel. For the Tathāgata cannot be delimited by anyone measuring or appraising him in reference to morality, concentration, or wisdom, etc., whereby one might say 'here is one with as many qualities, or is the same, or is his likeness.' And so there is no jewel like the Tathāgata with respect to being *inestimable.*"[40] Insofar as a jewel is priceless and unable to be adequately appraised, the only true case of such a jewel is the Tathāgata because in reference to him other jewels can be appraised (as of less value than he is). Only he is truly inestimable.

Similarly, the Buddha is *rarely seen* like the Wheel-Turning Emperor himself with his seven jewels. But compared to him, arising only after many eons, how can such emperors, arising many times in an eon, be considered jewels at all?[41] He is *used by high-status persons,* like the Seven Jewels of the Wheel-Turning Emperor, which can never be owned by lowly folk like "outcastes, bamboo workers, hunters, cartwrights, and scavengers," no matter how wealthy such persons may become.[42] The Buddha can be put to use by people with supporting conditions for understanding his teachings but not by the six non-Buddhist teachers of confused views.[43] Finally, something is a "jewel in the general sense of *generating pleasure.*"[44] People get utterly besotted with jewels of all kinds. But none can generate the pleasures of highest spiritual attainment like the Buddha, and recognizing this is the very transformation sought by the texts.

We may observe in passing that the comparison becomes an opportunity for the commentator, with typical scholastic enthusiasm, to elaborate in precise terms what these qualities are and thereby structure a complex pedagogy of the Buddha, the Dhamma, and the Saṅgha. Ever ready to provide lists as matrices to elaborate doctrine, Buddhaghosa lists and details the different kinds of Dhamma (the Dhamma of *nibbāna* and the Dhamma of the path) and the different kinds of Saṅgha (the various classifications of sacred persons: *buddhas, paccekabuddhas,* etc.). This commentarial device generates meaning, or, if one prefers, it draws out the extensive meanings present in the original *sutta.*

It is notable that Buddhaghosa draws attention to the presence of similes (*upamāvacana*) in the *sutta,* but not in connection to the jewel metaphor. He sees similes in two places, stanza 8 and stanza 12. In both, a clear comparison is set up and noted as such in the *sutta* ("similarly," *tathūpamam*). For example, in stanza 8:

> Just as a gatepost planted deep in the earth would be unshakable by the four winds—I speak of a good person like this who sees the Noble Truths with certainty.
> There is only a jewel in the sense of the Saṅgha. By this truth may there be safety![45]

The commentary sees the analogy of the gatepost and the good person as a simile, where an utterance of likeness indicates similitude here and in reference to some of the other extended similes in the commentary.[46] But he does not use the term "simile" in discussing the analogy and metaphor of the jewel. This suggests that he sees a different kind of practice with similitude and its limits in this case.

To sum up, the extended metaphor of the jewel constructs an elaborate parallel with the Three Jewels, where full use of the qualities of jewels creates evocative, aesthetic, and heuristic domains that extend how the Buddha, the Dhamma, and the Saṅgha may be known. But unlike an ordinary simile, content to point out likeness, the jewel metaphor develops a comparison that reorients one's understanding whereby the original jewels stop being jewels at all once one grasps the maximal greatness of the "true" jewels. The case may be likened to that of a little girl who considers her sparkly glass beads to be "jewels." When someday she realizes that her baubles are not real jewels, she undergoes a transformation in her knowledge, understanding, and taste and after that cannot see them in the same light.

The claim that there is "only a jewel in the sense of the Buddha," etc., gains its injunctive force from the transformation of vision and understanding made possible through the original analogy. This is why Buddhaghosa considers these truth utterances to be commands. The final verses of the *sutta* are Sakka's assent to the command on behalf of all beings present. We might also suggest that the Three Jewels become *refuges* at this point, where "refuge" is meant in the specific sense defined by Buddhaghosa elsewhere as "having awareness arise that 'this is my refuge, this is my all.' "[47] We can now begin to see the Jewel Sutta's effects reach beyond the story given by the commentary and why the Buddha claimed it would help 84,000 living creatures to grasp the Dhamma and impact beings in the 100,000 *koṭis* of world systems. The Jewel Sutta established the Three Jewels as refuges for all beings who might take them as their final end or support.

Conclusion

We began our exploration of this *paritta* text by noting its widespread ritual use to invoke ritual powers of protection, a usage that does not appear to rest on knowing the *sutta*'s meaning or how its power works. That many people may not know or care how it works, however, does not mean that no one ever knew this or that the hidden technologies of its power are unavailable to human understanding. As in this case, the commentaries often provide explanations whereby what may seem arbitrary or magical can be explained according to the causal factors involved. One is reminded of Arthur C. Clarke's third law, stating that any sufficiently advanced technology is indistinguishable from magic. Of course, once we understand its technology, it stops being magic.

The Jewel Sutta's technology may be explained via very precise and sophisticated understandings of language and speech acts developed in the Pali commentaries. First, among the many kinds of attributes something may have, there are some qualities of things and persons that are contextual and known principally (perhaps only) via our response to them: the qualities of my beloved are known to me in my response to him; the relevant qualities of jewels (in this *sutta*) are qualities that move us in that they give us pleasure, prompt worship, are hard for us to appraise, and so on. For the kind of transformative project in which the Buddhist thinkers were engaged, it is these kinds of relational attributes that are the qualities crucial to know, and thus the entire burden of the extended metaphor is carried by the *guṇas* of the jewels compared. This is a religious epistemology and pedagogy where humans learn the value of things not so much in and of themselves but *how they are, or can be, for us.*

Second, metaphors transform us—in this case, by first showing similitude and then revealing difference. The Three Jewels are like other jewels to a point but then surpass all jewels. To come to see that even Wheel-Turning Emperors' jewels pale in comparison is to be transformed and reoriented in such a way that one does not look at the things of this world—even its most precious things—in the same way again.

Finally, the reorientation is, in effect, a command. Truth statements are not really indicative sentences but rather have injunctive force precisely because they reorient and transform. The truth statement is the Buddha's command, an order followed by beings from Sakka on down to menacing nonhuman agents, securing their protection. To perceive the "only excellent jewels" is to assent to the injunctive force of the truth statement. This assent begins to suggest what it may mean to take the Three Jewels as a refuge.

Appendix: The Jewel Sutta

1. Whatever beings are gathered here, of the earth or in the sky,
   May all these beings be happy, and may they listen respectfully to what is said.

2. And so, beings, all of you, please attend and show lovingkindness to the human beings
   Who day and night bring you offerings; because of this, without being negligent, protect them!

3. Whatever treasure there is here or the other world, or whatever excellent jewel may be in the heavens,
   There is none on par with the Tathāgata. There is only an excellent jewel in the sense of the Buddha. By this truth may there be safety!

4. Destruction, dispassion, the deathless, and the excellent—Sakyamuni, concentrating, attained these;
   There is nothing on par with the Dhamma. There is only an excellent jewel in the sense of the Dhamma. By this truth may there be safety!

5. The highest one, the Buddha, praises what is pure, that which is called "concentration without gaps";
   There is nothing equal to that concentration. There is only an excellent jewel in the sense of the Dhamma. By this truth may there be safety!

6. There are eight persons, praised by the good, who constitute four pairs; they are disciples of the Sugata, worthy of honor, and gifts to them are very fruitful.
   There is only a jewel in the sense of the Saṅgha. By this truth may there be safety!

7. Those in Gotama's dispensation, intent, with steady mind, free of desire,

Having reached attainment, having entered the deathless, they are enjoying the peace they have obtained free of charge.
There is only a jewel in the sense of the Saṅgha. By this truth may there be safety!

8. Just as a gatepost planted deep in the earth would be unshakable by the four winds—
I speak of a good person like this who sees the Noble Truths with certainty.
There is only a jewel in the sense of the Saṅgha. By this truth may there be safety!

9. Those who have realized the Noble Truths well-taught by the one whose wisdom is deep may be very careless and yet will not take an eighth existence.
There is only a jewel in the sense of the Saṅgha. By this truth may there be safety!

10. Together with attainment in seeing, one lives having abandoned three phenomena: the view of personal identity, doubt, and whatever good works and ceremonial observances there are.
And one is saved from the four realms of hell and becomes incapable of six grave offenses.
There is only a jewel in the sense of the Saṅgha. By this truth may there be safety!

11. Although one might still do an evil act by body, speech or mind, one is not capable of hiding it; this incapacity is described for one who possesses this visible sign [of achievement].
There is only a jewel in the sense of the Saṅgha. By this truth may there be safety!

12. Just like a forest grove with its canopy blossoming in the first month of summer warmth, just so he taught the best Dhamma, the way to nirvana, for highest benefit.
There is only a jewel in the sense of the Buddha. By this truth may there be safety!

13. Best, knowing the best, bringing the best, most excellent, he taught the best Dhamma. There is only a jewel in the sense of the Buddha. By this truth may there be safety!

14. What is old is destroyed and there is no new arising in those disenchanted with future existence. Their seeds are destroyed and they have no desire for growth. Steadfast, they go out like a lamp.
There is only a jewel in the sense of the Saṅgha. By this truth may there be safety!

15. Whatever beings are gathered here, of the earth or in the sky, We honor the Buddha, the Tathāgata worshipped by gods and men. May there be safety!

16. Whatever beings are gathered here, of the earth or in the sky, We honor the Dhamma, the Tathāgata worshipped by gods and men. May there be safety!

17. Whatever beings are gathered here, of the earth or in the sky, We honor the Saṅgha, the Tathāgata worshipped by gods and men. May there be safety!

Notes

1. G. P. Malalasekera, *The Pāli Literature of Ceylon* (Kandy: Buddhist Publication Society, 1994). Malalasekera reports that the *Pirit Pota* would likely be found "in the meagre library of every Sinhalese home" (75). For a survey of *paritta* literature, as well as protective texts more generally across Indic Buddhist traditions, see Peter Skilling, "The Rakṣā Literature of the Śrāvakayāna." *Journal of the Pali Text Society* 16 (1992): 109–182; and Lily de Silva, *Paritta: The Buddhist Ceremony for Peace and Prosperity in Sri Lanka* (Peradeniya: National Museums of Sri Lanka, 1980). On the *Maha Pirit Pota,* see Lionel Lokuliyana, trans. *The Great Book of Protections* (Singapore Buddhist Meditation Centre, 1975).
2. *Milindapañha* 150. *Visuddhimagga* XIII.31. (See Bhikkhu Ñāṇamoli, trans. *The Path of Purification (Visuddhimagga)* [Seattle: Pariyatti Editions, 1999], 410).
3. *Mahāvaṃsa* xxxvii, vv.189–198. (See Wilhelm Geiger, trans. *Cūḷavaṃsa,* part 1 [London: Pali Text Society, 1973], 19).

4. Justin McDaniel, "*Paritta* and *Rakṣā* Texts," in *Encyclopedia of Buddhism,* edited by Robert E. Buswell (New York: Macmillan, 2004), 635.
5. The Ratana Sutta is found in both the *Suttanipāta* and the *Khuddakapāṭha,* and both are translated, with their commentaries, into English. See Bhikkhu Bodhi, trans. *The Sutta Nipāta: An Ancient Collection of the Buddha's Discourses* (Somerville: Wisdom Publications, 2017), and Bhikkhu Ñāṇamoli, trans., *The Minor Readings and Illustrator* (London: Pali Text Society, 1978). The commentaries to the Ratana Sutta are identical in both, with the exception of a few sentences at their beginnings. Both commentaries are called *Paramatthajotikā,* and they share much content as they each discuss the Metta, Ratana, and Maṅgala *suttas* (which are, incidentally, all well-known *paritta suttas*); they are conventionally rendered *Paramatthajotikā* I (Pj I) in the case of the *Khuddakapāṭha* commentary and *Paramatthajotikā* II (Pj II) for the *Suttanipāta* commentary. Both are attributed to Buddhaghosa in their colophons and by tradition, though modern scholars have disputed this attribution (see the introductions of both Bhikkhu Bodhi, 66–67, and Bhikkhu Ñāṇamoli, v-vi, on the question of authorship). The Jewel Sutta has parallel verses in the Sanskrit *Mahāvastu* I 290–295.
6. *Yaṃ kiñci vittaṃ idha vā huraṃ vā, saggesu vā yaṃ ratanaṃ paṇītaṃ; / Na no samaṃ atthi tathāgatena, idampi buddhe ratanaṃ paṇītaṃ. Etena saccena suvatthi hotu* (*Suttanipāta* 39 [verse 226]; *Khuddakapāṭha* 4). I am grateful to Steven Collins (personal communication) for help with the locative case here, where it gives the meaning of a word or indicates its range; hence my translation: "in the sense of."
7. Y*ānīdha bhūtāni samāgatāni, bhummāni vā yāni va antalikkhe;Tathāgataṃ devamanussapūjitaṃ, buddhaṃ namassāma suvatthi hotu* (*Suttanipāta* 41 [verse 239]; *Khuddakapāṭha* 9).
8. Later in the commentary, Sakka refers to this instance as a "truth statement" (*saccavacanaṃ*) (Pj I 278). Eugene Watson Burlingame suggests that it is equivalent to the better-known act of truth (*saccakiriyā*) in Pali literature as a formal utterance that has magical efficacy. See Burlingame, "The Act of Truth (*Saccakiriyā*): A Hindu Spell and Its Employment as a Psychic Motif in Hindu Fiction," *Journal of the Royal Asiatic Society of Great Britain and Ireland,* July, 1917, 434.
9. *Suttanipāta-aṭṭhakathā* (Pj II i.278. Usually the context is called the *nidāna,* but throughout the *Suttanipāta* the author calls it the *utpatti.* Both words can mean origin. In the *suttas* in the four *nikāyas,* the *nidāna* is mentioned at the beginning of the *sutta* itself, starting with

"thus have I heard" and the statement of the context of the teaching. But in both anthologies where the Jewel Sutta occurs, there is no "thus have I heard" and no context in the *sutta* itself, so all of the details and stories are supplied by the commentaries.

10. Pj I 157: *Yena vuttaṃ yadā yattha, yasmā cetaṃ imaṃ nayaṃ / Pakāsetvāna etassa, karissāmatthavaṇṇanaṃ.*
11. Pj I 161.
12. Pj I 162: *sā rakkhā koṭisatasahassaṃ cakkavāḷānaṃ pharissati, suttapariyosāne caturāsītiyā pāṇasahassānaṃ dhammābhisamayo bhavissatī.*
13. Pj I 164: *imaṃ, ānanda, ratanasuttaṃ uggahetvā balikammūpakaraṇāni gahetvā licchavirājakumārehi saddhiṃ vesāliyā tipākārantare vicaranto parittaṃ karohī"ti.*
14. Pj I 164.
15. Pj I 164: *upaddavānaṃ paṭighātatthāya vuttamidaṃ.*
16. Pj I 165.
17. *Mahāvaṃsa* xxxvii, vv. 189–198. (See Geiger, *Cūḷavaṃsa,* 19).
18. Pj I 168: *Adhippāyo panettha—nāhaṃ buddhoti issariyabalena vadāmi, api tu yaṃ tumhākañca imissā ca mānusiyā pajāya hitatthaṃ vadāmi "mettaṃ karotha mānusiyā pajāyā"ti.*
19. Pj I 169: *saccavacanaṃ payuñjitumāraddho;* Pj I 169: *buddhādiguṇap pakāsanena.*
20. Pj I 179, 180, 181, etc.: *Imissāpi gāthāya āṇā koṭisatasahassacakkavāḷesu amanussehi paṭiggahitāti* (The command [issued] with this verse also was accepted by the nonhumans in the 100,000 world spheres). This line is repeated in the commentary on stanzas 3–14.
21. Pj I 195: *Atha sakko devānamindo bhagavatā ratanattayaguṇaṃ nissāya saccavacanaṃ payuñjamānena nāgarassa sotthi katā, mayāpi nāgarassa sotthitthaṃ ratanattayaguṇaṃ nissāya kiñci vattabba nti cintetvā.*
22. For example, the commentary on stanza 6 says: "having stated the *quality* of the Saṅgha jewel he now made the truth statement based on just that *quality*" (*saṅgharatanassa guṇaṃ vatvā idāni tameva guṇaṃ nissāya saccavacanaṃ payuñjati;* Pj I 184). This line is repeated for many of the other stanzas, at Pj I 185, 186, 187. Another example: Pj I 179: "having stated the truth by way of the *qualities* of the Buddha" (*evaṃ buddhaguṇena saccaṃ vatvā*).
23. Pj I 179: *neva jātiṃ na gottaṃ na kolaputtiyaṃ na vaṇṇapokkharatādiṃ nissāya . . . loke sīlasamādhikkhandhādīhi guṇehi buddharatanassa asadisabhāvaṃ nissāya saccavacanaṃ payuñjati.*

24. As cited in Edwin Gerow, *A Glossary of Indian Figures of Speech* (The Hague: Mouton, 1971), 325 (Gerow's translation). I am grateful to Charles Hallisey for pointing this out about *guṇa,* this connection with Daṇḍin, and this example (personal communication).
25. See Maria Heim, *The Voice of the Buddha: Buddhaghosa on the Immeasurable Words* (New York: Oxford University Press, 2018), 202–206; see also Charles Hallisey, "Devotion in the Medieval Literature of Sri Lanka" (PhD diss., University of Chicago, 1988).
26. Mattia Salvini, "*Ratna:* A Buddhist World of Precious Things," in *Soulless Matter, Seats of Energy: Metals, Gems and Minerals in South Asian Traditions,* edited Fabrizio M. Ferrari and Thomas W. P. Dähnhardt, (Sheffield: Equinox, 2016), 224. Salvini notes that when practitioners are rightly appreciative, "the good disposition of the mind [referring to *saddhā* and *pasāda*] follows" from the *guṇas* of the Three Jewels.
27. *Arthaśāstra* 2.116–117: one "should become conversant with the size, price, characteristic, class, and color of jewels. . . ." (*ratnānāṃ pramāṇam mūlyalakṣāṇam jātiṃ rūpaṁ jānīyān. . . .*). It is interesting that the qualities of jewels that made them protective amulets against dangers and poison in ancient Indian religion are not referred to by Buddhaghosa. See, for example, the *Bṛhat Saṁhitā* of Varāhamihira, translated in S. R. N. Murthy, *Gemmological Studies in Sanskrit Texts* (Bangalore: Sri N. Subbaiah Setty, 1990), 24, 28–29; and Gyula Wojtilla, "Indian Precious Stones in the Ancient East and West," *Acta Orientalia Academiae Scientiarum Hungaricae* 27, no. 2 (1973): 213–215.
28. The *sutta* and commentary do not mention that other deities might be considered jewels, but we know that across India Hindu deities have been understood as jewels and worshipped as such. See Mikael Aktor, "Five Stones—Four Rivers—One Town: The Hindu *Pañcāyatanapūjā,*" in Ferrari and Dähnhardt, *Soulless Matter, Seats of Energy.* Such practices may furnish a context of a competitive landscape in which the Buddhist devotionalism evidenced in the Ratana Sutta and its interpretation are being forged.
29. Salvini, "*Ratna,*" 221–225. Salvini gets this definition (*ratnaṁ svajātiśreṣṭhe 'pi*) from the *Amarakośa* and the Pali lexica and commentaries that follow it. Nancy Lin's chapter in this volume suggests that the idea of a jeweled ornament being the best possible thing extends to seventeenth-century Tibet.
30. Pj I 169–170: *yaṃ manussānaṃ vohārūpagaṃ alaṅkāraparibhogūpagañca jātarūparajatamuttāmaṇiveḷuriyapavāḷalohitaṅkamasāragallā*

dikaṃ, yañca muttāmaṇivālukatthatāya bhūmiyā ratanamayavimānesu anekayojanasatavitthatesu bhavanesu uppannānaṃ nāgasupaṇṇādīnaṃ vittaṃ, taṃ niddiṭṭhaṃ hoti.

31. Pj I 170: *Ratananti ratiṃ nayati vahati janayati vaḍḍhetīti ratanaṃ. Yaṃkiñci cittīkataṃ mahagghaṃ atulaṃ dullabhadassanaṃ anomasattaparibhogañca, tassetaṃ adhivacanaṃ.*
32. See the articles in Ferrari and Dähnhardt, *Soulless Matter, Seats of Energy,* and, especially for the case of Buddhism, Salvini, "*Ratna,*" 219–254.
33. The seven royal jewels are described at length in the *Dīgha Nikāya* (D ii.16, ii.172–178).
34. Pj I 170: *rañño cakkavattissa cakkaratanaṃ maṇiratanañca, yamhi uppanne mahājano na aññattha cittīkāraṃ karoti, na koci pupphagandhādīni gahetvā yakkhaṭṭhānaṃ vā bhūtaṭṭhānaṃ vā gacchati.*
35. Pj I 170: *tampi ratanaṃ buddharatanena samaṃ natthi. Yadi hi cittīkataṭṭhena ratanaṃ, tathāgatova ratanaṃ.*
36. Pj I 179: "having stated the inequality of the Buddha Jewel with other jewels. . . ." (*buddharatanassa aññehi ratanehi asamataṃ vatvā. . . .*). Cf. 180, 182.
37. Pj I 171: *Yadi hi mahagghaṭṭhena ratanaṃ, tathāgatova ratanaṃ.*
38. Pj I 172: *rañño cakkavattissa cakkaratanaṃ uppajjati indanīlamaṇimayanābhi sattaratanamayasahassāraṃ pavāḷamayanemi rattasuvaṇṇamayasandhi.* One listing of the seven (nonroyal) jewels is in Milindapañha 267: gold (*suvaṇṇa*), silver (*rajata*), pearls (*muttā*), gemstone (*maṇi*), beryl (*veḷuriya*), diamond (*vajira*), and coral (*pavāḷa*). *Maṇi* as "gemstone" is of course vague; perhaps crystal is meant here. See T. W. Rhys Davids and William Stede, *The Pali English Society's Pali-English Dictionary* (Oxford: Pali Text Society, 1992 [1925]), 516.
39. Pj I 173: *maṇi veḷuriyo subho jātimā aṭṭhaṃso suparikammakato āyāmato cakkanābhisadiso vepullapabbatā āgacchati. Veḷuriyo* (Sanskrit *vaidūrya*) can be chrysoberyl or cats-eye, though cats-eyes are not cut with facets, and both of these stones are less precious than beryl (which in some instances can reach the status of precious stones in modern gemology, according to Wojtilla. See Gyula Wojtilla, "Ratnaśāstra in Kauṭilya's *Arthaśāstra,*" *Acta Orientalia Academiae Scientiarum Hungaricae* 62, no. 1 [2009]: 38). It is interesting that the superlative jewel of the *cakkavatti* is not one of the *mahāratna,* the "precious stones" listed in later *ratnaśāstra* literature as diamonds, sapphires, and rubies. But Kauṭilya's *Arthaśāstra,* one of the earliest texts describing gemstones, mining, and to some extent lapidary, does not

distinguish *mahāratnas*, and even diamond does not seem to occupy a central position in his treatise. Diamond (*vajira*) occurs seldom in the early Pali sources, present in the *Aṅguttara Nikāya* (I.124) and the *Milindapañha* (267), for example, but not regularly even in the commentaries.

40. Pj I 174: *Yadi hi atulaṭṭhena ratanaṃ, tathāgatova ratanaṃ. Tathāgato hi na sakkā sīlato vā samādhito vā paññādīnaṃ vā aññatarato kenaci tulayitvā tīrayitvā ettakaguṇo vā iminā samo vā sappaṭibhāgo vāti paricchindituṃ. Evaṃ atulaṭṭhenapi tathāgatasamaṃ ratanaṃ natthi.*
41. Pj I 174.
42. Pj I 174.
43. Pj I 175.
44. Pj I 175: *Yampi taṃ avisesato ratijananaṭṭhena ratanaṃ.*
45. Khp 4; Sn 40: *Yathindakhīlo pathavissito siyā, catubbhi vātehi asampakampiyo; Tathūpamaṃ sappurisaṃ vadāmi, yo ariyasaccāni avecca passati; Idampi saṅghe ratanaṃ paṇītaṃ, etena saccena suvatthi hotu.* The commentary notes that "just as" (*yathā*) is a "word for likeness" (*upamāvacana*). This stanza and its commentary are similar to stanza 12 and its commentary in noting a simile.
46. Pj I 185;191.
47. Pj I 16: *cittuppādena "esa me saraṇaṃ, esa me parāyaṇa"nti.* I am translating *parāyana* as one's "all," one's final end and support. This commentary on the *Khuddakapāṭha*, on the Three Refuges, has a lengthy discussion of what it means to take refuge, and this is just one sense of refuge but one in keeping with the reorientation to the Three Jewels described in the Jewel Sutta commentary.

Chapter 4

Jeweled Renunciation

Reading the Buddha's Hagiography

Vanessa R. Sasson

According to the *Jātakanidāna,* after encountering the Four Sights, the Bodhisatta commands his chariot driver to prepare Kanthaka for his Great Departure. Channa rushes toward the stables and finds the stately white horse standing beneath a silken canopy of jasmine flowers. While "lamps with scented oil burn," Channa saddles the majestic horse with ornate trappings.[1] Kanthaka apparently realizes the significance of the moment and neighs with pleasure.

The Bodhisatta then charges into renunciation (with Channa clinging to Kanthaka's tail), which under normal circumstances should have created a thunderous clamor. The gods, however, are committed to the success of this great escape and swallow Kanthaka's sounds by catching his mighty hooves in the palms of their hands. When the Bodhisatta reaches the gates that had imprisoned him for twenty-nine years (gates that required a thousand men to maneuver), the residing deity swings the doors open and waves the heroes through. The Bodhisatta soars past the sleeping guards on his brilliant white steed into unbridled freedom.

The *Jātakanidāna* points out, in no uncertain terms, that the Bodhisatta makes this Great Departure without a moment of hesitation: he abandons his kingship as though it is nothing more than "a blob of spit."[2] And yet . . . just before he disappears into the distance, the Bodhisatta is described as wanting one last look at the city. As soon as the thought arises in his mind, the great earth revolves like a potter's wheel, providing him with a view without his having to turn himself around. He wants to see the city, even though he has "no desire for it"—the paradox of the moment left to the readers to contemplate.[3] When he has had enough, the earth revolves back to position, and he is met with a dazzling sight: deities bearing torches manifest on the road in every direction. Sixty thousand deities bear torches behind him, sixty thousand bear torches ahead, and sixty thousand each on his right side and his left. Other deities carry torches all the way to the edge of the universe, and others still shower the Bodhisatta with heavenly perfumes, garlands, powders, and incense. The Bodhisatta is greeted like a heavenly sovereign into the next stage of his story.

This picture of the Bodhisatta's Great Departure embodies the paradoxical elements this book is attempting to negotiate. On the one hand, the Bodhisatta abandons his city and his kingship as though it is nothing more than a blob of spit. And yet, he is carried into his departure with divine attention, magical displays, and royal fanfare. The Bodhisatta is treated like a king even though he is determined to toss his crown away, and he is bejeweled at every turn. In this chapter, we will consider some of the scenes in the Buddha's hagiography that speak to his perpetually bejeweled status—both before his renunciation and after—and will argue that this paradox is threaded throughout his narrative. On the one hand, he is the monk, the teacher, the renunciant. And yet at the same time, he is the most bejeweled being in the cosmos. The Buddha is adorned like a cosmic king before and after he tosses his crown away.

His Surroundings

We will begin our tour of the Buddha's hagiographical opulence with the beginning (not the real beginning, given samsaric eternity, but the beginning of his last life).[4] It will come as no surprise that as heir to the throne, the Bodhisatta is described as having been raised in lavish luxury. Whether we use Pali canonical sources or move toward more extravagant texts like the Sanskrit *Lalitavistara,* the stage on which his narrative is set is one of material abundance. The *Sukhamalasutta* has the Bodhisatta "delicately brought up" with three palaces placed at his disposal (one for every season) along with man-made lotus ponds. His clothing comes from Kasi and a parasol is carried over his head.[5]

The commentarial literature fleshes some of this out, with the *Jātakanidāna* adding that the three palaces are many stories in height, each one bigger than the last. It also describes the prince surrounded by forty thousand dancing women. He is like "a god surrounded by groups of heavenly nymphs . . . entertained with music by an all-female orchestra, experiencing great bliss in these palaces that rotated in accordance with the seasons."[6]

The *Mahāvastu* describes the Bodhisatta's living quarters in more detail. When Asita soars into the city of Kapilavastu to investigate the birth of the Bodhisatta, he finds the palace to be like a heavenly realm, its upper chamber "gleaming like a brilliant mountain-top in the sky. . . . On the front of the mansion were pinnacles resplendent with silver and its corners gleamed like the flame of the sacrificial fire. The inner apartments were fair like pellucid shells. They sparkled like brilliant little suns or like moon-shaped ornaments. . . . There were seen arched portals of gold like burning fire. . . . On the ground with its heaps of jewels and piles of other splendours a lion sits and starts with fear at the rising sun which it has seen."[7] The city markets are, moreover, "busy in selling and buying" and thronged with joyful people.[8]

The *Buddhacarita* similarly presents us with a vibrant and prosperous city. Animals are decked in gold, cows produce abundant milk, and rain falls at the proper time. Even more, "there was no one in his realm who was rude to elders, not generous, untruthful, hurtful or non-observant."[9] And the king's coffers are filled with "untold treasures, all sorts of wealth and gems, gold, both wrought and unwrought." These treasures are so abundant that it is too much to bear even "for that chariot of the mind called desire!"[10] The kingdom that receives the future Buddha is, in other words, a glorious place, bursting with jewels and brimming with joy.

The *Lalitavistara* provides the most sumptuous descriptions of the Bodhisatta's fabulous life. One example worth noting is when he is carried from Lumbinī to Kapilavastu as a newborn. Here he is accompanied by a magnificent entourage that begins with a thousand urns of scented water carried ahead of him, followed by five thousand women sprinkling the road with scented water and another five thousand women covered in jeweled ornaments walking with them. There are also five thousand women wearing veils and five thousand women carrying flower garlands. There are five thousand women with peacock fans, five thousand women carrying *tāla* tree branches, and five thousand Brahmins ringing bells. Walking ahead of all of these are "twenty thousand elephants decorated with all their ornaments and twenty thousand horses all covered with golden garlands and with trappings."[11]

But that is not all. There are also eighty thousand chariots and forty thousand foot soldiers, and then there is the main chariot at the center of it all: the one carrying the newborn Bodhisatta, prince of the

Śākya kingdom. This chariot is decorated by the gods and is pulled by twenty thousand *apsaras,* who are adorned with jewels, flowers, and pearls. Between each two *apsaras* is a young woman and between each two women is an *apsara*—a cortège magnificently flanked by bejeweled female attendants in every direction.[12]

These descriptions, along with many others, highlight the extraordinary opulence with which the Bodhisatta is surrounded throughout his youth. It is obviously beyond the scope of this chapter to determine which text came first or the extent to which these texts borrowed from each other. My point is, moreover, not to suggest that textual representation serves as ultimate authority but only to demonstrate that insofar as some of the relatively early/pre-medieval Buddhist hagiographies are concerned, the narrative is consistent: some texts might be more restrained than others, but they agree that the Bodhisatta is raised on a very glamorous stage.

This glittering context undoubtedly serves to heighten the Bodhisatta's status—a direction toward which most traditions gravitate when they tell stories about their heroes. But the effect is more profound than it might at first seem. When the Bodhisatta makes his Great Departure, he is not abandoning a shack in the woods. His renunciation is of the highest order because he abandons the best of all possible worlds. The opulence with which he is raised is just one feature of the near-perfect world he abandons in favor of his quest for awakening.[13] The Bodhisatta is raised in a glittering, bejeweled world, and he renounces it all as though it is nothing more than a blob of spit.

Adornment

The Bodhisatta does not, however, toss his world aside right away. He first has to encounter the traditional Four Sights before he is ready. According to the *Jātakanidāna,* the prince encounters the Four Sights and then returns to his palace "to play in the park during the remaining hours of daylight and bathe in the royal lotus-pond."[14] When he is done, he lies down on a stone slab meant for royalty and waits to be adorned by his servants. They surround him with garments, ornaments, garlands, perfumes, and ointments. Before they begin the ritual, however, Sakka's seat in the heavens heats up, and he realizes that the Bodhisatta is about to be adorned (*alaṃkāra*) for the last time. After countless royal adornments (in this life and in previous lifetimes), the Bodhisatta is finally prepared to make his Great Departure. This would therefore be his last royal adornment. Sakka sounds the alarm and commissions Vissakamma with the task of orchestrating the prestigious event himself.

Known as the architect of the gods, Vissakamma has a reputation for managing the aesthetic needs of Great Beings. His most famous role is probably as Indra's builder in the story known as the "Parade of the Ants," when he is commissioned to build Indra's palace and is forced to maneuver impossible demands.[15] In Buddhist literature, he focuses on the Bodhisatta, providing him with the structures he needs at various points in his multi-life journey. He is responsible for the Bodhisatta's meditation hut in a number of previous lives, and in the Buddha's final life, Vissakamma creates the resplendent jeweled walkway the Buddha uses when he performs his miracle at Śrāvastī,[16] along with the jeweled staircase he requires to descend from Tāvatiṃsa Heaven.[17] It is therefore no surprise to find Vissakamma here, an emissary sent to adorn the Bodhisatta in royal regalia before the Great Departure. Who better to prepare the Great Being on such an important night?[18]

Vissakamma approaches the Bodhisatta with a magical head-dress and begins to wrap the cloth around the prince's head, but "as soon as the head-dress was wrapped around his head, a thousand layers of cloth rose up with jewels and precious gems on the top of his head. Wrapping the thousand layers of cloth ten times over, the ten-thousand layers [of the head-dress] rose up. One should not think, 'the head is too small for so many layers of cloth to stand up [on it].' "[19]

The delivery of this magnificent turban may be more than just symbolic. In a passionate philological essay, Jan Gonda argues that adornment (*alaṃkāra*) denotes not only the idea of "to beautify," but also that of "[to] provide, make ready and fit for a purpose, prepare, etc."[20] Near the end of his essay, he adds that it is difficult to determine where clothing ends and ornamentation begins: "A great many ornaments traced or trace their origin back to practical and serviceable things, such as clothes, etc., or amulets."[21] Throughout his paper, Gonda argues that ornamentation serves more than a decorative function. *Alaṃkāra* prepares the wearers and makes them fit for their office. Coomaraswamy argues that *alaṃkāra* also enhances and empowers the wearer.[22] Far from being a purely aesthetic feature, ornamentation, according to Coomaraswamy, makes the body complete and protects it. Likewise, Vidya Dehejia, in a marvelous study on adornment in early Indian art, reminds her readers that in India an unornamented body implies death and mourning.[23] Without adornment, one is without life.

In her chapter in this volume, Nancy Lin argues that modernist readings have diminished the concept of ornamentation and limited it to the superfluous, but if we take these Indic interpretations into consideration, then the scene of the Bodhisatta's adornment in the *Jātakanidāna* signals something significant about his status. The Bodhisatta is adorned because adornment serves to complete him, will protect him as he prepares to embark upon his journey, and will make him fit for the role he is about to play. The fact that divine beings intervene and dress him themselves (taking the place of more mundane, human servants) speaks volumes about his role in the larger Buddhist imagination. He is a royal being of the greater cosmic order, made whole by the jewels that crown his head like a budding flower. He is offered protection by these heavenly amulets moments before he charges into the next scene of his life.

We may, of course, argue that the Bodhisatta does not really need anything to make his Great Departure. He is karmically bound to achieve awakening, with or without Vissakamma's magical crown. But when ancient Indian rituals of kingship are added into the mix, his adornment appears to be much more important. The *Jātakanidāna* places his adornment immediately after he has bathed himself in his royal lotus pond. According to J. C. Heesterman, who produced an extensive survey of early Indian rituals of kingship, a bath is one of the key ingredients in what is otherwise a very lengthy process of royal consecration. We do not have in this hagiographical narrative a lengthy and explicit consecration ritual on a par with the early Vedic and Brahmanical manuals Heesterman studies, but bathing and adornment rituals were central elements, and as Heesterman reminds his readers, the early manuals were more like "encyclopedias recording the ritual in its ideal form" than reflections of particular ritual events that were performed all at once.[24] If we have here a reference to royal consecration, then his bath and adornment do more than point to his beautification. These rituals *transform* the Bodhisatta into the cosmic monarch he is destined to become. Ronald Inden argues that consecration ceremonies should not be understood as symbolic displays of royal power but instead should be read as transformative rituals, "universally performed acts by which men were transformed into kings."[25] These acts were, moreover, not performed once in a lifetime but repeatedly, at every turning point in a king's royal career, and they were specifically binary in structure, with the first half dedicated to the bath and the second half to the *paṭṭabandha*—the fixing of the turban, or the crowning.[26] When the Bodhisatta immerses himself in his royal pond and then hands himself over for ritual adornment (which was directed by the gods), we must surely see a reference to the Bodhisatta's cosmic consecration. He was crowned by the gods with a jeweled turban ten thousand layers strong—a ritual enthronement that marks his Great Departure, just before he tosses it all away.

Jewel Tossing

Having been properly adorned, the Bodhisatta returns to his city in his glittering chariot followed by a full retinue of musicians ("with majesty, glory, charm, and dazzling splendour");[27] is entertained by beautiful courtesans (who fail miserably in their quest to stir him); and then goes to see his wife and newborn son (who are fast asleep). He then mounts Kanthaka and charges into renunciation, still adorned with the heavenly turban Vissakamma had carefully wrapped around his head. He wears this ornament all the way to the Anoma River—a turban, we might recall, of ten thousand layers threaded with jewels. It could not have been easy to wear as he galloped at high speed, but comfort is probably beside the point. The narrative creates a dazzling picture with the Bodhisatta charging across the landscape wearing this jeweled turban of ten thousand layers on his head. If we allow ourselves a moment of creative engagement with the text, we might see it sparkling against a star-studded sky.

When he reaches the river, the *Jātakanidāna* tells us that he hands his royal ornaments to his chariot driver, grabs his topknot together with the diadem, and slices these both off in one quick stroke. The Bodhisatta then throws these into the air, saying, "'If I am to become a Buddha, let it stand in the sky; if not, let it fall to the earth.' Having risen one *yojana* into the sky, the topknot and jeweled head-dress stood there. Having seen this with his divine eye and having received it in a jeweled casket the size of a *yojana,* Sakka, the king of gods, named it the Topknot Jeweled Crest Shrine and established it in Tāvatiṃsa Heaven."[28] The extraordinary turban we have spent time considering has now been tossed away. The ten thousand layers fly into the sky, where they remain, enshrined in a casket to be cared for by the same deities who provided it for him.

Although the *Jātakanidāna* seems to be alone where ritual adornment (and potential consecration) are concerned, a number of early hagiographical accounts record the hair-(and-turban)-slicing moment, pivotal as it is for the Buddha's story. The *Buddhacarita,* for example, provides an exquisite image, as the prince

Took the sword with the hilt inlaid with gems;
He then drew out the sword from its scabbard
With its blade streaked with gold,
Like a snake from its hole.

Unsheathing the sword, dark as a lotus petal,
He cut his ornate head-dress along with the hair,
And threw it in the air, the cloth trailing behind—
It seemed he was throwing a swan into a lake.[29]

The imagery could not be more beautiful. His hair and head-dress trail through the sky like a swan gliding across a lake. Heavenly deities catch these in their palms and worship them in the sky.

We find this scene in other sources too, but the role played by the jeweled turban is not always clear. For example, the Bodhisatta's act of renunciation is twice described in the *suttas,* but in both instances, only the hair is specifically referred to. Consider the following description from the *Ariyapariyesanā Sutta:* "Later, monks, when I was young with very black hair, endowed with youth, in the prime of life, even though my parents were unwilling and were crying with tearful faces, I shaved off my hair and beard, put on a yellow robe, and went forth from home life into homelessness."[30] The head-dress is not part of the description. One might argue that the omission is irrelevant in such a brief text, but when the *Mahāvastu* makes a similar omission, the missing head-dress becomes problematic. On the other hand, when the Bodhisatta slices off his hair and tosses it up into the sky, according to the *Mahāvastu,* the hair is "taken up by Śākra, the lord of devas, and received worship in Trāyatriṃśa."[31] Likewise with the *Lalitavistara's* description: the Bodhisatta slices off his hair with his sword, tosses it into the wind, and the thirty-three gods catch it and worship it.[32] In neither of these accounts is the jeweled head-dress referred to, but in both accounts, the hair is received by the gods. We might wonder whether the gods received it because it was bound with the head-dress or whether they received it because anything that has to do with the Buddha is cherished. There is no clear answer, but in all the accounts, something is tossed into the sky, and what is tossed is received by the deities and enshrined.

This missing reference to the head-dress may, however, be the result of competing translations. The most common term used to describe that which the Bodhisatta slices off is *cūḍā.* Coomaraswamy argues that the word *cūḍā* designates the turban *with* the hair in it.[33] M. Monier-Williams provides support for this argument. Although the word is often translated as "protuberance" or "the hair on the top of the head, single lock or tuft left on the crown of the head after tonsure," Monier-Williams also suggests "crest, plume, or diadem" as alternatives.[34] It is therefore possible to suggest that the diadem is not missing after all but is folded into the *cūḍā*.[35]

But even if we decide not to follow the early translators and present the Bodhisatta as slicing off only his hair, the fact remains that there is—according to these very same texts—a jewel of some importance in the Bodhisatta's hair that is removed during his act of renunciation. In the *Buddhacarita*, for example, the Bodhisatta removes a jewel from his head-dress and hands it to Chandaka *before* he slices off his hair and head-dress:

> Taking the shining gem from his head-dress,
> A gem that performed the task of a lamp,
> He stood there as he made this oration
> Like Mount Mandara holding up the sun:
>
> "With this gem, Chanda, you must pay repeated homage to the king
> And beseech him without being diffident
> To relieve his anguish."[36]

Likewise, in the *Mahāvastu:* "The Bodhisattva handed over to Chandaka his jewels, his horse Kanthaka and his gem-studded sunshade and bade him greet his father, Mahāprajāpatī Gotamī, and all his kinsmen."[37]

Either way, then, it is clear that when the Bodhisatta makes his great act of renunciation, he removes not just his groomed hair (an obvious South Asian symbol of householder status), but also the many jewels that represent his royal status.[38] Some of these are returned to Kapilavatthu, while others are shipped to the god-realm, but none of them remain with him. They are all sent elsewhere, far from where he himself is going. John Strong argues that a Bodhisatta's relics (as opposed to a Buddha's relics) do not get enshrined on earth because they do not represent awakening—only the journey toward it. Bodhisattva relics (like the *cūḍā*) embody "what gets left behind" and are therefore not preserved here, in the human realm.[39] We may therefore conclude that the Bodhisatta's jewels—even those delivered by deities for ritual consecration—represent the antithesis of awakening. Jewels, turbans, and topknots belong to the discard pile.

Previous Departures

When the Bodhisatta discards his jewels on the road to awakening, he is not acting out of character. On the contrary, the jātakas tell us that he came to a similar conclusion many times before, making the act of renunciation a key pattern in his hagiography. Even more significant, his decision to renounce is often reached in a context of abundance and ease. Regularly in the jātakas, the Bodhisatta is positioned to inherit tremendous wealth, but he gives it all up in the hopes of achieving something higher. When he makes his Great Departure in his final life, his decision is the product of countless departures made in the past. Renunciation was therefore not a new experience for him. It was, rather, a recurring pattern in his multi-life narrative: over and over again, the Bodhisatta chooses to toss his jewels aside in the hopes of finding something better. It is no surprise that we have come to associate Buddhism with some level of austerity as a result.

One of the most famous past-life narratives in the Buddha's repertoire (but not a jātaka strictly speaking) can serve as a useful example here. Sumedha is often portrayed as the opening scene of the Buddha's multi-life journey, for the Bodhisatta has his first recorded encounter with a Buddha here, providing him with the coveted prediction that he will become a Buddha himself one day. Karen Derris describes the Sumedha narrative as a "prediction tale," which is what gives this story such special status.[40] It is precisely at this moment that the Buddha's cosmic biography (to use Jonathan Walters' language) takes root, launching him onto the Bodhisatta path.[41]

In the *Jātakanidāna,* Sumedha is described as having every desirable quality: he is handsome, amiable, endowed with excellent complexion, and of perfect lineage on both sides. He is, moreover, not just physically impressive. He is also of a contemplative nature, devoted as he is to his Brahmanical studies.[42]

Like many great heroes, however, Sumedha experiences suffering at a young age. Both his parents die early in his life, leaving him with virtually unlimited wealth. The officials in charge of his estate throw open doors to rooms filled with gold, silver, jewels, pearls, and other precious things, making all of it available to him. The young Sumedha looks at this wealth and realizes that neither his parents, nor his grandparents, nor anyone else has ever taken any of it with them after their death. He therefore decides to give it away and become an ascetic instead. He consults with the king before he renounces and, according to the *Madhuratthavilāsinī,* even offers to transfer it all to him, but the king claims to have no need "for the countless hundreds and thousands of crores," so Sumedha donates his wealth to the people instead.[43] The *Thūpavaṃsa* tells us that the people gathered greedily "like swarms of bees at the scent of the sounding drums" and spent seven days grabbing everything he had to give.[44] Their greed is contrasted with Sumedha's generosity, propelling him toward renunciation even more. He asks himself what good there is in watching "this taking of wealth as if it were a game?"[45] Although the text does not identify his emotional state at this moment, disgust is likely one way to describe it. He follows through on his decision to renounce and walks away.

If we are to understand this story as the beginning of the Bodhisatta path, then we may argue that there is a direct correlation between the road to awakening and the renunciation of wealth. The Bodhisatta is offered rooms filled with jewels, and he rejects it all—evidence once again that it is either one or the other but never both.

A similar situation arises at the tail end of his multi-life journey when he is reborn as Vessantara in the last of the canonical jātakas and his penultimate Bodhisatta rebirth. Indeed, we should note the remarkable symmetry between these two stories, with one opening the rebirth trajectory and the other closing it. In both of these, the Bodhisatta is reborn with extraordinary access to wealth, and in both of these he decides to toss it all away. In the *Vessantara Jātaka,* the Bodhisatta is described as coming out of the womb eager to practice generosity: "I wish to make a gift," he tells his mother. "Is there anything I can give?"[46] She places a purse with a thousand coins into his tiny hands. When he is a few years old, the king gives him a piece of jewelry worth ten thousand coins, and Vessantara gives it to one of his nurses. When his father finds out, he gives his son another necklace, but the baby Bodhisatta gives that away too.

This pattern continues throughout the narrative, culminating in the devastating gifting of his children to an evil slave driver, and eventually also his wife. Much has been written about this complex text;[47] the point I want to highlight here is the glaring contrast between the Bodhisatta's generosity and everyone else's more mundane responses. Indeed, the people surrounding the Bodhisatta do not even seem inspired by his example. His mother does not express amazement when he speaks to her right out of the womb, nor does she follow his magical lead. The nurses who receive the jewelry do try to return it (but this seems like a reasonable response given that they could have otherwise been accused of theft), and the king refuses to take the jewelry back, stating that

"What is given by my son is given well."[48] The king, however, does not seem inspired to practice generosity himself as a result. On the contrary, throughout the *Vessantara Jātaka*, the Bodhisatta practices generosity but never seems to inspire others to do the same.

When the Bodhisatta is finally kicked out of his kingdom for his excessive virtue, he decides to make "the gift of the seven-hundreds" on his way out: a gift of seven hundred elephants, seven hundred horses, seven hundred chariots, seven hundred women, seven hundred cows, seven hundred female slaves, and seven-hundred male slaves.[49] Each of these is decorated with gold and adorned with jewels, and the community charges toward it all like hungry ghosts. The Bodhisatta then prepares to depart, but his mother wants to support his generosity and gives him more to give: "wagons filled with seven kinds of jewels and other ornaments."[50] The Bodhisatta takes off his own jewelry and adds it to the pile, which he distributes as he drives into exile. People clamor around him to receive the valuables he tosses. When a group of Brahmins arrives late to the city and they realize that they missed the giving ritual, they react in a shocking way. Rather than accept their loss, they chase after the Bodhisatta until they catch up with his chariot and ask for his horses. The Bodhisatta (predictably) gives those away too.[51]

The *Vessantara Jātaka* is a masterful narrative with many layers of complicated material, but the point I am focused on here is the contrast between the Bodhisatta's generosity and everyone else's lack of it. What makes the Bodhisatta heroic in this narrative is that he goes against the grain, functioning in a fundamentally countercultural way by giving away what others would happily grab for themselves. He does not inspire generosity in others, but he is not a Buddha, so we may forgive him for not having yet developed pedagogical skill. He does appear to inspire his mother to some degree, but she seems to be participating to make her son happy and not because she herself has understood the lesson. Vessantara's generosity is therefore far from contagious, and it is highlighted by the avarice of everyone else. Both Sumedha and Vessantara toss their jewels aside while the rest of the world runs after them. The Buddhist argument appears to be that jewels need to be discarded, wealth is a trap, and renunciation is about leaving it all behind.

And Yet. . . .

Material renunciation is not the whole story. Although jewel hoarding is far from being a Buddhist priority, jewels are nevertheless scattered throughout the Buddha's hagiography. In her chapter in this volume, Maria Heim argues that jewels represent "the best in one's class"—that which is rare, honored, and of great value. When compared with the Buddha, however, jewels inevitably fade into the background because the Buddha is the most honored, the most valued, the most rare. He is the most precious jewel of the Buddhist *imaginaire,* and material jewels are rendered insignificant by comparison. But as the most precious jewel, the Buddha deserves the most precious offerings the material world has to offer. Jewels are therefore strewn at the Great Being's feet, not just when he is a prince, but at every step of his narrative.

The *Lalitavistara* includes a wonderful scene in which the gods lay down their jewels in the Bodhisatta's presence. Before he leaves for his Great Departure, the Bodhisatta goes up to the palace roof to make obeisance to the Buddhas. The gods immediately fill the sky around him, "holding flowers, incense, perfumes, and garlands, aloes, perfumed powders, and monastic garments, parasols, standards, banners, earrings of flowers and garlands of precious stones."[52] The Bodhisatta sees the Four Great Gods joined by all kinds of magical beings floating among the clouds, each one holding a fiery weapon. And then, "As was fitting, they all laid down their crowns and diadems of pearls and bowed before the Bodhisattva."[53] Just as the Bodhisatta is about to leave the palace (and all the jewels that are in it), the gods appear before him and lay down their celestial crowns. When I think of this scene, I imagine the palace roof covered with jewels, scintillating and sparkling and shimmering in the evening light, as gods in every direction bow their heads toward him. The Bodhisattva is more precious than all the jewels of the ten thousand realms, but this does not mean that jewels must be removed from his narrative. On the contrary, the jewels remind the reader that he is the most precious because the jewels—what others spend their lives chasing (the Sumedha narrative and the *Vessantara Jātaka* cases in point)—are as nothing in his presence. Jewels continue to play a role in his narrative, even if he himself plans on discarding them.

Another scene that speaks to the Bodhisatta's bejeweled renunciation is his enthronement at the Bodhi tree. Like the mansions in which he is raised, the Bodhi tree is described in some sources as a palace in its own right. The *Mahāvastu* describes it as draped in fine cloth and decorated with strings of jewels. When the gods look down, some of them see the tree that stands above the throne as though it is made of gold, while others think it is made of silver, and others see it as beryl, crystal, or emerald. Some even think it is made of a hundred thousand precious stones, each deity seeing it in accordance with their virtue. The glittering gods fill the sky, draped in their own majestic splendor and dripping with their own gems, creating a courtly scene that far surpasses any possible worldly enthronement ceremony.[54]

The *Lalitavistara* embellishes this moment with even greater splendor, beginning its description with the road leading up to the tree as being perfumed by the gods and covered in a shower of heavenly flowers. The trees throughout the many universes "all bent their crowns" toward the Bodhi tree, recognizing Mahabodhi's supremacy the way the gods earlier recognized the Bodhisatta.[55] Altars made of the seven precious things line the road and are sheltered by jeweled nets with royal parasols and banners. Palm trees of seven precious substances produced by magic fill the area, while the tree itself is encircled by seven altars made of seven precious stones. Seven rows of trees line these altars, and beyond these are seven precious nets encircled by seven golden cords. There are also holy books covered with cloths made of gold and golden lotuses woven into the fabric, and the tree is sheltered by a jeweled lattice. When the gods see the magnificence of this stage, they compare their own heavenly realms to a cemetery and exclaim, "Ah! This is indeed the incomprehensible result of the complete maturation of merit!"[56]

These scenes take place before the Bodhisatta becomes the Buddha, but the jewels only get brighter *after* his awakening. One of the most fantastical narratives in the Buddha's hagiography is undoubtedly the scene of his jeweled walkway—a scene the *Buddhavaṃsa* uses as preamble to its listing of previous Buddha encounters. The text opens with Brahmā beseeching the Buddha to make his Dhamma available because some beings "have little dust."[57] The Buddha agrees and decides to respond by demonstrating the "unsurpassed power of a Buddha": he creates a jeweled walkway in the sky.[58] The entire world is illuminated by this magical feat, and even "the dark spaces between the worlds" see its doom temporarily dissipated.[59] This walkway is described as being like a course of pillars, with all the sides made of gold and the walk itself being made of jewels.

> The junction of beams was symmetrical; the floor boards were covered with gold. The railings were all gold, well measured out from both sides. Sand made of jewels and pearls was spread out, illuminating all the directions, just like he who rises with 100 rays. Walking up and down on that, he, the self-reliant one of the 32 marks, the

> illuminated one, self-awakened, the Conqueror, walked up and down the walk.[60]

The commentary tells us that the Buddha does not merely walk up and down this glittering sky-bridge. He also performs the marvel of twinning (*yamakapāṭihāriya*)—a feat he uses later in his life to vanquish his competition in the town of Śrāvastī. The *Madhuratthavilāsinī* explains this marvel as being an accomplishment reserved exclusively for Buddhas (arahants do not share this power).[61] Indeed, according to the *Divyāvadāna,* the twinning miracle is one of the indispensable acts of a Buddha—a necessary component of a Buddha-life-Blueprint.[62] When he performs it, the upper part of his body becomes a flame and the lower part a stream of water; then, the lower part of his body becomes a flame and the upper part becomes a stream of water. He then creates this feat alternating between the front and back of his body; then he limits it to each of his eyes, then his ears, his nostrils, his shoulders, his hands, his feet, his fingers, and even the spaces between his fingers. Then a flame erupts from every pore of his skin and hair, and a moment later every pore shoots a stream of water. Finally, his whole body glows in a variety of colors: blue, yellow, red, white, crimson, and opaque brilliant. The Buddha walks up and down his jeweled walkway in the sky, manifesting all of these extraordinary illusions, and then he adds one more: he twins himself so that one of him walks while the other sits, and then they switch roles. Then one sits while the other lies down, and then they also switch positions. All of this together is known as the Twinning Marvel, and this is what he performs while strutting along a jeweled bridge in the sky.

There is nothing more marvelous than this image, and I suspect some narrators of the tradition agree, given how often reference is made to it in both narrative and art. The *Buddhavaṃsa* places this scene almost immediately after he achieves awakening (according to the commentary, Brahmā approaches the Buddha with his request to teach on the eighth week), but in other sources, the scene takes place just as the Buddha is establishing himself at Jetavana in the town of Śrāvastī. The context is, moreover, quite different: in the *Buddhavaṃsa,* the scene serves as introduction to its long list of previous Buddha encounters, while the Śrāvastī version provides an almost humorous account of the Buddha's takedown of local heretics. Either way, though, this scene plays a pivotal role in the Buddha's hagiography with Śrāvastī becoming one of the eight pilgrimage sites as a result. By twinning himself (and producing the twinning of fire and water), the Buddha demonstrates his ability to be in two places at once. Strong has suggested that because the Śrāvastī version often takes place just before the Buddha disappears into Trāyastriṃśa Heaven for the rains retreat, it also serves to prepare the community for his absence, representing a kind of "dry-run for his more permanent absence in nirvāṇa."[63] If Strong is right (and he usually is), it would explain the scene's importance in the Buddha's developing hagiography—a scene, I must reiterate, where he is at his most bejeweled.

There is no question that generosity is one of the pillars of the Buddhist tradition. Renunciation is likewise a central feature of most Buddhist narratives. Taken together, we may easily conclude that jewels have no role to play in the literature, but I hope this chapter serves to counter that assumption because the jewels are, in fact, everywhere.[64] Although the Bodhisatta tosses his jewels every chance he gets, the storytellers always manage to sneak them back in. Either they are draped around his head in a magical turban of ten thousand layers, or they are scattered at his feet, or they are transformed into a jeweled walkway in the sky, but one way or another, the Buddha remains bejeweled—at the beginning, in the middle, and in the end.

Notes

1. *gandhatelapadīpesu jalantesu* (*Jātakanidāna* 62).
2. *kheḷapiṇḍaṃ* (*Jātakanidāna* 63; see also *Madhuratthavilāsinī* 283 for an identical reference).
3. *anapekkho* (*Jātakanidāna* 63).
4. For discussion of the Bodhisatta's childhood (in this opulent context), see Vanessa R. Sasson, "The Buddha's 'Childhood': The Foundation for the Great Departure," in *Little Buddhas: Children and Childhoods in Buddhist Texts and Traditions*, edited by Vanessa R. Sasson (New York: Oxford University Press, 2013), 75–96.
5. *Sukhamalasutta* AN 3.39; i 145. See also *Māgandiyasutta* MN 75; i 514.
6. *Bodhisatto devo viya accharāsaṅghaparivuto, alaṅkatanāṭakaparivuto, nippurisehi tūriyehi paricāriyamāno mahāsampattiṃ anubhavanto utuvārena tesu pāsādesu viharati* (*Jātakanidāna*, 58).
7. *Mahāvastu* ii 35. Translations of the *Mahāvastu* are from J. J. Jones, trans. *The Mahāvastu*, 3 vols. (London: Pali Text Society, 1987; Sacred Books of the Buddhists).
8. *Mahāvastu* ii 35.

9. *Buddhacarita* 2.11; for a translation, see Patrick Olivelle, trans. *Life of the Buddha by Ashvaghosha.* (New York: New York University Press, 2008; Clay Sanskrit Library).
10. *Buddhacarita* 2.2.
11. *Lalitavistara* 1:147–148. For a translation, see Gwendolyn Bays, trans. *The Lalita Vistara Sūtra, Voice of the Buddha: The Beauty of Compassion,* 2 vols. (Berkeley: Dharma Publishing, 1983; Tibetan Translation Series). Also see Dharmacakra Translation Committee, *The Play in Full (Lalitavistara),* 2019, http://read.84000.co/translation/UT22084-046-001.html; and R. L. Mitra, trans. *The Lalita-Vistara: Memoirs of the Early Life of Sakya Sinha* (chs. 1–15) (New Delhi: Sri Satguru, 1998).
12. In what seems like a humorous side note, the text adds that "through the power and glory of the Bodhisattva, the goddesses did not perceive the disagreeable odor of the women and the women were not humiliated by the beauty of the *apsaras*" (*Lalitavistara* 1:148). It is a point not directly related to the theme of this chapter but too entertaining to pass up.
13. We may also include his near-perfect parents, his idealized wife, and eventually his son, but that is material for another book.
14. *so tattha divasabhāgaṃ kīḷitvā maṅgalapokkharaṇiyaṃ nhāyitvā* (*Jātakanidāna* 59).
15. Brahmavaivarta Purāna, Kṛṣṇa Janma Khanda 47.50–161. See Heinrich R. Zimmer, *Myths and Symbols in Indian Art and Civilization* (New York: Pantheon, 1946), 3–11.
16. For a list of some of Vissakamma's Buddhist appearances, see the entry on Vissakamma in G. P. Malalasekera's *Dictionary of Pāli Proper Names* (Oxford: Pali Text Society, 1997), 3:906–907.
17. Jātaka no. 483; see E. B. Cowell, *The Jātaka or Stories of the Buddha's Former Births,* 6 vols. (Oxford: Pali Text Society, 1995), 4:168.
18. Vissakamma also dresses the Bodhisatta when he prepares himself to leave the palace in his rebirth as Temiya in the *Mugapakkha Jātaka.* For a wonderful translation, see Naomi Appleton and Sarah Shaw, *The Ten Great Birth Stories of the Buddha: The Mahānipāta of the Jātakatthavaṇṇanā,* 2 vols. (Chiang Mai: Silkworm, 2015), 1:66.
19. *Veṭhanena veṭhitamatte sīse moḷiyaṃ maṇiratanākārena dussasahassaṃ abbhuggañchi. Puna veṭhentassa dussasahassanti dasakkhattuṃ veṭhentassa dasa dussasahassāni abbhuggacchiṃsu. "Sīsaṃ khuddakaṃ, dussāni bahūni, kathaṃ abbhuggatānī" ti na cintetabbaṃ* (*Jātakanidāna* 60). A briefer version of this narrative appears in the *Madhuratthavilāsinī* (280). Here, he is adorned by Vissakamma with "deva-like adornments." There is, unfortunately, no description of his elaborate head-dress.

20. Jan Gonda, "The Meaning of the Word *Alaṃkāra*," in *Selected Studies Presented to the Author by the Staff of the Oriental Institute, Utrecht University, on the Occasion of His 70th Birthday* (Leiden: Brill, 1975), vol. 2: *Sanskrit Word Studies* (Leiden: Brill, 1975), 263.
21. Gonda, "The Meaning of the Word *Alaṃkāra*," 274.
22. A. K. Coomaraswamy, "Ornament," *Art Bulletin* 21, no. 4 (1939): 377.
23. Vidya Dehejia, *The Body Adorned: Dissolving Boundaries between Sacred and Profane in India's Art* (New York: Columbia University Press, 2009), 38.
24. J. C. Heesterman, *The Ancient Indian Royal Consecration: The Rājasūya Described According to the Yasju Texts and Annotated* (The Hague: Mouton, 1957), 4.
25. Ronald Inden, "Ritual, Authority, and Cyclic Time in Hindu Kingship," in *Kingship and Authority in South Asia,* edited by J. F. Richards (Delhi: Oxford University Press, 1998), 54.
26. Inden, "Ritual, Authority, and Cyclic Time in Hindu Kingship," 61.
27. *mahantena yasena atimanoramena sirisobhaggena* (*Jātakanidāna* 60).
28. *"Sacāhaṃ buddho bhavissāmi, ākāse tiṭṭhatu, no ce, bhūmiyaṃ patatū," ti antalikkhe khipi. Taṃ cūḷāmaṇiveṭhanaṃ yojanappamāṇaṃ ṭhānaṃ gantvā ākāse aṭṭhāsi. Sakko devarājā dibbacakkhunā oloketvā yojaniyaratanacaṅkoṭakena sampaṭicchitvā tāvatiṃsabhavane cūḷāmaṇicetiyaṃ nāma patiṭṭhāpesi* (*Jātakanidāna* 65); a virtually identical passage can be found in the *Madhuratthavilāsinī* 284.
29. *Buddhacarita* 6.56–6.57.
30. MN 26; i 163; see also MN 36; i 240.
31. *Mahāvastu* ii 165.
32. *Lalitavistara* 1:339.
33. A. K. Coomaraswamy, "The Buddha's *Cūḍā*, Hair, Uṣṇīṣa, and Crown," *Journal of the Royal Asiatic Society* 60, no. 4 (1928): 20. For further discussion of this issue in narrative and early Gandhāran art, see also A. Foucher, *L'art greco-bouddhique du Gandhāra: Étude sur les origines de l'influence classique dans l'art bouddhique de l'Inde et de l'Extrême-Orient* (Paris: Imprimerie Nationale, 1922), 363–366.
34. M. Monier-Williams, *A Sanskrit-English Dictionary* (Delhi: Motilal Banarsidass, 1997), 400–401.
35. It bears noting, however, that the *Buddhacarita* does not use the word *cūḍā* in the passage cited above but instead makes a clear reference to both the head-dress and the hair as separate objects (*mukuṭaṃ sakeśam*).
36. *Buddhacarita* 6.14–15.

37. *Mahāvastu* i 165.
38. For a wonderful book on the subject of hair, see Alf Hiltebeitel and Barbra D. Miller, eds. *Hair: Its Power and Meaning in Asian Cultures* (New York: SUNY, 1998). See also Patrick Olivelle, "Hair and Society: Social Significance of Hair in South Asian Traditions," in *Language, Texts, and Society: Explorations in Ancient Indian Culture and Religion,* edited by Patrick Olivelle (Cambridge: Cambridge University Press, 2011), 321–350.
39. John S. Strong, *Relics of the Buddha* (Princeton, NJ: Princeton University Press, 2004), 67.
40. Karen Derris, "When the Buddha Was a Woman: Reimagining Tradition in the Theravāda." *Journal of Feminist Studies in Religion* 24, no. 2 (2008): 29–44. Worth noting is Derris's argument that there is, in fact, an earlier prediction tale preserved in a few medieval Theravāda sources when the Bodhisatta is reborn as a woman. The Bodhisatta receives a prediction that in a future life she will be reborn as Sumedha, when she will receive the official prediction. This is, in her words, "a prediction of a prediction" tale (35). Naomi Appleton has challenged Derris in her interpretation of this jātaka tradition in her article "In the Footsteps of the Buddha? Women and the Bodhisatta Path in Theravāda Buddhism," *Journal of Feminist Studies in Religion* 27, no. 1 (2011), 33–51.
41. Jonathan S. Walters, "Stūpa, Story, and Empire: Constructions of the Buddha Biography in Early Post-Aśokan India," in *Sacred Biography in the Buddhist Traditions of South and Southeast Asia,* edited by Juliane Schober (Honolulu: University of Hawai'i Press, 1997), 160–192.
42. *Jātakanidāna* 2.
43. *Madhuratthavilāsinī* 74.
44. Stephen C. Berkwitz, *The History of the Buddha's Relic Shrine: A Translation of the Sinhala Thūpavaṃsa* (New York: Oxford University Press, 2007), 37.
45. Berkwitz, *The History of the Buddha's Relic Shrine,* 37–38.
46. Appleton and Shaw, *The Ten Great Birth Stories of the Buddha,* 2:542.
47. It would be impossible to cite every study that touches on the *Vessantara Jātaka*, but to provide a sample, consider the following: Steven Collins, ed. *Readings of the Vessantara Jātaka* (New York: Columbia University Press, 2016); Steven Collins, *Nirvana and Other Buddhist Felicities* (Cambridge: Cambridge University Press, 2009), 497–562; Richard F. Gombrich, "The Vessantara Jātaka, the Rāmāyaṇa and the Dasaratha Jātaka," *Journal of the American Oriental Society* 105, no. 3

(1985): 427–437; Maria Heim, "The Aesthetics of Excess," *Journal of the American Academy of Religion* 71, no. 3 (2003): 531–554; Susanne Mrozik, "Astonishment: A Study of an Ethically Valorized Emotion in Buddhist Narrative Literature," in *Embedded Languages: Studies of Sri Lankan and Buddhist Cultures, Essays in Honour of W. S. Karunatilllake,* edited by Carol S. Anderson et al. (Colombo: Godage International, 2012), 261–288; Vanessa R. Sasson, "Stories of Excess: Abraham and Vessantara," in *To Fix Torah in Their Heart: Essays on Biblical Interpretation and Jewish Studies in Honor of B. Barry Levy,* edited by J. Du Toit et al. (Cincinnati: Hebrew Union College, 2018), 171–198.

48. Appleton and Shaw, *The Ten Great Birth Stories of the Buddha,* 2:543.
49. Appleton and Shaw, *The Ten Great Birth Stories of the Buddha,* 2:551.
50. Appleton and Shaw, *The Ten Great Birth Stories of the Buddha,* 2:566.
51. This tradition of gifting everything prior to a life of renunciation continues today. For a wonderful contemporary description of a Jain "jewel-tossing" episode, see Suketu Mehta, *Maximum City: Bombay Lost and Found* (New York: Vintage, 2004), 511ff.
52. *Lalitavistara* 1.316.
53. *Lalitavistara* 1.316.
54. *Mahāvastu* ii 309ff.
55. *Lalitavistara* 2.417.
56. *Lalitavistara* 2. 423.
57. *Buddhavaṃsa* 1.1.
58. *Buddhavaṃsa* 1.5.
59. *Buddhavaṃsa* 1.7.
60. *Tulāsaṅghāṭānuvaggā, sovaṇṇaphalakatthatā; vedikā sabbasovaṇṇā, dubhato passesu nimmitā. Maṇimuttāvālukākiṇṇā, nimmito ratanāmayo; obhāseti disā sabbā, sataraṃsīva uggato. Tasmiṃ caṅkamane dhīro, dvattiṃsavaralakkhaṇo; virocamāno sambuddho, caṅkame caṅkamī jino* (*Buddhavaṃsa* 1.14–16).
61. For discussion of this event, see David Fiordalis, "Buddhist Miracles in Narrative and Doctrine," *Journal of the International Association of Buddhist Studies* 33 (2010): 381–408, and Sara McClintock, "Compassionate Trickster: The Buddha as a Literary Character in the Narratives of Early Indian Buddhism," *Journal of the American Academy of Religion* 79 no. 1 (2011): 90–112.
62. For discussion, see John S. Strong, *The Buddha: A Short Biography* (New York: Oneworld, 2001), 107–112.
63. Strong, *Relics of the Buddha,* 177.

64. For a discussion of these omnipresent jewels, see also Phyllis Granoff's article, "Maitreya's Jewelled World: Some Remarks on Gems and Visions in Buddhist Texts," *Journal of Indian Philosophy* 26, no. 4 (1998): 347–371.

Chapter 5

Are We All Merchants?

Buddhists, Merchants, and Mercantilism in Early India

Andy Rotman

It has frequently been argued in scholarly articles and devotional tracts that Buddhism developed as "a counter or alternative to the materialist society of . . . new cities where money ruled."[1] According to this origin story, Buddhism took hold in India during a time of intense urbanization, when domestic and foreign trade boomed and the production and consumption of luxury goods increased the status—and, it seems, desires—of an emerging and emboldened middle class. Buddhism, it is said, offered a remedy for those enmeshed in the commercial world and the inevitable give and take, earn and spend, that it entails. But did Buddhism really develop as an antidote to the market and consumerism? Did it, so to speak, make jewels lose their luster? The short answer is no.[2]

Buddhism had a close and formative relationship with merchants and mercantilism from a very early period, if not from its inception then certainly from the beginning of the Common Era.[3] This relationship, in turn, helped guide Buddhism's development in important ways, leaving the market's imprint on the very foundations of Buddhism. One important byproduct of this relationship was a resultant market-based morality. Merit and virtue were now subjected to the forces of commodification and as such could be bought, earned, stockpiled, transferred, cashed in, and depleted.[4]

Traces of the mercantile, in fact, are evident throughout Indian Buddhism. Śāntideva's *Bodhicaryāvatāra* (A guide to the Bodhisattva's way of life), an eighth-century Sanskrit text that many Buddhists venerate as a paragon of writing on ethics and wisdom, likewise bears the mark of the mercantile. As we read in the first chapter, verse 11,

> You who are accustomed to traveling abroad among
> the trading centers that are the realms of rebirth,
> grasp firmly the jewel that is *bodhicitta!*
> It is precious, and it has been evaluated
> by the unique caravan leaders of the world
> who are of immeasurable intelligence.[5]

Here the bodhisattva path is explained, or perhaps equated, with merchant activity. Buddhas and bodhisattvas are configured as wise caravan leaders, existence in saṃsāra as an overseas trading expedition, and *bodhicitta*—or "awakening mind"—as a precious jewel. The Indian commentator Prajñākaramati (950–1030 CE) offers this insight into these parallels:

> Here "trading centers"—that is, cities where there is the buying and selling of goods and wares—are actually the realms of rebirth. Likewise, "the trading centers that are the realms of rebirth" are the places where there is the buying and selling of goods and wares, which are good and bad karma. . . . The intention here is this: you who desire to obtain the wealth that is happiness are, in fact, merchants. Therefore, you should grasp this great jewel with great care. Why? Because it is precious. This expresses the reason.[6]

Notice that Prajñākaramati, after explaining the religious path as a series of commercial trading centers, tells his readers that they are merchants or perhaps that they should think of themselves as merchants. But why? Why use merchant activity as a model for spiritual activity? And what does it tell us about jewels that they were likened to *bodhicitta?* Did they possess a special power?

Worth pondering here is that although the infamous "two truths" (*satyadvaya*) of Buddhist philosophy are frequently translated as "conventional truth" and "ultimate truth," the former, also known as *vyavahārasatya,* could likewise be rendered as "commercial truth," "market truth," or "transactional truth," for *vyavahāra* is often a term for "business" or "trade." Nāgārjuna has famously written in his *Mūlamadhyamakakārikā* (Fundamental verses on the Middle Way) that "the ultimate is not taught without depending upon the conventional,"[7] so perhaps an understanding of the "mercantile" is somehow expedient or, for the likes of Prajñākaramati, necessary for understanding "ultimate truth."[8] Living as we do in "the trading centers that are the realms of rebirth," maybe all of us are, in fact, merchants. And maybe at times in the past this insight really mattered.

In what follows, in an effort to think through this mercantilizing of Indian Buddhism, I will offer an overview of merchant-monastic relations in the Kuṣāṇa and Sātavāhana empires; explore some of the ways that Buddhism offered power and prestige to the merchant community, and vice versa; and consider the interconnectedness in early Buddhism of jewels, magnificence, and virtue. The abiding question is the extent to which early Buddhists were, in fact, merchants—and the ways that this interpenetration, or at least intimacy, of identities might have mattered.

Buddhism, Mercantilism, and the Kuṣāṇas

Along with the rise and fall of the Mauryan Empire and its unification of much of the Indian subcontinent, a complex system of trade routes was established, enabling the merchant community that exchanged goods between cities on these routes to grow in financial and social power.[9] By the third century BCE, according to James Heitzman, "the first network of long-distance trade routes is discernible" and also "the first surviving Buddhist monastic sites," all of which "were located close to non-monastic sites or along routes connecting urban locations."[10] This connection of Buddhist monasticism with trade and urbanism becomes even clearer in the second century BCE.[11] During this time we find a steady growth of monastic sites in the western Deccan that were likewise connected with urban centers or trade routes. A few centuries later in the eastern Deccan, circa 200 CE, there was a sudden increase in the number of Buddhist sites near Ikṣavāku cities and trade routes with the rise of their empire and a corresponding decrease one hundred years later with its decline.[12] "Equally striking," Heitzman observes, "is the growth of Buddhist sites in Gandhāra [in northwest India] and the concurrent influence of the Kuṣāṇa empire between 0 and 300 [CE]."[13]

Now if we examine the connection between Buddhist monasticism and the Kuṣāṇa empire, once again we observe that Buddhist monastic sites arose on trade routes or near urban centers—that here as well Buddhism seems to have had close ties with trade and urbanism. But if we look more closely at Kuṣāṇa urban centers—and at those urban centers throughout India in which Buddhism developed during this period—we see that the foundation of this urbanism was an economy based on trade, mostly foreign trade in luxury goods. During this period, for the first time in history, the Silk Route, which proceeded from the Ganges River to Central Asia, came under unified control. This meant that the main trade routes that connected China with the Egyptian city of Alexandria, one of the major focal points of Asian trade, passed through the Kuṣāṇa-controlled territory of northwest India. Taking advantage of their strategic position, Kuṣāṇa traders profited from a brisk overland exchange of goods with foreign partners, particularly the Chinese.[14]

Overseas trade with Rome was also booming.[15] Thanks to the Greeks' discovery of the monsoon winds in the first century CE, the travel time between Italy and India was reduced to sixteen weeks.[16] Almost one ship a day is said to have left Rome on this commute. In this trade relationship, with India mostly importing raw materials and exporting luxury goods, Rome incurred a substantial trade deficit.[17] As Pliny laments in his *Natural History* in the first century CE, "There was no year in which India did not drain the Roman empire of a hundred million sesterces. So dearly do we pay for luxury and our women."[18]

While internal trade within India at the time was brisk—cotton was being transported from the Deccan, perfume from the north, numerous articles from the south, and so on—this trade was apparently less a matter of bringing goods to domestic consumers than of consolidating goods for easy export. The final destination of these commodities was frequently foreign consumers, most notably those in Rome. The most telling indicator of the importance for India of this trade with Rome was the de-urbanization that occurred throughout India after the breakup of the Roman Empire in the fourth century CE. While other factors surely led to this condition—the fall of the Sātavāhanas and Kṣatrapas, the decline of towns on the Silk Route in Central Asia and Bactria, and perhaps a regional onset of arid weather[19]—the principal cause, as the historian R. S. Sharma argues at length, was the decline of foreign trade.[20]

The Kuṣāṇa administration actively promoted foreign trade with both its monetary and commercial policy.[21] The Kuṣāṇas were the first rulers in India to cast gold coins—coins that matched the Roman gold aurei in size and weight—and their copper coins accorded to Persian and Attic standards.[22] More important, they encouraged the proliferation of merchant guilds, which promoted and regulated trade in the empire.

The literature and epigraphy of the Kuṣāṇa period suggest the presence of these guilds not only in the realm of commerce, but also in the realm of religion. One Kuṣāṇa inscription mentions that two Mathura guilds of flour makers received perpetual endowments in cash under the proviso that they use the interest that accrued to feed one hundred Brahmins every day.[23] Other inscriptions refer to a timber merchants' monastery and a cloak makers' monastery, attesting to direct guild involvement with Buddhism.[24]

It is important to note that a monastery given to the Buddhist monastic community was not a debt-free gift. On the basis of various passages in Mūlasarvāstivādin texts, Gregory Schopen argues that monks who received such gifts were obligated to perform a number of acts benefiting the monastery's donor, such as the recitation of verses and the assigning of the resultant merit. "This arrangement," Schopen remarks, "looks . . . less like a gift than an exchange of mutual benefits."[25]

So how did the guilds in the Kuṣāṇa realm benefit from their donations to the Buddhist monastic community? Could these inscriptions be indicative not just of Buddhism's spiritual appeal, but also of its increasing political clout under the patronage of Kuṣāṇa kings? Did guilds make donations to many religious institutions as a way of buying favor with the powers that be? Did Brahminism's lack of a centralized officiating body like the Buddhist monastic community make it less likely to receive donations? Did the Buddhist monastic community exploit this difference, implementing and lobbying for measures that those enmeshed in the commercial world would view as a kind of probusiness "remedy" or "antidote," ushering in a robust "Buddhist rate of growth"?[26] Many questions linger.

Several seals from the city of Bhita (near present-day Allahabad) also refer to merchant corporations known as *nigamas*. S. K. Maity has suggested that *nigama* means "township" and that "these seals represented the authority of some autonomous urban administrations."[27] In the Gupta period, at least, a *nigama* functioned like a glorified chamber of commerce, looking after a town's commercial and financial interests, as well as helping with its administration.[28] It is indicative of the influence of *nigamas* under the Kuṣāṇas that they were empowered to issue coins.[29] Of the five pre-Indo-Greek coins on which the term *nigama* appears, four bear the names of the different quarters of Taxila, one of the most important cities in Gandhāra and a major center for Buddhism under the Kuṣāṇas. Another coin from Taxila also bears the term *pañcanigama* (five *nigamas*). "It is evident," R. S. Sharma notes, "that on the eve of the Greek occupation of Taxila its government was carried on either by a single corporation of artisans and merchants or by a joint body comprising five corporations."[30] The relationship between the merchants who peopled these *nigamas* and the guilds to which these merchants belonged is, unfortunately, still unclear.[31] The connection, financial or otherwise, between these *nigamas* and the Buddhist monastic community is likewise unclear, but elsewhere there is evidence that *nigamas* funded the monastic community directly: the *nigama* of Karāhakaṭa made an offering at Bharhut, and the *nigama* of Dhānyakaṭaka made offerings at Amarāvatī.[32]

During the Kuṣāṇa period, however, it was another type of merchant alliance—the lay association—that provided the Buddhist monastic community with much of its increased patronage. While the epigraphic record attests to the donations of individual merchants and their family members,[33] as well as those made by foreigners (Greeks, Bactrians, and Iranians) who were probably merchants,[34] and even to the joint donations of individuals and monastics,[35] more common in the Kuṣāṇa realm were group donations made by lay associations.[36] Unlike the administrative guild or the political *nigama,* these lay associations, Xinru Liu concludes, "sprang up from the development of guild-caste organizations in urban centers" and may have been "merchants' associations founded for the purpose of organizing donations."[37] It seems that a group of merchants was "employed by the monastic community" (*saṅghaprakṛta*) to organize the lay community at large so that it could make collective donations to them to fund large-scale construction.[38] Liu observes that "the purpose of making substantial donations motivated lay devotees to organize themselves according to the model of their own guilds and that of saṅgha administration," suggesting connections and similarities among various donative, administrative, and religious institutions.[39]

Now we can extend the previous proposition. It's not just, as the archaeological evidence indicates, that Buddhist monasticism was connected with trading centers and the routes that connected trading centers. We can also say that Buddhist monasticism was connected with individual merchants—mostly in their role as donors—but far more frequently with merchant associations: with the mercantile bodies that constituted the world of trade (guilds), with the political bodies that administered it (*nigamas*), and with the donative bodies that acted as its benefactors (lay associations).

Buddhism, Mercantilism, and the Sātavāhanas

We find a similar connection between the mercantile world and Buddhism, at more or less the same time, in the western Deccan under the Sātavāhanas and, although I won't discuss it here, in the eastern

Deccan under the Ikṣavākus.[40] The similarities are striking. Here too we find a thriving merchant community whose fortunes were dependent on foreign trade; here too merchants organized themselves into guilds, which became powerful institutions, helping in the organization of trade and, perhaps, in the administration of towns;[41] and here too we find evidence of a significant increase in the patronage that merchants, both individually and collectively, gave to Buddhism.[42]

Even though the Sātavāhanas, unlike the Kuṣāṇas, were "zealous champions of the varṇa system" and apparently provided the Buddhist monastic community with only meager financial support, Buddhism nonetheless thrived under their rule.[43] The stone railing encircling the stūpa at Jagannāth in Pauni, for example, bears inscriptions recording the donations of merchants, householders, monastics, and lay disciples, with little evidence of royal support.[44] Buddhism's development at Pauni and its extensive growth throughout the western Deccan was primarily funded by nonroyal donors, so perhaps it was the ordinary citizenry in India, not its royalty, that provided the financial lifeline that allowed Buddhism to flourish in this period.

Since guilds were very involved in financial and political affairs under the Sātavāhanas, even offering banking services, their direct funding of the Buddhist monastic community, without lay associations acting as intermediaries, raises questions about the motives and benefits involved in their providing such support.[45] Like the merchants under the Kuṣāṇas, the merchants under the Sātavāhanas were power brokers, almost subsidiary potentates, in their communities.[46] What could have been the reasons then for Sātavāhana merchants in their collective status as guilds to support the Buddhist monastic community? No doubt the answer involves a variety of religious, social, and political reasons: to earn religious merit, to gain social standing, and perhaps to buy influence with the monastic community, as it in turn had considerable influence with the Sātavāhana government.[47]

Another aspect of Buddhism under the Sātavāhanas that might help us understand more about Buddhism in this period is the self-referential accounts found in the inscriptions recording donations of individual donors. Judging from these inscriptions, caste affiliation didn't figure significantly in an individual's choice of profession or in how individuals chose to identify themselves. These donors, representing a large cross-section of society, chose to mention "only their occupations and professions together with their place of residence."[48] Since these inscriptions were written when the balance of power among the state, religious institutions, and the laity was in flux, "the recording of donations by different occupational groups at the cave sites may be seen as a means of stating their economic power which in turn would determine their position in the new social hierarchy."[49]

Himanshu Ray also claims that it was within the caste system "that social mobility was sought,"[50] but I think it's quite likely that these inscriptions, as well as those from the Kuṣāṇa realm, bear testimony to the partial fulfillment of the famous prediction from the *Viṣṇu Purāṇa*—which was probably more a statement of fact than of fear—that one day "property alone would confer prestige ... wealth alone would be the source of dharma ... and fine clothes alone would indicate dignity."[51]

An examination of Sātavāhana art also provides insight into the dynamics of the relationship between the merchant community and the Buddhist monastic community. For example, the artwork on the balustrades and gateways that surround the stūpas in and around Sanchi put the interactions between the two groups into relief. At stūpa 1 in Satdhāra, which was likely constructed during the Aśokan period in the third century BCE, and eighteen kilometers away at stūpa 2 in Sanchi, which was constructed during the Śuṅga period in the last quarter of the second century BCE, the balustrade posts are decorated with carved medallions. At stūpa 1 in Satdhāra, these medallions are completely floral except for one medallion that contains an image of a Bodhi tree and another an image of a *yakṣa*.[52] At stūpa 2 in Sanchi, as at Bodhgaya and Bharhut, these medallions contain images of plants, animals, demi-gods, Bodhi trees, stūpas, and some "singularly crude and archaic" figures of humans, all depicted within delicately wrought floral settings.[53] By contrast, a few hundred meters to the east of stūpa 2 are the main gateways of stūpa 1, which were built during Sātavāhana rule in the first century BCE. The images on these gateways are crowded with people, each individual rendered with a naturalism not found on the earlier balustrades. These carvings depict thickly populated cities, couples in love play, and women decked out with costumes and ornaments. Although there are still images of Bodhi trees and stūpas, they are now surrounded by people, shoulder to shoulder, facing them, with hands raised in veneration.

It's curious that at stūpa 1 in Sanchi, as well as at the Karle monastery in the Sātavāhana-controlled Deccan and at Buddhist sites in Kuṣāṇa-controlled Mathura, there are numerous carvings of amorous couples and sensuous depictions of women obviously enjoying a variety of material pleasures. Considering this "bourgeois sophistication,"[54] this new urban and sensual quality to the art being produced at Buddhist pilgrimage and monastic sites during this period, I wonder to what degree and in what ways Buddhism was catering to the desires of its patrons. Sex sells, but did it back then? And if so, to whom?

As D. D. Kosambi has written in regard to Karle, "The sculpture is beautiful, even voluptuous, of handsome couples of opulent men and women, dressed in the height of style, riding horses and elephants; hardly what one would expect in an assembly place of monks, but precisely what rich merchants would have liked."[55] And how did these elaborately decorated monasteries like Karle actually function? Were they somber rain retreats in which monastics would engage in meditation practices, or were they places for the upwardly mobile to visit on weekend outings and gape at representations of handsome men and buxom women indulging in sexual play? Moreover, why did merchants, guildmasters, and monastics fund the construction of so many of these carvings?[56]

It is also worth noting that Buddhism wasn't the only heterodox religion in India to have close ties with the merchant community. In the early centuries of the Common Era in the northern plains and in the western Deccan, where the Kuṣāṇas and the Sātavāhanas held power, Jainism also grew and prospered from the patronage of merchants.[57] Like Buddhism, Jainism thrived in towns around trade routes where many merchants and craftspeople lived; its "social base . . . was primarily confined to the urban middle class"; and—like Buddhism in the western Deccan, if not in the north—its funding came primarily from merchants, not royalty.[58] Likewise, Jainism was also very popular in Taxila and even preeminent in Mathura[59]—at the time, the two most important cities in the northern plains for Sarvāstivādin Buddhism and both hubs for trade and commerce. Considering that both Buddhism and Jainism suddenly began to thrive in basically the same places and at the same time and with the same support base, what individual and collective needs were these heterodox religions fulfilling, and what transformations had occurred to stimulate these needs? What was it that nascent merchant communities, in particular, weren't getting from elsewhere but thought they could get from these religions?

Merchants, Status, and Magnificence

To judge by Brahmanical literature, merchants—generally members of the vaiśya caste—were distrusted by the constituency of the upper castes and offered little praise and prestige. Both the *Arthaśāstra* tradition, which glorifies the supremacy of kṣatriyas, and the dharmaśāstra tradition, which does the same for Brahmins, recognize the potential threat that a powerful merchant class represents to their respective political and sacerdotal powers.[60] In the *Arthaśāstra* (Science of politics), Kauṭilya maps out a labyrinth of rules and regulations to ensure that the government not only accrues ample revenue from taxing merchants, but also controls the production and exchange of numerous commodities. Kauṭilya, as B. G. Gokhale writes, "obviously favors the growth of the monopolistic power of the state and often betrays the feelings that a wealthy merchant class and the power of its guilds may contribute to the erosion of the majesty of the state."[61]

The merchant fares far worse in dharmaśāstra texts. The *Manusmṛti* (Manu's code of law), for example, recognizes that society needs merchants and their services and therefore instructs the king to make sure that vaiśyas engage in trade, lend money, farm the land, or keep livestock.[62] Still, it advises the king to keep firm control over mercantile activity: fixing the rates for buying and selling merchandise, setting the prices every five days, and so on.[63] While vaiśyas are expected to know how to evaluate trade goods and the profit and loss from a trade, those individuals who nevertheless "make a living through trade are to be excluded from offerings to the gods and ancestors."[64] And they will fall into disrepute, if not ruin.[65]

The merchant, in short, was something of an outcaste. He—for merchants were presumed to be male[66]—was wealthy beyond his prescribed social status, he associated with individuals "beneath" him (like śūdra craftsmen and foreign barbarians), and his travels made him a conduit and harbinger for new ideas and practices. Perhaps that is why seafarers are grouped with clear social reprobates: arsonists, poisoners, false witnesses, gamblers, drunks, and madmen.[67] The merchant may have brought wealth to the community, but he was still a threat to the Brahmanical social world that the *Manusmṛti* was so desperate to preserve.

Though the merchant fares better in Brahmanical materials from later centuries, there is a lingering sense that merchants are a little crooked, if not outright crooks. Writing about Guṇāḍhya's *Bṛhatkathā* (Great romance) and the narrative tradition more generally, J. A. B. van Buitanen offers this insight:

> Kauṭilya, who could hardly qualify as a moral arbiter himself, describes the merchants whose spirit pervades the narrative literature as "thieves except for the name." It is not just profitable dishonesty that the Indian

> success story advocates, however, but a very effective sort of oneupmanship. This happy attitude supposes a good many virtues, among which the Indians prized presence of mind highest and practical knowledge second. Words for "witty," "clever," "worldly," and "crooked" are often the same, and this combination characterizes many heroes of the success stories.[68]

In Buddhist narratives, however, merchants tend to be more clever than crooked, rich by dint of their accumulated merit and the results that this manifests. Many of these stories read like merchants' fairy tales, with merchants gaining wealth easily, almost inevitably, and their large stockpiles of wealth indicating their equally large stockpiles of virtue. As Russell Sizemore and Donald Swearer explain, "Because the law of kamma guarantees that each receives the fate merited by his [or] her acts and because wealth, being good, is a fit reward for meritorious action, prosperity is a proof of virtue."[69] Prayudh Payutto, in *Buddhist Economics,* makes this clear: "The common tendency (in Thailand) [is] to praise people simply because they are rich, based on the belief," which he thinks is mistaken, "that their riches are a result of accumulated merit from previous lives."[70]

The high regard accorded to merchants in Buddhist literature is made explicit in the *Supriya-avadāna,* one of the stories in the *Divyāvadāna* (Divine stories), a "greatest hits" collection of Indian Buddhist narratives.[71] In the story, Supriya converts all of India to Buddhism. He does so, however, not as a buddha or a bodhisattva, but as a merchant who first satisfies everyone's material needs and then establishes them on the tenfold path of virtuous actions. Merchants, it seems, can turn the wheel of dharma too, and they can do so quite well.

The *Supriya-avadāna* also features a particularly bold claim about the status of merchants. It is said that the great city of Rohitaka (present-day Rohtak, northwest of Delhi) "is inhabited by a great king and served by merchants who are great men."[72] To equate merchants with "great men" (*mahāpuruṣa*)[73]—a technical term in this text, to be sure—is to make strong claims about the destiny of merchants, for it is frequently said in Buddhist texts that only two options are open to such a being: to become a *cakravartin* king or a buddha, the respective pinnacles of religious and political power.[74] At the end of the *Supriya-avadāna,* it is said that Supriya was the Buddha-to-be in a previous lifetime, but in terms of converting beings to the dharma, Supriya seems to have been every bit the match of his later incarnation.

But why did merchants give to the Buddhist monastic community? What did they gain from making these offerings? The easy answer is "merit." Giving to such a great field of merit as the Buddhist monastic community generates merit, and merit leads to wealth and happiness. But giving can also generate a kind of status—a claim that is hardly new.

Paul Veyne, for example, in his work on gift giving in ancient Rome during the Hellenistic and Roman periods (ca. 300 BCE–300 CE), describes in detail how acts of public patronage were a crucial way for notables to express their membership in the upper class and by doing so prime themselves for political careers and a certain "prestige." Elsewhere, as well, Veyne discusses the connection between giving and the Aristotelian notion of "magnificence." Within a South Asian context, R. A. L. H. Gunawardana likewise claims that the earliest Brāhmī inscriptions in Sri Lanka, most of which were to the Buddhist monastic community, "reflect a state of intense competition for status conducted through acts of conspicuous generosity."[75]

We also find a similar logic of giving in James Laidlaw's ethnographic work on the Jains of Jaipur.[76] After describing the varieties of giving in which Jains engage, Laidlaw discusses the reasons that he can discern for their making such gifts. Among the beneficiaries of these gifts, Laidlaw explains, are the benefactors themselves: "There is a sense in which public religious giving can be seen as a social investment strategy. It advertises the wealth of a rich merchant family in a morally approved way, and so augments its standing in the community."[77] As Laidlaw remarks,

> To understand their generosity, it would be as much a mistake to look for a functional explanation to demonstrate that they are really acting in narrow self-interest, as it would to think we had explained anything by piously indicating a religious motivation. Euergetism is not actually necessary for rich merchants with a successful business, and there are few who, as their co-religionists see it, do not play their part. What euergetism is necessary for is honour or reputation (*izzat, nam*), being regarded as a leader of the community, one of the "big men" (*bare log*), a *seth*. And it is this, I think, which motivates it.[78]

Such claims to status can also be made for Indian merchants in the Buddhist tradition. In James Heitzman's archaeological work on the connection between Buddhism and trade, he questions why it is that Buddhist monasteries in the early centuries of the Common Era were consistently associated with cities, empires, and trade but always located at the peripheries of these urban trading centers, for being located "at a distance from the scenes of political and economic power made their direct participation in such activity inefficient."[79] As Heitzman notes, "The location of monasteries in relation to urban structures suggests that the Buddhist institutions had little discernible role in the political or economic activities of their patrons. Why then did people whose main concern was power apportion some of their wealth to organizations that apparently did nothing to add to that power?"[80]

Heitzman's assessment of Buddhist institutions and their motivations and alliances may be in need of revision, but his answer is nonetheless telling: "Buddhism may have provided an opportunity for those persons at various class and status levels within the urban environment to express and confirm their positions through ostentatious display ... [and] here status rather than class was the crucial determinant of donated magnificence."[81]

According to Heitzman, "donated magnificence" was accessible only to a small group of economic elites. As he explains, "The relative magnificence of donations was a method for establishing the divisions in a hierarchical elite. Only the wealthy could afford to have a monument built; only the wealthiest could afford the richest and most ornate of designs."[82] It is perhaps this quest for "magnificence," to echo Aristotle, that helps explain why Buddhists at this time incorporated various luxury goods into their rituals. As Neelis notes, "Commodities referred to as the 'seven jewels' (*saptaratna*), including gold, silver, crystal, beryl, carnelian, coral, and pearls, are frequently found among the contents of reliquary deposits and valorized as laudable donations in Buddhist texts (especially but not exclusively Mahāyāna sūtras)."[83]

Correlating textual materials regarding the "seven jewels" and archeological finds at Taxila, Xinru Liu argues that it was precisely those goods that were being traded by Kuṣāṇa merchants that were singled out in Buddhist texts as being efficacious in ritual offerings.[84] She then makes the bold claim that "the demand for many commodities in the Eurasian trade was *prompted* by Buddhist ritual" and that "Buddhist values *created and sustained* the demand for certain commodities traded between India and China during the first to the fifth centuries AD."[85] It's also possible that Buddhist monasteries simply became repositories for these objects, which were already in circulation, because valuable commodities were thought to make valuable gifts—and maybe become relics themselves, as John Strong suggests in his chapter in this volume.[86] But even being a bank of this kind is not benign. As Thomas Jefferson once wrote, echoing the fearmongering in the śāstras, "Banking establishments are more dangerous than standing armies."[87]

Regardless of the precise explanation for why the "seven jewels" became so heavily trafficked, it does seem that when Śāntideva and Prajñākaramati described *bodhicitta* as a jewel in the *Bodhicaryāvatāra,* they may have been being more than metaphoric. It seems quite possible that precious jewels were recognized as material forms of Buddhist virtue—catalysts for "awakening mind" or even manifestations of it. This might not have "prompted," "created," or "sustained" the demand for precious jewels, but it wasn't a deterrent.

Still, all this was surely only part of Buddhism's allure. Buddhism, as Kathleen Morrison notes, "overcame many of the problems Brahmanical Hinduism presented to merchants, including strict rules of commensality, limited avenues for social advancement, and a prohibition against overseas travel."[88] Buddhism also offered a model for a mobile community, unlike the śāstras, which imagined a world much more settled and fixed. Renunciants and merchants were both outcastes in that world, and one could imagine them joining forces against a common Brahmanical enemy.

Some of Buddhism's appeal, I imagine, also lay in its solution to a perennial problem, especially for rich merchants: "You can't take it with you when you die."[89] According to Buddhism's "market morality"—which I discuss elsewhere and which is a prominent feature of early Buddhist literature[90]—merit and money are convertible forms of capital, much like Bourdieu's symbolic and economic capital, but the places and procedures that allow individuals to exchange one form of capital for the other are much more explicit and readily accessible than anything Bourdieu describes.[91] In this way, Buddhism is like a convenient currency exchange. It allows one to convert money and moral action into merit, and merit into money and moral attainment. And it offers excellent rates of return. One can accrue merit by giving to Buddhist saints and shrines, and merit can be transformed into roots of virtue for fervent aspirations that promise future wealth, be it economic or spiritual. Numerous merchants in the *Divyāvadāna,* for example, "cash in" the merit they've accrued from an offering in order to be reborn "in a family that is rich, wealthy, and prosperous."[92]

Monks and merchants, it seems, were playing in overlapping fields with interchangeable forms of capital. This play, I would suggest, generated a kind of intersubjectivity between the two groups, such that the two shared similar kinds of experience—a form of moral economics—and each helped constitute for the other certain confines and dispositions for that experience. Scholars have observed the ways that religion has often been built on the backs of merchants—most notably in the case of Islam, "with its special affinity to trade and traders and its urban character"[93]—but I think the case of Buddhists and merchants in early India exhibits a more intimate form of reciprocity, with each developing on the back of the other. Studying the two in tandem lets one see the connections between the monk and the merchant, the saṅgha and the guild, morality and the market, and, perhaps, the monastery and the bazaar.

So to return to the question I asked at the beginning of the chapter: are we all, in fact, merchants? Well, not exactly, but I do think that Buddhists and merchants were very closely allied in the early centuries of the Common Era in India and that they had mutually constitutive and interpenetrating identities that developed in tandem. This is similar in many ways to the relationship between Protestants and merchants that Max Weber describes in *The Protestant Ethic and the Spirit of Capitalism,* although Buddhism is far more lavish than Protestantism with its encomiums to merchants. To claim, as does the *Bodhicaryāvatāra,* that buddhas are caravan leaders is lavish indeed.[94] And it's worth thinking hard about why such a claim was ever made.

Notes

1. Greg Bailey and Ian Mabbett, *The Sociology of Early Buddhism* (Cambridge: Cambridge University Press, 2003), 25.
2. One might look to the earliest Buddhist texts, like the last two books of the *Suttanipāta,* "which belong to the oldest of the Pāli texts," and notice how they focus on forms of renunciation. Luis Gómez, "Proto-Madhyāmika in the Pāli Canon," *Philosophy East and West* 26, no. 2 (1976): 139. Then one could try to argue that early Buddhism as an institution wasn't concerned with commerce, but the argument would be weak, conjured from a textual absence (*argumentum ex silentio*). Gregory Schopen and now many others have cautioned us against such presuppositions and romanticizations and have shown us the complex ways that Indian Buddhist monastics and monasteries became connected to social and economic institutions. See, for example, Gregory Schopen: "Archaeology and Protestant Presuppositions in the Study of Indian Buddhism," *History of Religions* 31, no. 1 (1991): 1–23, and

"Dead Monks and Bad Debts: Some Provisions of a Buddhist Monastic Inheritance Law," *Indo-Iranian Journal* 44 (2001): 99–148; Shayne Clarke, *Family Matters in Indian Buddhist Monasticisms* (Honolulu: University of Hawai'i Press, 2013).

3. See, for example, the numerous accounts and representations of the two merchants Trapuṣa and Bhallika, who were the Buddha's first lay disciples. Phyllis Granoff, "The Gift of the Two Merchants: Defining the Buddhist Community through Story," *East and West* 55, no. 1/4 (2005): 129–138. A telling example of this close relationship comes from the more than one thousand official, business, and private documents that have been discovered in and around Niya, near the southern edge of the Taklamakan Desert. These documents, written in a dialect of Gāndhārī in the third-fourth centuries CE, give us some sense of what monks in the area were doing at that time. Apparently, at least some of them owned servants, slaves, and vineyards; were involved in property disputes, camel trading, and negotiating state regulations for a monastery; and were responsible for fines levied in court. A. M. Boyer, E. J. Rapson, E. Senart, and P. S. Noble, eds., *Kharoṣṭhī Inscriptions Discovered by Sir Aurel Stein in Chinese Turkestan* (Oxford: Clarendon Press, 1920–1929), nos. 437, 473, 425, 516, 546, 489, 345. Translations in T. Burrow, *A Translation of the Kharoṣṭhi Documents from Chinese Turkestan* (London: Royal Asiatic Society), 1940. To be sure, these monks were involved in the commercial world and not, as we read in the *Suttanipāta* (verses 35–75), living "alone like a rhinoceros horn." Bhikku Bodhi, trans., *The Sutta Nipāta: An Ancient Collection of the Buddha's Discourses* (Boston: Wisdom Publications, 2017), 162–167. My thanks to Timothy Lenz for his help with the Niya documents.

4. For more on the logic and practice of this moral economy, see Andy Rotman: *Thus Have I Seen: Visualizing Faith in Early Indian Buddhism* (New York: Oxford University Press, 2009), and "Marketing Morality: The Economy of Faith in Early Indian Buddhism," in *Śrīnidhiḥ: Professor Shrikant Shankar Bahulkar's Gratitude Volume,* edited by Shripad G. Bhat, Shilpa Sumant, and Ambarish Vasant Khare (Pune: Saṁvidyā Institute of Cultural Studies, 2009), 253–290.

5. Dwarikadas Sastri, ed. and trans., *Bodhicāryāvatāra of Ārya Śāntideva with the Commentary of Śri Prajñākarāmati* (Varanasi: Bauddha Bharati, 1988), 12:
suparīkṣitam aprameyadhībhir bahumūlyaṃ jagadekasārthavāhaiḥ |
gatipattanavipravāsaśīlāḥ sudṛḍhaṃ gṛhṇata bodhicittaratnam ||

6. Sastri, *Bodhicāryāvatāra,* 12, *gataya eva pattanāni paṇyadravyakrayavikrayanagarāṇi iha pattanāni* | *tadvat śubhāsubhakarmapaṇyadravyakrayavikrayasthānāni gatipattananāni ... ayam abhiprāyaḥ vāṇija eva sukhasampattilābhārthino yūyam* | *ataḥ idam eva mahāratnaṃ mahatādareṇa gṛhṇata* | *kutaḥ* | *bahumūlyam iti* | *hetupadam etat.*
7. Mark Siderits and Shoryu Katsura, trans., *Nāgārjuna's Middle Way* (*Mūlamadhyamakakārikā*) (Boston: Wisdom Publications, 2013), 273–274, chapter 24, verse 10, *vyavahāram anāśritya paramārtho na deśyate.*
8. For more on conventional truth in Buddhism, see The Cowherds, *Moonshadows: Conventional Truth in Buddhist Philosophy* (New York: Oxford University Press, 2011). For more on conventional truth in Vedānta, see Andrew Nicholson, *Unifying Hinduism: Philosophy and Identity in Indian Intellectual History* (New York: Columbia University Press, 2010), 87–88. And for more on *vyavahāra* in Hindu law, see Donald Davis, *The Spirit of Hindu Law* (Cambridge: Cambridge University Press, 2010), "Doubts and Disputes (*vyavahāra*)," 108–127.
9. I wrote the first draft of the remaining sections of this chapter in India in the mid-1990s. At the time my primary source for reference materials was the library maintained by Pune University's Pali and Buddhist Studies Department. In the interim, I have updated my arguments but only partially updated the references. Some of them will seem dated (or obscure), and some more obvious ones are missing. For more up-to-date citations, see Jason Neelis's excellent account of the symbiotic relationship between early Buddhist monastic institutions and trade networks: *Early Buddhist Transmission and Trade Networks: Mobility and Exchange within and beyond the Northwestern Borderlands of South Asia* (Leiden: Brill, 2011).
10. James Heitzman, "Early Buddhism, Trade and Empire," in *Studies in the Archaeology and Palaeoanthropology of South Asia,* edited by Kenneth A. R. Kennedy and Gregory L. Possehl (Oxford: Oxford University Press and IBH Publishing, 1984), 124. For an updated account, see James Heitzman, "The Urban Context of Early Buddhist Monuments in South Asia," in *Buddhist Stūpas in South Asia: Recent Archaeological, Art-Historical, and Historical Perspectives,* edited by Jason Hawkes and Akira Shimada (Delhi: Oxford University Press, 2009), 192–215.
11. As Neelis (*Early Buddhist Transmission and Trade Networks,* 20–21) notes, Kathleen Morrison criticizes "an overemphasis on connections between urban and monastic centers patronized by powerful and wealthy donors at the expense of smaller Buddhist establishments in

rural hinterlands with significant agricultural resources supported by a broad array of donors. . . . Such critiques do not invalidate the general model of a symbiosis between Buddhist monastic institutions and trade networks, but do illustrate local and regional complexity." Kathleen Morrison, "Trade, Urbanism, and Agricultural Expansion: Buddhist Monastic Institutions and the State in Early Historic Western Deccan," *World Archaeology* 27, no. 2 (1995), 203–221.

12. Heitzman, "Early Buddhism, Trade and Empire," 131. See too Ram Sharan Sharma, *Urban Decay in India (c. 300–c. 1000)* (Delhi: Munshiram Manoharlal, 1987), 100.
13. Heitzman, "Early Buddhism, Trade and Empire," 131.
14. Xinru Liu, *Ancient India and Ancient China: Trade and Religious Exchanges AD 1–600* (Delhi: Oxford University Press, 1988), 53–87.
15. Moti Chandra, *Trade and Trade Routes in Ancient India* (Delhi: Abhinav Publications, 1977), 109–128. See too E. H. Warmington, *The Commerce between the Roman Empire and India* (London: Curzon Press, 1974), and Mortimer Wheeler, *Rome beyond the Imperial Frontiers* (London: Bell, 1954).
16. M. Chandra, *Trade and Trade Routes in Ancient India,* 112. Manfred Raschke, however, suggests that the increase in overseas trade at this time wasn't because the technique of harnessing the monsoon winds was newly discovered, but rather that it was only now exploited, as it was economically expeditious to do so. Manfred Raschke, "New Studies in Roman Commerce with the East," in *Aufstieg und Niedergang der römischen Welt: Geschichte und Kultur Roms im Spiegel der neueren Forschung,* vol. 2.9.2 (New York: W. de Gruyter, 1978), 662. "The best possible explanation then for the 'discovery' attributed to Hippalus," Himanshu Ray explains, "would be to suggest that the Greeks crystallized what had hitherto been hearsay"; *Monastery and Guild: Commerce under the Sātavāhanas* (Delhi: Oxford University Press, 1986), 3.
17. For a list of these goods, see M. Chandra, *Trade and Trade Routes in Ancient India,* 123–128.
18. H. Rackham, trans., *Natural History,* by Pliny (Cambridge, MA: Harvard University Press, 1956–1962), 7:41. Pliny's claim might be an exaggeration. See A. Bernardi, "The Economic Problems of the Roman Empire at the Time of Its Decline," in *The Economic Decline of Empires,* edited by Carlo M. Cipolla (London: Methuen, 1970), 22–23; Ray, *Monastery and Guild,* 145–147; and Neelis, *Early Buddhist Transmission and Trade Networks,* 225–226.

19. M. K. Dhavalikar, "Environment: Its Influence on History and Culture in Western India," *Indica: Journal of the Heras Institute of Indian History and Culture* 33, no. 2 (1996): 112–113.
20. Sharma, *Urban Decay in India (c. 300–c. 1000)*, 132–142.
21. Neelis, *Early Buddhist Transmission and Trade Networks,* 137–145. The Kuṣāṇa monarch Wima may even have invaded Gandhāra because the region was already a flourishing trade center. Excavations at the Taxila site Sirkap revealed a rapid urban development in the century preceding the Kuṣāṇa era. B. N. Mukherjee, *The Economic Factors in Kushana History* (Calcutta: Pilgrim Publishers, 1970), 16; cited in X. Liu, *Ancient India and Ancient China,* 10.
22. B. N. Puri, *India under the Kushanas* (Bombay: Bharatiya Vidya Bhavan, 1965), 213–223; F. De Romanis, "Aurei after Trade: Western Taxes and Eastern Gift," in *Dal denarius al dinar—L'oriente e la moneta Romana (Atti dell'incontro di studio, Roma 16–18 settembre 2004*), edited by F. De Romanis and S. Sorda (Rome, 2006), 54–82.
23. D. C. Sircar, *Select Inscriptions Bearing on Indian History and Civilization,* vol. 1 (Calcutta: University of Calcutta, 1942), 151–153, no. 4.
24. Heinrich Lüders, *List of Brahmi Inscriptions from the Earliest Times to about A.D. 400 with the Exception of those of Aśoka* (Appendix to *Epigraphia Indica,* vol. 10), edited by Sten Konow (Calcutta, 1912), 191–192, §157; 110, §74, K24. For more on the lay ownership of monasteries, see Gregory Schopen, "The Lay Ownership of Monasteries and the Role of the Monk in Mūlasārvāstivādin Monasticism," *Journal of the International Association of Buddhist Studies* 19, no. 1 (1996): 81–126.
25. Schopen, "The Lay Ownership of Monasteries and the Role of the Monk in Mūlasārvāstivādin Monasticism," 100.
26. India's annual growth rate from the 1950s to the 1980s has often been referred to, disparagingly, as a "Hindu rate of growth," suggesting that Hinduism fostered a mercantile complacency and sluggishness that was displaced only by the economic liberalization begun in the 1990s. During the colonial period, outside observers likewise criticized Indian markets, suggesting that local forms of religiosity impeded the development of capital. See C.A. Bayly, *Rulers, Townsmen and Bazaars: North Indian Society in the Age of British Expansion 1770–1870* (Cambridge: Cambridge University Press, 1983), 453.
27. S. K. Maity, *Economic Life of Northern India* (Calcutta: World Press, 1957), 157.

28. Ram Sharan Sharma, *Aspects of Political Ideas and Institutions in Ancient India,* 4th rev. ed. (Delhi: Motilal Banarsidass, 1996), 389.
29. A. Ghosh, *The City in Early Historical India* (Simla: Indian Institute of Advanced Study, 1973), 46; K. D. Bajpai, "Authority of Minting Coins in Ancient India," *Journal of the Numismatic Society of India* 25, no. 9 (1963): 17–21.
30. Sharma, *Aspects of Political Ideas and Institutions in Ancient India,* 380. See too Vijay Kumar Thakur, *Urbanisation in Ancient India* (New Delhi: Abhinav Publications, 1981) 250–252, and Johannes Bronkhorst, "Why Is There Philosophy in India?" *1998 [Sixth] Gonda Lecture* (Amsterdam: Royal Netherlands Academy of Arts and Sciences, 1999), 12–13n28.
31. Sharma, *Aspects of Political Ideas and Institutions in Ancient India,* 281.
32. Lüders, *List of Brahmi Inscriptions,* nos. 705, 891. R. P. Chandra, "Some Unpublished Amaravati Inscriptions." *Epigraphia Indica* 25 (1919–1920): nos. 4 and 5; cited in Ray, *Monastery and Guild,* 198. For more on the role of *nigamas* in the construction of Amarāvatī, see Akira Shimada, *Early Buddhist Architecture in Context: The Great Stūpa at Amarāvatī (ca. 300 BCE–300 CE)* (Leiden: Brill, 2013), 155–158.
33. For example, there are inscriptions recording the donations from builders, a caravan leader's wife, and a goldsmith's wife. See, respectively, Sten Konow, *Kharoṣṭhī Inscriptions with the Exception of Those of Aśoka,* Corpus Inscriptionum Indicarum, vol. 2, part 1 (New Delhi: Director General, Archaeological Survey of India, 1991), 150, LXXVI and 151, LXXVIII; Lüders, *List of Brahmi Inscriptions,* 199–200, §172, K88; 187–188, §150, K14.
34. Lüders, *List of Brahmi Inscriptions,* 91–92, §60, K189; 92–93, §61, K204; 93–94, §62, K190; 103–104, §68, K196; 171–172, §135; and Konow, *Kharoṣṭhī Inscriptions,* 77, XXVII; 98, XXXVII.
35. Lüders, *List of Brahmi Inscriptions,* 86–87, §52, K175; 87, §53, K176; and Konow, *Kharoṣṭhī Inscriptions,* 141, LXXIV.
36. Lüders, *List of Brahmi Inscriptions,* 83–84, §47, K181; 84, §48, K182; 84–85, §49, K183; 85, §50, K185; 85–86, §51, K184.
37. X. Liu, *Ancient India and Ancient China,* 111, 117.
38. That these *saṅghaprakṛta*—or "commissioners of the Community," to follow Lüders's translation—were merchants is made explicit in an inscription that records that a cooking stone "had been put up by the commissioners of the Community, the merchants, whose [names are] . . ."

(*saṅghapr[a]kitehi vyavahārihi upaṭapito yeṣam n[ima.i]*). Lüders, *List of Brahmi Inscriptions,* 100–103, §65, G5.

39. X. Liu, *Ancient India and Ancient China,* 112.
40. See Elizabeth Rosen Stone, *The Buddhist Art of Nāgārjunakoṇḍa* (Delhi: Motilal Banarsidass, 1994), 10–11, and Haripada Chakraborti, *Early Brāhmī Record in India (c. 300 B.C.—c. 300 A.D.)* (Calcutta: Sanskrit Pustak Bhandar, 1974), 76. See too D. C. Sircar, "Some Brahmi Inscriptions," *Epigraphia Indica* 34 (1961–1962): 207–212, and H. Sarcar and B. N. Misra, *Nagarjunakonda* (Delhi: Archaeological Survey of India, 1972), 13ff.
41. Ray, *Monastery and Guild,* 130, 198.
42. X. Liu, *Ancient India and Ancient China,* 125. It isn't known, however, whether this attests to a marked increase in the number of merchants who patronized Buddhism or to a marked increase in the number and size of the donations of those merchants who already patronized Buddhism. It is also possible that merchant donations to Buddhism remained more or less the same and that instead this evidence attests to significant changes in inscriptional habits.
43. Sharma, *Aspects of Political Ideas and Institutions in Ancient India,* 275. See too Sheldon Pollock, *The Language of the Gods in the World of Men: Sanskrit, Culture, and Power in Premodern India* (Berkeley: University of California Press, 2006), 61–62. A representation of the Sātavāhana king named Sātakarṇi making a donation to Buddhist monks at the Kanaganahalli stūpa hints at some degree of closeness between the two, but "nothing is known about donations made by Sātavāhana kings to the monasteries." Monika Zin, *The Kanaganahalli Stūpa: An Analysis of the 60 Massive Slabs Covering the Dome* (New Delhi: Aryan Books International, 2018), 124. See too Andrew Ollett, *Language of Snakes: Prakrit, Sanskrit, and the Language Order of Premodern India* (Berkeley: University of California Press, 2017), 33–34; R. C. C. Fynes, "The Religious Patronage of the Sātavāhana Dynasty," *South Asian Studies* 11 (1995): 43–50.
44. Vasudev Vishnu Mirashi, *The History and Inscriptions of the Sātavāhanas and the Western Kshatrapas* (Bombay: Maharashtra State Board for Literature and Culture, 1981), 244.
45. Ray, *Monastery and Guild,* 129. The majority of donations were of the interest that accrued from perpetual endowments with guilds or the Buddhist monastic community (Ray, *Monastery and Guild,* 103, 157). See too James Burgess and Bhagwanlal Indraji, *Inscriptions from the Cave-Temples of Western India* (Delhi: Indian India, 1976), 47, Junnar

no. 16, and Mirashi, *The History and Inscriptions of the Sātavāhanas and the Western Kshatrapas,* 96–100.

46. Sharma, *Aspects of Political Ideas and Institutions in Ancient India,* 281.
47. Some of this influence arose concomitantly, no doubt, as the Sātavāhana rulers made use of Buddhism's ability to function as a nonviolent instrument of authority—one that could validate royal claims, disseminate information, legitimize social transformations, and create politically neutral buffer zones (Ray, *Monastery and Guild,* 101, 182).
48. Ray, *Monastery and Guild,* 192–193.
49. Ray, *Monastery and Guild,* 208.
50. Ray, *Monastery and Guild,* 176.
51. V. A. Bhattacarya, ed., *Viṣṇu Purāṇa* (Calcutta, 1882), iv 24, 74, 88, 90, *tataś cārtha evābhijanahetur ... dānam eva dharmahetuḥ ... sadveṣadhāryeva pātram.*
52. There may be more nonfloral medallions at Satdhāra, but when I visited the site in December 1997, only two had been unearthed in the excavations. See too R. C. Agrawal, "Stupas and Monasteries: A Recent Discovery from Satdhara, India," in *South Asian Archaeology, 1995: Proceedings of the 13th International Conference of the European Association of South Asian Archaeologists,* edited by R. and B. Allchin (New Delhi: Published for the Ancient India and Iran Trust, 1997), i 403–415.
53. Debala Mitra, *Sanchi* (New Delhi: Archaeological Survey of India, 1992), 64.
54. Sushma Trivedi, "Impact of Trade on Early Art of India (circa 200 B.C.–300 A.D.)," *Journal of the Asiatic Society of Bombay* 70 (1995): 153.
55. D. D. Kosambi, *The Culture and Civilization of Ancient India in Historical Outline* (Delhi: Vikas Publishing, 1997), 183.
56. Heinrich Lüders lists hundreds of inscriptions bearing testimony to such donations in *List of Brahmi Inscriptions,* nos. 162–568.
57. Lüders, *List of Brahmi Inscriptions,* nos. 30, 32, 39, 41, 53, 54, 74, 76, etc.
58. Smita Sahgal, "Spread of Jinism in North India between circa 200 B.C. and circa A.D. 300," in *Jainism and Prakrit in Ancient and Medieval India,* edited by N. N. Bhattacharya (Delhi: Manohar Publications, 1994), 216–229. Jain monastic sites are also similar to Buddhist sites in terms of location, structure, and artifacts. James Fergusson and James Burgess, *The Cave Temples of India* (Delhi: Oriental Books Reprint

Corporation, 1969), 490–512, and Vincent Smith, *The Jain Stupa and Other Antiquaries of Mathura* (Varanasi: Indological Book House, 1969; Archaeological Survey of India Reports); cited in Heitzman, "Early Buddhism, Trade and Empire," 123.

59. Sahgal, "Spread of Jinism in North India," 220, 228–229.
60. See Radhakrishna Choudhary, *Kautilya's Political Ideas and Institutions* (Varanasi: Chowkhamba Sanskrit Series Office, 1971), 430ff.; Balkrishna Govind Gokhale, "The Merchant in Ancient India," *Journal of the American Oriental Society* 97, no. 2 (1977): 125–130.
61. Gokhale, "The Merchant in Ancient India," 125.
62. Patrick Olivelle, ed. and trans., *Manu's Code of Law: A Critical Edition and Translation of the Mānava-Dharmásāstra* (New York: Oxford University Press, 2005), ch. 8, v 410.
63. Olivelle, *Manu's Code of Law,* ch. 8, verses 401–406.
64. Olivelle, *Manu's Code of Law,* ch. 9, verses 329, 331, and ch. 3, verse 152.
65. Olivelle, *Manu's Code of Law,* ch. 3, verses 64–65.
66. Women are more likely to be represented as being traded (especially in marriage) than being traders. See Garima Kaushik, *Women and Monastic Buddhism in Early South Asia: Rediscovering the Invisible Believers* (Abington: Routledge, 2016), 148–220.
67. Olivelle, *Manu's Code of Law,* ch. 3, verses 158–161.
68. J. A. B van Buitenen, *Tales of Ancient India* (Chicago: University of Chicago Press, 1959), 6.
69. Russell F. Sizemore and Donald K. Swearer, "Introduction," in *Ethics, Wealth and Salvation: A Study in Buddhist Social Ethics,* edited by Russell F. Sizemore and Donald K. Swearer (Columbia: University of South Carolina Press), 4.
70. Prayudh Payutto, *Buddhist Economics: A Middle Way for the Market Place,* 2nd ed., revised and enlarged (Bangkok: Buddhadhamma Foundation, 1995), 76.
71. For translations from the *Divyāvadāna,* see Andy Rotman: *Divine Stories: The Divyāvadāna, part 1* (Boston: Wisdom Publications, 2008), and *Divine Stories: The Divyāvadāna, part 2* (Boston: Wisdom Publications, 2017).
72. E. B. Cowell and R. A. Neil, eds., *Divyāvadāna* (Cambridge: Cambridge University Press, 1886), 108.7–8, *mahārājādhyuṣitam mahāpuruṣabaṇignisevitam.*
73. It is interesting that a similar though less loaded equation still occurs in India. James Laidlaw remarks that "all Jain and Hindu traders can also

be referred to as Baniyas . . . [and] Baniya is exactly synonymous with 'Mahajan.'" Though the term *mahājan* means "great person" and in modern Hindi is a near synonym for *mahāpuruṣ* or "great man," it generally refers to merchants, bankers, and moneylenders. These merchants, known as *mahājans*, are among the people who Laidlaw later argues offer "really large scale financial contribution[s]" in the Jain community as part of their jockeying for status. James Laidlaw, *Riches and Renunciation: Religion, Economy, and Society among the Jains* (New York: Oxford University Press, 1995), 88, 142ff.

74. See, for example, the *Lakkhaṇa-sutta* in the *Dīghanikāya* (iii, 142); Maurice Walshe, trans., *Thus Have I Heard: The Long Discourses of the Buddha* (*Dīgha-nikāya*) (Boston: Wisdom Publications, 1987), 441.
75. Rotman, *Thus Have I Seen,* 144, citing Paul Veyne, *Bread and Circuses: Historical Sociology and Political Pluralism,* translated by Brian Pearce (London: Penguin Books, 1990), 122–124, 13–18, 380, and R. A. L. H. Gunawardana, "Social Function and Political Power: A Case Study of State Formation in Irrigation Society," in *The Study of the State,* edited by Henri J. M. Claessen and Peter Skalnik (The Hague: Mouton, 1981), 136.
76. The forms of giving that Laidlaw enumerates also parallel the forms of giving represented in the *Divyāvadāna.* He explains that "the bulk of the euergetism which gem merchants in Jaipur engage in provides for collective Jain religious life: [1] maintaining temples and other buildings, [2] providing religious feasts, and [3] financing religious ceremonies" (*Riches and Renunciation,* 144). Included in this first category would be the incident in the *Kotikarṇa-avadāna* of a merchant giving a jeweled earring to an old couple so that they can take care of a dilapidated stūpa (Cowell and Neil, *Divyāvadāna,* 23.6–9), and in the third category would be King Aśoka's gift of a quinquennial festival (Cowell and Neil, *Divyāvadāna,* 403.6ff.). The second category is the best represented of the three in the *Divyāvadāna*. In a large number of *avadānas* there are examples of meals being provided to the community of monks (Cowell and Neil, *Divyāvadāna,* 65.4ff., 66.11ff., 81.18ff., 85.17ff., etc.).
77. Laidlaw, *Riches and Renunciation,* 146.
78. Laidlaw, *Riches and Renunciation,* 146.
79. Heitzman, "Early Buddhism, Trade and Empire," 132.
80. Heitzman, "Early Buddhism, Trade and Empire," 132.
81. Heitzman, "Early Buddhism, Trade and Empire," 132. For more on the connection between merchants and status in Buddhism, see Gokhale,

"The Merchant in Ancient India," 128–129; Ray, *Monastery and Guild,* 202, 208; and X. Liu, *Ancient India and Ancient China,* 90.

82. Heitzman, "Early Buddhism, Trade and Empire," 132. Further complicating Heitzman's account is the problem that many of these inscriptions are not located for easy reading; from the ground below they are often no more than distant, tiny scrawls. Perhaps, as Robert Brown contends, they were not intended to be "'read,' or even looked at in any logical or analytical fashion." Robert L. Brown, "Narrative as Icon: The Jātaka Stories in Ancient Indian and Southeast Asian Architecture," in *Sacred Biography in the Buddhist Traditions of South and Southeast Asia,* edited by Juliane Schober (Honolulu: University of Hawai'i Press, 1997), 72.
83. Neelis, *Early Buddhist Transmission and Trade Networks,* 22.
84. X. Liu, *Ancient India and Ancient China,* 88–102.
85. X. Liu, *Ancient India and Ancient China,* 120, 125 (italics added). Neelis finds Liu's claim "highly debatable, since commodities such as gold with intrinsic economic values can be adopted for religious purposes, even in traditions (like Buddhism and Christianity) that explicitly reject worldly riches" (*Early Buddhist Transmission and Trade Networks,* 23).
86. See Christoph Emmrich's chapter in this volume, which offers a case study of "the power that jewels have in their own right, a power that Buddhists and Buddhist texts plug into and from which they derive their own respective power."
87. Letter from Thomas Jefferson to John Taylor, May 28, 1816. https://founders.archives.gov/documents/Jefferson/03-10-02-0053 (accessed January 23, 2019).
88. Kathleen Morrison, "Commerce and Culture in South Asia: Perspectives from Archaeology and History," *Annual Review of Anthropology* 26 (1997): 95. See too Ellison Banks Findly, *Dāna: Giving and Getting in Pali Buddhism* (Delhi: Motilal Banarsidass, 2003), 16–18. Furthermore, while Brahmanical Hinduism had strict and onerous rules regarding debt, Buddhism was far more lenient and forgiving. Charles Malamoud, "The Theology of Debt in Brahmanism," in *Debts and Debtors,* edited by Charles Malamoud (London: Vices, 1983), 21–40.
89. And so in the *Jātakanidāna*—as Vanessa R. Sasson notes in her chapter in this volume—when Sumedha's parents die and he inherits their fortune, he realizes that his parents couldn't take their wealth with them to the next world, for no one can, and he immediately gives away his

entire inheritance. N. A. Jayawickrama, trans., *The Story of Gotama Buddha (Jātaka-nidāna)* (Oxford: Pali Text Society, 1990), 3.

90. Rotman, "Marketing Morality."
91. See too Harry Falk, "Money Can Buy Me Heaven: Religious Donations in Late and Post-Kushan India," *Archäologische Mitteilungen aus Iran und Turan* 40 (2008): 137–148.
92. Cowell and Neil, *Divyāvadāna,* 23.18–19, 192.14–15, 289.6–7, 313.22–23, etc., *āḍhye mahādhane mahābhoge kule.*
93. Morrison, "Commerce and Culture in South Asia" 98, citing P. Risso, *Merchants and Faith: Muslim Commerce and Culture in the Indian Ocean* (Boulder, CO: Westview, 1995); M. Ibrahim, *Merchant Capital and Islam* (Austin: University of Texas Press, 1990); A. Reid, "Islamization and Christianization in Southeast Asia: The Critical Phase, 1550–1650," in *Southeast Asia in the Early Modern Era: Trade, Power, and Belief,* edited by A. Reid (Ithaca, NY: Cornell University Press, 1993), 151–179; cf. Richard Eaton, *The Rise of Islam and the Bengal Frontier 1204–1760* (Berkeley: University of California Press), 1993.
94. For more on the Buddha as caravan leader, see Neelis, *Early Buddhist Transmission and Trade Networks,* 33–34.

Chapter 6

"I Don't Want a Wife without Ear Cuffs"

Jewels, Gender, and the Market among the Newars of Nepal

Christoph Emmrich

This chapter is driven by the question of what role jewels play in how people relate to each other. More precisely, it asks how jewels, on the basis of the difference between those who display them and those who take note, help to create the difference between the desired and the desiring. The most obvious domains in which this difference plays out are in the relations between women and men, be they human or superhuman, and between classes or castes, shaping how members of specific gender or status groups understand themselves and relate within the groups in which they find themselves—through jewels. That involves looking at jewels, at least as a first step, as a commodity and at the market conditions under which they are produced, owned, and circulated. It further also requires looking at the way jewels figure in literary discourse that has shaped historically enduring ways of understanding the implications of the deployment and enjoyment of jewels and creating and reconfirming what jewels are meant to and happen to do.

Buddhism, and more specifically the Buddhism of the Newars of Nepal, appears to be a particularly productive field for asking these questions for two main reasons. First, the Newar jewelry market has been dominated over the last centuries by members of castes self-identifying as Buddhist; this means that Buddhist or not, Newars have to deal with Buddhists when they deal with jewels. Further, those Buddhists understand themselves as being in charge of the Newar jewelry business, just as they take pride in being the largest manufacturers and exporters of religious artifacts in Nepal. These Buddhist Newar groups are well aware of the significance of jewels for caste and class differences and of the influence of Buddhist material culture on Nepalese society. It hence behooves us to trace jewels into territory that may not be specifically Buddhist but allows for the Buddhist and not-Buddhist to illuminate each other to help us understand how jewels work.

Second, Buddhism is well known for having a particular interest in the relation between the householder status involving possession and the monastic status involving renunciation. The acquiring of riches, including jewels, is celebrated just as much as is their rejection, and the way in which the two are balanced or made to remain at odds with each other is something Buddhist communities have articulated throughout their history. Buddhist Newars both share that heritage and deal with the unique historical circumstances in which they find themselves, such as their elite castes' complex status as both monks and householders; their role as makers, sellers, and consumers of jewels; their role as composers of songs that celebrate the beauty of jewels and of those wearing them; or their role as transmitters of old and revered stories that speak or are made to speak in the Newar idiom both of the power of jewels and of the power that lies in divesting oneself of them. This situation is additionally productive as it throws a particularly sharp light on sexual difference and the difference between the desiring and the desired: Newar jewelers and authors, being, in the words used above, those who take note, have been predominantly men, while those who display, both in and outside of Newar texts (mostly written by men), and marked as desire-inducing are predominantly women. Those differences become more complicated and tell us even more about the power of jewels when we read, for example, of bejeweled bodhisattvas or of women who, following Buddha Śākyamuni's example, become ascetics themselves. The Buddhism-inspired rejection of the jewel, understood as a breaking of the cycle of desire and initiated by a more-than-human man, is one that both repeats and holds the promise of change or further differentiates old differences. This chapter will try to address all this in three steps: by elaborating first on the fashioning, then on the singing, and finally on the narrating of jewels.[1]

Fashioning Jewels

Being a goldsmith was, at least until the last century, the dominant occupation of Vajrācārya and Śākya men, but nowadays they also follow a variety of other occupations, such as those in the fields of miscellaneous shopkeeping, education, civil administration, and medicine. Vajrācāryas are members of the priestly caste associated with conducting the fire sacrifice and with shrines that involve tantric worship, while Śākyas serve more generally as guardians and curators of most major traditional Newar monasteries.[2] It is Śākyas who are more specifically known as *bares*, a Newar term derived from Sanskrit (Skt.) *vandya,* "venerable," which refers to the status of monks that the ordination rite boy children of both castes undergo bestows upon them. High-caste Hindus, however, are said to refer to members of both castes, slightly derogatorily, as *bares*; hence the general use of this term to denote goldsmiths.[3] It has been men, not women, who work on the primary materials and fashion. Goldsmithing has been their dominant economic activity both in the cities (particularly in Lalitpur, less so in Kathmandu) and also outside the urban centers.[4] Involvement in the jewelry (*tisā*) business has remained almost as strong an identity marker of these two caste communities as Buddhism.[5] The history of an influential Śākya clan, the Dhakvas, is said to go back to a Newar goldsmith who spent only half of the Tibetan donations in gold he received for a lama's throne and used the other half to start a textile retail business, thus laying the foundation for the family's fortune.[6] A well-known Vajrācārya, Duṇḍabahādur, can to this day be found sitting behind the counter of his precious metal shop in the Lalitpur locality of Gābāhāḥ, just across the street from the impressive Buddhist studies private library he has built, chipping away at his lifetime's work: the translation of the entire Theravāda canon into Newar.[7] On the whole, however, with the general decline of the small goldsmith business due to rising gold prices and other changes in this sector worldwide, lines of business have increasingly shifted toward tourist curio production and sales, which include less jewelry than images and tourist souvenirs. It needs to be remarked that it has been men, not women, who work on the primary materials and fashion the artifacts. Traditionally and until today women have to a limited degree, if at all, been involved in the sale.

The Vajrācāryas' and the Śākyas' traditional handling of precious metals and their occupation as jewelry makers has been associated, especially among non-Buddhist Newars, with a relatively low caste status that such occupational castes share with those in the non-Newar Parbatiyā communities. While Buddhist Newars traditionally tend to put the blame on the local legendary version of Śaṅkarācārya for Vajrācāryas and Śākyas, David Gellner assumes that the perception of goldsmithing as a low-caste activity may be the effect of the Newars' taking over views dominant among the Parbatiyā, where we find a much less clearly differentiated caste system in which a much vaster range of occupations is regarded as low caste.[8] That stands in contrast both with the high caste status that Vajrācāryas and the Śākyas enjoy within the traditional Buddhist Newar caste hierarchy and with the general respect Newar society has toward artisans.[9] Scholars have also remarked on the internal hierarchies that exist among the Newar artisan castes themselves depending on their primary resources, which form part of the set of Eight Substances (Skt. *aṣṭadhātu*) or Metals: gold, silver, copper, lead, mercury, zinc, iron, and tin.[10] Here the Vajrācāryas rank highest due to their handling of gold (*lum̐*), associated with the sun, while the Śākyas rank second with silver (*vaha*), associated with the moon.[11] A partly diverging hierarchy of metals is reflected by the body parts on which they may be worn: gold only as low as the fingers, copper only down to the waist, and silver down to the feet being good for walking.[12] A somewhat different list reflecting a similar hierarchy, but more comprehensively dealing with the division of labor in the fabrication of jewelry, mentions first the Śākya, or *bare,* as the goldsmith or silversmith; the jeweler (*jvāri*), often from the Śreṣṭha and Mānandhar castes; the blacksmith (*kau*) working with iron; the copper and brass worker (*tamo*); the tailor (*suikā*); and, finally, the artisan working with molten glass, with glass pearls, and with cotton and silk threads, identified by his religious identity, the *musmā,* or Muslim.[13]

What these lists make clear is that making jewelry is a joint project. As Bruce McCoy Owens has shown regarding the procession of Buṃgadyaḥ, or the Red Matsyendranāth, and as Niels Gutshow and Axel Michaels have shown for Newar life-crisis rituals, individuals from different castes and of unequal social status need to come together to create these events.[14] Just like Newar rituals, Newar jewelry encapsulates, in the process of its production, Newar society as a whole and refers back to its diversity, its inequality, and the insistence on the complementarity of its social order. Structurally, the roles cover the manufacturing of the various settings; the filaments joining, if necessary, their parts; the more or less precious inlays; and, always at the final stage, the work in gold or silver. Just as the Vajrācārya is the main officiating priest (*mūlpurohit*) in a rite, it is the Buddhist goldsmith who stands, or rather sits, at the end of this lineup and completes the event of beauty, which the wearing of a piece of jewelry is meant to be, by adding the metal work and fashioning the piece into a consummate whole. Having even more absolute control than the priest, the goldsmith is the only artisan with whom the client gets to directly interact throughout the process, including the ongoing financial transactions, the other specialists being merely called upon to make their contributions by the Buddhist chief artisan.[15]

The special position held by the goldsmith is further highlighted by the fact that his responsibilities do not end with the handing over of the merchandise to the customer. For a child's first rice feeding (*macā jaṃkva;* Skt. *annaprāśana*) at five or six months of age he is asked to pierce the child's earlobes ahead of the ritual event, nowadays often in his shop, and is then called into the family home, bringing, together with his pincers, the earrings that he twists into the infant's pierced earlobes, as well as the pair of heavy anklets (*kalli*) he or she has to wear for the first time on that occasion.[16] And once the child, if she is a girl, is grown up and gets married, it is usually the same goldsmith who manufactures and slips on the golden bracelets the bride gets to show off.[17] The goldsmith not only helps individuals to achieve relative ritual seniority; he also, in his role of facilitating the extensive wedding gifts that are involved as part of the exchanges, dowry-related or not, helps to ritually create alliances between families. This speaks of the intimate relationship the goldsmith, traditionally a neighbor, has with the families he services. Just as every Newar family has a priest who accompanies the members through the domestic cycles of annual, life-cycle, and occasional rites and whose own family and priestly lineage are usually tied to the patron family over generations, so the goldsmith not only supplies the family with his artifact, but is also well aware of all the key events and social changes marked by rites in which his services are required. On these occasions he is allowed into the homes of his clients. But more than that: similar to the priest and to the range of para-priests (to which one could easily add him) the jeweler has the most direct access to the bodies and the well-being of his clients.[18] The goldsmith, on certain occasions, himself attaches the artifacts to ears, arms, and legs. What he has wrought with his own hands is what makes his clients look their best, represents their status, and celebrates their bodies and their auspiciousness and prestige on key occasions in their lives. His work is in constant contact with their bodies most of their waking time (and much of their sleeping time) and has become one with their skin and flesh more than almost any other service or artifact in the Newar world.

Jewelry forms a substantial part of any Newar family's capital; the stakes are high and with them the fear that one may be taken for a ride. It thus comes as no surprise that among the Newars these fears have taken the shape of stereotyping and derogatory adages that warn about the greedy and treacherous goldsmith: "The *bare* sells lead at the price of gold" (*baray lisānā lum̐yānā mī*) or "The *bare* cannot sleep after failing to have the gold stolen from his mother's jewelry" (*mānyā tisān lum̐ khuyākāy machine bareyā nhya mavā*).[19] The South Asian traditional male-oriented proverb culture also has the female family members, thanks to the expenses their demand in ornaments run up, foolishly supply with food somebody who is neither a husband nor their children: "A woman's jewelry is the *bare*'s food" (*misāyā tisā bareyā nasā*).[20] Because of the perceived inevitability of the family's fortune bleeding into the pocket of the goldsmith, trust is of the essence in this relationship. This implies that the goldsmith is also keenly aware of the economic fortunes of the family to whom he is tied. He knows how much his patrons can and are likely to spend at which point in time. He is also the one who pawns or, if things come to a crunch, buys family jewelry when his patrons go through rough patches, and he is expected to do so discreetly.[21] The first bank in the Kathmandu Valley and in Nepal, the Nepāl Baiṃk Limiṭeḍ, opened only in 1937, and life insurances began to be offered a good thirty years later.[22] This means that right until the middle of the twentieth century among the Newars, as among most other communities in South Asia before that and in some right unto the present day, the jewelry that women wore on their bodies functioned as a family's most readily divestable asset and the Buddhist goldsmith as their personal banker.[23] It was women who handled that part of the domestic capital, even if, as Doranne Jacobson points out, the relative control of commodities with such a high prestige value should not make us ignore persisting economic inequalities.[24] On the other side, it was the goldsmith on whom families relied for their jewelry-related investments, as it was his choice of materials that would guarantee that the family could resell the jewelry close to market value. In fact, families still consult with their goldsmith even when independently purchasing jewels from a *jvāri*.

Another responsibility of the goldsmith that adds to his profile as a para-priest is his expertise regarding gems (Skt. *ratna*).[25] As we have seen, while the *jvāri* may sell them, the *bare* is the one who integrates them into his work, deciding which particular jewels of which size and shape are needed for which item, on which occasion, for which person, and, if more than one jewel is required, in which combination. As mentioned above, each gem is affiliated with a specific celestial deity (Skt. *graha*) and its specific powers, from which the wearer profits. These powers range from protecting against physical illnesses, such as the ruby or gold; bringing health, happiness, and prosperity and protecting against blame, such as the white pearl; or strengthening one's memory and facilitating childbirth, such as the emerald.[26] The particularly powerful piece of jewelry that includes all nine gems (Skt. *navaratna*), requires the arrangement of the individual stones in a prescribed fashion (with the ruby, or the piece of gold, at the center, then proceeding down the list starting in the east, continuing clockwise around the ruby with coral, garnet, sapphire, lapis lazuli, topaz, emerald, diamond on the top, and ending with the pearl) and other rules concerning the stones' size, color, and conjoining metals. The way gems are otherwise chosen and arranged depends on the wearer's gender, which determines the range of carat a stone should be and on her or his horoscope. The main gem a person should wear is the birth gem (*janma ratna*) or astrological stone (*rasi ratna*), which depends on that person's ruling celestial deity (*svāmī graha*).[27] Thus all jewelry involving gems requires a mediation not only of a host of artisans by the goldsmith, but also of the two para-priests' work by the client. Astrologers and goldsmiths both have the knowledge to prescribe certain kinds of jewelry, including semiprecious stones, to serve specific purposes in life. For example, a client who worries about a trip is recommended to have a ring with a pearl and another with a moonstone (Skt. *candrakāntā*) made to appease the moon deity who clears the way. An elderly client may be advised to commission a ring with a turquoise (*yū*) to keep her or him from feeling stiff or cold.[28]

Readers need to be reminded at this point that the Vajrācārya and Śākya goldsmiths have not only fellow Buddhists as their clients, but also the large population of Hindu Newars and Hindu non-Newars, who depend on them as much as the Buddhists Newars. In this function, too, the goldsmiths are more similar to the para-priestly barbers, who provide their services regardless of their own and their client family's priestly lineage. Just as the idiom of most Newar ritual practices or the language Newar itself, the vernacular of jewelry, in which the goldsmiths are naturally fluent, is one and the same across religious affiliations. Motifs and meanings differ, but the experienced and well-trained Buddhist goldsmith is familiar with that range and more so with one or the other, depending on which families his family has been servicing. In having held what comes close to a pan-Newar monopoly on jewelry making, the *bare* is comparable to other Newar ritual institutions such as the Kumārīs, or "Living Goddesses"; Hāratī, or the goddess of smallpox and small children; Buṅgadyaḥ, or the "Red Matsyendranāth"; and Janabāhāḥdyaḥ, or the "White Matsyendranath," all four of which are historically rooted in Buddhist communities but which are of importance to the Newars as a whole and also to the much larger community of non-Newar Nepalis.

Though jewelry remains a gender and age marker even outside those contexts of heightened attention and expenditure, the largest visibility the Buddhist Newar goldsmith's work has today is during the deployment of traditional Newar jewelry on the occasion of the celebration of life crisis rites, when Newars experience belonging and perform Newarness.[29] In fact, these events are the only occasions on which most of the jewelry, known or forgotten among the Newars today, still is, or has been traditionally, worn. As most of this jewelry has to be understood as forming an array of ritual implements, the degree to which the handling and understanding of this jewelry is still alive depends to a great deal on how much the performers today decide to include these implements in the life crisis rites they organize. Jewelry as marker of ritual seniority through a life span thus is mainly applied and displayed on the occasion of these very events, and not, as popular depictions in song and video culture may suggest, in everyday usage. The jewelry used during each and all of these rites in the life of a Newar is either manufactured for the occasion or, mostly for the domestic rites, part of the treasure trove passed on from one generation to the next, mostly as part of the traditional form of financial insurance held by women, but also dispersed due to the inevitable divisions inheritance in large families involve. Alternatively, it is loaned from the many goldsmiths and jewelry shops that have sprung up in the last several decades, specialized in servicing families who cannot rely on the last generation's coffers.

Early childhood rites deploy a range of jewelry functionally connected to the acquisition of knowledge and to protection, particularly on the occasion of the first rice feeding; they involve earrings (*mārlicā, luṁcācā*), pendants (*tāyo, jāṃtar*), as well as massive silver anklets (*kalli*). The childhood rite *ihī,* the marriage involving the *bilva* fruit, is the first big challenge for every family with girl children: they are expected to produce golden hair ornaments (*sāthwācā*) and headgear, such as the celebrated five chains (*nyāpu sikhaḥ*), the goldflower (*luṁyā svāṃ*), and a drop-shaped golden jewel for the forehead (*siṃcā*), earrings (*riṃcā, mārlicā*), studs (*tapacā*), colliers (*suttā, tikhamā*), bracelets (*culyā, bāi*), rings (*āṃgū*), and anklets (*kalli, pāuju*). The same range needs to be reproduced at the conclusion of the confinement rite for girl children called *bārhā tāyegu,* adding more coiffure jewelry, such as a hair bun ornament (*sapva tisā*), a hair needle (*candrasūrya*) and, again, more bracelets. Even Vajrācārya and Śākya boy children traditionally require for their Buddhist temporary ordination, called *bare chuyegu,* bracelets (*bāi*), a collier (*suttā*), and studs (*pāyti* or Nep. *cāpari tapa*), while for the Brahmanical tonsure rite called *busā khākegu*, families need to provide the boy with a ring made of gold (*luṁ āṃgu*) or of the Five Precious Metals (*pañcadhātuyā aṃgu*) and studs (*tapacā*) or earrings (*jyāpucā*). During the elaborate series of Newar wedding rites the gifting of specific items marks the stages from engagement to integration into the groom's family through rites of request, encounter, and transfer performed by individual members of both bride givers and bride takers. Much of the jewelry used during the girl children's earlier rites is expected to be redeployed, adding to those even more ornaments to head (*nyāpu sikhaḥ, jhuppā, nhakosā*), ears (e.g., *hira* or *navaratnayā tapa, jhuṃkā,* and *degaḥ tukki,* all particular to urban Buddhist brides), and neck, such as a chain of gold coins (*asarphimā*), a coral necklace (*bhiṃpūmā*), a large protective collier pendant (*tāyomā*), and a necklace (*candrahāra*) reaching down to the height of the belly. Marriage, involving the move from one family to another, is, in economic terms, one of the most precarious moments in a Newar woman's life, and it makes the gift of jewelry, particularly from her own family to her, over which she holds most control, so important. What Doranne Jacobson writes about women in rural Madhya Pradesh holds equally true of the Newar woman: "Within each kin group, jewelry is owned by those who control the fewest other economic resources, particularly young brides. Conversely, within each household those who have most control over other material assets tend to own the least jewelry."[30] Rites for senior Newars feature the old-age rite called *jyāḥ jaṃkva,* in which couples are celebrated, the woman wearing many of the jewelry highlights from her earlier life crisis rituals and the man a golden ring, the most marked new piece of jewelry being earrings in gold (*punāycā*) to be worn by the couple for the rest of their lives and accumulating, depending on the age of the celebrated, as the ritual is repeated roughly every eleven years. Consecrations to become a Newar association's (a *guthi*'s) seniormost member (*thakāli luyegu*) also involve the ritual wearing of a new set of gold earrings, as does the consecration as an *ācārya,* or tantric master, of a member of the Vajrācārya caste (*ācā luyegu*), who gets to wear a type of earring called *gokula* (or *gogula*), made of gold with three tiny pearls. Jewelry accompanies the Newar even on his or her journey out of this life: Śākya families place a golden stud or a gold ring into the mouth of a deceased woman or man, respectively, usually accompanied by a piece of coral or even a *navaratna* jewel, to ensure the compliance of all the celestial deities on the family member's journey to Sukhāvatī, the World of Bliss. That last gift is removed before the cremation and may, if given to the Newar association dealing with death rites (*si guthi*), cover the expenditures of this costly last rite. The dead moves on without any of the jewelry she or he has worn during his or her lifetime. And even the living, if she is a woman, may, following her husband's death, live a life deprived of adornment. In many families the surviving widow's glass bracelets are ritually broken, and the widow refrains from wearing jewelry. On the other hand, I am aware of several Newar women who performed their old-age rites well after their husbands' cremations and donned the jewelry required on that occasion.

Such an ambivalence regarding the wearing of jewelry after or during certain life crisis events among the Buddhist Newars is found not only at death. Contemporary temporary ordination rituals for Vajrācārya and Śākya boys ostentatiously do without any jewelry, even if in the past the gifting of rings, bracelets, and studs was part of the requirements. In the big, representative temporary ordinations at Kvābāhāḥ in Lalitpur the boy children today go jewel-less. The alternative childhood and adolescence rite for girl children is *ṛṣiṇī pabbajā,* "the going forth [i.e., into homelessness] as a female seer," which involves girl children spending several days in a Theravāda monastery or meditation center to learn Buddhist practice and doctrine. It was introduced in the 1970s to replace the traditional confinement rite (mentioned above), which on its last day requires the girl children to wear a full set of bridal jewelry, both for their visit to the Gaṇeśa shrine and to present themselves to the larger community in that outfit during a reception as post-menstrual potential brides. *Ṛṣiṇī pabbajā,* in contrast, requires that the girl child follow the eight vows, the seventh including the vow to abstain from wearing ornaments. She hence needs to take out any studs and remove any necklaces she may be wearing and leave them at home before entering the monastic space. The nuns who run these camplike events stress in their sermons, directed at the temporary recluses, the risks of early marriage and the importance of discipline, doctrine, and meditation for the girl children's empowerment. Ironically, it is the very fact that this practice is so closely designed along the lines of the traditional Newar seclusion rite, making it seem, in traditional Newar women's eyes, just another *bārhā tayegu,* that on the concluding day of *ṛṣiṇī pabbajā* the jewelry makes its grand return. When the adults come to pick up their daughters, granddaughters, or nieces from the monastery, they bring all the finery that Newar girls are expected to wear on that day, have them put on all the *tāyos, pāyos,* and golden headgear—often while still on the monastic premises in the presence of the nuns who taught them otherwise, making everybody join in for the group photo—and walk them over to the family home's Ganeśa shrine to make their obeisance dressed up as little brides.

It also needs to be noted that there is an acute awareness of what has come to be seen as an endangered tradition of doing things the Newar way. This anxiety is not new and in its present form goes back at the very least to the 1980s, when particularly among the Buddhist Newars it spurred priests to introduce dramatic changes in the way traditional knowledge was passed on, leading to the public being rediscovered as an arena for self-affirmation. This anxiety has deeper roots in Newar religious resistance to the monarchy and the Newar language nationalism movement, both dating back to the early twentieth century. There is a widespread complaint that jewelry deemed "traditional" and "originally Newar" is seen less and less in public, less manufactured and sold, and even more rarely worn and displayed. Observers note a general tendency to wear smaller, lighter, cheaper jewelry with less gold, or gold-plating, and with fewer to no stones.[31] One trend is to break up single larger pieces to have smaller ones made out of the materials. Another is to go for jewelry imported from India, particularly from Bengal, or to have jewelry designed following models from south of the border.[32] While this is lamented by some and can be argued to be a weakening of the traditional hold by women on this specific form of capital, Doranne Jacobson reminds us that at the same time these new developments may be "indicative of a potential increase in women's overall economic power."[33]

As in the case of ritual culture or the artistic and architectural heritage, these developments and perceptions have led, in the field of Newar jewelry, to an increased interest in documentation and preservation, on the one hand, and practices of celebration and revival, on the other. Publications like the ones by Suśilā Mānandhar and Motilakṣmī Śākya are one expression of this trend.[34] Motilakṣmī's book's title even stresses that the jewelry is "ours" (*jhigu*), meaning the Newars', or more specifically that it belongs to high-status Buddhist Newar castes who have their own claims to represent the pan-Newar gemeinschaft. Efforts made since the 1980s by the Hastakalā Prabardhan Śākhā (a government department dedicated to artisanal industries) to document and promote technologies for the production of traditional jewelry, including jewelry identified as Newar, are driven by concerns that are similar, with the ethnic at the service of the national. A similar self-folklorization occurs in the nostalgic celebration of Newar material culture in films and music videos with female models bedazzling in stage versions of the real things. These musical productions transport and recreate a song culture in which, as we shall see in the next section, jewelry plays a central role in the articulation of desire, in this case for the traditional and self-identical.

It is difficult to say how much of the current handling of jewelry associated with Newarness carries on old practices or betrays an attention to and stress on jewelry that is new. In other words, how much of it is indeed "lost," as the conversationists claim, and how much of it has found uses and a prominence it only acquired due to the discourses and performances of crisis is yet to be ascertained. It is safe to assume that these developments reach at least as far back as to the fall of the Malla kingdoms and the appropriation of Newar ornamentation customs by the victorious Śāha dynasty in the second half of the eighteenth century or the introduction of Victorian forms of jewelry, such as the brooch or the watch with its chain, at the Śāha and Rāṇā courts in the second half of the nineteenth century, to mark only two incisive events in the history of Newar jewelry.[35]

This takes us full circle from the production via the divestment to the reappreciation of jewelry among Buddhist Newars. However, such practices need to be contextualized both historically and in terms of the popular literary culture that contributes toward giving these practices meaning and continuity through time. An ideal place to look for that is the rich lyrical culture that, as with jewelry, is both a fragile and endangered resource and a bastion of nostalgic, retraditionalizing discourse that may tell us as much about a disappearing world as about a reinvented one of material culture and sexual difference on both sides of the Buddhist/non-Buddhist divide.

Singing Jewels

Jewelry plays a key role in what is arguably the most popular of Nepalese songs, "Rājamatī,"—famous from the first time we know it was sung, during Prime Minister Jaṅg Bahādur Rāṇa's visit to London in 1850, until today on occasions when Nepali and particularly Newar folklore are celebrated.[36] The song is written in almost rudimentary Newar, bordering on what may have been nineteenth-century slang, and, as one may expect from folkloric material dealing with the marketability of women in the eyes of men, comes with a generous helping of objectifying and demeaning language:

> Crazy Rājamatī! / If she comes to me,—luv! / Coo-chi-koo, Rājamatī Baby! / If I don't get Rājamatī, / I'm gonna go to Benares. / O Daddy, get me Rājamatī Baby! //1//
>
> Curly, swirly hair, / Bedroom eyes. / A Saṃkhu chick, right? / Face, white. / Face with two spots. / Tāhānani's Rājamatī Baby. // 2//
>
> Egg-shells in a cranny, / Beaten rice dust from a shop: / Rājamatī is a mess. / Where is Rājamatī? / There is one in Ituṃbāhāḥ. / Get me Rājamatī Baby! //3//
>
> Walking in front is Big Bossypants. / Walking behind is Li'l Bossypants. / After her goes Rājamatī Baby. / I don't care for Big Bossypants. / Couldn't care less about Li'l Bossypants. / Get me married to Rājamatī! //4//
>
> Big Bossypants got a *tāyo*. / Li'l Bossypants got *pāyos*. / Rājamatī Baby got *bijakanis*. / I don't want a wife without *bijakanis*. / O Daddy, get me Rājamatī Baby! // 5//
>
> Thaṃhiti is uptown. / Kohiti is downtown. / Maruhiti is half way. / While fetching water at Maruhiti / She tripped on a broad stone / And Rājamatī slammed flat on her back. //6//
>
> Dress her up in jewellery! / Let the Gujaratis play! / Get me married to Rājamatī! / If you get me Rājamatī, / I will not go to Benares. / O Daddy, get me Rājamatī Baby! //7//[37]

It is the jewelry mentioned in verse five that makes Rājamatī particular and particularly attractive to the male singer. The other girls too are wearing jewelry. A *tāyo,* worn by "Big Bossypants" (which, depending on the tone one may want to adopt in the translation, could also be rendered as "Great Mistress"),[38] is an oblong metal pendant with pointed ends that hangs horizontally on the person's breast and may include an image of a protective deity, most often the Buddhist deity Hāratī.[39] It is part of an array of jewelry deployed to ward off diseases, the evil eye, or any kind of demonic attacks, similar to the pendants known as *jāṃtar*, some of them worn as early as in infancy. Anklets, of which the *pāyos* worn by "Li'l Bossypants" (or "Little Mistress") are one kind, bear a similar protective function and are worn by girl children from early childhood.[40] *Tāyo* and *pāyos* may be all right. *Bijakanis*, or ear cuffs, though, are way better.[41] They point ahead to the type of jewelry worn at a wedding: the prospective bride already carries in part what the son anticipates she will comprehensively be showered with in the celebration of his family's economic prowess, complete with the sound of flutes imported from Gujarat and in the fulfillment of his wish. Referencing the Hindu wedding rite in which the groom ritually threatens to leave for Benares only after having his father ritually change his mind and getting him to marry the bride, the son says it is either all or nothing, either the ear-cuff-wearing Rājamatī or renunciation in a faraway land. But just as in the wedding the future-son-in-law's emotional blackmail is ritualized, so in the song the threat teeters between the empty and the fanciful. More important, the deranged son is already mentally performing his own wedding. The dominant feature of the song, being an address of one male to another, is, in line with a certain aesthetic of South Asian love discourse, the transgressive male, here embodied by the son demanding from his father to agree to a love marriage. The transgressive male gaze is poeticized by the attention to detail in the evocation of the circumstances surrounding the appearance of the desired figure: the order of the line in which the girls move, including their size or seniority, and, most important, the kinds of jewelry they wear. Other details include materials traditionally referred to in Newar poetry, such as discarded eggshells and rice dust, standard Newar poetic indicators that a secret erotic meeting has taken place, as well as the song climaxing with Rājamatī's fall. But it is the detail pertaining to jewelry that helps formulate most strongly the son's desire. In fact, when he specifies not only which of the three women he desires, but also which woman he sees himself marrying, it is ear cuffs that make the prospective bride. Of course, Rājamatī happens to be adorned that way, and his insistence on marrying only a woman who wears those is a way of poetically framing his exclusive love for Rājamatī: those very earrings are crucial because the only one wearing them is Rājamatī. But this very insistence and the preoccupation with detail are also indicative of the transgressive side of poetic speech of the enamored and the beauty of the conventionally bizarre. The love-crazed poet cannot help but establish a connection between the detail of the intimate ornamentation of Rājamatī's ears and the prospective framing of the bride's body at her wedding, as if he were acting at the command of the jewel's beauty. A reading of the song by its male Jyāpu (or farmers' caste) singers and noted by Manandhar even goes so far as to understand the jewelry as coded references to the women's bodies: "Big Bossypants" wearing a *tāyo* is a poetic way of saying that she has a goiter; "Li'l Bossypants"' *pāyos* stand in for her deformed feet; and *bijakani* is, in this reading, a veiled reference to nothing less than Rājamatī's uterus. In this most forced decoding of a jewel, the name of which may not be too familiar anymore, *bija-* is said to be derived from Skt. *bīja,* "seed" and in a compound with (the not further explained) *-kani* comes to mean the womb (*macāchem̐;* literally "the house of the child").[42] In what sounds like a secondary reading meant to appeal to a male audience's thirst for misogynistic innuendos, the niceties of an imagined wedding and a threatened renunciation make place to fantasies of body shaming, on the one hand, and sex and impregnation, on the other.

Whether respectable or crass, the son's appeal to his father may in all likelihood be futile anyway, as the criterion for selecting a bride, or rather excluding every other woman, on the basis of the jewelry worn on the day the son fell in love with its wearer, or, for that matter, using jewels to both code and convey his physical preferences or advertise the childbearing potential of his pick, would sound highly unconvincing to his father, his family, and pretty much anybody else, stressing, again, the transgressive side of jewel talk. As the centrality of the bejeweled object of desire in the song seems to suggest, there is no poetic beauty without the poeticized jewel. And it is the jewel that makes the boy lose his marbles.

Another significant detail of the song is Rājamatī's provenance: the singer identifies her as coming from Sankhu, a city known for its trade with Tibet and its Buddhist hill shrine, and the son spotted her at Itumbāhāḥ, a locality that has its name from one of the oldest and largest Buddhist Newar monasteries of Kathmandu. According to a local tradition, it was founded by a certain Keśacandra, a gambler who is said to have lost his late father's inheritance but regained an even greater fortune when the pigeons, which had eaten an offering of rotten rice made to him by a Paśupati Bhairava, left golden droppings. The amount of precious metal guano with which he was left allowed him to establish the vihāra.[43] The bejeweled Rājamatī is said to inhabit a Buddhist space famed for its treasure-hunting founding father, which recalls the association of jewelry with Buddhist goldsmiths from specific monastic communities. Despite all his zaniness—and a nineteenth-century Hindu boy's desiring a Buddhist girl would certainly also belong to that department—there is no doubt that the son is still rational enough to be looking for a bride whose parents can afford some serious frippery.

Though much of Nepalese literary poetry is part of a larger and older South Asian, Prakritic, or Sanskritic tradition of versification, Lienhard also notices in Newar compositions "a human and individual spirit which is rarely found in Indian lyrics," and he continues: "Not infrequently the poet or singer allows the listener to partake of his very personal experiences, his sufferings, his repentance, his passion, amorousness or disappointment in love."[44] The affective dimension of these texts is something we will need to bear in mind when thinking about the way the poet or singer deploys jewelry. In fact, the interest in this specific detail is, in Lienhard's eyes, a characteristic of Newar poetry: "Love poems repeatedly praise various details of a woman's or girl's appearance: her fair complexion, her elegant gait, her jacket and skirt, the vermillion mark as well as the flower stuck into her hair and, most frequently, her finery and adornments."[45] These descriptions are, of course, standardized, and the depicted situations are meant to echo each other. But it is the interest in the material and sensual aspect of these objects and in the recurrence of an array of very specific items that betrays a specifically Newar aesthetics.

In another song from possibly the mid-nineteenth century, we have the girl, also on the move and on display, wearing little bracelets on her arms,[46] a little *tāyo* (the same powerful pendant as "Big Bossy-pants" above) around her neck, and little golden bud-shaped ear studs (*luṁyā mukhuḥcā*), which are called "strikingly beautiful" (*bāna*), highlighting, just as with the *bijakanis* above, the auricular (*nhāypaṃ*) regions as the spot where desirability peaks.[47] The persistent use of the Newar diminutive affix *-cā* for the various jewelry items contributes in the cute-ification and eroticizing of the woman, just as the famous "Rājamatīcā" above.[48] The "baby" of twentieth-century Anglophone crooner lyrics here is one who wears jewelry that fits her size. As its recurrence shows, a crucial aspect of display are jewels appearing in a specific place and jewels in motion. In a song that dates back probably to the same period as "Rājamatī" the singer asks, "Which backstreet is that? Which backstreet is this?" as he observes the girl, this time called Pānabatī, on her way to the inevitable well, thus opening the song. "It is the backstreet of Makhaṃ Square," he himself supplies the answer, making the Kathmandu Valley reader immediately think of the shrine of Taleju, the tutelary goddess of the Newar kings, and announces "The girl Pānabatī approaches," coming directly to the point: "This is the lion head anklet (*siṃkhvā kiyā kalli*)." The next stanza stays with the ornament, insisting that "The lion anklets' ring, 'tārā-tārā,' is irresistible," and it has such a powerful effect on the young man that he exclaims, "Dragging my mind with you, swish-swish, you brushed past."[49] The image is linked to motion and, through the sound hereby produced, to the materiality of the lion head anklets.[50] The song traces the bodily trajectory of the girl's line of flight, along which the singer has lost his sound-bound mind. Both the "Rājamatī" and the "Panābatī" song capture that moment and that place of encounter, which is surprising and fleeting. It is the jewelry through which the singer manages to slow down, to zoom in, to capture, to stay with that which has hit him. And it is through the jewelry that that moment and that place are extended for the duration of the song, allowing the singer and the listener to stay with that which cannot stay, to follow that which cannot be followed, to have what cannot be owned.

A song that Lienhard highlights for dating back as far as to the sixteenth or seventeenth century and for its indebtedness to Maithilī poetical forms sees a young man on the lookout for a girl he lost sight of.[51] Similarly to the Rājamatī song,[52] the singer draws an identikit of the desired person, moving from garment via makeup, hairstyle, flower ornaments, and facial features, occasionally returning to garment, only to end up with her jewelry: "Wow, the bracelet is made of silver, the mukhuli of gold. /" (*culyā jā ohayā mukhuli lum̐yā re /*), "Gosh, how expensive those little ear studs must be!" (*tukicā guliyā re /*), "Hey, that girl's *maichu* (?) is made of silver" (*maichu ohayā hlākahma lyāseya re /*).[53] It is the ear ornaments, in this case a pair of studs called *tuki*, worn by both women and men, that call for an exclamation of surprise about their market value.

The demonstrative promise of the son craving to cover little Rājamatī in jewelry can also be found reversed, such as in the first-person perspective song in which the unfortunate Siṃtali complains that her lover, who "has been gone for a while, said 'I will have you wear *tāyo* and *tukis*.'"[54] A song in which the singer claims to know all about marriage and women, in which he sententiously proclaims that, once married, "Her arms and legs will be covered, friend," that they will be covered with nothing less than "jewelry" is self-understood.[55] Jewelry is seen as tying women to men in the commitment that beauty is meant to seal, as female voices themselves are made to demand commitment in terms of a nuptial deployment of jewelry: "One string of tiny *magathyā* (?),[56] two strings of flower-plait jewellery, / Colour me red. Lift the palanquin. Send me off!"[57] Similarly, for the female voice, love is also beyond the conventions and the trappings of wedding: "I thought not of feasting and putting on (*tiya*) [jewelry]. / I only knew you through love."[58] So the jewelry associated with wedding becomes the language of dashed hopes, of broken promises, of lost affection, of severed ties, of sorrow. "Desiring bracelets (*culyā*) and *tāyos* I was trapped by the master /."[59] And yet, it is still love and the pain of not finding it that lurks behind all the stuff: "Not that there is not enough to eat. Not that there is not enough to dress up with (*tiyayāta*). / Suffering (*duḥkha*) is not to have had even a single love"[60]—a definition of *duḥkha* strikingly different from the one found in Buddhist texts.

Inversely, Newar song also imagines female desire for the jewel-bestowing patron, such as mid-twentieth-century lyrics in which the female first-person singer dismissively demands, "You better give me one red (?) ring, Mr. Cad (*gunnā* [= Hindī *guṇḍā*] *dāju*)"[61] and continues in heavy jewel talk: "If you, Mr. Cad, give me a *tāyo* and two *tucikās,* / My ear will be lined with *muṃdris*,"[62] the *muṃdrā* or *muṃdri* being a large-looped earring. In the woman's formidable demand fantasized by the male poet we reencounter the crescendo of jewelry items already noted in the Rājamatī song, leading from the modest piece dangling over her breast and tied around the neck right up to the pieces adorning her ears. Only here the ear is literally lined with cuffs, and it is the woman who is made to predict an almost miraculous climactic serialization with multiplication almost magically bursting forth from those one, two little bijoux she demands. While jewelry is the embodiment of the desiring singer's infatuation, it can be also turned by the man into the curse of the rejected to resemble something close to what today would be termed slut shaming. The male singer holds it against the woman who rejected him that she beautified herself in the first place and, as the refrain of a certain song goes, got "courted and carried away" due to—and here the singer addresses her directly—"the anklets on your feet, the golden bracelets on your arms, / [And] when you flash your ring."[63] It is the reductive identification of woman and jewelry that stands at the core of this poetics. But just as the song seems to absorb the woman into her jewelry, so jewelry also seems to be the way for the poet to project himself into the most intimate realms of female space. The serenaded female figure failing to make it to the window to expose herself to the appropriating male gaze of the singer is said to be close to wearing out the chunky coral beads: "Your big *bhiṃpūs* are half gone. / Precious lady, don't you need to come out?"[64] Lienhard, no doubt by relying on an oral commentary, tries to solve the puzzle by suggesting, "Since the girl wears her corals even when sleeping, these ornaments have become worn-out."[65] This poetic intrusion into the girl's bedroom could be understood as trying to evoke the eroticism of the languid, evoking the frisson of coral for days on end relentlessly pushing against sheets. Wasting away is also a common South Asian poetic motif, either a physical sign of the prolonged separation of lovers or the hallmark of impermanence. With the big *bhiṃpūs* likely to be the jewelry-talk version of the woman's breasts, the poet may be suggesting that she is either secretly pining for him and wasting away what is meant to be enjoyed or foolishly saving herself up as age inexorably cuts into her assets.

Another song probes even deeper into female interiority. A lovesick woman, tentatively identified by the commentary as Narendralakṣmī, the queen of King Yoganarendra Malla of Lalitpur (r. 1684–1705), sings about herself and about her love: "I am an extremely feeble woman. I see jewellery (*tisā*) inside my heart."[66] Here jewelry becomes something different from what we have seen so far. Though it is still the most powerful medium through which to articulate love, it is no longer the outward application, something the man sees as applied by the woman to instill desire or bestowed upon the desired in order to claim ownership. Here the beloved has been completely absorbed by the precious, and the precious is no longer an artifact but one's beloved. She or he is not close to one's body like a pendant or an ear cuff but in one's heart. In a modern song the pining lover addresses his beloved as "Love, oh, jewel" (*māyā re ratna*),[67] but after awaking from the dream he had of her, he realizes: "There was no beloved, no Kṛṣṇa, no Rāma," but first of all "no diamond."[68] As a song ascribed to Jagatajaya Malla of Kathmandu (r. 1722–1736) puts it, having seen Kṛṣṇa or Hari, the epitome of the desired person, means "having seen the jewel among men" (*puruṣaratana khanyāva*).[69] Calling the beloved a jewel extends to humans and superhumans, Hindu and Buddhist. But the jewel-like nature of the beloved is not all about the *bhakti* that transcends the world of things. In a nineteenth-century poem, attributed to a male Jyāpu poet and that was sung on the occasion of the carnivalesque annual Sāpāru, or Gāijātrā, the singer ends a long list of recommendations regarding women by warning: "Friend, inspect [her] just as you inspect a diamond or a pearl." In the topsy-turvy time of Sāpāru the song reminds the listener that the beloved may be the most precious, but even the precious remains a commodity. It also reminds us that the man may be a fool, but he is still the buyer.

In a nineteenth-century poem composed by the scholar Amṛtānanda, Buddha Śākyamuni himself is the jewel (not Skt. *ratna,* as in the Triple Gem, but Skt. *maṇi*) of his lineage (*Śākya-kulayā*), rhyming on the verse that calls him the lord of the Three Worlds (*tribhubanayā dhanī*).[70] Another identification of the sacred with a jewel is the Newar designation of their nine most revered books, the Nine Dharmas (Skt. *navadharma*), Nine Books (Skt. *navagrantha*), or Nine Sūtras (Skt. *navasūtra*) as the "Nine Gems" (Skt. *navaratna*), which appear in rituals that include the worship of the Triple Gem in the form of a maṇḍala splayed out on the floor of the ritual arena, the set of nine making up the Dharma Gem (Skt. *dharmaratna*).[71] The parallelism to one of the most prized, powerful, and popular ornaments in South and Southeast Asia, the nine-gemmed gold-framed composite piece of jewelry called the *navaratna,* popular in the shape of rings, pendants, or studs, is not accidental. Each jewel, most often arranged, just as the texts, in the form of a maṇḍala, is associated with one of the nine celestial bodies (Skt. *navagraha*): the ruby (*mānika*) with the sun (Sūrya), sometimes replaced by gold, which has the same celestial affiliation; the white pearl (*moti*) with the moon (Candra); the coral (*mugā*), preferably red, with Mars (Mangala); the emerald (*pannā*) with Mercury (Budha); the topaz (Skt. *puṣparāja*) with Jupiter (Bṛhaspati); the diamond (*hira*) with Venus (Śukra); the sapphire (*nira*) with Saturn (Śani), preferably blue, as the black type amplifies this god's negative powers; the hessonite or garnet (Skt. *gomeda*) with the ascending lunar node (Rāhu); and the cat's eye or lapis lazuli (*lasune;* Skt. *vaidūrya*) with the descending lunar node (Ketu). Due to its association with the celestial bodies, each gem has a specific power that contributes to the joint ritual effect of the ensemble—a point we already encountered when dealing with the goldsmith as ritual specialist.

In an eighteenth-century song, the Buddha Śākyamuni, apart from being one of the Triple Gems, also wears jewels, particularly and not surprisingly for us at this point, on his ears: "Your ears are bedecked with many jewels. / Your ears shine twice as brightly as the sun /."[72] The Newar deity of Mt. Cobhāla, called Covāḥ or Lokeśvaram, on his "body, the color of dawn, wears a garland of diamonds and pearls" (*aruṇayā barṇa vasa hīrāmotī mālā hmasa /*) and his body "radiates effulgence" (*jājvalyamāna vasa thika*).[73] The most obvious and visible effect of the jewels is that of self-produced, inextinguishable light, with the sun as a model. Addressing the even more famous Newar deity Buṅgadyaḥ, also known as the red *nāthyogi-bodhisattva* Matsyendranātha-Lokanātha and protagonist of the largest festival of the Kathmandu Valley, another poet compares the extraordinary beauty of the face of the bright red processional image first, again, with that of the dawn (*atina sundara khvāla aruṇa samāna*), then as being "equal to a golden ṭikā applied [to the forehead] that resembles the sun" (*suraja thye thika luyā cithayā samāna*). The jewels added to the beautiful god in the following verse—"bedecked with jewellery containing various gems and precious stones" (*aneka ratana mānika tisāna tiyāva*)[74]—help set the theme: gold and stones. A verse, heavily alliterative in Newar, goes: "In the golden crown: a golden screw pine flower. / On the ears: golden rings" (*kanakamatukasa kanakaketakisvāna / karaṇasa kanakakuṇḍala*), reminding the listener that just as the deity assembles jewelry, he is also a place of compassion (*karuṇānidhāna*) and is known by his name Karuṇāmaya, "the compassionate." The poet continues composing a similar parallel between "the bejeweled ornament" (*maṇimaya tilahila*) and "the oil lamps radiating splendor" (*mata una teja thika*), which surround the god's chariot during one of his nightly ritual stops, like "a necklace made of jewels he has been adorned with" (*maṇimaya hālana tiyāva*), lights that remind the poet of the bodhisattva's "own physical form [being] made of mind" (*manomaya svarūpa*).[75] The bodhisattva's jewelry is made out of nothing less than precious stones, just as the deity himself is made out of the purest substance a being possesses. Fashioning and material refer to each other, just as the adorned and the adorning. Jewels are not celebratory add-ons but lead the listener and are revealed to the listener to be one with the very essence and evanescence of him who is being celebrated. The buddha is the jewel because he both rejects jewelry and attracts and allows for more jewelry.

These lyrics celebrate the symbolic and real capital that goes into the ornamentation of Buddhist or Hindu Newar devotional images. In fact, there is a whole branch of the Newar goldsmithing industry that produces jewelry that clients buy not for themselves or to distribute within the family, but to gift to monasteries that hold charismatic images onto whom these donations are bestowed. There is a specific type of traditional Newar association exclusively dedicated to the management of ornaments donated to a particular image, called *tisā bicā pujā guthi,* an association dedicated to worship involving the handling of jewelry. On particular days of worship—big festivals in the case of the most important images, more intimate events in the case of lesser known ones[76]—the *guthi* members retrieve the jewelry from the temple custodian; report, under his supervision, damaged or missing pieces; make, if necessary, amends; cleanse and polish; and then return the objects to the image for worship.[77] While some of the most basic types of jewelry, such as *gokulas*, *tāyomās*, *kallis*, or glass bangles (the latter offered to the Kumārī, Vāgeśvarī, Dakṣiṇkālī, and Satyanārāyaṇa), are shared between humans and images, there is a range that is worn only by deities and some by certain deities only.[78] Images of buddhas and bodhisattvas, of Viṣṇu, Lakṣmī, and Sarasvatī, all take gold, silver, and gemstones, fashioned as crowns, earrings (though there are cases where Śākyamuni may not be given ear ornaments), necklaces, and anklets with specific iconographic features such as lotuses or *tulsi* leaves. Famous images like that of Buddha Śākyamuni at Kvābāhāḥ or the Bhaktapur Dīpaṅkara buddhas could not be more heavily adorned. Śaiva and Śākta images and the wrathful Buddhist ones, including Bhairava and the *yoginīs*, tend to have a preference for snake- and otherwise fright- and charnel-ground-themed jewelry.[79] Just as with humans, jewelry is not only made anew and donated, but is also made to remain with the deity and establishes continuity and a personal or familial relationship with a deity over time. Beyond that, specific singular pieces of jewelry may also help in turning a human into a deity, such as with the Kumārīs, "the Living Goddesses," who become who they are by wearing a serpentine necklace that is passed on from one incumbent to the next,[80] just as family jewels are passed on, as we saw above, from women to girl children, from one generation to the next. Be it through a unique dedication renewed through care or through a serial handing down, which too involves a renewal of ritual involvement, there is no beautification that does not conspicuously signal generosity.

Narrating Jewels

Of the princely protagonists of *avadānas* who figure in lyrical and prose narratives and are regarded as extremely beautiful, more than one comes with a jewel embedded in the top of his skull, such as the beautiful prince (Skt. *sundararājakumāra*) Kavikumāra, "who had a crown-jewel on his head and bore beautiful auspicious marks" (*sundarasulakṣanasaṃyukta śirasaṃ cūḍāmaṇi-duhma*).[81] The most famous throughout the Buddhist world is, of course, Prince Maṇicūḍa, literally "whose head crown [bears] a jewel," of the eponymous *avadāna*. He figures so prominently in Newar literature that his story forms part of the corpus known as the *Svayaṃbhūpurāṇa*, a family of works of various scale, content, and time period that celebrate the Kathmandu Valley's most prominent Buddhist site, and that has been integrated into the *Maṇiśailamahāvadāna*, a *sthalapurāṇa* celebrating the goddess Vajrayoginī, worshipped in a temple above the Kathmandu Valley town of Sankhu. The Newar-language *Maṇicūḍāvadānoddhṛta* (An extract of the *Maṇicūḍāvadāna*) is a stand-alone text derived from the version found in the Sanskrit *Mahajjātakamālā*, also preserved in Nepal, but also related to the one contained in the *Avadānakalpalatā*.[82] All versions include a passage that elaborates on the gem (*maṇi* or *ratna*) that emerges out of the prince's fontanelle and that gives him his name. This is not a jewel that is bestowed in order to beautify but one that emerges from within and remains an integral part of the bodhisattva's body, right until the bitter end, when the decision by the prince to perform generosity (*dāna*) involves its being surgically removed from his skull. Consequently, its effect dramatically exceeds that of ordinary jewelry; the *Maṇicūḍāvadānoddhṛta*, at variance with the *Mahajjātakamālā* and closer to the *Avadānakalpalatā*, has the jewel "emitting 1,000 rays of merit" (*dol-chi puṇyayā tej pi-hāṃ vasyaṃ coṅ*), the merit (Skt. *puṇya*) being, as the the *Avadānakalpalatā* version explains, "carried over from a previous birth" (Skt. *prāgjanmāntarasaṃsakto*) and comparable (Skt. *iva*) to the light of the mental faculty of "discrimination" (Skt. *viveka*).[83] In the Sanskrit we find a trace of what Phyllis Granoff has identified as the main quality of jewels in South Asian Buddhist literature: to allow for "visions as expanded realities" with the jewel as a literary motif in which "the deeds of the Buddhas, and Bodhisattvas are either visible or actually manifested."[84] While the *Avadānakalpalatā* version opens a window for a view beyond the present existence, just as in the *Gaṇḍavyūha* and the other texts on which Granoff focuses, which reveal entire worlds and buddha bodies made of gems, the *Maṇicūḍāvadānoddhṛta* expands on the bodhisattva's meritorious deeds as they spill over into this world. Like the sun at night, the light issued by the newborn's jewel spread beyond the palace and illuminated the entire royal city of Sāketa, making people believe that day had broken.

More dramatically, the jewel's rays bore miraculous properties, such as turning warm what was cold and cool what was hot, allaying famines, transmuting water into anti-venom and (of significance for the *avadāna*'s plot and this book's focus on jewelry) iron into gold. In keeping with Granoff's view that the jewel helps the deeds of the buddhas and bodhisattvas to be actually manifested, this ability for metallurgical upgrade works into the hands of the prince's inclination toward generosity, allowing him to perform at will the most upmarket instantiations of *dāna*. An organically grown, embodied jewel framed by a body that is not quite yet that of a buddha, a jewel that is, as Granoff so insightfully writes, "at once reflection, reflecting surface and creative matrix," produces the stuff jewelry is made of that can be gifted and worn.[85] That virtue pervades the bodhisattva's mother as soon as he enters her womb. Queen Kāntimatī immediately feels the urge to preach the dharma and to donate too and does so by presenting herself in public, ascending the lion throne, preaching and giving away conspicuous quantities of gold. The *Maṇicūḍāvadānoddhṛta* does not fail to mention that before performing the meritorious deed, the queen had made sure to slip into a dress made of brocade and gilt thread cloth (*tās jadijabāpayā bastranaṃ hilava*) and had put on gemstone ornaments (*māṇikyayā ābharaṇ tiyāo*)—in other words, had "adorned herself with jewellery as well as she could" (*phayān phayāthya til-hilanaṃ tiyāva*), so much so that "she lit up the assembly round by the splendour of her own body" (*thava śarīlayā tejan sabhāmaṇḍalas khayakava*).[86] The jewel that is the embryo kicks off a series of deeds his mother is compelled to carry out, and it shines forth through the regalia in which she presents herself. The jeweled world of the buddhas and bodhisattvas and the world of jewelry of queens and kings are one and many. It is the power the jewels hold, the setting in which they unfold, and the connections the jewels are believed to establish that join these various realms into one.

The other story, popular among the Newars and with a jewel in a prominent role, is the *avadāna* or *jātaka* named after Viśvantara, in his Newar variant Bisvaṃtara (or Bisvantara).[87] In the most accessible Newar version, the edition and study by Siegfried Lienhard of a scroll painting featuring the narrative in both visual and the textual form, the climax is built up by serial acts of giving that almost always involve jewels.[88] The prince's father, upon the birth of his son, makes "a donation of vestments, grain, precious metals, gems etc." (*bastra dhana drabya ratna ityādina dāna*).[89] The prince himself gifts money and precious metals (*anega dhana drabya ityādina dāna*), and when to him too a son is born, he proffers "a multitude of gems, precious metals etc." (*anega ratna dravya ityādina*), with the provisional climax being that the prince establishes a donation hall and donates to monks and Brahmins coming from all over the word "a multitude of gems, gold, silver, vestments etc." (*anega ratna subarṇṇa rūpya bastra ityādina*).[90] The donative initiative, however, that shall cap it all and that leads to the banishment of the generous prince from the kingdom is that of the royal elephant to the ruler of another country: "When there were no more [potential] recipients of donations left, Prince Bisvaṃtara packed a multitude of gems (*anega ratna*), mounted the elephant (*kisi*), who was the Elephant Gem (*hastiratna*), and went on the hunt for beggars." The neighboring king decides to send a Brahmin to meet the traveling, prince and "then prince Bisvaṃtara gifted the Elephant Gem together with the gems to the brahmin envoy."[91] In another version quoted by Lienhard, the Elephant Gem is explicitly identified by the greedy king as protecting its country from military defeat: "Thanks to his power nobody can conquer that country."[92] Here, again, we find an accumulation and condensation of materials, faculties, and meaning: The (usually albino) elephant is one of the eight palladium-like gems a wheel-turning monarch has at his disposal. As if that were not enough, in the story the elephant is made to carry part of that king's wealth for distribution abroad. Jewels, whether figurative or literal, tend to attract or to produce more jewels, creating an overspill of jewels, just as the bodhisattva's urge to give without limit. Giving away the source of the multiplication of riches thus becomes one of the ultimate forms of *dāna* and one of the tragic events on the path of Bisvaṃtara's dissolution and glory. Thanks to his outrageous gifts, Maṇicūḍa receives back a jewel twice as radiant as the first, and Bisvaṃtara, whose counterpart in most other versions becomes king, acquires a superior dharma body in the Newar version. In both stories, in fact, the theme that surrounds the jewel is that of the bodhisattvas giving it away and Bisvaṃtara foregoing for himself and for others close to him the overspill it embodies and produces. Both heroes pay dearly for that—the former with his life, the latter with his royal birthright. Owning jewels is a privilege; giving them away can be dangerous. Replicating the jewel's overspill through its gift represents a form of transgression that produces horror or censure or both. Jewels are for keeps. Gifting a jewel is inherently gifting something one cannot afford to gift. It is a gift by which one is bound to ruin oneself. But because of that, it is also the gift for which one cannot be but rewarded in unexpected and extraordinary ways. It is through one's acceptance of self-ruination that one is, or has the hope of becoming, reestablished as more prosperous and more recognized than before.[93]

A key text of modernist Buddhism in which this Newar poetic economy of jewels unfolds in old and new ways is the *Sugata Saurabha* (The perfume of the Buddha), a *mahākāvya* on the life of the Buddha

Śākyamuni composed by the most celebrated twentieth-century Newar writer, Chittadhar Hṛdaya (1906–1982), while in prison, with the Newar translation of the *Lalitavistara* by Niṣṭhānanda Vajrācārya (1858–1935) from 1914 as his main inspiration, and published in Calcutta in 1948.[94] Jewels play a central role in celebrating the future buddha's royal background, on the one hand, and, on the other hand, his renunciation, consisting, among other things, in the rejection of ornamentation altogether. Jewels are introduced in the first canto, called "Lumbinī," in the entrance of Śākyamuni's mother's female entourage, with the women's "gold anklets [going] 'kling-klang'" (*chilichili svarṇāgū ghaṃgalā*), "their nipples dancing like pearl necklaces" (*amigu nugale motimālā saṃgu theṃ*), "their hair in plaits decorated with flower gems (*jiṃmha ahiyā thīgu maṇitheṃ satabate svaṁ*), "teeth of pearl in mouths of coral" (*mhutusi bhiṃpū dathvī dugu danta paṃktī motiyā*), "emerald-inlayed gold bracelets on both wrists, diamond-spangled earrings seen jiggling" (*nikhyara nāḍī kanaka kaṃkaṇa taḥgu pannā naṃ thunāḥ nhāypane nicvaṃgu hīrakayāgu kuṇḍala saṃ khanā /*)—to just name only a few items of a very long list.[95] The praise of king Śuddhodana's two queens displays a similar profile drawn with pearls, gold, and emeralds.[96] But all this is only the framing of the central jewel that appears in the "Birth" (*Janma*) canto, where, in verse 12 (my numbering) the bodhisattva is called "this gem of a child" (*thī umha macā*) and—among other things to explain the absence of defiling birth fluids in a future buddha's birth—is compared to a spotless jewel wrapped in cloth (*pāṭavastre niṣkalaṅkagu ratna theṃ*), prefiguring the emergence of *ratna* number one of what would soon assemble as the Three Jewels. Here *bhakti*, which we have encountered above as directed toward the beloved, the god, or, in the song by Amṛtānanda, Buddha Śākyamuni, is directed toward the precious child.[97] The baby returns as the jewel in verse 19 after his first round of breastfeeding, when he makes all darkness disappear being "the jewel of the heart whose splendor extends in all directions" (*hṛdayamaṇiyā teja dvāra nyaṃka he*).[98]

Gautama's first rice feeding, by contrast, is the first occasion on which the bodhisattva displays his predilection for rejection. The poetic rendering of the rite sees his father following Newar tradition in having a dish placed in front of his son with objects that the infant is encouraged to touch, ritually determining his future professional career. This being a Newar text and the king wanting his son to be a prince, the reader is not surprised to find the dish filled almost exclusively with "expensive jewellery" (*bahumūlya bhūṣaṇayā chulyāḥ*): "three-faced amulets" (*svapho dugu jantra*), "lion-headed bracelets" (*siṃhakhvāḥ dugu culyā*), a garland with mostly organic protective objects, but also "hard-to-obtain heavenly jewels" (*durlabha dibya ratnata*), "a gold-and pearl-ringed rudrākṣa garland" (*moticāḥcā phosikhaḥ dugu luṃ bhunāḥ rudrākṣamāḥ*), "necklaces of white pearl" (*tuyūgu mauktika*) and "top-quality red-hued coral" (*rakta varṇagu bhiṃgu bhiṃpūmāḥ*), "anklets of gold" (*luṁyā goṁcā*), "gold anklet bells" (*luṁyā . . . ghaṃgalā*), apart from, as de rigeur for this rite, among other things, a pen, a ball of clay, a brick, and a book.[99] To the king's consternation, the bodhisattva child grabs it all and flings it away.

The canto called "Marriage" (*Ihī*) sees the next substantial ornament-heavy passage. It is artfully initiated in the preceding canto by the prince's first meeting with his future wife and the gift, his travel chest being empty, of "the ornament, the priceless necklace of his own beautiful neck" (*thilahila thaḥgu sundar kaṇṭhayā bahumūlya hāra*),[100] just as in the *Lalitavistara* the prince gifts his future bride a ring and more, which she there, however, refuses.[101] Gautama's life as a Newar prince and householder begins as it shall end: by his getting rid of the entanglements of jewelry. But first Yaśodharā will have to arrive on her wedding day in a palanquin and step out of it in a riot of bling: "The fingers were covered with rings twinkling like stars /"[102] and "See the gem-covered golden hairband and goldflower ornaments blazed. / The string pearl earrings and golden fivefold hair chains quivered, displaying the incipient emotions coming from the beating heart."[103] As she wears the most prized and recognizable items of the traditional female Newar wedding attire—including the goldflower headgear (*luṁsvāṃ*), a filigree composite of gilt copper in the shape of leaves, vines, flowers, and little bird figures, attached to the hair like a cap, and the five chains (*nyāpusikhaḥ*), attached similarly and reaching down along the scalp like the fingers of a hand—the jewelry speaks of what the bride, wordless and demure, dare not, while the modernist and Newar revivalist poet makes her jewelry say what it wouldn't have in the past. The bodhisattva then leaves behind him a trace of gems as he extricates himself from the life of desires that are not his: his famous chariot is decorated with gems (*ratna maya*); the bodhisattva gives a pearl necklace (*mauktika māḥ*) as a farewell gift to his aunt and foster-mother, who takes the gift as an expression of affection (*bhāḥpa premayā*), just before the prince himself remembers the gift he gave to his wife as "a vine of the heart" (*hṛdayalatā*).[104] Before leaving the city, even Māra tempts the determined prince by offering him that he will make the prince "replete with the seven gems" (*saptaratnaṃ pūrṇa*) of the world monarch.[105] Māra will try again, just before Gautama calls the earth goddess to bear witness, offering to the ascetic "an overflowing treasury of various gems and riches" (*jāḥgu yakva dhukūta nānāratna dhana*).[106]

The decisive act is, of course, the moment when the prince takes off his "crown encrusted with precious stones" (*bhiṃgu maṇi maya mukuṭa*), his "pearl-embroidered shoes" (*motimaya lākāṃ*), and all other royal accouterments, asks his charioteer Candaka to return all to the palace, and then uses "his own jewel-crowned sword" (*thaḥgu maṇimaya cudugu khadgaṃ*) to cut off his hair.[107] This step will be repeated by Yaśodharā, in the next, eponymous canto, who there decides to become a domestic *yoginī* (*cheyṁ cvanāḥ naṃ yogini theṃ*) who teaches her female entourage the five precepts, including, as part of the seventh of the eight precepts (Skt. *aṣṭaśīla*), that they "should vow to give up the wearing of jewellery and of all gem-studded ornaments."[108] The women of the Newar court, whose excesses of ornamentation served as the show opener in the first canto, now turn the inner chambers of the royal palace into a jewel-free, semi-monastic space.

One of the most visible motifs of the whole first third of the poem leading up to Gautama's great renunciation is the celebration of beauty and wealth, on the one hand, and its rejection, on the other: the more breathtaking the jewelry, the more extraordinary the bodhisattva's and his followers' abandonment. But there is more to it: Todd Lewis has noted the excision of the supernatural in Chittadhar Hṛdaya's hagiography of Buddha Śākyamuni and, instead, an attention to the realia of Newar heritage, such as the prince undergoing a Newar life crisis rite and his wife a Newar wedding, all missing, of course in the poem's model, the *Lalitavistara*.[109] The degree to which jewelry, and specifically Newar jewelry, is celebrated throughout the first half of *Sugata Saurabha* is striking. I would take Lewis's point a step further and suggest that the supernatural returns in the guise of a heightened poetic attention to a hyperbolically Newarized ritual and material culture, to a legendary past in which the rich, the powerful, and the stunning-looking were Newars and to a poetic utopia in which the world is beautiful and the good is possible. One needs to read this as stemming from the pen of a poet who was thrown into prison by a non-Newar political elite who, while having themselves appropriated much of the Newar tangible heritage, suppressed the Newar people, their language, their literature, and their Buddhism. Opulence and renunciation are two sides of a Newar modernity born out of repression and resistance and its utopian

Buddhist poetry: jewelry that is put on speaks of the rich, self-confident, unabashed, traditionalist Newar, while jewelry that is taken off holds the promise of individuals and of a society in charge of and not weighed down by its own wealth and desires. Buddhist modernism, which among the Newars comes in many forms and particularly those associated with Theravāda, stresses the renunciatory as a transformative, innovative, and liberating moment. Traditional Newar Buddhism, in which every desirable god or human comes with jewels, is poetically rethought and retraditionalized by giving jewels a new function that is both gendered, ethnic, and ethical. Jewels, embraced or renounced, allow the Newar Buddhist to be both authentic and renewed. Chittadhar Hṛdaya also stands for an early twentieth-century modernist Nepalese Theravāda-inspired Buddhism still very much in the hands of men. Similar to the Newar songs, it is the man who imagines women wearing jewelry, the man rejecting it, and the women following his example. That changes in the second half of the twentieth century, when it is Theravāda Newar women who begin having the greater impact on a changing Buddhist ritual world. What returns here is the event described in the closing passage of this chapter's first part: the Newar girl children who need to remove their studs for their stay in the meditation center, where they learn about the empowerment Buddhism offers to girl children and who, once that stay is over, are hastily gussied up by their mothers and grandmothers to make sure the empowerment gestured at remains a Newar one.

As this chapter ends with the poetic, it may be useful to contrast what it has tried to do with Vanessa Sasson's contribution to this volume, "Jeweled Renunciation: Reading the Buddha's Hagiography," which shows how jewels are an integral part of the poetic texture of the Buddha Śākyamuni's life story. Sasson's text demonstrates how in poetry, no matter what and no matter when on the Gautama Siddhartha's trajectory toward nirvāṇa, the influence he has on his environment is jewelification or, more generally put, ornamentation. Jewels are the material manifestation and self-celebration of a buddha's effect on the world. This chapter, reversely, has been about trying to understand the power that jewels have in their own right, a power that Buddhists and Buddhist texts plug into and from which they derive their own respective power, the power that empowers Buddhism and that empowers those who invoke Buddhism for their empowerment. For this reason this chapter has been primarily concerned not so much with the bejeweled place that is the Buddhist cosmos but with jewels that are worn by humans, real or imagined, jewels that through their use shape the differences that make up human relations, and by doing that mediate transformations in humans. Jewelry is the language of the unreal and unaffordable dear, of the affective that cannot be named otherwise but by evoking the highest possible condensation of the precious. The jewels are left to do much of the talking as much of the talking is done through jewels. And yet in these contexts, although jewels have a power of their own and always do something—sparkle, shine, magically change and convey things, impact the observer, be she or he inside or outside the text—they are also never just thus. As we have seen, they are either worn and owned, or they are gifted or rejected, always named, described, praised, desired, or given up. And it is in the rejection of the jewel that we experience not only the merging of he who takes note and she who displays. More important, the desired that is the jewel turns into the jewel that is the promise of an end to desire.

Notes

1. The two most important studies dealing with the sociology, semiotics, and material culture of Newar jewelry are Sushila Manandhar's monumental "Bijoux et parures traditionnels des Néwar au Népal: Une approche anthropologique et historique" (PhD diss., Université de Paris X, 1998), which extends to other kinds of ornamentation and attire, and Motilakṣmī Śākya's *Jhigu tisā, kāsā va bhvayghāsā (svanigaḥ nevāḥta madhyeyā svaṃgū jāti śākya, bajrācārya, udāsataygu)* [Our jewelry, games, and dishes (of three castes among the Newars of the Kathmandu Valley, the Śākyas, the Vajrācāryas, and the Urāys)] (Khvapa [Bhaktapur]: Kutaḥ pikāk, 2016). Hannelore Gabriel's *The Jewelry of Nepal* (New York: Weatherhill, 1999), 60–85, includes one substantial chapter on the Newars, while John Clarke's *Jewellery of Tibet and the Himalayas* (New York: V&A Publications, 2004), 50–61, presents Newar jewelry as if from within the Tibetan context.
2. A study of the role of jewels among the Newars cannot do without pointing to the fact that the priestly Newar Buddhist caste, named after the title of the tantric priest, the *vajrācārya* or "diamond master," bears in its name the preeminently tantric Buddhist jewel, the *vajra,* which also gives the name of one of the "vehicles" (*yānas*) Newar Buddhists follow, the Vajrayāna. The idea, image, and potency of the indestructible pure jewel is as central as the use of this term prefixed to a vast array of names and objects is ubiquitous, turning the tantric world into one pervaded by *vajra,* which covers much more than the mere

meaning of "diamond." It also needs to be remembered that the *vajra* (made out of metal, not precious stone) is also a key ritual implement in tantric Buddhist liturgy for which the *vajrācārya* adepts need to receive initiation to become practicing tantric priests.

3. David N. Gellner, and Declan Quigley, eds. *Contested Hierarchies: A Collaborative Ethnography of Caste among the Newars of the Kathmandu Valley, Nepal* (Oxford: Oxford University Press, India, 1995), 217.
4. The Newar scholar Hemrāj Śākya names the two Lalitpur monasteries Ha Bāhāḥ an Oṁ Bāhāḥ as the communities most famous for goldsmithing and refining gold dust (*dhūsāḥ*). See Hemrāj Śākya, *Mayūrvarṇa mahāvihāryā saṃkṣipta itihās* (Lalitpur: Bhiṃcheṁ bāhāyā sarvasaṃgha [2571 V.S.], 1973), 57; quoted in David Gellner, *Monk, Householder, and Tantric Priest: Newar Buddhism and Its Hierarchy of Ritual* (Cambridge: Cambridge University Press, 1992), 265.
5. All original source language words in parentheses are in Newar if not otherwise stated.
6. Michael Allen, referred to in Gellner, *Monk, Householder, and Tantric Priest,* 372n17.
7. For an interview with Duṇḍa Bahādur Vajrācārya for Bodhi Television, December 14, 2018, see https://www.youtube.com/watch?v=wmou8P_ScvI.
8. Such castes include the Sunār, who belong to the Dalit Kāmī caste, which, according to a Śākya source quoted by David Gellner, claims to be related to the Śakya and Vajrācārya caste (Gellner, *Monk, Householder, and Tantric Priest,* 91). Gellner explains this as being due to a little differentiated caste system among the Parbatiyā (*Monk, Householder, and Tantric Priest,* 354n18).
9. Gellner and Quigley, *Contested Hierarchies,* 213–214.
10. S. Manandhar, "Bijoux et parures," 127, quotes the Lalitpur goldsmith and translator of Buddhist scriptures Duṇḍabahādur Vajrācārya as saying that all eight substances are used, directly or indirectly, for the manufacture of any kind of jewelry: five directly and three for alloying, assembling, coating, casting, or the purifying of gold and silver.
11. The Tāmrakārs rank third with copper (*sijā*), associated with Mercury, and the Kaṃsakārs working in bronze (*kayṁ*). These are followed by the Śilpakārs working in wood (*siṁ*) and the Lohākārs working in iron (*na*), associated with the notoriously difficult Saturn. See Joyce W. Shepard, "Symbolic Space in Newar Culture" (PhD diss., University of Michigan, 1985), 59, and Siegfried Lienhard, "The Monastery and the

Secular World: Saṅgha-Buddhism and Caste-Buddhism," *Journal of the American Oriental Society* 11 (1989): 594; both quoted in Gellner and Quigley, *Contested Hierarchies,* 213.

12. S. Manandhar, "Bijoux et parures," 108.
13. S. Manandhar, "Bijoux et parures," 111. For the Muslim jewelry sellers of Lalitpur, see Megan Adamson Sijapati, *Islamic Revival in Nepal: Religion and a New Nation* (London: Routledge, 2011), 25.
14. For a detailed description of such a division of labor, see Bruce McCoy Owens, "The Politics of Divinity in the Kathmandu Valley: The Festival of Bungadya/Matsyendranath" (PhD diss., Columbia University, 1989), ch. 8, 260–297. Nils Gutschow and Axel Michaels: *Handling Death: The Dynamics of Death and Ancestor Rituals among the Newars of Bhaktapur, Nepal* (Wiesbaden: Harrassowitz Verlag, 2005); *Growing Up: Hindu and Buddhist Initiation Rituals among Newar Children in Bhaktapur, Nepal* (Wiesbaden: Harrassowitz Verlag, 2008); and *Getting Married: Hindu and Buddhist Marriage Rituals among the Newars of Bhaktapur and Patan, Nepal* (Wiesbaden: Harrassowitz Verlag, 2012).
15. Sushila Manandhar gives a beautifully simple example of such a collaboration: "Three Newar castes participate in making a bracelet made of five metals (*pañcarasimyā cullyā*) . . . : a Śākya goldsmith makes the gold wire, *lūṁ tāra,* and the silver wire (*waha tāra*), a Tamrakār makes the copper wire, *sijā tāra,* and the brass wire, *lī tāra,* and a blacksmith makes the iron wire, *na tāra.* . . . Finally, the goldsmith takes the three wires, winds the silver wire around them and covers them with a golden encasement, with lion face tips or with pointed ends" ("Bijoux et parures," 111). Unless otherwise noted, all translations from this article are my own.
16. At our daughter's first rice feeding in Lalitpur, 2007, my former Vajrācārya friend and landlord had his family's goldsmith, who happened to be his brother-in-law, perform this task for us.
17. S. Manandhar, "Bijoux et parures," 112.
18. Such para-priests are the barber and his wife (the *nau,* viz. the *naunī*), who pair the toes and paint crimson red the lower part of the feet of those who undergo life crisis rites, or the astrologer (*jośī*), who may also happen to be from the Vajrācārya caste and who is asked by the family to produce the astral chart of a newborn that will determine which celestial powers will rule her or him throughout life.
19. S. Manandhar, "Bijoux et parures," 113. Manandhar refers to the well-known Hindi proverb "The *Sunār* steals [the gold] from his own

mother's nose ring" (*sunār āpnī māṃ ki nāt meṃ se bhī curtā hai*), also found in William Crooke, *The Tribes and Castes of the Western Provinces and Oudh* (Calcutta: Office of the Superintendent of Government Printing, 1896), 4:340.

20. Roland Barthes's view that in the pre-contemporary understanding *"la femme est à la fois mangeuse d'hommes et de diamants"* betrays a similar view on the relation among gemstones, gender, and nutrition (Roland Barthes, "Des joyaux aux bijoux," in *Œuvres complètes,* edited by Éric Marty, vol. 1: *Livres, textes, entretiens, 1942–1961* (Paris: Seuil, 2002), 1091.
21. The idea that the clients only own the representation and only for some time while the value stays with the goldsmith is expressed in a proverb from south of the border: "The jewellery belongs to the people, the gold belongs to the *Sunār*" (*sonā sunār kā, ābharaṇ saṃsār kā*). Crooke, *The Tribes and Castes of the Western Provinces and Oudh,* 340.
22. S. Manandhar, "Bijoux et parures," 113.
23. Doranne Jacobson, "Women and Jewelry in Rural India," in *Women in India: Two Perspectives,* edited by Doranne Jacobson and Susan S. Wasley (New Delhi: Manohar, 1999 [1977]), 210.
24. Jacobson, "Women and Jewelry in Rural India," 173.
25. The classical South Asian practice of "the assessment of gems" (*ratnaparīkṣā*) has been codified in the vast, venerable, and specialized literature of *ratnaśāstras,* traditionally consulted by jewelers, traders, ministers, and poets, but most of all the reference point for the *maṇḍalin,* the mediator between seller and buyer, mentioned in premodern sources (Louis Finot, *Les lapidaires indiens* [Paris: Émile Bouillon, 1896, ii–v]). They generally cover the gems' origin (*utpatti*), location (*ākara*), color (*varṇa* or *chāyā*), kind (*jāti*), qualities (*guṇas*) and defects (*doṣas*), effect (*phala*), price (*mūlya*), and counterfeits (*vijāti*) (Finot, *Les lapidaires indiens,* xx). The two most prominent texts are the (probably) sixth-century *Ratnaparīkṣā* of Buddhabhaṭṭa (or Buddhabhaṭa), with a similar yet incomplete variant of this text appearing in Varāhamihira's *Bṛhatsaṃhitā,* both texts probably going back to a common source, now lost, and the (maybe south Indian) post-sixth-century *Agastimata* (Finot, *Les lapidaires indiens,* vi–xii). Worthy of note is that the *Ratnaparīkṣā,* the earliest complete extant *ratnaśāstra* text, was composed or redacted by a Buddhist and that the Nepal German Manuscript Cataloguing Project database contains fifteen (undated) manuscripts and the Asha Archives hold two (undated) manuscripts with Newar versions of the text (Premśānti Tulādhar, *Nepalbhāṣā*

sahityayā itihāsa [The history of Nepalbhasa literature] [Yeṁ (Kathmandu): Nepālbhāṣā ekedami, 2000], 32); cp. *Āśā saphū kuthiyā abhilekh granthayā varṇātmak dhalaḥ* (A descriptive catalogue of selected manuscripts preserved at the Āśā Saphū Kuthi [Āśā Archives]), edited by Janak Lāl Vaidya and Prem Bahādur Kaṃsakar (Kathmandu: Cvasāpāsā, 1991), 247, for the description of one of the manuscripts, which says something about its circulation among the Newars.

26. For a complete list of these powers given by Duṇḍabahādur Vajrācārya, see S. Manandhar, "Bijoux et parures," 138.
27. S. Manandhar, "Bijoux et parures," 140.
28. S. Manandhar, "Bijoux et parures," 142.
29. For more details on the utilization of jewelry in Newar life crisis rites, see the second part of Sushila Manandhar's dissertation, "Bijoux et parures dans les stades de la vie," 187–380, and M. Śākya, *Jhigu tisā, kāsā va bhvayghāsā,* section on jewelry in chapter 3, "Saṃskār svarūp viśeṣayā tisāyāgu dhala" (List of ornaments of the various life crisis rituals), 153–168.
30. Jacobson, "Women and Jewelry in Rural India," 172–173. Jacobson also points out that "[a] woman's ability to secretly transfer wealth received or taken by her affines into *maika* jewelry [i.e., given by her natal family] controlled only by herself is an important means of adding to the economic power of an economically disadvantaged group—women" (210).
31. This is a trend observable across South Asia and, indeed, globally, occurring regionally at different historical times over the last half a century. This shift lies at the heart of Roland Barthes's famous essay "Des joyeaux au bijoux," in which he writes about fashion, which *"ne connaît plus le joyeau, mais seulement le bijou,"* a secularized, democratized *"rien,"* or nothing, which *"règne sur le vêtement non plus parce qu'il est absolument précieux, mais parce qu'il concourt d'une façon decisive à le faire signifier"* (1093).
32. For a discussion of some of these developments, see S. Manandhar, "Bijoux et parures," 430–439.
33. Jacobson, "Women and Jewelry in India," 211.
34. S. Manandhar, "Bijoux et parures," and M. Śākya, *Jhigu tisā, kāsā va bhvayghāsā.*
35. For a splendid documentation of Shāh and Rāṇa jewelry, see the collection of court photographs in Marcella Sirhandi, *Royal Nepal through the Lens of Richard Gordon Matzene* (Chicago: Serindia Publications, 2009).

36. *Rājamatī kumatī / jike va:sā pirati / hāya bābā Rājamatīcā / Rājamatī ma bila dhā:sā / Kāśī vane tela bubā / hayā byu Rājamatīcā // 1 // saṁ dhā:sā kuli kuli / mikhā dhā:sā bālā bālā / Sakvamiyā hmyāyamacā lā / khvā: dhā:sā tuyū khvā: / khvāle niga: tī du / Tāhānaniyā Rājamatīcā //2// kheṁkholā dhyākve daṃ / pasa:-baji dhū daṃ / Rājamatī bhulusulu daṃ / Rājamatī gana du / Ituṃbahāle chamha du / hayā byu Rājamatīcā //3// hnāpā va:hma Tahrithakuṃ / lipā va:hma Cihrithakuṃ / vayā lipā Rājamatīcā / Tahrithakuṃ ma yo jita: / Cihrithakuṃ mile ma jū / Rājamatī byāhā yānā byu //4// Tahrithakuṃyā tāyo: du / Cihrithakuṃyā pāyo: du / Rājamatīyā bijakani du / bijakani marumha / kalā: jita: ma yo bubā / hayā byu Rājamatīcā //5// Tha:neyā Thaṁhiti / Ko:neyā Kohiti / bice lāka Maruhiti / Maruhiti la: kā: vanaṃ tago / loṃhate luphiṃ hānā: / Rājamatī thasa: pāla hnāṃ //6// tisānaṃ tiyakā: / Gujarātī puyakā: / Rājamatī byāhā yānā byu / Rājamatī bila dhā:sā / Kāśī vane ma khu bubā / hayā byu Rājamatīcā //7//.* See Siegfried Lienhard, *Nevārīgītimañjarī: Religious and Secular Poetry of the Nevars of the Kathmandu Valley,* vol. 10 (Stockholm Oriental Series. Stockholm: Almqvist and Wiskell International, 1974; Acta Universitatis Stockholmiensis), 59 (for the Newar version), and 160–161 (for Lienhard's translation and notes). While I retain Lienhard's Newar transliteration when quoting from his edition (except for inserting forward slashes for the verse and stanza breaks and numbering where Lienhard uses spaces and brackets), I otherwise follow the contemporary conventions of the academic transliteration of Old (or Classical) Newar; see Kamal P. Malla et al., eds., *A Dictionary of Classical Newari Compiled from Manuscript Sources* (Kathmandu: Nepal Bhasa Dictionary Committee, 2000).
37. Lienhard, *Nevārīgītimañjarī,* 59.
38. Indra Māli, *Nepālbhāṣā taḥkhaṁgvaḥdhukū* (Practical Nepal Bhasa dictionary) (Yeṁ: Nepālbhāṣā ākādemiyā niṃtiṃ, 1130 NS, VS 2066 [2009/10 CE]); s.v. *tāyo,* 254.
39. Manandhar writes that when given to infants, its dedication happens in a rite called *tvāy cinegu,* through which the child "makes friends" (*tvāy cinegu*) with one of Hāratī's five children, Wasībhāju, Wasīmayaju, Latabhāju, Latimayaju, or Jilānbhāju (S. Manandhar, "Bijoux et parures," 213). On special occasions, *tāyos* are also offered to deities, as the following line from a song celebrating the ritual immolation (*sati*) of Bijyālakṣmī, a queen of Rāṇa Bahādur Śāh (1777–1799), demonstrates: "Then she returned, arrived at [the shrine of] Jayavāgīśvarī, / And, hey, offered a gold-plated *tāyo*" (*anaṃ niseṃ libāṃ bijyāta Jayabāgīśvarī*

thenakala bijyāta / ana lubhītayā tāyo: chāyā bila re //); Lienhard, *Nevārīgītimañjarī*, 120.

40. Māli, *Nepālbhāṣā taḥkhaṁgvaḥdhukū;* s.v. pāyo, 358.
41. For the identification of *bijakani* I follow Māli, *Nepālbhāṣā taḥkhaṁgvaḥdhukū* ; s.v. *bijakāni*, 414: "A kind of jewelry for women made of gold with floral ornaments inlayed with gems shaped along the ear" (*misātay nhāypanay taṃgu buttā tayāḥ thī thunātaḥgu tuki theṃjyāḥgu chatāji luṁyā tisā*). Lienhard, who has "ear ornaments," refers to the illustration in Dilli Ram Regmi, *Medieval Nepal*, vol. 2 (New Delhi: Rupa, 2007 [1965]), 1080, where the word *bijakānni* (note: Newar is well known for its only weakly normative orthography) is part of the header of a drawing that depicts various types of jewelry, including, but not restricted to, ear ornaments. However, Kamal P. Malla et al., eds., *A Dictionary of Classical Newari Compiled from Manuscript Sources* (Kathmandu: Nepal Bhasa Dictionary Committee, 2000), s.v. *bicakani*, 328, has "a kind of ornament worn around the neck," just as Thakur Lal Manandhar and Anne Vergati, eds., *Newari-English Dictionary. Modern Language of the Kathmandu Valley* (Delhi: Agam Kala Prakashan, 1986), s.v. *bija kani* [*sic*], 177, has "an ornament of the neck." Ulrike Kölver and Iswarananda Shresthacarya, eds., *A Dictionary of Contemporary Newari. Newari—English* (with the assistance of Daya Ratna Sakya and Nirmal Man Tuladhar, edited by Bernhard Kölver and Siegfried Lienhard), vol. 8: *Nepalica* (Sankt Augustin: VGH Wissenschaftsverlag, 1994), s.v. *bicakani* (var. *bijakani*), 236, play it safe with "kind of ornament (for the ear or the neck)." John Clarke in the note to fig. 42, "Woman's neck ornament, *tayo bizakani*," calls the latter "a version of the more elaborate form of *tayo* . . . the *tayo bizakani* which always features the nine-(or up to thirteen-) headed protective cobra set above a jewel setting" (*Jewellery of Tibet and the Himalayas*, 60). What Clarke does not mention, but what is visible in the figure he provides, is that each of the cobras' snouts holds a metal ring, making it a curved row of multiple cuffs, just like one would find with ear *ornaments*. Thus *bijakāni* alone may actually refer to a row of rings as ornamental feature. Manandhar takes the lexicographical confusion around the term *bijakāni* as the prime example for a progressive loss of knowledge among the Newars about their own jewelry culture: "*Nombreux sont les Newar qui ne savent plus distinguer les bijoux par leur nom*" (S. Manandhar, "Bijoux et parures," 18; see also 433).

42. S. Manandhar, "Bijoux et parures," 434, as well as fn. 388.
43. John K. Locke, *Buddhist Monasteries of Nepal: A Survey of the Bāhās and Bahīs of the Kathmandu Valley* (Kathmandu: Sahayogi Press, 1985), 287.
44. Lienhard, *Nevārīgītimañjarī,* 22–23.
45. Lienhard, *Nevārīgītimañjarī,* 23.
46. Here and elsewhere, naturally, the grammatical singular used for the Newar terms for the jewelry in the texts needs to be rendered as plural in the case for those ornaments worn in pairs or in rows.
47. *lāhātisa culyācā galapatasa tāyo:cā / hnāyapanasa dava bāna lum̐yā mukhu:cā /;* Lienhard, *Nevārīgītimañjarī,* 60.
48. "-cā" does not translate well into English, where one would need to use "little." It would find a much better parallel in the eponymous Italian *-ina* ("*Madamina, il catalogo è questo*"), the French ending *-ette* ("*Alouette, gentile alouette*"), or the German *-lein* ("*Mein schönes Fräulein, darf ich wagen*").
49. *va chu galli thva chu galli Makhaṃtvāyā galli re / Pānabati maiyāṃ hnyānā va:gu siṃkhvā kiyā kalli re . . . / hisidu hāi kalliyāgu tārā tārā sala re / jigu mana lākā: cha lā suru suru vana re /;* Lienhard, *Nevārīgītimañjarī,* 58.
50. Lion-head anklets, usually made out of silver, are ornaments traditionally reserved for girls above the age of five and worn for the first time during *ihī,* the first of the two Newar marriage-related premenstrual life-cycle rituals. According to S. Manandhar ("Bijoux et parures," 109), they help clear the way and impart the girl with the strength of the lion and can be worn by the girl throughout her life. With traditional Newar jewelry being acutely age-specific, to speak about jewelry means also to speak about age without referring to figures. Since at least the last decade of the twentieth century, lion-head anklets have barely been worn anymore and, except for the above-mentioned ritual occasions, have been replaced by a pair of fine anklets called *pāuju,* similar to the Indian *pājeb.* Lienhard calls the song "modern" (*Nevārīgītimañjarī,* 159), and S. Manandhar claims that this "*prouve leur usage quotidian jusqu'au vingtième siècle,*" ("Bijoux et parures," 288), but the dating is vague, and the occurrence of an item in a song is not reliable data for documenting actual practice. What is safe to say is that as the song ages, through time, specific jewelry becomes part of the inventory of nostalgia. Jewelry again and differently, historically, becomes the cypher of the unobtainable.
51. Lienhard, *Nevārīgītimañjarī,* 154.

52. That this is a genre that crosses languages, literatures, and times is proven by "Has Anybody Seen My Girl (Five Foot Two, Eyes of Blue)," known best in its version by Sam M. Lewis and Joseph Widow Young and first recorded by The California Ramblers in 1925. The part of it most strikingly similar to the Newar song above (including the reference to jewels) runs as follows: "Now if you run into a / Five foot two, covered with fur / Diamond rings and all those things / Betcha' life it isn't her, / But could she love, could she woo? / Could she, could she, could she coo? / Has anybody seen my girl?"
53. Lienhard, *Nevārīgītimañjarī*, 56. At *Nevārīgītimañjarī*, 155n8, Lienhard overcautiously, it seems, given the little import, surmises "A certain type of ornament (?)."
54. *tayo: tuki suike dhakā: hekā vaṃgu tā he data;* Lienhard, *Nevārīgītimañjarī*, 64.
55. *lāhā-tuti-nānā dayakāva juyu pāsā //;* Lienhard, *Nevārīgītimañjarī*, 123.
56. The dictionaries are silent, but Lienhard tentatively identifies it as "some ornament (?)" (*Nevārīgītimañjarī*, 182n7).
57. *chatā tam̐yā magathyācā nitā tam̐yā tvākasvāna / hyāuka duli thanā chvava //;* Lienhard, *Nevārīgītimañjarī*, 73.
58. *naya tiya ma bhā:lapā / sihehanaṃ chi chahma siyā hnāṃ /;* Lienhard, *Nevārīgītimañjarī*, 73.
59. *latā yo ji prabhuna culyā tāyo: lobha kenā: / lakhabhukhapati kenā:* Lienhard, *Nevārīgītimañjarī*, 75.
60. *nayayāta ma gā: ma khu tiyayāta ma gā: ma khu / rasa chatā ma dayāva duḥkha //;* Lienhard, *Nevārīgītimañjarī*, 75.
61. *akhbarīyā aṃgu chapā phvane e gunnā dāju /;* Lienhard, *Nevārīgītimañjarī*, 64.
62. *tāyala tukicā china jita bilasā / hnāyapana daṃka du mundri re gunnā dāju /;* Lienhard, *Nevārīgītimañjarī*, 64.
63. *tutisa pāyo: maiju lāhātisa lum̐yā culyā / akhabarīyā aṃgū kenā;* Lienhard, *Nevārīgītimañjarī*, 58.
64. *tata:go:gu bhiṃpū bājyo: vane dhuṃkala;* Lienhard, *Nevārīgītimañjarī*, 60.
65. Lienhard, *Nevārīgītimañjarī*, 162n3.
66. *abalā ji ati misā cittasa bhā:lapā tisā /;* Lienhard, *Nevārīgītimañjarī*, 67. Lienhard adds "(You) are," stressing the identification of the addressee with the jewelry and making him the one to whom the feeling is directed (174). For the historical identity of the poem's lyrical subject, also see *Nevārīgītimañjarī*, 174.

67. Lienhard, *Nevārīgītimañjarī,* 59.
68. *ma du hīrā ma du jyāna ma du kṛṣṇā madu rāmā;* Lienhard, *Nevārīgītimañjarī,* 60.
69. Lienhard, *Nevārīgītimañjarī,* 80.
70. Lienhard, *Nevārīgītimañjarī,* 39.
71. They consist of, in the common Newar version of their titles, (1) the *Aṣṭasāhasrikā prajñāpāramitā sūtra,* (2) the *Gaṇḍavyūha sūtra,* (3) the *Daśabhūmika sūtra,* (4) the *Samādhirāja sūtra,* (5) the *Saddharmalaṅkāvatāra sūtra,* (6) the *Saddharmapuṇḍarīka sūtra,* (7) the Tathāgataguhyaka (or *Guhyasamāja tantra*), (8) the *Lalitavistara sūtra,* and (9) the *Suvarṇaprabhāsottamasūtrendrarāja.* For a discussion of their ritual context through history, see Will Tuladhar-Douglas, *Remaking Buddhism for Medieval Nepal: The Fifteenth-Century Reformation of Newar Buddhism* (Abingdon: Routledge, 2006), 144–146, where the author suggests that this may be a development unique to medieval Kathmandu Valley Buddhism.
72. *aneka ratnana tiyā chi karṇaṃ / duguṇa sūryayā teja chi karṇam /;* Lienhard, *Nevārīgītimañjarī,* 40.
73. Lienhard, *Nevārīgītimañjarī,* 54.
74. Lienhard, *Nevārīgītimañjarī,* 44.
75. Lienhard, *Nevārīgītimañjarī,* 43.
76. For the case of Bhaktapur's Dīpaṅkaras on the occasion of the festival of Pañcadān, see Junu Bāsukalā Rañjitkār, *Bhaktapurko Pañcadān Parva (Saṃskṛtibāre Viśleṣaṇātmak Adhyayan)* (Kāṭhmāḍauṃ and Lalitpur: Nhūjaḥ guṭhī samāj; Bauddha adhyayan samāj Nepāl, 2007) (NS 1127, VS 2064), 116–117.
77. Daya Ratna Shakya, a Portland-based Newar linguist and activist, remembered his grandfather narrating that on the establishment of the Guṭhī Saṃsthān, the state-run association for the management of public religious affairs, the association's officers came and took into their custody temple jewelry, following which devotees were less willing to continue making donations of this kind (personal communication, Portland, November 2, 2019).
78. For a list of those, see S. Manandhar, "Bijoux et parures," 65–70.
79. Motilakṣmī Śākya typologizes jewelry depending on who wears it, following her categories: deities, royals, ordinary (i.e., traditional, higher-caste) people, low-caste people, wrathful deities, animals, Buddhists (given the Buddhist orientation of her book), and contemporary trendy buyers (*Jhigu tisā, kāsā va bhvayghāsā,* 140–141).
80. S. Manandhar, "Bijoux et parures," 67, 71.

81. Lienhard, *Nevārīgītimañjarī,* 84.
82. Siegfried Lienhard, *Maṇicūḍāvadānoddhṛta: A Buddhist Re-Birth Story in the Nevārī Language* (Stockholm: Almqvist and Wiksell, 1963), 17. Lienhard's position that the *Maṇicūḍāvadānoddhṛta* represents a Newar composition at variance with its Sanskrit predecessors has been criticized by de Jong and Hahn: Willem de Jong, "Review of Lienhard *Maṇicūḍāvadānoddhṛta,*" *Indo-Iranian Journal* 9, no. 1 (1965): 75; Michael Hahn, *Candragomins Lokānandanāṭaka* (Wiesbaden: Otto Harrassowitz, 1974; Asiatische Forschungen 39), 15.
83. *Avadānakalpalatā* 3.24 has "He was born with a jewel as an ornament on the crown of the head, spotless like the discrimination carried over from a previous birth. //" (*ajāyatāsya sahajaścūḍālaṃkaraṇaṃ maṇiḥ / prāgjanmāntarasaṃsakto viveka iva nirmalaḥ //*); P. L. Vaidya, ed., *Avadānakalpalatā,* (Darbhanga, Bihar: Mithila Institute, 1959; Sanskrit Texts no. 22). In contrast, *Mahajjātakamālā* 49.97b-98a has "He had on his head's circle (*uṣṇīṣamaṇḍalaṃ*) a blazing great self-emerged jewel. // Its heavenly beams bursting forth, spreading out . . . (*ātmarūḍhamahāratnavyañjtoṣṇīṣamaṇḍalam // tanmaṇe raśmayo divyā niścarantaḥ pasāritāḥ / . . .*); Michael Hahn, ed., *Der große Legendenkranz (Mahajjātakamālā). Eine mittelalterliche buddhistische Legendensammlung aus Nepal* (Wiesbaden: Otto Harrassowitz, 1985).
84. Phyllis Granoff, "Maitreya's Jewelled World: Some Remarks on Gems and Visions in Buddhist Texts," *Journal of Indian Philosophy* 26, no. 4 (1998): 364.
85. Granoff, "Maitreya's Jewelled World," 365.
86. Lienhard, *Maṇicūḍāvadānoddhṛta,* 17. The two main Sanskrit versions are less elaborate and also less jewelry-oriented. *Mahajjātakamālā* 49.62 has: "Then Mahārānī Kāntimatī, bedecked with all ornaments (*sarvālaṅkārabhūṣitā*), ascended the Lion Throne in the assembly," and *Avadānakalpalatā* 3.18 focuses on the *dharmadeśana* aspect of the scene and compares the *mahārānī* to Sarasvatī.
87. For more on the role of this text in Newar Buddhist ritual, see Christoph Emmrich, "How Bisvaṃtara Got His Dharma Body: Story, Ritual and the Domestic in the Composition of a Newar Jātaka," *Journal of the American Oriental Society* 132, no. 4 (2012): 539–566.
88. Siegfried Lienhard, *Die Legende vom Prinzen Viśvantara. Eine nepalesische Bilderrolle aus der Sammlung des Museums für Indische Kunst Berlin* (Berlin: Museum für Indische Kunst Berlin, 1980; Veröffentlichungen des Museums für Indische Kunst Berlin, vol. 5).
89. Lienhard, *Die Legende vom Prinzen Viśvantara,* caption 7, 53.

90. Lienhard, *Die Legende vom Prinzen Viśvantara,* caption 18, 54; caption 20, 54; and caption 24, 55.
91. *thana Bisvantara rājakumārana dāna kālaopiṃ ma dayāo anega ratna thaṅāo hastiratna kisi gayāo jācaka māla bijyāka julo // . . . thana Bisvantara rājakumāraṇa dūta brāṃhmaṇayāta ratna sahitanaṃ hastiratna kisi dāna biyāo coṅa julo //;* Lienhard, *Die Legende vom Prinzen Viśvantara,* captions 25 and 27, 55.
92. *thvayā prabhāvana sunānaṃ thva rājya jitaya yāya ma phu;* Lienhard, *Die Legende vom Prinzen Viśvantara,* 118, fn. 12.
93. As it seems, another way to have jewelry produce the miraculous is to lose it: according to the *sthalapurāṇa* of Sankhu, the *Maṇiśailamahāvadāna,* Vajrayoginī sporting around in the woods of Mt. Maṇicūḍa inadvertently dropped her left serpent earring (*nāgakuṇḍala tisā chatā baym̐ kutu vana*), which upon touching the ground created the Maṇikuṇḍala *tīrtha* (Barṇa Bajra Bajrācārya, *Maṇiśaila Mahāvadāna* (Bhom̐ta: Sāgar Pres, N.S. 1119 [1998 CE] (1st ed. NS 1082 [1961 CE]), 30.
94. Todd T. Lewis and Subarna Man Tuladhar, eds. and trans., *Sugata Saurabha. An Epic Poem from Nepal on the Life of the Buddha by Chittadhar Hṛdaya. Annotated Newari-English Translation and Introduction* (Cambridge, MA: Harvard University Press, 2007).
95. Lewis and Tuladhar, *Sugata Saurabha,* 10–12. The *Lalitavistara,* usually known for its hyperbolic descriptions, merely mentions the one thousand Śākya girls (*śākyakanyāsahasraiḥ*) in the queen's retinue but does not mention any jewelry they might be wearing (P. L. Vaidya, ed., *Lalitavistara* [Darbhanga: Mithila Institute, 1958], 60). The bodhisattva's mother does travel in a jeweled chariot (Vaidya, *Lalitavistara* 7.15, p. 60), and the procession that leads the bodhisattva to his father's home is opulently portrayed in terms of royal material culture. But merely one of the many sets of five thousand girls (*pañca ca kanyāsahasrāṇi*) is said to be "wearing ornaments made auspicious by gems [or pearls]" (*ratnabhadrālaṃkāraparigṛhītāni*) and the twenty thousand heavenly girls (*viṃśati ca devakanyāsahasrāṇi*), mentioned later and duly ignored by the modernist and rationalist Hṛdaya, are said to be "adorned with all kinds of ornaments, wearing strings of gems [or pearls]" (*sarvālaṃkāravibhūṣitāni ratnasūtraparigṛhītāni*) (Vaidya, *Lalitavistara,* 71). Compared with the *Sugata Saurabha*'s stunningly fashion-conscious Newar women, the *Lalitavistara*'s girls appear to be shockingly underdressed.
96. Lewis and Tuladhar, *Sugata Saurabha,* 28–29.

97. The Newar poet Nātibajra Bajrācārya's (1938–2019) last collection of poems, all poems for or about children, is tellingly called *Ji herā. Macākavitā* (My diamond. Children's poems) (Yeṁ: Īlohaṃ Prakāśan, NS 1130 [CE 2010]).
98. Lewis and Tuladhar, *Sugata Saurabha,* 38.
99. Lewis and Tuladhar, *Sugata Saurabha,* 67–68.
100. Lewis and Tuladhar, *Sugata Saurabha,* 96.
101. "After taking off a ring costing several hundred thousands, he proffered it [to her]. . . . She said: 'We will not rid the prince of ornaments'" (*sa tasyai cānekaśatasahasramūlyamaṅgulīyakaṃ nirmucya prādāt // . . . sā āha—na vayaṃ kumāraṃ vyalaṃkariṣyāmaḥ . . .*); (*Lalitavistara,* 100).
102. *lusita nagu theṃ thīgu pacine cvaṃguliṃ / Sugata Saurabha,* p. 114.
103. [. . .] *thīgu so jhuppā va takkā, ratna śirbandī, luṁsvāṃ / jhoticāḥcāy* [read: *moticāḥcāy*; note by author] *cvaṃgu durubaccā va nyāpusikhaḥ sanāḥ nhūgu bhāvaṃ madika kampita jūgu hṛda gati cvana kanāḥ /*; Lewis and Tuladhar, *Sugata Saurabha,* 114.
104. Lewis and Tuladhar, *Sugata Saurabha,* 125, 132, 140.
105. Lewis and Tuladhar, *Sugata Saurabha,* 143.
106. Lewis and Tuladhar, *Sugata Saurabha,* 183.
107. Lewis and Tuladhar, *Sugata Saurabha,* 146, 147.
108. *kāñcana, ratna-vibhūṣaṇa dhākva, / dhāraṇa yāyagu totyagu byākka /*; Lewis and Tuladhar, *Sugata Saurabha,* 166.
109. Lewis and Tuladhar, *Sugata Saurabha,* xlv–lii and lvii–lix.

Chapter 7

Ornaments of This World

Materiality and Poetics of the Fifth Dalai Lama's Reliquary Stūpa

Nancy G. Lin

One of the most sumptuous sights in the Buddhist world is the reliquary stūpa (*mchod rten*) of the Fifth Dalai Lama, Ngawang Lobzang Gyatso (1617–1682), in Lhasa's Potala Palace (plates 1 and 2). Completed late in 1697 and containing his embalmed body, together with other precious things, the stūpa is coated almost entirely with gold and bedecked with jewels and ornamental metalwork. It soars 12.6 meters high and extends 7.65 meters wide at its base in a narrow gallery adjacent to the west side of the main assembly hall in the Red Palace.[1] The mastermind behind the stūpa's construction, the Dalai Lama's regent, Desi Sangyé Gyatso (1653–1705), designed the Red Palace to the scale of its most valuable object: the pinnacle of the stūpa rises to the third story of the Red Palace, while the golden roof of its chapel extends to the Red Palace's full height of four stories.[2] In all its glittering, vertiginous monumentality, the stūpa can scarcely be taken in at once.

Given its imposing appearance, opulent decoration, and staging as the centerpiece of the newly built Red Palace, it comes as no great surprise that Desi Sangyé Gyatso dubbed this stūpa the "Sole Ornament of the World" (*'dzam gling rgyan gcig*). The superlative name asserts that this was an object that could not be duplicated and further implies that the Fifth Dalai Lama himself was unique. Such rhetoric of uniqueness is consistent with the Desi's wide-ranging efforts to cement the religious, political, and cultural dominance of the Fifth Dalai Lama and his Ganden Podrang government throughout the Tibetan-speaking world and to affirm the spiritual authority of the Dalai Lama and his Gelukpa lineage tradition throughout the Buddhist world.[3] Still, the materiality of the stūpa itself—along with its epithet—invites us to consider it specifically in terms of ornament.

This chapter explores the uses and conceptions of ornament in early modern Tibet through a case study of the Fifth Dalai Lama's reliquary stūpa. My work considers how its materiality and poetics work in shared aesthetic, religious, social, and political contexts. What did it take in material terms to make this monumentally luxurious object? What was being accomplished or conveyed by heavily ornamenting the stūpa's surface, placing precious things in its interior, naming it the Sole Ornament of the World, and poetically praising it as such? What theoretical or functional definitions and capacities of ornament are thus articulated or implied by the stūpa and sources around it? How might all this help us think about ornaments, jewels, and the study of material things in Tibetan and Buddhist contexts and beyond? In response to these questions, I trace how the reliquary stūpa substantiated the wealth, power, and networks of the Ganden Podrang government, as well as the aspirations of those connected with it. I then argue that the extravagance of the stūpa's production was deemed inextricable from its transformative capacities as a Buddhist agent that effects outcomes in the world. An ornament, especially one marked as the best of its kind, can be indispensable to, even exceed and radically change, what it adorns.

The modernist rejection of ornament in Europe and America since the early twentieth century has led to its vilification in visual and material culture, the effects of which continue to be felt today. Ornament has been dismissed as superfluous to the function of an object, as mere embellishment. The words "ornamental" and "decorative" have come to be used pejoratively, to signify that something is useless or, at best, lacking in creativity and inferior to fine art. Further still, ornament is often associated with excessive luxury, corruption, and deceit, a fraught assessment that acknowledges the close link between aesthetics and ethics while relegating ornament to a position of disrepute.[4] In a series of fateful lectures beginning in 1909, the Vienna-based architect Adolf Loos argued that advanced societies must reject ornament, for in his view "ornament is no longer a natural product of our culture, but a symptom of backwardness and degeneracy."[5] The ensuing denigration of ornament among modern designers has persisted for more than a century, although it has been mitigated somewhat by a recent resurgence of interest in architecture and other media.[6]

Such historical baggage should give us pause in any attempt to study ornament in Tibetan contexts, given that Tibetan Buddhism and

Tibetan culture have been perceived as backward, degenerate, and corrupt by outsiders, while Tibetan Buddhist art has been pigeonholed as lacking in originality.[7] Yet in recent decades a number of scholars have challenged historically fraught assumptions about ornament in art and architecture, suggesting alternative definitions, capacities, and values, most frequently with respect to Islamic, European, and American art.[8] Among historians of Asian art, Vidya Dehejia has drawn widely from premodern Indian sculptural and poetic representations of the idealized human body to argue that ornament played a consistent set of roles: ornament made the body complete, whole, beautiful, and desirable; furthermore, ornament protected the body through its auspicious qualities.[9] Jonathan Hay has argued that Chinese luxury objects from the Ming-Qing period not only advertised taste, status, and power, but also worked as decorative objects through the pleasures of their sensuous surfaces.[10] Such scholarship endeavors to rehabilitate ornament and decorative art in the wake of more than a century of normative critiques. Much of it also strives to understand ornaments and ornamented objects in the specific historical, geographic, religious, and/or cultural contexts where they were made and used. By examining historical Tibetan and Buddhist ways of applying and valuing ornament (*rgyan*), my work shows how such practices and perspectives challenge our understanding of what an ornament is and what it can do.

In addition to art historical scholarship on ornament, my work is informed by Buddhological scholarship, especially Stephen Teiser's investigation of the semantic range of *zhuangyan* 莊嚴 ("to ornament") in Dunhuang liturgies and other sources, John Kieschnick's observations about splendor and wealth in Chinese and Buddhist material culture, and Phyllis Granoff's study of jewels in Sanskrit and Pali Buddhist texts.[11] Along with other essays in this volume, my study joins a growing body of work on materiality and Buddhist traditions in Asia.[12] In particular, the act of placing precious and semiprecious substances on, inside, or underneath stūpas and pagoda temples—or otherwise in proximity to relics—recurs through Buddhist history. The interpretation of such acts invites intriguing comparisons (see the chapters by Strong, Huang, and Tarocco in this volume).

Unlike most of the objects studied or referred to in prior scholarship in Buddhist and Tibetan studies, the Fifth Dalai Lama's reliquary stūpa was written about extensively by its creator in two textual

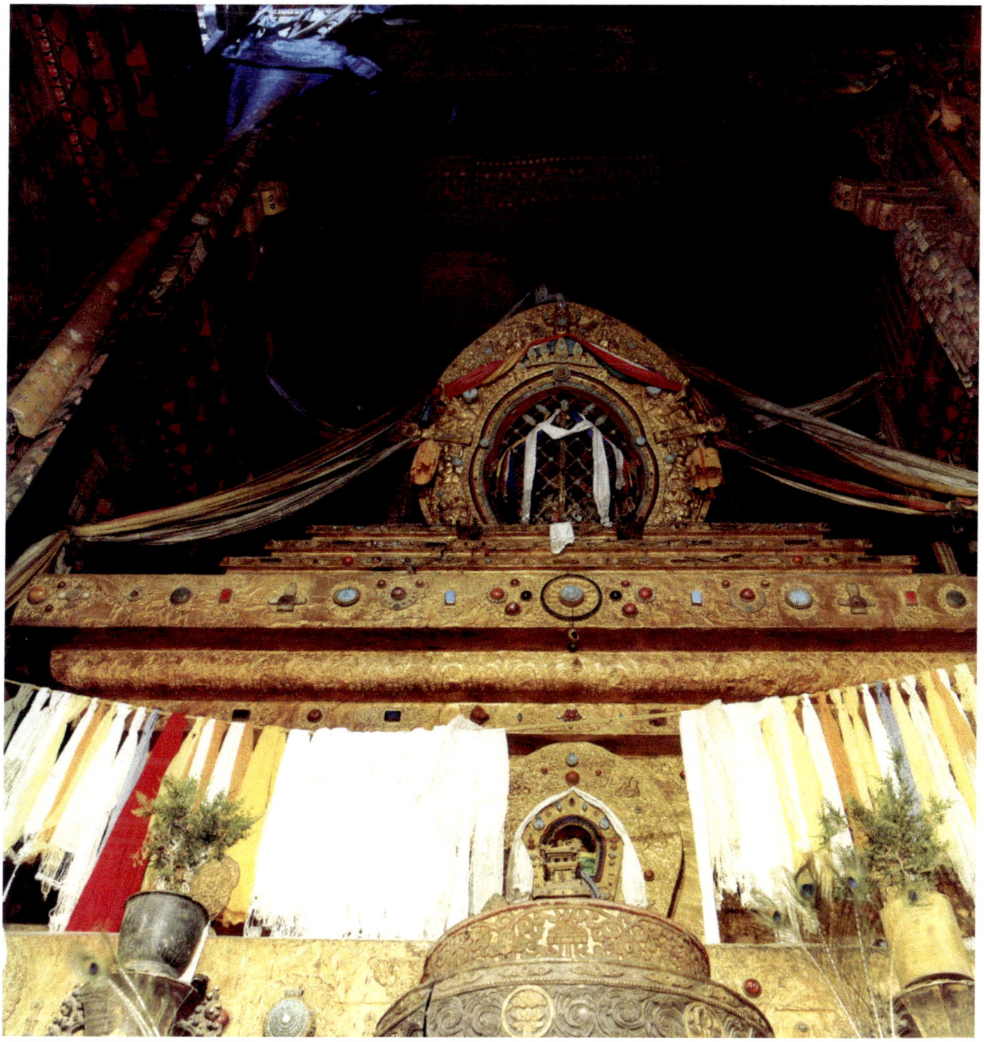

Plate 1. View of the Fifth Dalai Lama's reliquary stūpa from the base. Height, 12.6 meters; width, 7.65 meters. Red Palace of the Potala, Lhasa, Tibet. Completed in 1697. After Liu Lizhong, *Buddhist Art of the Tibetan Plateau* (Hong Kong: Joint Publishing, 1988), 246.

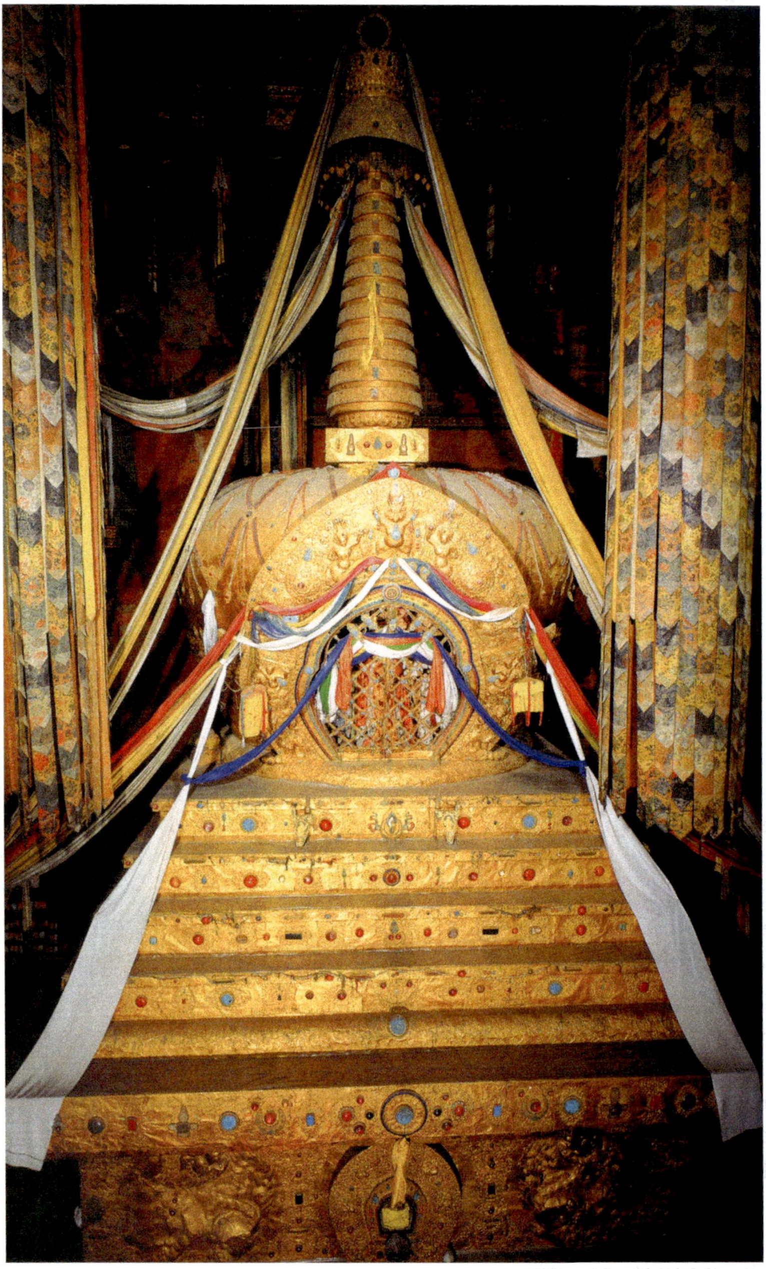

Plate 2. Frontal view of the Fifth Dalai Lama's reliquary stūpa. After Tibetan Administrative Office of the Potala, ed., *The Potala: Holy Palace in the Snow Land* (Beijing: China Travel and Tourism Press, 1996), 100.

sources. One is a two-volume account entitled *Boat for Crossing the Ocean to the Island of Liberation, Treasury of Blessings: Catalog of the Support-Objects and Temple for the Sole Ornament of the World Reliquary,* published in 1697 (hereafter *Catalog*).[13] The other is the three-volume supplement to the Fifth Dalai Lama's autobiography, *Fine Silken Dress*.[14] Elements of both the exterior and interior of the Fifth Dalai Lama's stūpa may have changed since its original construction and consecration. Among other vicissitudes, the Fifth Dalai Lama's stūpa was reportedly looted by Dzungar Mongols late in 1717.[15] Nevertheless, along with other parts of the Potala, it was spared destruction during the Cultural Revolution under Communist rule.[16] The survival of both the stūpa itself and related texts poses an opportunity to learn in detail about the formation of a specific Buddhist object in both its material and its discursive contexts. As I will demonstrate, close analysis of these sources can provoke us to reconsider and add to theories of ornament.

Making the Fifth Dalai Lama's Stūpa

Desi Sangyé Gyatso designed the Fifth Dalai Lama's reliquary according to iconographic and iconometric guidelines he adapted from canonical sources and Tibetan precedents. In particular, the Sole Ornament of the World was modeled after the "great awakening" stūpa (*byang chub chen po'i mchod rten;* cf. Skt. *mahābodhicaitya*), a basic type that features four square, terraced steps below the vase-shaped dome (*bum pa*) (fig. 2). Like other Tibetan Buddhist stūpa types, the "great awakening" stūpa also features other standard components divided into the "lion-throne" base up to and including the cap; the midsection up to and including the square *harmikā;* and the upper section including a lotus support, thirteen tiered wheels, an umbrella with its cover, a moon, a sun, and a pinnacle. The various elements of the stūpa have been ascribed symbolic meanings, and authors have proposed differing sets of iconometric proportions, as previous studies have documented.[17]

What concerns me here, however, are decisions not specifically accounted for by prescriptive literature on stūpas. Nowhere in the Desi's manual on stūpa construction—completed in 1687, three years before the commencement of work on the Red Palace—does he discuss the absolute height of a properly made stūpa. Nor does he mention the use of gilding, precious stones, or decorative motifs

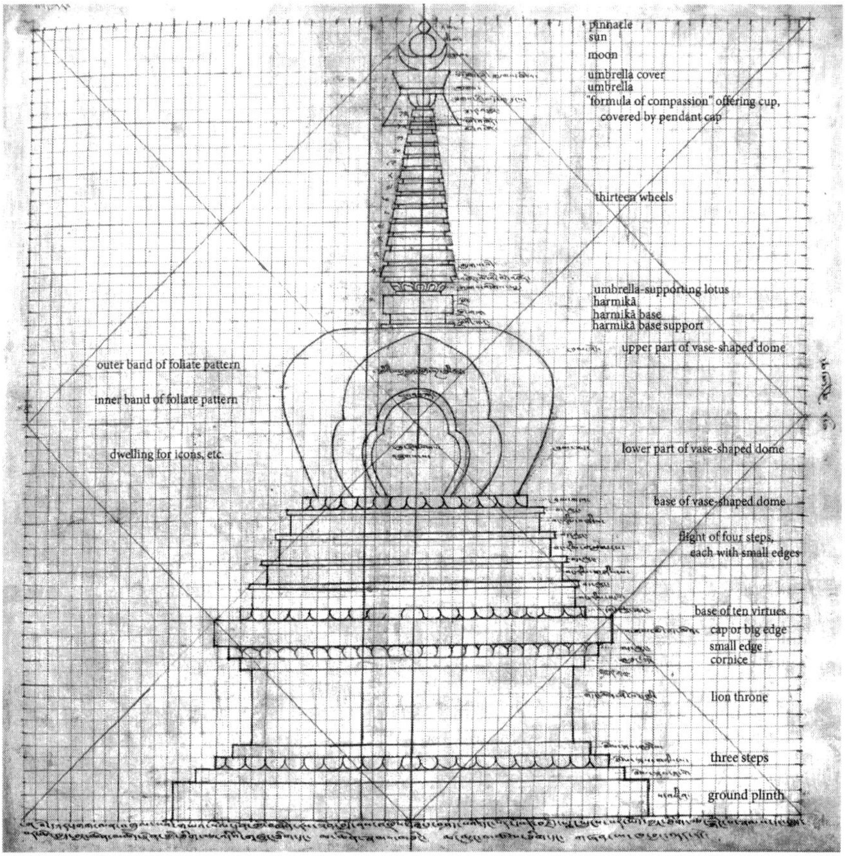

Fig. 2. Drawing of "great awakening" stūpa type according to the proportions advocated by Desi Sangyé Gyatso (English translations and glosses by Nancy G. Lin.) From *Cha tshad kyi dpe ris dpyod ldan yid gsos* (Illustrations of measurements: A refresher for the cognoscenti), fol. 127 recto, ca. 1687; reproduced in Christoph Cüppers, Leonard van der Kuijp, and Ulrich Pagel, eds., *Handbook of Tibetan Iconometry* (Leiden: Brill, 2012), pl. 290.

worked in repoussé in its surface.[18] Yet it is these very adornments, executed at an outsize scale, that make the Fifth Dalai Lama's stūpa a visually singular object. This has been apparent even to casual foreign observers. Visiting in 1904, L. Austine Waddell—who was underwhelmed by the city of Lhasa, the Jokhang, and much of the Potala's interior and who dismissed Tibetan Buddhism as primitive and corrupt "Lamaism"—dwelled on the impressive presence of the Fifth Dalai Lama's stūpa in *Lhasa and Its Mysteries,* his account of the British invasion of Tibet led by Colonel Younghusband (fig. 3).[19] "The base of the great relic shrine," he wrote, "is richly adorned with gold and inlaid with precious stones, and the steps of its plinths are used as altars for the countless votive-offerings of princes for ages, and wreaths of pearls and other jewelled necklaces hang from its upper structure, which can be seen towering up some 40 feet overhead." Navigating the stairs and corridors upstairs, Waddell praised the stūpa's "gorgeously jewelled top" and remarked on its "colossal dimensions" in comparison to the reliquary stūpas of subsequent Dalai Lamas, affirming that among all the Dalai Lamas, the Fifth "still dominates the whole in death."[20] The stūpa achieves its awe-inducing effect through the extravagantly proportioned application of ornament.

The staggering array of resources and networks across Asia that were marshalled to create this object emerges in dizzying detail in the Desi's *Catalog* of the reliquary stūpa. As was immediately obvious to Waddell and other visitors, conspicuous wealth was poured into raw materials and skilled labor in order to produce the Sole Ornament of the World and the structure built to house it. To gild the stūpa's wooden armature 119,082 *srang* of gold were reportedly used (perhaps something in the range of 4,440 kilograms).[21] Thousands of precious and semiprecious stones were attached to its surface. Some fifteen hundred artisans were employed from Tibet, Nepal, India, Kashmir, China, and areas north of Tibet to complete the stūpa and its chapel: woodworkers, stone masons, painters, goldsmiths, and more.[22] The cost of construction, calculated in terms of loads of grain, was more than 30.5 million bushels (*khal*), while the cost of ritual performances and processions was the equivalent of more than 8.8 million bushels.[23] For comparison, Kurtis Schaeffer has researched the cost of printing the eighteenth-century Degé Tengyur (the second and longer of two divisions of the Tibetan Buddhist canon), which totaled a little more than 443,000 bushels of barley for labor and materials. As Schaeffer has pointed out, this amount could have financed Dakpo Shedrub Ling, a large monastery of about eight hundred monks in Central Tibet, for fifty years based on figures from the first half of the twentieth century.[24] By this measure, the cost of producing the Fifth Dalai Lama's stūpa could have financed eighty-eight such monasteries for fifty years.

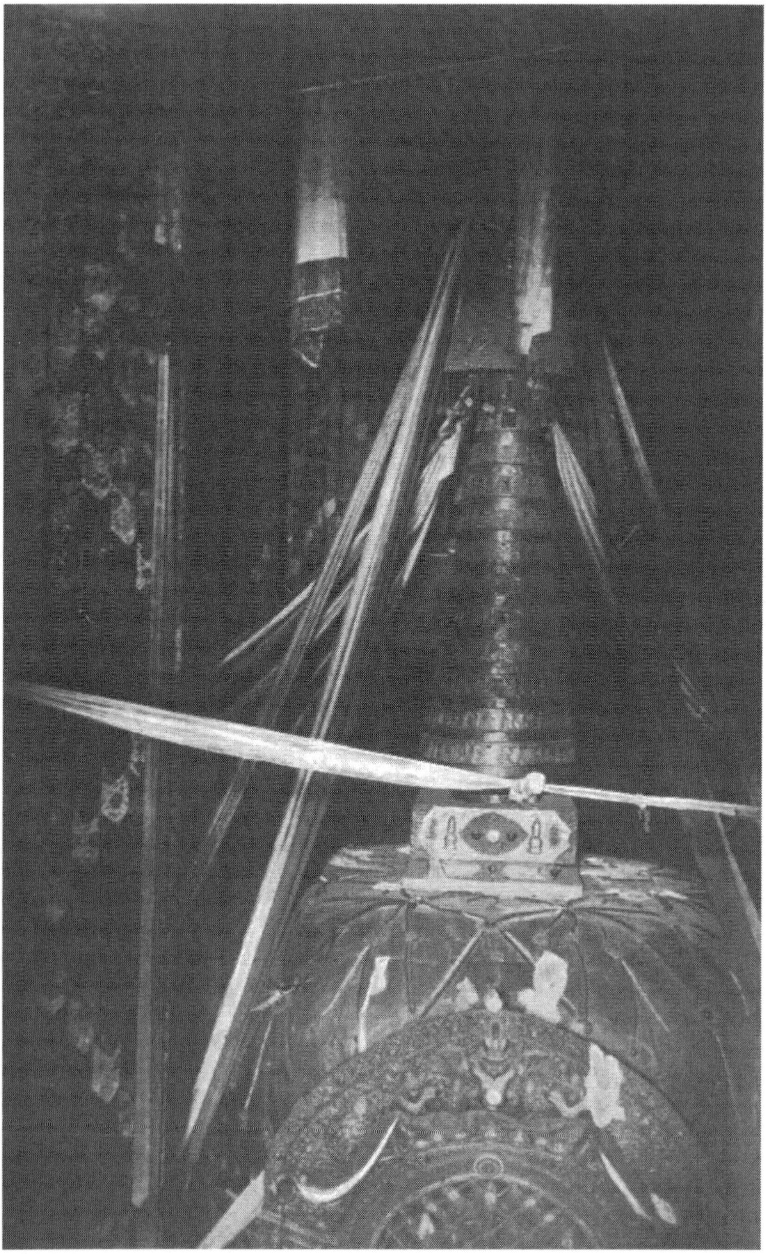

Fig. 3. View of the Fifth Dalai Lama's reliquary stūpa from the upper gallery, 1904. After Waddell, *Lhasa and Its Mysteries* (New York: E. P. Dutton, 1905), 396.

The material resources needed to complete this grand reliquary did not come from the Desi and the coffers of the Ganden Podrang alone. Thousands of people are acknowledged for their offerings in the *Catalog,* named either individually or corporately by monastic assembly, family, or locale. Gold and silver are recorded as the most common forms of offering; donated metals also included brass, zinc, iron, and bronze. Among the gems given were amber, carnelian, coral, crystals of various kinds, lapis lazuli, pearls, rubies, and turquoise. Other valuable donated items included silk, satin, wool, saffron, vermilion, and matchlocks. Some kinds of gifts may have been traded or used to compensate laborers, including yaks and hybrid yaks (*mdzo*), horses and their harnesses, mules, sheep, tea, and butter. Icons, relics, and ritual objects were more rarely given, such as a spontaneously appeared Avalokiteśvara image from the house of Rinpung, the brain relics of the arhat from the Nenying Zhabdrung, golden images of the Buddha and Tsongkhapa, a golden stūpa, a silver maṇḍala, a silver skull cup, a conch turning to the right, and musical instruments. The donors hailed from all over the Tibetan polity as well as from Ladakh, Sikkim, Chinese border areas such as Dartsedo (Kangding 康定), Mongolia, and the Qing court. They included reincarnating lamas (*sprul sku*) and the Lamo Oracle, monks and nuns, spirit mediums and an itinerant reciter (*ma ṇi ba*), aristocrats and government officials, servants and retainers, painters and goldsmiths, doctors and anonymous villagers. Each individual's or group's offerings ranged from precious items valued at more than one thousand *srang* to no more than one *zho* of silver, equivalent to one-tenth of a *srang.*[25]

Those who specifically gave bodily ornaments also varied in religious and social status. To illustrate with a cross section of examples within Tibetan society, these donors included the Desi's mother, Magen Butri Gyelmo, who gave her forehead turquoises, crown turquoise, and amber, worth 602 *srang* and 5 *zho*. From Gyaltsen Tönpo, the estate of the Paṇchen at Trashilhünpo, came pearl mālā(s), gold, and silver worth 2,593 *srang* and 3 *zho*. The monastery committee of Pendé Lekshéling Dratshang—the personal monastery of the Dalai Lamas—principally gave forehead turquoise(s), as well as gold worth 1,220 *srang* and 5 *zho*. The noble lady of Zurkhang Sharpa principally gave her forehead turquoise; the value of her gifts totaled 225 *srang* and 5 *zho*. Gyitang Norbu gave "lotus petal" earrings in the archaic style, a crown turquoise, and other items valued at 142 *srang,* 9 *zho,* and 5 *skar.* A group of five servants of Püntsok Changlochenpa gave one or more earrings, worth 30 *srang* and 8 *zho*. The painter Genyen gave his crown turquoise and amber, valued at 24 *srang* and 6 *zho,* while the painter Ragkha Sönam gave his crown turquoise and gold valued at 3 *srang* and 5 *zho.* Women and men not marked as aristocratic also gave personal jewelry, such as Tseten Pelmo, Chokden, and Sönam Gölha of Lhasa.[26]

According to the *Catalog,* many of these bodily ornaments were affixed to the surface of the Fifth Dalai Lama's stūpa itself. For example, two forehead turquoises and one crown turquoise from the Desi's mother were set into the fourth (uppermost) step on the flight of four terrace steps (see fig. 2), along with a large amber that had been in her possession. A *gajamukta* "pearl," said to come from inside an elephant's head, that had adorned the Desi's hat was set into the third of the four terrace steps. An earring offered by the five servants of Püntsok Changlochenpa was placed on the bulbous upper part of the vase-shaped dome, along with a mālā made of black *vajranāga* clay from the emperor of China. The Fifth Dalai Lama's ornaments were placed on the stūpa as well, including a rare *gajamukta* set into the fourth terrace step and several bodily ornaments placed around the icon niche.[27] As John Strong suggests in this volume, following the work of Wannaporn Rienjang, gems could stand in for their owners among Buddhist donors of northwest India and Gandhāra. While practices of donating personal jewelry in early modern Tibet await further investigation, this raises the interesting possibility that donors' personal ornaments simultaneously adorned the Fifth Dalai Lama's reliquary stūpa and enabled their "extended bodies" to be placed in proximity with the corporeal remains and other relics of the deceased master, in a manner analogous to the practice of burial *ad sanctos.*[28] Certainly Tibetans have treated gift offerings to lamas and deities as a means for the giver to cultivate karmic connections (*rten 'brel;* cf. Skt. *pratītyasamutpāda*) with the recipient, thereby extending the cycle of affective bonds, merit, and compassion.[29] This principle resonates with Christoph Emmrich's contemporary observation in this volume that people cultivate relationships with Newar deity images by donating personal or familial jewelry to them. Beyond the karmic merit (*bsod nams;* Skt. *puṇya*) accrued by donating their jewelry for the stūpa, donors established or continued their particular relationships with the Dalai Lama into future lifetimes.

The Sole Ornament of the World is thus a material substantiation of the wealth and cosmopolitanism of the Fifth Dalai Lama and his court, along with their religious followers, polity, and allies. The prosperity of this period was due in no small part to Gushri Khan's military unification of Tibetan territories and the political stability maintained by the Ganden Podrang, which enabled trade to flourish with Lhasa as a key node on major trade routes.[30] The bulk of tax revenue was redistributed to monasteries—mostly in the Gelukpa order to which the Dalai Lama belonged—to sustain their monks, to offer religious services, and to found new monasteries.[31] Yet the Desi's record of donations from laypeople as well as lamas and monks of non-Gelukpa lineage traditions attests to the surplus of wealth that could be directed to a single monument.

The stūpa is also a culmination of the extensive networks of relationships and resources required to make such a singularly magnificent object. These would have included artisans and donors from various regions and socioeconomic levels; gold dust from rivers and mines across Tibet; turquoise from Persia; coral from Mediterranean shores; amber from Kashmir, China, and Burma; and other precious stones and beads from India and elsewhere. In addition to activating social obligation and political cooperation, these networks supported spiritual aspirations and invested the reliquary stūpa itself with authority. The Sole Ornament of the World has served as a site for donors and visitors to accumulate merit, as well as to cultivate personal karmic connections with the Dalai Lama. In turn, the corporeal relic of the Fifth Dalai Lama—his embalmed body—is framed, or better yet *adorned,* by the myriad gems, motifs in precious metals, and pieces of jewelry that form the exterior surfaces of the stūpa.[32] Collectively this ornamentation affirms, a hundred thousand times over, that in all the world here is an object of maximal significance: worthy of utmost devotion and immensely powerful.

Given the multitude of people and resources involved, it is astonishing that the Desi kept the Fifth Dalai Lama's death a secret from all but a tight inner circle at the Potala. The Fifth Dalai Lama in fact had passed away in 1682, but the Desi did not publicly disclose this information until 1697, when he dramatically unveiled the stūpa and publicly introduced the young Sixth Dalai Lama. Up until that year, the construction of the stūpa was presented as a means to secure the Dalai Lama's long life and the welfare of Tibet.[33]

In the meantime, the interior of the stūpa was also being prepared. The Desi records that on April 30, 1693, both Dharma treasures (*chos gter*) and wealth treasures (*nor gter*) were placed in the base of the reliquary, invoking a binary classification of religious treasures (*gter ma*) that came into use in Tibet by the twelfth century.[34] The textual "Dharma treasures" included canonical tantras, literature from the five subjects of

Gelukpa curriculum (Abhidharma, Prajñāpāramitā, Madhyamaka, pramāṇa, and Vinaya), the *Perfection of Wisdom in 8,000 Lines* and the *Bhadrakalpikasūtra,* collections of *dhāraṇī* texts, the seventeen Nyingma tantras, and the *Five Chronicles* of the fourteenth-century treasure revealer Orgyen Lingpa. The "wealth treasures" listed included "precious substances of many kinds such as beryl, sapphire, ruby, chrysoberyl, rose quartz, *nal* spinel, diamond, turquoise, coral, lapis, pearl, patterned *gzi* stone, amber, rhinoceros horns, elephant tusk, sheep's suet jade, carnelian, *mchong* chalcedony, crystal, seven *zho* of gold granules, four *srang* of silver, and white silver," along with other items such as textiles; tea, fruit, grain, and other foods; botanical medicines; musical instruments; a vajra and bell; bowls and plates; basins and cauldrons; armor and weaponry; and a spotted antelope hide.[35] The collection of luxury items may be compared to those found in or beneath other stūpas and pagoda temples (see Strong and Tarocco in this volume). "Heaping up all the articles that could be wished for, with nothing lacking," the Desi sums up, "these profound and fine treasures were concealed."[36]

Outside and in, the Fifth Dalai Lama's reliquary stūpa was lavishly outfitted with precious metals, stones, and other rarities. Buddhist predilections for "donated magnificence" were already evident in the early centuries of the Common Era, as Andy Rotman has observed in this volume, following the work of James Heitzman. Yet the Sole Ornament of the World exemplifies not only the conspicuous generosity of donors, but also the broader courtly aesthetic of the Fifth Dalai Lama's Ganden Podrang. This aesthetic was captured in the phrase *srid zhi'i phun tshogs,* "existence and peace replete," or alternatively "all the marvels of saṃsāra and nirvāṇa," the name the Desi gave to the Red Palace assembly hall adjacent to the stūpa gallery. It celebrated radical ornateness and luxurious abundance that, as I have suggested elsewhere, also entailed bodhisattvic generosity culminating in the ultimate fruits of liberation.[37] For the Fifth Dalai Lama's court, such marvelous plenitude therefore constituted not only an aesthetic, but also an ethos that was fundamental to their broader project of religious governance, the "integration of Dharma with worldly existence" (*chos srid zung 'brel*).[38] In the next section I explore how this aesthetic and ethos of marvelous plenitude is articulated by considering the Desi's rhetoric about the stūpa as ornament in concert with the material qualities of the stūpa itself.

Theorizing Ornaments of the World

Perhaps the most-cited definition of *rgyan,* "ornament," in Tibetan sources is translated from Daṇḍin's late seventh- or early eighth-century Sanskrit treatise on poetics: "The factors that make poetry beautiful are called ornaments."[39] In common usage, *rgyan* refers to ornaments that adorn bodies, built structures, and so forth, often appearing in the phrase "beautiful ornament(s)" (*mdzes pa'i rgyan*). At first glance, such definitions and usages might appear to accord with the common English-language concept of ornament as embellishment, as a beautifying feature that is not necessary or inherent to the object or work of literature. However, this may or may not correspond to how "ornament" was understood in the context of the reliquary stūpa's epithet, the Sole Ornament of the World. To find more specific and relevant clues for theorizing ornament with respect to the Fifth Dalai Lama's stūpa, I investigate textual references to the stūpa itself and uses of relational phrases like "ornament of the world" in Tibet and South Asia.

Desi Sangyé Gyatso offered his own commentary on the name of the stūpa in a poem appearing in his supplement to the Fifth Dalai Lama's autobiography, *Fine Silken Dress* (hereafter *Supplement*). Written in the heavily figural style of courtly Tibetan poetics (*snyan ngag;* cf. Skt. *kāvya*), the poem opens as follows:

> Aho! Chief to emerge from the ocean of merit of beings
> is this golden reliquary stūpa, treasury of a hundred thousand plays
> of light,
> sole ornament beautifying vast Jambudvīpa,
> rising in the pure and clear sky![40]

For anyone who might not recognize either the allusion or the poetic figure employed, an annotation to the verse in the woodblock edition helpfully states that it is "sweetened by the taste of undivided action in a conjoined metaphor (*ldan pa'i gzugs can;* Skt. *yuktarūpaka*) that puns on an old legend in which the sun emerges from the ocean of milk."[41] This refers to the Indic myth in which the gods and demigods churn the ocean to extract the nectar of immortality (*bdud rtsi;* Skt. *amṛta*), using a colossal mountain that is named Mandara in the Purāṇas and often conflated with Meru in Buddhist sources.[42] While many precious items emerge from the ocean of that myth, the Desi takes poetic license to claim that the sun is paramount. And so, just as the sun has emerged from the ocean of milk, the Fifth Dalai Lama's stūpa has emerged from the metaphorical ocean that is the merit of sentient beings; both rise high into "the pure and clear sky."[43] As such, the sun and this stūpa are simultaneously praised as the "sole ornament beautifying vast Jambudvīpa," Jambudvīpa being the name for the continent on which humans live—that is, the world we inhabit.

Commonplace notions of ornament as superfluous embellishment are clearly inadequate in this case, for surely the sun is indispensable to our world, or at least to the sentient beings and plants in it. Nor would it be an exaggeration to observe that the Ganden Podrang repeatedly presented the Fifth Dalai Lama as indispensable to the Tibetan people and to this world at large, through his identification with the bodhisattva Avalokiteśvara, the construction of his rebirth lineage, and other strategies.[44] As implied by the Desi's verse, the Fifth Dalai Lama's reliquary stūpa is likewise indispensable. But even recent scholarly definitions of ornament may not serve us particularly well here since they mostly deem ornament as a subset of decorative art, as motifs or "imagescapes" that induce pleasure through visual messages.[45] Ornament, as James Trilling succinctly proposes, "is the art we add to art: shapes and patterns worked into an object or building for the pleasure of outline, color, or fantasy."[46] According to such views, the stūpa's surface is ornamented, but the stūpa itself would not qualify as an ornament. The Desi's poetry claims otherwise, at least in using the Tibetan word *rgyan,* which I have translated as "ornament." The remainder of this chapter works to unpack the implications of taking the Fifth Dalai Lama's entire stūpa as ornament.

Earlier and contemporaneous references provide literary, religious, and historical context for interpreting the phrase "sole ornament beautifying Jambudvīpa," which itself glosses the name of the reliquary stūpa. The Desi was hardly the first poet to use this kind of phrasing. Indeed, Sanskrit variations on the epithet "ornament of the world" were often used to praise members of royal families in South Asia. For example, in stone inscriptions at Khajuraho, King Yaśovarman is called "the ornament of royal families" (*nṛpakulatilaka*), while his mother, Queen Kañcukā, is called the "sole ornament of the world" (*bhuvanaikabhūṣaṇa*) as well as a "jewel among women" (*strīratna*).[47] Such references should be understood in the context of medieval Indian courtly culture in which, as Daud Ali has shown, decorating the human body and its surroundings was a key practice and gems were thought to enhance virtues like beauty, strength, goodness, and wisdom.[48] The thirteenth-century epic poem *Līlāvatīsāra* is another rich source for this kind of phrasing: kings are an "ornament of the world" (*mahītilaka*), an "ornament of the earth" (*kṣititilaka*), and an "ornament of the solar dynasty" (*ikṣvākukulabhūṣaṇa*). A royal palace is a "three-storied ornament for the world" (*tribhūmam bhūmimaṇḍanam*); one capital city is a "forehead ornament for the country of Lāṭa" (*lāṭalalāṭatilaka*); another is the "chief ornament of Jewel Island" (*ratnadvīpālaṃkārasāra*).[49] Contemporaneous with the Fifth Dalai Lama, in a 1655 stone inscription Jayapratāpamalla, king of Nepal, called himself "ornament of the Solar dynasty" (*ravikulatilaka*).[50]

By invoking this metaphor, the Desi was demonstrating the participation of the Ganden Podrang court in what Sheldon Pollock has termed the "Sanskrit cosmopolis," which extended across much of South and Southeast Asia for well over a millennium. The involvement of the court was material and interpersonal as well as literary: paṇḍitas from Varanasi, Allahabad, and Mathura were invited or welcomed to the court and well recompensed with gold and other gifts. After studying Sanskrit grammar with Balabhadra and Gokula, Darpa Lotsāwa Ngawang Püntsok made use of his knowledge on a number of publication projects at the behest of the Fifth Dalai Lama, including translations of Sanskrit grammatical texts, a new Tibetan commentary on Kṣemendra's *kāvya* work *Avadānakalpalatā* (*Rtogs brjod dpag bsam 'khri shing*), and a compilation of the Tibetan Buddhist canon (the Kangyur and Tengyur), which incorporated new translations made by him.[51]

Given their familiarity with Sanskrit literary culture, we might expect that the Ganden Podrang court would apply its superlative epithets to Tibetan objects or people. Indeed among the Fifth Dalai Lama's collected writings, we find that the Potala Palace is called the "sole ornament of the well-formed earth" (*legs bskrun 'dzin ma'i rgyan gcig pho brang che*); the Lhasa Jokhang is called the "sole ornament of Jambudvīpa" (*'dzam bu gling gi rgyan gcig lha ldan sprul pa'i gtsug lag khang*); and the Jowo image is given the same epithet (*'dzam gling rgyan gcig shākya mu ne'i sku*).[52] Thus a correspondence is implied between a principal object—the Fifth Dalai Lama's reliquary stūpa or the Jowo—and the structure that houses it—the Potala or the Jokhang. In his supplement to *Fine Silken Dress,* Desi Sangyé Gyatso called the Fifth Dalai Lama himself "the grand crown ornament of saṃsāra and nirvāṇa, the sole ornament of all that is Dharmic and worldly in Jambudvīpa" (*srid zhi'i gtsug rgyan chen po 'dzam gling chos srid kun gyi rgyan gcig*).[53] Such phrasing suggests that the reliquary stūpa is an extension of the

Fifth Dalai Lama, in terms of both his bodily person and the singular status of his life accomplishments.

The phrase "sole ornament of the world" and similar expressions were applied to yet more objects in Tibet before and during the time of the Fifth Dalai Lama. The Fifth Dalai Lama's collected works contain further references: Drepung Monastery is called "the sole ornament of the snowy earth" (*gangs can 'dzin ma'i rgyan gcig*), using a common name for Tibet. The fortress of Neudong, headquarters of the Pakmodrupa dynasty (1349–1435), is referred to several times as "the palace that is the sole ornament of the world" (*'dzam gling rgyan gcig pho brang sne'u sdong rtse, pho brang 'dzam gling rgyan gcig sne'u sdong rtse*), suggesting that this may have been an epithet established during its rule.[54] Beyond the Fifth Dalai Lama's works, the Second Karmapa, Karma Pakshi (1204–1283), made a monumental cast-bronze image of the buddha Śākyamuni named "Ornament of the World" (*'dzam bu gling gi rgyan*) for Tsurpu Monastery, with a reported height of about twenty meters.[55] His successor, the Third Karmapa, Rangjung Dorjé (1284–1339), included this dedicatory statement in his anthology of birth stories of the Buddha, later painted on the walls of the circumambulatory at Zhalu Monastery: "May the world be ornamented with gloriously blazing auspiciousness (*bkra shis dpal 'bar 'dzam gling rgyan du shog*)!"[56] The great encampment of the Karmapas was known as "Ornament of the World" (*'dzam gling rgyan*).[57]

From these examples, we can see that while epithets like "sole ornament of the world" could be applied to multiple people or objects, at least until the late seventeenth century it was generally reserved for what stood at the apex of political and/or spiritual power. In this usage "ornament" may have effectively shared one of the definitions of "jewel" as glossed by the *Amarakośa* lexicon: "what is best in its class."[58] As Maria Heim points out in this volume, the Jewel Sutta (*Ratana Sutta*) expresses a similar sentiment, asserting that "there is only an excellent jewel in the sense of the Buddha," and likewise for the Dhamma and the Saṅgha, respectively. Seventeenth-century Tibetan usage was informed and inflected by earlier Buddhist sources such as the *Uttaratantra* (*Ratnagotravibhāga*) verse on why the Buddha, Dharma, and Saṃgha are called jewels:

> They are jewels because their appearance is difficult to encounter,
> Because they are stainless, because they are powerful,
> Because they are the ornaments of the world,
> Because they are supreme, and because they are changeless.[59]

The prose commentary further states that like jewels, "they are the ornaments of the world because they are the causes of the splendid intentions of all beings."[60] The word for "splendid" in Sanskrit here is *śobha,* which also means "brilliant," "lustrous," or "beautiful" and is broadly associated with virtue. Tellingly, the Tibetan translation is *dge ba,* which primarily means "virtuous" or "good." Since "morality is never far away from beauty or pleasure," as Oleg Grabar observed, "esthetics and ethics are . . . automatically the issues of ornament."[61] According to the Buddhist standards articulated here, beautiful intentions are those that are virtuous, and virtuous intentions are themselves beautiful.

Desi Sangye Gyatso's next verse praising the Fifth Dalai Lama's stūpa resonates with this characterization:

> Dwelling inseparably from the *jñānasattva,*
> it conquers the *kleśas* of discordant conflict and disease
> with the sound of the right-turning conch of *dhāraṇīs* inserted for
> excellent consecration,
> ushering in festivities of a new Perfected Age.[62]

Like the Three Jewels, the Sole Ornament of the World is presented as a powerful, supreme, and changeless entity that brings about virtue. While it takes particular material form, the stūpa is inseparable from the "gnosis being" (*ye shes sems dpa';* Skt. *jñānasattva*), a tantric term designating the true liberated form of a deity. In his *Catalog,* the Desi reinforces this characterization by calling the stūpa "unprecedented" (*snga na med pa*), as well as "an illusory display (*sprul*) made from the visionary intuition of the noble lotus-bearing one"—that is, the Fifth Dalai Lama as an emanation of the bodhisattva Avalokiteśvara.[63] The living physical body of the Dalai Lama and the stūpa are implicated to be of the same kind: illusory displays emanated by a liberated being for the benefit of Tibet and the world at large. Even after the Fifth Dalai Lama's passing, the stūpa remains to conquer *kleśas*, karmic impurities that incite unwholesome thoughts and actions—and, therefore, bad karmic outcomes. With the collective virtue that ensues, the stūpa is promised to lead sentient beings into a new age of harmony, prosperity, and goodness.

Based on this brief survey, to say that an ornament of the world—whether the Three Jewels, the Fifth Dalai Lama's stūpa, or others—enhances that which it ornaments would seem to be an understatement at best. Rather, for Desi Sangyé Gyatso and other Buddhist authors, an ornament of the world is the best of all possible things, something that can and does effect radical transformation of that which it adorns: the world with its beings. This understanding overlaps with Pali commentarial interpretations of the Three Jewels "in their ability to bring about beneficial results," although in Pali sources the emphasis is on producing delight in devotees based on recognition of their worth rather than on transforming the entire world.[64] Further, unlike Buddhaghosa (see Heim's chapter in this volume), the Desi is interested in the material qualities of the jewels that ornament the stūpa itself, as their extensive documentation in the *Catalog* indicates.

More specifically, the Desi's writings further suggest that the stūpa's radical capacities are necessarily accomplished through its material qualities. Here I would like to return to the Desi's first verse in the *Supplement,* comparing the stūpa to the sun. As productive a metaphor as this turned out to be in literary terms, more can be said about its material significance. For in the Desi's poetic language, it is the sun that most resembles the Fifth Dalai Lama's stūpa: each is a "treasury of a hundred thousand plays of light," where the Tibetan word for "light" (*snang ba;* cf. Skt. *avabhāsa, āloka*) could equally denote sunbeams or the dazzling plays of light cast by the glittering, intricately textured surface of the stūpa, with its gilt repoussé work and its jewels of alternating colors. Beyond its hue, the physical properties of gold—its malleability, ductility, and inability to tarnish—lend themselves to the laborious creation of such effects and, like the sun itself, to their imperishability.[65] Gold's potential to be worked to such splendor was taken seriously by the Desi. Elsewhere in the *Catalog,* he claims that for key parts of the Red Palace such as the grand assembly hall, "Tibetan gilding alone is so extremely sumptuous that it can overpower even the radiance of the sun."[66] His boast is made explicitly in comparison with Chinese gilding. We must take this to mean the quality of gilding that Tibetans could commission, for the goldsmiths employed by the construction of the Red Palace were mostly Newars from the Kathmandu Valley. (On contemporary Newar goldsmiths see the chapter by Emmrich in this volume.) Nevertheless, this flash of competitive spirit confirms that the visual appearance of the stūpa and its housing mattered a great deal: it had to be made using preeminent materials and techniques, or at least remembered as such.[67]

Snang ba can also refer to phenomenal appearances, echoing the Desi's claim that the stūpa is an "illusory display made from the visionary intuition" of Avalokiteśvara. Such language evokes jeweled, paradisiacal heavens and buddha-fields; and indeed, the *Catalog* compares the Red Palace to the bodhisattva Maitreya's palace in Tuṣita Heaven.[68] As

Phyllis Granoff has demonstrated, Maitreya's marvelously jeweled palace in the *Gaṇḍavyūha*—and the succession of jeweled palaces that the seeker Sudhana encounters before it—give rise to clear visions through plays of light and reflection, facilitating liberative insight into the very nature of things. Crucially, jewels (including gold) are "active creative agents" in this process: they "appear in response to meritorious deeds" and "have the power to create a visionary world."[69] The Sole Ornament of the World may be read as a bid to actualize some of the miraculous experience and effects of encountering a bodhisattva in his fabulously ornamented home.

After all, the Fifth Dalai Lama's stūpa was built as the crowning glory of the Potala, itself named after Avalokiteśvara's mountain abode. The Desi may well have strived to imitate the monumental opulence of Avalokiteśvara's palace, if not the particulars of its design. He cites this detailed description in the *Supplement:*

> The palace at the top of Mount Potala is filled with precious substances from all parts such as gold, silver, pearls, beryls, conches, crystals, corals, emeralds, and furthermore, with various kinds of flowers. . . . [It has] four steps, three leagues in height and five leagues wide. The first side is made of precious crystals; the second side is made of silver; the third side is made of rubies; and the fourth side is made of sapphires. The four corners are made of precious emeralds. . . . The first parapet is made of gold, the second parapet is made of silver, the third parapet is made of turquoise. They are adorned with nets and tassels of pearls. . . . In the middle of that house, a lion throne with lovely and colorful sun, moon, and lotus cushions has been arranged. Many gods, nāgas, yakṣas, gandharvas, asuras, garuḍas, kinnaras, mahoragas, humans, spirits, and so forth will gather there. And they will stay there joyfully honoring you, Avalokiteśvara, O child of enlightened heritage.[70]

Such descriptions of Avalokiteśvara's palace on the mythical Mount Potala(ka) resonate with the luxurious materials used in the exterior and interior of the Fifth Dalai Lama's stūpa, as well as its awe-inducing scale. In practice, any attempts in this world to imitate a paradisiacal abode must inevitably fall short. Yet this hardly deterred Desi Sangyé Gyatso, or the Fifth Dalai Lama's court before him, from imagining and enacting the aesthetics of luxurious plenitude on a grand scale. And among the many ambitious projects of the Ganden Podrang, the Sole

Ornament of the World may have come closest to heaping up all the marvels of saṃsāra and nirvāṇa.

In turn, the splendor of the stūpa's assemblage empowers it to act efficaciously for the general welfare. Celebrating in verse the Dharma and wealth treasures that had been placed in the base of the stūpa, the Desi wrote:

> The kin of the golden mountain manifests what is immaterial into
> concrete things.
> Beneath his reliquary whose crest touches the sky,
> the excellent Dharma beginning with the Words and treatises of sūtras
> and tantras,
> examples of fine, fine jewels, silks, and fruits
> of gods, humans, nāgas, and gandharvas,
> vast, vast Jambudvīpa's extraordinary kinds of wealth,
> many, many rich treasures to be enjoyed as requisites
> were concealed so that virtue may abide in this good, good world.[71]

Although the textual works placed in the stūpa are duly acknowledged, the praise heaped on the wealth treasures, further heightened through repetition, is telling. Precious substances have been gathered from all over this vast world and compressed into the stūpa. Their splendor brings about virtue (*dge ba*) in the inhabitants of this world, which the Desi auspiciously declares to be good. All this was made possible by the prosperity and peace ushered in by the reign of the Fifth Dalai Lama himself. To fulfill its promise as the sole ornament of this world, the stūpa is filled with the finest and most beautiful things that this world can offer. In turn, it effects the virtue that is necessary for both worldly ease and spiritual liberation. In this regard the Sole Ornament of the World resembles the fabulous wish-fulfilling gem (*cintāmaṇi*) of Buddhist lore: it is uniquely precious in its material composition, and it bestows both material and soteriological benefits.[72]

The Fifth Dalai Lama's reliquary stūpa both celebrates the generous use of ornament and endures as testament to what an ornament can be and what it can do. Virtuous in itself, an ornament (*rgyan*) can be the best of all possible things. Ornament can exceed that which it adorns, even as it beautifies and transforms it; the world needs this best of ornaments, but this ornament does not need the world. As an object that required adornment, the reliquary stūpa spurred the mass mobilization and materialization of wealth and cosmopolitanism, devotion and obligation, in nearly infinite variety and with striking inclusiveness. As the impetus for building the Red Palace, the Sole Ornament of the World effected the making of a magnificently arrayed space, a worldly counterpart of a cosmic bodhisattva's abode. As ornament, it promises to transform this world into a perfected one, free of discord and disease, virtuous and ultimately liberated—the most radical beautification possible. So articulated by the Desi, ornament has the capacity to bring out the full potential of that which it adorns. Crucially, its material and aesthetic value are inextricable from its capacity as a transformative agent in the world. The splendor of the object is key to its efficacy.[73]

In my analysis, the Sole Ornament of the World does away with the hierarchy and dependency assumed between the object and its ornament. Ornament is far more than embellishment, enhancement, protection, or source of pleasure: it is radically transformative. Its maximal significance should prompt us to investigate whether ornaments are more central to Tibetan and Buddhist thought and practice than is generally recognized, given their widespread material and rhetorical use in these historical contexts. Broadly speaking, it should also prompt us to ask what capacities ornament may exercise in other contexts. Like material things in general, ornaments may be more than what we assume, yet this only becomes apparent when we examine particular objects and the sources around them, thereby yielding details, perspectives, and theories we would have missed by contenting ourselves with standard definitions, textual witnesses, or generalized claims about materiality. Through such efforts, we can expand our horizon of possibilities for how things and humans act on and constitute each other.

Appendix

Wylie Equivalents for Tibetan Proper Names

Phonetic transcription	*Wylie equivalent*
Chokden	mchog ldan
Dakpo Shedrub Ling	dwags po bshad grub gling
Dartsedo	dar rtse mdo
Dalai Lama	tā la'i bla ma
Dalai Lama Ngawang Lobzang Gyatso	tā la'i bla ma ngag dbang blo bzang rgya mtsho

Darpa Lotsāwa Ngawang Püntsok	’dar pa lo tsā ba ngag dbang phun tshogs
Desi Sangyé Gyatso	sde srid sangs rgyas rgya mtsho
Drepung	’bras spungs
Ganden Podrang	dga’ ldan pho brang
Gelukpa	dge lugs pa
Genyen	dge bsnyen
Gyaltsen Tönpo	rgyal mtshan mthon po
Gyitang Norbu	sgyid thang nor bu
Jokhang	jo khang
Jowo	jo bo
Kangyur	bka’ ’gyur
Karmapa Karma Pakshi	karma pa karma pakṣī
Karmapa Rangjung Dorjé	karma pa rang byung rdo rje
Lamo	la mo
Lhasa	lha sa
Magen Butri Gyelmo	ma rgan bu khrid rgyal mo
Nenying Zhabdrung	gnas snying zhabs drung
Neudong	sne’u sdong
Nyingma	rnying ma
Orgyen Lingpa	o rgyan gling pa
Pakmodrupa	phag mo gru pa
Paṇchen	paṇ chen
Pendé Lekshéling Dratshang	phan bde legs bshad gling gra tshang
Potala	po ta la
Püntsok Changlochenpa	phun tshogs lcang lo can pa
Ragkha Sönam	rags kha bsod nams
Rinpung	rin spungs
Sönam Gölha	bsod nams dgos lha
Tengyur	bstan ’gyur
Trashilhünpo	bkra shis lhun po
Tseten Pelmo	tshe brtan dpal mo
Tsongkhapa	tsong kha pa
Tsurpu	mtshur phu
Zhalu	zhwa lu
Zurkhang Sharpa	zur khang shar pa

Notes

An early version of this chapter was presented at the symposium New Directions in the Study of Tibetan Buddhist Art History, Harvard-Yenching Institute, Harvard University, April 28–29, 2018. I thank the organizers and participants for the opportunity to receive feedback on my work, particularly Zhang Changhong, Leonard van der Kuijp, Wen-shing Chou, and Karl Debreczeny. I also thank Ellen Huang, Linda Lin, Briana Foley, Vanessa Sasson, Roy Tzohar, and two anonymous reviewers for stimulating comments and suggestions on drafts of this essay. Finally, I am grateful to Jane and Frank Lin for prompting me to deliberate over the materiality of ornament in serendipitous ways.

1. The gallery is measured at 11.65 meters wide by 38 meters long; it was later populated by the reliquary stūpas of the Tenth and Twelfth Dalai Lamas. Liu Hongxiao 刘鸿孝, *Gsang ba kun 'dus pho brang po ta la / Bu da la gong mi bao* 布达拉宫秘宝/ *Gems of the Potala Palace* (Beijing: Krung go'i mi rigs par ris sgyu rtsal dpe skrun khang, 1999), 170; Pingcuo Cidan 平措次旦, "Bu da la gong nei de wu shi da lai ling ta 布达拉宫内的五世达赖灵塔," *Wenwu* 文物 9 (1985): 95.
2. At the time it was built, before the reliquary stūpas of later Dalai Lamas were added, the Fifth Dalai Lama's stūpa was one of only two Potala objects marked by a golden roof; the other was the 'Phags pa Lokeśvara icon. On the significance of the latter object as the palladium of Tibet, see Per K. Sørensen, "Restless Relic: The Ārya Lokeśvara Icon in Tibet: Symbol of Power, Legitimacy and Pawn for Patronage," in *Pramāṇakīrtiḥ: Papers Dedicated to Ernst Steinkellner on the Occasion of His 70th Birthday,* edited by Birgit Kellner et al., 2 vols. (Vienna: Arbeitskreis für Tibetische und Buddhistische Studien, Universität Wien, 2007), 2: 857–885.
3. For a concise overview see Kurtis R. Schaeffer, "The Fifth Dalai Lama Ngawang Lopsang Gyatso," in *The Dalai Lamas: A Visual History,* edited by Martin Brauen (Chicago: Serindia Publications, 2005): 64–91.
4. E. H. Gombrich, *The Sense of Order: A Study in the Psychology of Decorative Art* (Ithaca, NY: Cornell University Press, 1979), chaps. 1–2; James Trilling, *Ornament: A Modern Perspective* (Seattle: University of Washington Press, 2003).
5. Adolf Loos, "Ornament and Crime," in *Ornament and Crime: Selected Essays,* translated by Michael Mitchell (Riverside, CA: Ariadne Press, 1998), 170; Christopher Long, "The Origins and Context of Adolf Loos's 'Ornament and Crime,'" *Journal of the Society of Architectural Historians* 68, no. 2 (June 2009): 200–223.

6. Gülru Necipoğlu and Alina Payne, eds., *Histories of Ornament: From Global to Local* (Princeton, NJ: Princeton University Press, 2016), introduction, 1–6.
7. Donald S. Lopez Jr., *Prisoners of Shangri-La: Tibetan Buddhism and the West* (Chicago: University of Chicago Press, 1998).
8. In addition to the work of Trilling and the volume edited by Necipoğlu and Payne as cited above, a significant earlier intervention was made by Oleg Grabar, *The Mediation of Ornament* (Princeton, NJ: Princeton University Press, 1992).
9. Vidya Dehejia, *The Body Adorned: Dissolving Boundaries Between Sacred and Profane in India's Art* (New York: Columbia University Press, 2009).
10. Jonathan Hay, *Sensuous Surfaces: The Decorative Object in Early Modern China* (Honolulu: University of Hawai'i Press, 2010).
11. Stephen Teiser, "Ornamenting the Departed: Notes on the Language of Chinese Buddhist Ritual Texts," *Asia Major,* 3rd Series, vol. 22, no. 1 (2009): 201–237; John Kieschnick, *The Impact of Buddhism on Chinese Material Culture* (Princeton, NJ: Princeton University Press, 2003); Phyllis Granoff, "Maitreya's Jewelled World: Some Remarks on Gems and Visions in Buddhist Texts," *Journal of Indian Philosophy* 26, no. 4 (Aug. 1998): 347–371.
12. Recent works on this topic include Fabio Rambelli, *Buddhist Materiality: A Cultural History of Objects in Japanese Buddhism* (Stanford, CA: Stanford University Press, 2007); Dominique Townsend, "Materials of Buddhist Culture: Aesthetics and Cosmopolitanism at Mindroling Monastery," PhD dissertation, Columbia University, 2012; and James Duncan Gentry, *Power Objects in Tibetan Buddhism: The Life, Writings, and Legacy of Sokdokpa Lodrö Gyeltsen* (Leiden: Brill, 2017).
13. Sde srid Sangs rgyas rgya mtsho, *Mchod sdong 'dzam gling rgyan gcig rten gtsug lag khang dang bcas pa'i dkar chag thar gling rgya mtshor bgrod pa'i gru rdzings byin rlabs kyi bang mdzod: A Detailed Account of the Funeral Ceremonies and Entombment Rites of the Fifth Dalai Lama Ṅag-dbaṅ-blo-bzaṅ-rgya-mtsho,* 2 vols. (New Delhi: T. Tsepal Taikhang, 1973), TBRC W8223 (hereafter *Dkar chag*). Other relevant sources include a 1697 proclamation on the use of salt to embalm the corpse of the Fifth Dalai Lama; it has already been treated in an excellent case study on relics and materiality. Kurtis R. Schaeffer, "Salt and the Sovereignty of the Dalai Lama," in *Images, Relics, and Legends: The Formation and Transformation of Buddhist Sacred Sites,* edited by

James Benn, Jinhua Chen, and James Robson (Oakville, Ontario: Mosaic Press, 2012): 298–322.

14. Sde srid Sangs rgyas rgya mtsho, *Drin can rtsa ba'i bla ma Ngag dbang blo bzang rgya mtsho'i thun mong phyi'i rnam thar Du kū la'i gos bzang* (hereafter *Du kū la*), vols. 8–10 of Tā la'i bla ma V Ngag dbang blo bzang rgya mtsho, *Rgyal dbang lnga pa Ngag dbang blo bzang rgya mtsho'i gsung 'bum*, 28 vols. (Beijing: Krung go'i bod rig pa dpe skrun khang, 2009).
15. Luciano Petech, *China and Tibet in the Early XVIIIth Century*, rev. ed. (Leiden: Brill, 1972), 49.
16. Other prominent reliquary stūpas have not been so fortunate: those of Tsong kha pa at Dga' ldan Monastery, the First Dalai Lama at Bkra shis lhun po Monastery, and the Paṇ chens at Bkra shis lhun po Monastery were all destroyed and have since been rebuilt. It would thus be difficult to undertake a comparison of the Sole Ornament of the World as an object with other monumental reliquary stūpas of Tibet, although such a project would be worthy and fascinating in its own right.
17. On literary sources and examples of the eight types of stūpas from South Asian and Tibetan regions, see Pema Dorjee, *Stupa and Its Technology: A Tibeto-Buddhist Perspective* (New Delhi: Indira Gandhi National Centre for the Arts, 1996), and Elena Pakhoutova, "Reproducing the Sacred Places: The Eight Great Events of the Buddha's Life and Their Commemorative Stūpas in the Medieval Art of Tibet (10th–13th Century)," PhD dissertation, University of Virginia, 2009.
18. The Sde srid's manual largely agrees with the color scheme prescribed in Sahajavilāsa's commentary on *Vimaloṣṇīṣa*, but it differs on some points. Quoted and translated in Dorjee, *Stupa and Its Technology*, 130, 135, 158, 169.
19. On Waddell's assessment of Tibetan Buddhism, see Donald S. Lopez Jr., *Prisoners of Shangri-La: Tibetan Buddhism and the West* (Chicago: University of Chicago Press, 2008), 34–40.
20. L. Austine Waddell, *Lhasa and Its Mysteries: A Record of the Expedition of 1903–1904* (New York: E. P. Dutton, 1905), 391–393.
21. Precise equivalents between the Tibetan *srang* and our current metric system may not be possible to ascertain, in part because the weight of *srang* could vary; this rough estimate is based on the equivalence of one *srang* with 37.3 grams. Sde srid Sangs rgyas rgya mtsho, *Dkar chag*, vol. 1, 647.2–647.3=319a2–319a3. I thank Ian MacCormack for supplying this reference.

22. Dan Martin, "Tables of Contents (*dKar chag*)," in *Tibetan Literature: Studies in Genre,* edited by José Ignacio Cabezón and Roger R. Jackson (Ithaca, NY: Snow Lion, 1996), 502; Sde srid Sangs rgyas rgya mtsho, *Dkar chag,* vol. 1, 388.6–408.5=191b6–201b5.
23. A *khal* may have weighed about thirty pounds, and twenty *bre* equal one *khal.* Tsepon Wangchuk Deden Shakabpa, *One Hundred Thousand Moons: An Advanced Political History of Tibet,* 2 vols., translated and annotated by Derek F. Maher (Leiden: Brill, 2010), 1:401. The Sde srid calculated the total value of materials at just over 1,041,828 *srang* of silver, or the equivalent of a little more than 18,752,905 *khal.* Ian MacCormack, "Buddhism and State in Seventeenth-Century Tibet: Cosmology and Theology in the Works of Sangyé Gyatso," PhD dissertation, Harvard University, 2018, 291.
24. Kurtis R. Schaeffer, "The King's Canons," in *The Culture of the Book in Tibet* (New York: Columbia University Press, 2009), 109; Ngawang L. Nornang, "Monastic Organization and Economy at Dwags-po Bshad-grub-gling," in *Reflections on Tibetan Culture: Essays in Memory of Turrell V. Wylie,* edited by Lawrence Epstein and Richard F. Sherburne (Lewiston, NY: The Edwin Mellen Press, 1990; Studies in Asian Thought and Religion 12), 249–268.
25. Sde srid Sangs rgyas rgya mtsho, *Dkar chag,* vol. 2, 432.4–493.2 =600b4–630a2.
26. A *skar* is equivalent to one-tenth of a *zho*. Sde srid Sangs rgyas rgya mtsho, *Dkar chag,* vol. 2, 434.2–434.4=601b2–601b4, 441.1–441.2=605a1–605a2, 441.6=605a6, 452.2=610b2, 454.2=611b2, 477.4=622a4, 459.5=613a5, 461.5–461.6=614a5–614a6, 463.2–463.3=615a2–615a3.
27. Sde srid Sangs rgyas rgya mtsho, *Dkar chag*, vol. 1, 659.1=325a1; 660.1–660.5=325b1–325b5; 662.2=326b2, 662.4–662.6=326b4–326b6. I thank Ian MacCormack for generously sharing his notes on these details. According to oral accounts, the practice of using personal jewelry to adorn the reliquary stūpas of the Dalai Lamas and the Paṇchens has continued, with members of the aristocracy invited to donate such items for this purpose. Jane Casey, "Ornaments of Faith: Himalayan Jewelry and Jeweled Objects," in *Vanishing Beauty: Asian Jewelry and Ritual Objects from the Barbara and David Kipper Collection,* edited by Madhuvanti Ghose (Chicago: Art Institute of Chicago, 2016), 36, 39nn72–73. I thank Iwona Tenzing for suggesting this reference.
28. Wannaporn Kay Rienjang, "Honoring the Body: Relic Cult Practice in Eastern Afghanistan with Comparison to Dharmaarajika Pakistan," PhD dissertation, University of Cambridge, 2017, as quoted in John

Strong in this volume. On this point her work builds on that of Gregory Schopen, "Burial *Ad Sanctos* and the Physical Presence of the Buddha," in *Bones, Stones and Buddhist Monks: Collected Papers on the Archaeology, Epigraphy, and Texts of Monastic Buddhism in India*, edited by Gregory Schopen (Honolulu: University of Hawai'i Press, 1997), 114–147. The Tibetan association of turquoise with one's vital principle (*bla*) may be relevant here. Samten G. Karmay, "The Soul and the Turquoise: A Ritual for Recalling the *bla*," in *The Arrow and the Spindle: Studies in History, Myths, Rituals and Beliefs in Tibet*, 2 vols. (Kathmandu: Mandala Book Point, 1998), 310–338.

29. For a study on the calibration of karmic bonds through gift exchange, see Wen-shing Chou and Nancy G. Lin, "Karmic Affinities: Rethinking Relations among Tibetan Lamas and the Qing Emperor," in *Water Moon Reflections: Essays in Honor of Patricia Berger*, edited by Ellen Huang, Nancy G. Lin, Michelle McCoy, and Michelle H. Wang (Berkeley: IEAS Publications, forthcoming).
30. On Tibetan participation in the burgeoning of Eurasian overland trade in the seventeenth century, see Luce Boulnois, "Gold, Wool and Musk: Trade in Lhasa in the Seventeenth Century," in *Lhasa in the Seventeenth Century: The Capital of the Dalai Lamas*, edited by Françoise Pommaret (Leiden: Brill, 2003), 132–156.
31. Peter Schwieger, *The Dalai Lama and the Emperor of China: A Political History of the Tibetan Institution of Reincarnation* (New York: Columbia University Press, 2015), 60.
32. Here I follow John Strong's characterization (in this volume) that jewels "adorn" relics, which draws from the work of Wannaporn Rienjang. The more general point that a relic must be framed to signal its importance has been noted in previous scholarship. See Patrick J. Geary, *Furta Sacra: Thefts of Relics in the Central Middle Ages*, rev. ed. (Princeton, NJ: Princeton University Press, 2011), 5; Robert H. Sharf, "On the Allure of Buddhist Relics," *Representations* 66 (Spring 1999): 81.
33. Michael Aris, *Hidden Treasures and Secret Lives: A Study of Pemalingpa (1450–1521) and the Sixth Dalai Lama (1683–1706)* (London: Kegan Paul International, 1989), 124.
34. Ronald M. Davidson, "Imperial Agency in the Gsar ma Treasure Texts during the Tibetan Renaissance: The *Rgyal po bla gter* and Related Literature," in *Tibetan Buddhist Literature and Praxis: Studies in Its Formative Period, 900–1400*, edited by Ronald M. Davidson and Christian K. Wedemeyer (Leiden: Brill, 2006), 127.

35. I take *su ganti* here to be an alternate spelling of *su gandhi,* or rose quartz. *Gzi* can refer to agate or carnelian with banding and other patterns. *G.yang tri* is spelled *g.yang ṭi* in other sources, both apparently transcriptions of "sheep's suet" (*yangzhi* 羊脂) jade. See, for example, the whitish jade object described in Yannick Laurent, "An Important Documentary Tibetan Gilt-Inscribed Jade River Pebble 'Kapala' Box and Cover," in *Water, Pine and Stone Retreat Collection: Treasures,* Sotheby's, Hong Kong, October 3, 2017, 54–63.
36. Sde srid Sangs rgyas rgya mtsho, *Du kū la,* 10:124–125.
37. Nancy G. Lin, "Recounting the Fifth Dalai Lama's Rebirth Lineage," *Revue d'Etudes Tibétaines* 38 (February 2017): 119–156.
38. I analyze this ethos of the Fifth Dalai Lama's Ganden Podrang court in my book manuscript in progress.
39. *snyan ngag mdzes par byed pa yi// chos rnams rgyan zhes rab tu brjod//* (Skt. *kāvyaśobhākarān dharmān alaṃkārān pracakṣate*). Daṇḍin, *The Kāvyādarśa of Śrí Daṇḍin,* edited, with a commentary, by Paṇḍita Premachandra Tarkabágíśa (Calcutta: Asiatic Society of Bengal, 1863; Bibliotheca Indica 40), 2.1; Dbyug pa can (Daṇḍin), *Snyan ngag me long ma,* in *Tā'i si tu pa kun mkhyen chos kyi 'byung gnas bstan pa'i nyin byed kyi bka' 'bum,* 14 vols. (Kangra, H. P., India: Sherab Gyaltsen, 1990), vol. 6, 645.6=*cha* 9a6. The figures of sense and sound (*rgyan;* Skt. *alaṃkāra*) classified in Daṇḍin's work have pervaded Tibetan classical belles-lettres (*snyan ngag*) since the late thirteenth century.
40. *a ho 'gro ba'i bsod nams rgya mtsho las// 'thon pa gser gdung snang ba 'bum gyi mdzod// rab yangs 'dzam gling mdzes pa'i rgyan gcig tu// dag pa'i mkha' la shar ba 'dis gtsos pa//.* Sde srid Sangs rgyas rgya mtsho, *Du kū la,* 10:165.
41. *nyi ma 'o mtsho las thon pa sngon byung gtam dang sbyar ba ldan pa'i gzugs can la bya ba tha dad min pa'i ros mngar ba/.* Sde srid Sangs rgyas rgya mtsho, *Du kū la,* 10:165.
42. R. Mayer, "Observations on the Tibetan Phur-ba and the Indian Kīla," in *The Buddhist Forum,* edited by Tadeusz Skorupski (London: School of Oriental and African Studies, 1991), 2:166–167.
43. Hence the actions are integral or literally "unbroken" (*bya ba tha dad min pa*) because both subjects perform them; and the metaphor is described as conjoined (*ldan pa*) because the metaphors—sun and ocean—are conventionally associated with each other in the Indic myth.
44. Yumiko Ishihama: "On the Dissemination of the Belief in the Dalai Lamas as a Manifestation of the Bodhisattva Avalokiteśvara," *Acta*

Asiatica 64 (1993): 38–56, and "The Dalai Lama as the *Cakravarti-rāja* as Manifested by the Bodhisattva Avalokiteśvara, *Cahiers d'Extrême-Asie* 24 (2015): 169–188; Lin, "Recounting the Fifth Dalai Lama's Rebirth Lineage."

45. Even Alfred Gell, who is perhaps the most radical in asserting that "decoration is intrinsically functional," apparently assumes that it must be seen to be functional. Alfred Gell, *Art and Agency: An Anthropological Theory* (Oxford: Clarendon Press, 1998), 73–95; Grabar, *The Mediation of Ornament,* 226–230; Jonathan Hay, "The Passage of the Other: Elements for a Redefinition of Ornament," in Necipoğlu and Payne, *Histories of Ornament,* 62–69.
46. Trilling, *Ornament,* xiii.
47. James Burgess, ed., *Epigraphia Indica: A Collection of Inscriptions Supplementary to the Corpus Inscriptionum Indicarum of the Archaeology Survey,* 2 vols. (Calcutta: Superintendent of Government Printing, 1892–1894), 1:126, 143.
48. Daud Ali, *Courtly Culture and Political Life in Early Medieval India* (New York: Cambridge University Press, 2004; Cambridge Studies in Indian History and Society 10), 162–170.
49. Jinaratna, *The Epitome of Queen Lilávati,* 2 vols., translated by Richard Fynes (New York: NYU Press, 2006; Clay Sanskrit Library), 1:460–461, 30–31, 234–235, 499, 370–371, 380–381.
50. Sheldon Pollock, *The Language of Gods in the World of Men: Sanskrit, Culture, and Power in Premodern India* (Berkeley: University of California Press, 2006), 327–328.
51. Lobsang Shastri, "Activities of Indian Paṇḍitas in Tibet from the 14th to the 17th Century," in *Tibet, Past and Present: Tibetan Studies I: PIATS 2000: Tibetan Studies: Proceedings of the Ninth Seminar of the International Association for Tibetan Studies, Leiden, 2000,* edited by Henk Blezer (Leiden: Brill, 2002), 139–141.
52. Tā la'i bla ma V Ngag dbang blo bzang rgya mtsho, *Rgyal dbang lnga pa Ngag dbang blo bzang rgya mtsho'i gsung 'bum* (hereafter *Gsung 'bum*), 28 vols. (Beijing: Krung go'i bod rig pa dpe skrun khang, 2009), 19:37; 6:296; 19:71.
53. Sde srid Sangs rgyas rgya mtsho, *Du kū la,* 8:221; translation adapted from Sde srid Sangs rgyas rgya mtsho, *Life of the Fifth Dalai Lama,* vol. 4, part 1, translated by Zahiruddin Ahmad (New Delhi: International Academy of Indian Culture, 1999; Śata-Piṭaka Series 392), 234. On the singularity of the Red Palace in comparison to famed Indic and Tibetan Buddhist structures, as represented by the Sde srid, see

MacCormack, "Buddhism and State in Seventeenth-Century Tibet," 260–264.

54. Tā la'i bla ma V Ngag dbang blo bzang rgya mtsho, *Gsung 'bum,* 5:246; 12:127, 194; 18:440; 20:189, 362.

55. Irmgard Mengele, "The Artist's Life," in *The Black Hat Eccentric: Artistic Visions of the Tenth Karmapa,* edited by Karl Debreczeny (New York: Rubin Museum of Art, 2012), 36. Tragically, this icon was also destroyed during the Cultural Revolution; in 1997 it was rebuilt by the Seventeenth Karmapa. Lama Kunsang et al., *History of the Karmapas: The Odyssey of the Tibetan Masters with the Black Crown* (Ithaca, NY: Snow Lion, 2012), 54.

56. Karma pa III Rang byung rdo rje, *The Tibetan Rendering of the Jātakamālā of Āryaśūra, Supplemented with Sixty-Seven Additional Jātaka Stories,* 2 vols. (Darjeeling: Kargyud Sungrab Nyamso Khang, 1974), 2:621.4; Sarah Aoife Richardson, "Painted Books for Plaster Walls: Visual Words in the Fourteenth-Century Murals at the Tibetan Buddhist Temple of Shalu" (PhD diss., University of Toronto, 2016), 145–146n288.

57. For example, see Franz-Karl Ehrhard, "A Thousand-spoke Golden Wheel of Secular Law: The Preamble to the Law Code of the Kings of gTsang," in *Secular Law and Order in the Tibetan Highland: Contributions to a Workshop Organized by the Tibet Institute in Andiast (Switzerland) on the Occasion of the 65th Birthday of Christoph Cüppers,* edited by Dieter Schuh (Andiast: Andiast International Institute for Tibetan and Buddhist Studies, 2016), 111, 121.

58. *ratnaṃ svajātiśreṣṭhe 'pi.* Mattia Salvini, "*Ratna:* A Buddhist World of Precious Things," in *Soulless Matter, Seats of Energy: Metals, Gems and Minerals in South Asian Traditions,* edited by Fabrizio M. Ferrari and Thomas W. P. Dähnhardt (Sheffield: Equinox, 2016), 221. My use of this reference is thanks to Maria Heim's chapter in this volume.

59. Adapted from Karl Brunnhölzl trans., *When the Clouds Part: The Uttaratantra and Its Meditative Tradition as a Bridge Between Sūtra and Tantra* (Ithaca, NY: Snow Lion, 2015), 351. *ratnāni durlabhotpādān nirmalatvāt prabhāvataḥ / lokālaṃkārabhūtatvādagratvān nirvikārataḥ. 'byung ba dkon phyir dri med phyir// mthu ldan phyir dang 'jig rten gyi// rgyan gyur phyir dang mchog nyid phyir// 'gyur ba med phyir dkon mchog nyid//. Ratnagotravibhāga* 1.22; *Theg pa chen po rgyud bla ma'i bstan bcos rnam par bshad pa,* Tōh. 4025, 169.2=85a2. The verse is cited by Sde srid Sangs rgyas rgya mtsho in a longer discussion on the preeminence of the stūpa as a material "support" (*rten*) of the

dharmakāya (*Dkar chag,* vol. 1, 516.4–516.5=254b4–254b5). I am grateful to Ian MacCormack for pointing me to the Sde srid's citation.

60. Translation adapted from Brunnhölzl, *When the Clouds Part,* 351. *lokālaṃkārasādharmyeṇa sarvajagadāśayaśobhānimittatvāt. 'jig rten gyi rgyan du chos mthun pas ni 'gro ba thams cad kyi bsam pa dge ba'i rgyu yin pa'i phyir ro/. Ratnagotravibhāga* 1.22 (20.16–20.17); *Theg pa chen po rgyud bla ma'i bstan bcos rnam par bshad pa,* Tōh. 4025, 169.4–169.5=85a4–85a5.
61. Grabar, *The Mediation of Ornament,* 27, 39.
62. *ye shes sems dpa' 'bral med bzhugs pa la// mi mthun rtsod pa'i nyon mongs rim nad chos// byin rlabs phul byung gzungs 'bul g.yas 'khyil sgras// bcoms te gsar pa'i rdzogs ldan mgron 'gugs pa//.* Sde srid Sangs rgyas rgya mtsho, *Du kū la,* 10:165.
63. *'phags pa lag na padma'i ye shes rang snang las grub pa'i sprul.* Sde srid Sangs rgyas rgya mtsho, *Dkar chag,* vol. 1, 438.3–438.4=216b3–216b4.
64. Salvini, "*Ratna,*" 224.
65. As Trilling has pointed out, apart from its rarity, such physical properties make gold a particularly suitable material for ornament (*Ornament,* 80).
66. *bod shog kho na nyid shin tu phyug pas nyi mdangs kyang zil gyis gnon nus shing.* Sde srid Sangs rgyas rgya mtsho, *Dkar chag,* vol. 1, 447.5–447.6=221a5–221a6.
67. Although fuller exploration is beyond the scope of this chapter, the healing and protective properties of gems as recognized by Tibetan medical traditions could add to this discussion. See, for example, Desi Sangyé Gyatso, *Mirror of Beryl: A Historical Introduction to Tibetan Medicine,* translated by Gavin Kilty (Boston: Wisdom Publications, 2010), 326–327.
68. Sde srid Sangs rgyas rgya mtsho, *Dkar chag,* vol. 1, 454.5–454.6=224b5–225b6.
69. Granoff, "Maitreya's Jewelled World," 363, 359.
70. Translation modified from Sde srid Sangs rgyas rgya mtsho, *Life of the Fifth Dalai Lama,* vol. 4, part 1, translated by Zahiruddin Ahmad (New Delhi: International Academy of Indian Culture, 1999; Śata-Piṭaka Series 392), 37–38. Sde srid Sangs rgyas rgya mtsho, *Du kū la,* 8:37–38.
71. *dngos med dngos por sprul ba gser ri'i spun// gtsug tor mkha' la reg pa'i gdung rten 'og / mdo rgyud bka' bstan gnyis sogs dam pa'i chos// lha mi gdengs can dri za la sogs kyi// bzang bzang rin chen gos dar 'bras mtshon pa// yangs yangs 'dzam gling khyad 'phags nor gyi rigs// mang*

mang mkho dgu'i longs spyod 'byor ba'i gter// legs legs 'jig rten dge ba gnas phyir sbas//. Sde srid Sangs rgyas rgya mtsho, *Du kū la,* 10:125.

72. For analysis of the *cintāmaṇi* in Pali and Sanskrit Buddhist texts, see Salvini, "*Ratna*," 242–247. For a study of the *cintāmaṇi* cult in medieval Japan and its links with imperial power, see Bernard Faure, *Gods of Medieval Japan*, vol. 1, *The Fluid Pantheon* (Honolulu: University of Hawai'i Press, 2016), chap. 6.
73. In some respects, this theory of ornament shares affinity not only with Indic theories of jewels, but also with older meanings of the Sanskrit *alaṃkāra* as that which strengthens, adds power to, renders fit or capable, and/or expedites divine outcomes. Jan Gonda, "The Meaning of the Word *Alaṃkāra*," in *Selected Studies Presented to the Author by the Staff of the Oriental Institute, Utrecht University, on the Occasion of His 70th Birthday*, 5 vols. (Leiden: Brill, 1975), 2:257–274; Andrew Ollett, "Making It Nice: Kāvya in the Second Century," *Journal of Indian Philosophy* 47 (2019): 269–287.

Chapter 8

Beads and Bones

The Case of the Piprahwa Gems

John S. Strong

In January 1898, an important archaeological discovery was made near the village of Piprahwa in Northern India, not far from the Nepalese border—a place that some later came to identify as the site of the Buddha's hometown, Kapilavastu.[1] Inspired by the recent discovery of an Aśokan pillar at nearby Lumbinī (just fifteen kilometers across the frontier), William (Willie) Peppé, the manager of a local plantation known as the Birdpore Estate, decided to excavate the largest of the mysterious mounds of which he was aware on his vast property. The hillock soon proved to be an ancient brick stūpa, and, sinking a shaft straight down from the top, at a depth of about twenty feet, he discovered a chamber in which was a great stone coffer. Inside the coffer were five reliquary vases, and inside the vases (unfortunately, Peppé does not tell us which) there were found pieces of bone and also ornaments of various sorts (mostly beads, gold jewelry, and semiprecious gems).[2]

The discovery of "beads and bones" mixed together in reliquaries is, in fact, rather common in North Indian Buddhist archaeological finds.[3] Just to give one example: in 1794, when Jagat Singh, a minister of the rāja of Banaras, was digging for reusable building materials (bricks and cut stones) in the ruins of a large ancient mound in Sarnath (later realized to be the site of the Buddha's first sermon), his laborers came across a round stone box containing a green marble vase, inside of which they found "40 to 46 pearls, 14 rubies, 8 silver and 9 gold ear-rings, and three pieces of human arm bone."[4] The workers, thinking that the bones were the remains from someone's cremation fire or from a rich woman who had committed satī, quickly disposed of them in a proper Hindu fashion by consigning them to the waters of the nearby

Ganges. The reliquary and the jewelry they took to Jonathan Duncan, the local East India Company official, who eventually donated them to the Asiatic Society of Bengal.[5] This may, in fact, have been one of the earliest discoveries of Buddhist relics in India—perhaps of the Buddha himself or of some arhat of renown—and, despite the fact that the bones were cast into the river, it exhibits well the typical pattern of Buddhist reliquaries containing bone relics and/or ashes and various types of jewelry in close contiguity.[6]

A number of features were different about the Piprahwa case, however. First, one of the soapstone reliquary vases turned out to have an inscription, in Brāhmī characters, explicitly proclaiming that this was the receptacle of relics of Śākyamuni Buddha. Second, the corporeal relics themselves were not immediately disposed of (as at Sarnath) but were soon made over to the king of Siam, as a gift of the British Raj.[7] Finally, the number and variety of beads, gems, and ornaments found with the relics, amounting to well over a thousand individual pieces, were far greater and richer than those found at Sarnath or anywhere else in India. As Harry Falk put it, "Gemstones in small numbers have been found with many reliquaries. By contrast, the amount found at Piprahwa is stunning, not to speak of the[ir] quality."[8]

It was indeed the gems that first struck Peppé's eye when he opened the stone box and took the lids off the reliquaries. In his own words, here were "ornaments in gold; gold beads; . . . several pieces in gold leaf stamped with the figure of a lion, [of an elephant], with the impression of the Buddhist cross [svastika]; . . . quantities of stars or flowers both in silver and gold . . . , pearls of [different] sizes, leaves serrated and veined, Buddhist tridents, pyramids, pierced and drilled beads of various sizes and shapes, cut in white or red cornelian, amethyst, topaz, garnet, coral, and crystal."[9] It is on the fate and significance of these gems and jewels and beads that I shall focus in this article, but it may be useful to say a few words first about what happened to the reliquaries, the inscription, and the bodily relics.[10]

The Reliquaries

According to the 1878 Indian Treasure Trove Act, the British colonial government laid claim to all and any materials excavated from Indian soil of a value of more than ten rupees.[11] The finds at Piprahwa thus did not belong to Willie Peppé but to the Raj, and it was up to the government to decide what to do with them. Most of the gems (as well as the stone coffer and the reliquary vases) were deemed to be *of antiquarian interest* and so were sent to the Indian Museum in Calcutta.[12] The relics, however, were thought to be *religious items* of value to Buddhists but not appropriate for display in a secular museum.[13] Of the five reliquaries, four were made of soapstone, but one was of crystal, with a lid topped by an exquisitely carved handle in the shape of a fish (also of crystal), hollowed out and stuffed with "minute flowers of gold [and] precious stones"[14] This, as Falk has made clear, was an exceptional and expensive work of art. Falk suspects it could only have been the gift of a very prominent person, and he suggests it was commissioned by Aśoka to contain relics of the Buddha and kept in the great stone coffer, which was originally situated in Lumbinī and moved to Piprahwa for security reasons during the persecution of Buddhists that followed the demise of the Mauryan Empire.[15]

The Inscription

Of the four soapstone reliquaries, only one bore an inscription. Though he could not read the Brāhmī script, Peppé diligently copied out the text as best he could and sent it to his friend Vincent Smith, the indologist and historian, who was then serving as district judge in the nearby town of Gorakhpur.[16] Smith could not decipher the whole thing, but he immediately realized its importance, and, a few days later, on January 23, 1898, he wrote back: "My dear Peppé, your find turns out to be of greater interest than we thought as the bones were believed by their depositor to be those of Buddha himself."[17] After that, news of Peppé's discovery spread fast—first among scholars and then in the popular press.[18] Soon, many of the scholarly and semi-scholarly luminaries of the day went to work on the inscription.[19] For a while, there was some debate about the interpretation of some parts of it, but in due time a consensus, defined by Auguste Barth, seems to have emerged: "This deposit of the relics of the blessed Buddha of the Sākyas [is the pious work] of the brothers of Sukīrti, jointly with their sisters, with their sons and their wives."[20]

That might have settled the issue of the inscription, except for one thing that complicated the picture: some people thought it wasn't genuine—that it was a forgery. The question arose mostly because not long after the 1898 discovery, Anton Führer, one of the scholars initially consulted by Peppé, who, moreover, had visited Piprahwa just after the excavation was over, was found to be a charlatan.

Much has been written about Dr. Führer and his high crimes and misdemeanors, and I cannot go into the details here. Suffice it to say that an inquiry into his activities revealed Führer as someone who had tried to build up his reputation by faking archaeological finds, and he was known in particular to have forged Brāhmī inscriptions—adding some to pieces in his own museum! Confronted with the accusations, he pleaded no contest and promptly resigned.[21] Though none of the formal accusations against Führer pertained to the Piprahwa inscription, his association with that dig and with Willie Peppé raised suspicions about the genuineness of the inscription. Some even suggested that the relics themselves had been planted; others thought they were not human bones at all.[22]

Today, the scholarly consensus seems to be that the inscription on the reliquary should be accepted as authentic.[23] Some, however, still maintain the opposite,[24] or they hypothesize that shortly after the discovery, there was collusion among certain scholars and British colonial government officials at the highest levels to systematically quash or cover over any doubts about the relics because, as we shall see, the decision had been made to offer the Piprahwa relics to the king of Siam, and British authorities had a vested interest in silencing any questioning of their authenticity.[25]

The Afterlives of the Corporeal Relics

Let me now turn to the fate(s) of the corporeal relics (the "bones") that were found at Piprahwa. Mention was made above that according to the provisions of the Treasure Trove Act, the British colonial government decided not to send the corporeal relics to the Indian Museum in Calcutta along with their reliquaries. Instead, it asked Peppé to have them stored in the government treasury in the local district town of Basti.[26] Once there, the corporeal relics were safely in the government's hands; the only question was what to do with them. The answer was not long in coming. Shortly after Peppé's finds were made, while the relics were still at Piprahwa, a Thai monk named Jinavaravaṃsa arrived at Birdpore House and asked to see them.[27] Jinavaravaṃsa was the disciple of a prominent Sri Lankan monk, the Venerable Waskaduwa Subhuti, who himself was a Pali scholar well known to British buddhologists.[28] This alone gave him a certain pedigree, but even more than that, Jinavaravaṃsa also turned out to be Prince Prisdong Chumsai, the London-educated cousin of the Siamese king Chulalongkorn; he had taken all the first-prize honors at King's College and, among other things, had acted as the Siamese envoy plenipotentiary to twelve European countries, as well as to the United States. His diplomatic career behind him, he had, for a host of complex reasons, decided to become a monk.[29] After his visit to Piprahwa, he wrote to Willie Peppé, asking that the corporeal relics that were now in storage be turned over to the king of Siam, who would give them the care they were due as the king was "the only reigning Buddhist Monarch in the world." Besides, he added, Europeans did not care for ashes and bone.[30] Peppé passed Jinavaravaṃsa's petition on to William Hoey, the commissioner of Gorakhpur, who expressed his opinion that the idea was a good one, especially because the Buddhists in India were upset over their perceived loss of the Bodhgaya temple to the Hindus and would be somewhat assuaged by this gesture.[31] At the same time, the gift might be good for strengthening relations with the Siamese, who were, at this point, feeling squeezed between Britain, which had just conquered Burma, and France, which had just moved into Cambodia and Laos.[32] Hoey's opinion was endorsed by Vincent Smith, and the whole thing made its way up the bureaucratic chain, and by late July 1898, the government of India decided that the Piprahwa relics "should be entrusted by the Government of the North West Provinces and Oudh to the King of Siam." A later proviso was added that it was expected that King Chulalongkorn would "not object" to sharing a portion of the relics with the Buddhists of Burma and Ceylon.[33]

Thus the die was cast. A representative from the king of Siam came all the way to Piprahwa (along with gold-plated miniature pagodas of his own) to receive the relics, which were brought back there from Basti.[34] They were then ceremoniously transported to Thailand, where, the following year, 1899, they were enshrined in the newly built Golden Mount (at Wat Saket) in central Bangkok, still a major tourist attraction today.[35]

The history of the Piprahwa bones, now owned by Siam, was, however, just beginning, for Chulalongkorn soon decided to use them for his own diplomatic and political purposes.[36] In February 1899, the Siamese handed over some portions of their collection to representatives from various pagodas in Burma and various temples and sects in Sri Lanka.[37] A year later, it was Japan's turn since Japanese Buddhists, hearing of the distributions to Burma and Ceylon, also petitioned for a share. The relics given to them were eventually enshrined in 1904 in a newly built temple in Nagoya, the Nissenji (日籛寺 Japan-Siam temple), after having been received at and housed in the interim in an imperial temple in Kyoto, the Myōhōin (妙法院).[38] Three decades later, long after Chulalongkorn's death, the Thais resumed their relic distribution activities. In 1935, at the instigation of the Buddhist Mission of North America (today, the Buddhist Churches of America), some more Piprahwa relics were sent from Bangkok to the Buddhist Church of San Francisco. They are still today enshrined in a stupa built onto the roof of their temple building.[39] Then, in 2009, yet another share (four small bones) of this seemingly inexhaustible supply was sent to the Union Bouddhiste de France.[40] Today, they are housed in what was formerly the Cameroon Pavilion from the 1931 Paris Universal Colonial Exposition but which has now become the Grande Pagode du Bois de Vincennes. There they were enshrined on May 17, 2009, after being exhibited at the Hôtel de Ville (City Hall), where they were received by the mayor of Paris.[41]

The Afterlives of the Gems

We come now, at last, to the gems. During all this time, while the "bones" were traveling the world, the Piprahwa "beads" were experiencing afterlives of their own. It should be said that the Indian Treasure Trove Act, which decreed that the gems belonged to the British state (and so were sent to the Indian Museum in Calcutta) also allowed for the discoverer to retain some portion of the finds if they were deemed to be "duplicates"—that is, identical to others in the trove. Accordingly, Vincent Smith (as district judge) and Willie Peppé sat down together and drew up an inventory of the entire collection of gems, carefully marking how many of each type had been found and agreeing how many were to be retained by Mr. Peppé and how many were to be made over to the museum.[42]

It should be said that by the time this inventory was made, Peppé had already started categorizing his finds and storing them in different containers. He seemed to have placed most of the gold and silver ornaments and pearls in fourteen glass cases. Here were to be seen, among other things, a largish gold leaf umbrella, various small gold figurines (a coiled snake, a female figure, an elephant), pieces of gold and silver leaf stamped with various items (trident, svastikas, lions), 58 gold and silver stars, 41 pearls of different sizes, and 105 beads of various materials (gold, amethyst, garnet, topaz, coral), as well as a quantity of semiprecious stones. All together there were about 307 pieces. None of these, apparently, was to be retained by Peppé.[43]

In addition, however, there were well over a thousand other items to be sorted through that had been placed in thirteen makeshift receptacles—small bags, empty pill boxes, pen boxes, an empty medicinal bottle of quinia—apparently whatever was at hand. The contents of these containers were also duly detailed by Smith and Peppé, who listed them in four columns entitled "I. Description of jewels etc.," "II. Total Number Found," "III. Number retained by Mr. Peppé," and "IV. Number Made over to Museum." Space does not permit the reproduction or even summary of this list, which includes hundreds of pieces of different sorts. Suffice it to say that most of the items are non-gold perforated beads that are described according to their shapes ("stars," "cups," "drops," "leaves," "bugle beads," "long beads," "lotus-pod beads," "flat beads," "small beads," etc.) and the substance of which they were made (various types of amethyst, crystal, cornelian, various types of topaz, metal, garnet, lapis lazuli, pearl, etc.).[44] In addition there were 64 rolls of gold leaf in one pillbox and quantities of seed pearls in a red bag. All told, in these various receptacles, there were 1,153 counted items, of which Peppé got to retain 433 "duplicates."[45]

Travels of the Gems

On August 6, 1898, not long after the bulk of the gems had been delivered to the Indian Museum, the well-informed Jinavaravaṃsa wrote to Willie to ask if he might be willing to give him some of his duplicate gems (which he called "ornamental offerings") "as souvenirs of his visit" to Birdpore, adding that, in exchange, he would be happy to send him anything he might want either from Siam or Sri Lanka.[46] We do not know if Peppé complied with this request, but it is likely he did, for a month later, Jinavaravaṃsa sent him "a complete collection of Siamese postage & revenue stamps . . . several [of which were] very rare."[47]

Then, on August 15, 1898, Peppé also sent a total of twenty gems and one gold roll to Jinavaravaṃsa's Sri Lankan mentor, the Venerable Subhuti, which he received in his temple in Waskaduwa, near Kalutara, south of Colombo, on October 7.[48]

Peppé returned to England in 1903 and took the remainder of his gems with him. After giving a few specimens to his sister and some more to the Royal Asiatic Society, he had the rest of them arranged in three double-sided glass cases, which he labeled "Relics from the Piprahwa Stupa."[49] These remained in England until Willie's death in 1936, at which point Willie's son Humphrey, who succeeded his father as manager of the Birdpore estate, got the consent of his siblings to take the gems back to Birdpore so that they could be shown to pilgrims passing by on their way to or from Lumbinī and to other visitors.[50] In 1952, the newly independent government of India nationalized all private estates, and Birdpore House became a Government Inspection Bungalow. Even so, Humphrey and his wife stayed on for a few years, being permitted to rent three rooms in what had been their home. There, they continued to show the gems to occasional visitors, not the least of whom were the Dalai Lama and the Panchen Lama, who visited in 1956, when they were in India for celebrations of the Buddha Jayanti. The Dalai Lama returned again in 1960, shortly after his flight from Tibet, and had dinner at Birdpore House on his way to visit Lumbinī. The menu and the list bearing all the guests' signatures was kept by the Peppés and has survived.[51] Soon thereafter Humphrey and his wife left India for good and took the gems with them to London, where they remain in the possession of the family.[52]

For years, various generations of Peppés kept the gems in an old chest. As Willie's grandson Neil later put it, no one really thought much of them; they were sort of family curios.[53] Things changed, however, in the early 2000s due to an interesting set of events. It turned out that the Peppés were not the only ones in London to possess Piprahwa gems. In June 2003, Paul Seto, then president of the British Buddhist Society, was making an inventory of the organization's possessions when he happened to find, under the bottom shelf of a display case, a cardboard box. In it were various conference badges that had belonged to Christmas Humphreys, the founder of the society, and also a smaller box, neatly tied with a red ribbon and labeled as containing "Relics of Buddha. From the Piprawah Stupa. Birdpore Estate. Gorakhpur N.W.P. India 1898."[54] When Seto opened the box, he found twelve Piprahwa gems inside. Seto had never heard of Piprahwa, and no one had any idea where this box had come from,[55] but a little research informed him about Willie Peppé, and some more inquiries led him to Willie's grandson Neil, then living in England, who revealed to him that he too had quite a collection of similar pieces (i.e., his family's gems).[56]

If Christmas Humphreys, whose view of relics was that they had nothing to do with the Buddhism that enthused him, had stashed the gems away in a box where they were soon forgotten, Paul Seto, by contrast, was tremendously excited about them. "Everything stopped," he later told the *London Sunday Times*. "My first thought was 'It can't be true!' My second was '[This] should be in a venerated place, not in a cardboard box in a cupboard. . . . I feel a responsibility to every Buddhist in the world and every Buddhist who will come, to establish what these objects truly are so they can be given proper respect.'"[57] And he began to hatch plans (never realized) to build a stupa for the gems in Eccleston Square.[58] Eventually, however, Seto left the presidency of the society. Today, the gems are still in their cardboard box—not in a cupboard but in a safe in the office of the president of the Buddhist Society, Desmond Biddulph. He told me no one had asked to see them in a very long time.

Discussion

The discovery made at Piprahwa in 1898 remains one of the most spectacular finds in Buddhist archaeological history, but it is exceptional not for its bone relics, nor even for its inscription (since other such inscribed reliquaries have subsequently been found), but for its gems.[59] One of the scholars who has studied and thought systematically about the gems and beads in Buddhist reliquary finds is Wannaporn Rienjang. In her work on archaeological finds in Greater Gandhāra, she touches on several reasons for devotees to place beads in reliquaries together with the cremains of great saints or the Buddha. In what follows, I want to comment on four of these.

(1) The beads can be seen as offerings intended to honor the deceased saint and thereby to make merit for the devotee. In the event of relics buried inside stupas (as at Piprahwa),[60] these beads would have been put in the reliquaries prior to interment, "during which time the relics may have been temporarily placed on display."[61] This would have been done by Buddhist devotees—certainly laywomen, but also laymen and possibly monks.[62] According to Rienjang, the range of quality and artistry reflected in the gems and beads "suggest[s] that the donors included both extremely wealthy individuals and people with less valuable offerings."[63]

The same may be true in the case of Piprahwa, although it should be said that at the high end of the spectrum there, the quality of the gems is truly exceptional. Thus, the first thing that struck Jack Ogden, the gemologist whom the Peppés asked to examine their collection, was that he was looking at pieces that were far superior in craftmanship to all the other jewelry he had ever studied from Buddhist stupas in India. For him, this indicated "that [they] must have been made or collected for a person or purpose of considerable importance."[64] Much the same conclusion was reached by Harry Falk, who is even more specifically inclined to see the stone coffer, the crystal reliquary, and a special (almost unique in India) class of beads he calls "star-shaped flowers" as being Aśokan in origin.[65]

Regardless of their provenance, one of the purposes of these offerings would have been for the donor to make merit and perhaps also aspire to some form of enlightenment. The acts of merit implied in the Piprahwa finds may, in fact, be found described in Buddhist literature. For example, in the second story of the Sanskrit collection of legends, the *Avadānaśataka*, the laywoman Yaśomatī, makes, among other things, an offering to the Buddha of "flowers made from gold, silver and jewels" and then vows to achieve Buddhahood. She is assured that, as a result, she will become, in a future aeon, the buddha Ratnamati (Bejeweled).[66] Or again, in story 77, the daughter of a rich merchant, meeting the past Buddha Kāśyapa, spontaneously takes off her garland of pearls and offers it to the Blessed One.[67] As a result, in a subsequent life, she is reborn with the name Muktā (Pearl) and attains arhatship.[68]

It is interesting to compare such gifts of gems to the more ordinary routine devotional offerings in Buddhism. Typically, today, in Theravāda countries, a devotee, in front of a Buddha image or stupa, will at least make a meritorious offering of a fresh flower blossom. This is accompanied by a recognition (sometimes expressed in a ritual verse) that, in time, this flower will fade, just as one's own body will die.[69] Flowers made of gold or jewels, on the other hand, do not fade. In this regard, the Piprahwa gems are different from ordinary offerings: they are a gift that keeps on giving, an act of merit that keeps on acting.

(2) In addition to being meritorious offerings, the beads and gems may be seen as adornments of the bones with which they are placed.[70] As such, they give meaning to that which they adorn. Patrick Geary has pointed out that the "bare relic—a bone or a bit of dust—carries no fixed code or sign of its meaning."[71] It needs to be framed—to be "adorned"—in order to have significance. One of the functions of beads and gems (and reliquaries) is to provide such a frame. Simply put, in terms of our discussion, bones become "relics" when they are adorned by beads. In this way too, they can be distinguished from the "sepulchral bones" of the ordinary dead that are never accompanied by beads.[72]

(3) As the examples from the *Avadānaśataka* above suggest, donors were existentially involved in their offerings, to the point that the gems they gave came to be reflected in their names (Bejeweled, Pearl). Rienjang makes a similar point when she suggests that, as personal

ornaments or possessions, gems could stand in for their owners, whether deceased or alive. According to her, microscopic examination of Gandhāran beads shows that they "appear to have been used and worn before being deposited in the relic caskets." In other words, these *were* items of personal jewelry and not pieces "prepared specifically for ritual offering."[73]

That being the case, Rienjang goes on to make an interesting interpretative move. Stupa sites, it should be remembered, were often places not only where the relics of saints were interred, but also the remains of the ordinary dead, who had been buried "ad sanctos"—the nearer to the relics of the departed saint, the better.[74] Assuming that the beads represent their donors, Rienjang goes on to propose that they and the other gems may have been an alternative or additional way to actual burial for devotees to get close—indeed very close—to the holy relics. By placing their own personal jewelry in the reliquaries themselves, the owners of these ornaments could "have their 'extended bodies' close to the . . . corporeal remains of the venerated entity, as in the case of *burial ad sanctos*."[75]

(4) Finally, in addition to being meritorious offerings that adorned the bones and embodied their donors, the beads and gems may also be seen as themselves Buddha-relics, but of a slightly different kind. Based on her work on Gandhāran materials, Rienjang suggests that the hardness and brilliance of gemstone beads "may reflect the incorruptibility and the excellent virtue of the Buddhahood and arhathood."[76] Indeed, in time, beads may have come to be preferred to bones.[77] For example, in later phases of finds in Gandhāra, corporeal relics actually disappear from reliquaries altogether, and all that is found in them are beads, especially pearls, which had "actually become the body, or rather bodies . . . of the Buddha and arhats themselves."[78]

At Piprahwa, of course, beads and bones *were* found together. In this context, the beads do not replace the bones so much as complement them. As is well known, in the broad context of ancient India, dead bodies and remains of dead bodies, such as bones and ashes, were generally considered to be impure. Like the bones found by Jagat Singh's workers in Sarnath, with which this chapter began, they were to be disposed of quickly and thoroughly. In this regard, the development of the relic cult in Buddhism was, at least according to some, a definite anomaly.[79] Johannes Bronkhorst has argued that some Buddhists may have had lingering general cultural worries about the impurity of relics, or they may have worried about the opinions of non-Buddhists or wanted to reassure potential converts about the legitimacy of relic worship.[80] As a result, various ways were found in Buddhism to mitigate these sentiments about the potential impurity of relics. One of these, I would like to suggest, was to introduce gems into reliquary deposits, as symbols of purity and also (to contrast further with bones and ashes) as symbols of permanence.[81] In this light, the beads and gems at Piprahwa can indeed be seen as relics—as embodiments of the Buddha himself—but they are relics of a rather different kind, stressing purity and permanence in contrast to corporeality and impermanence.

In this the gems at Piprahwa may be said to resemble the "hard glittering particles" that form—in addition to bones—one of the major types of Buddhist relics.[82] These jewel-like relics—which are sometimes thought of as transmogrified somatic substances—are often looked for in the ashes of the cremation pyres of great teachers, but they may be said to appear in other places as well. Indeed, in East and Southeast Asia and Tibet today, they are by far the more numerous kind of relic.[83]

Is it possible that the devotees who placed their beads and gems among the bones at Piprahwa wanted thereby to replicate the post-funerary situation in which these two types of relics coexisted? While evidence for ancient India is missing, this notion that there are two kinds of relics may be traceable at least back to Buddhaghosa in the fifth century CE. While acknowledging that some of the Buddha's relics (e.g., his eyeteeth) were bona fide bones, the great systematizer of the Theravāda tradition, in his commentary on the *Mahāparinibbāna Sutta*, also stated that the Buddha's relics were of three types—"like jasmine buds, like washed pearls, and like [nuggets] of gold."[84] As we have seen, flowers made out of different semiprecious substances, pearls, and pieces of gold were all among the gems found among the bones at Piprahwa.

Beads apart from Bones

The question must be asked, however, what happens to the "beads" when they are separated from their "bones"? The Piprahwa case perhaps makes it possible to answer this since, as we have seen, the British colonial government brought about such a separation by its decision to send the bones to Siam and the beads to the Indian Museum. One might think that one of the results of this situation would be that the beads would lose their religious meanings, but in fact this does not appear to be the case: they continue to be seen as relics—both by Buddhists and by the Peppés.

It is noteworthy that in the inventory of items from Piprahwa to be sent to the museum, the gems were called "jewels"; but when Willie Peppé placed the ones that he retained in glass cases, he labeled them "relics of the Buddha." That is also, as we have seen, the phrase he wrote on the box of gems he donated to the Asiatic Society (now at the Buddhist Society) and the way he described (i.e., as "relics") the twenty gems and one gold roll he sent to the Venerable Subhuti.[85] It may be, of course, that in all these cases he was using the term "relic" in its wider meaning of "an object of historical or sentimental interest surviving from an earlier historical time,"[86] but I think not. From Jinavaravaṃsa, Peppé was clearly aware of the religious importance of these objects to Buddhists, and the glass cases were intended to show the gems to pilgrims (such as the Dalai Lama) passing through Piprahwa.

In any case, the transformation was far more than lexical for the Venerable Subhuti, who, having received the twenty gems and the gold roll sent by Peppé, treated them as though they were bona fide relics and promptly enshrined them in his temple at Waskaduwa.[87] There, they have been worshipped up to the present day (by no less than the president of Sri Lanka), and over the decades, successive abbots have used them to establish ties with other temples, in much the same way that bone relics sent to King Chulalongkorn have been used. For example, from 1908 to the present, Waskaduwa has gifted some of its gem/relics to the following: the Dīpaduttamārāma (Jinavaravaṃsa's vihāra, known as "the Thai temple" in Colombo);[88] the Bodhiya temple in Kalutara; the crown prince of Thailand in Bangkok; and a Buddhist community of disciples in Moscow. In all of these cases the gems were viewed as though there were no difference between them and bone relics.[89]

Envoi

In April 2015, Willie's great-grandsons, Daniel Peppé and his cousin Chris Peppé, were invited to attend a public exposition of some of the Piprahwa gems still at Waskaduwa. They were greatly impressed by the fervor and the sheer number of the thousands of devotees present for that occasion, and gradually a realization dawned. As Chris Peppé later put it: "[Before my travels] I still viewed the gems as something that would be [seen] primarily in museums. However, my trip seemed to indicate otherwise. Although I insisted that the gems should really only be regarded as relic offerings, I was ... made aware of a much larger religious significance.... It seemed as if the jewels were almost being treated as relics themselves."[90] Chris Peppé's realization echoes that of his great-grandfather Willie and that of the many Buddhists who flocked to view the gems.

In this chapter, after a retelling of the saga of the Piprahwa finds, it has been suggested that the "beads" found there may be viewed in a variety of ways. They may be seen as ongoing offerings meant to make merit. They may be viewed as adorning their bones and so highlighting the latter's relic status. They may also be seen as embodiments of their donors, who thus could be ongoingly in the presence of the Buddha, even after death. Finally, they can be viewed as fully relics in their own right—something they achieved not merely by proximity to the Buddha's bones, but also by their own intrinsic qualities and by their resemblance to the "glittering particles" that are commonly thought of as relics. In their new situation—of being apart from those bones—the beads seem to have lost the first three of these functions, but they have retained their fourth aspect of acting as bona fide relics on their own.

Notes

I would like to thank Wannaporn Kay Rienjang and Sraman Mukherjee for sending me some of their articles—both published and unpublished; Chris Peppé for allowing me to quote from one of his emails; and the Guggenheim Foundation for a fellowship in 2015–2016 that enabled me to start research on a broader topic, of which this chapter is a part.

1. See, e.g., K. M. Srivastava, *Buddha's Relics from Kapilavastu* (Delhi: Agam Kala Prakashan, 1986). For a discussion of the controversy concerning the location of Kapilavastu, see Max Deeg, *The Places Where Siddhārtha Trod: Lumbinī and Kapilavastu* (Lumbini: Lumbini International Research Institute, 2003), 24–36, and Harry Falk, "The Ashes of the Buddha," *Bulletin of the Asia Institute* 217 (2013; pub. 2017), 56–57. In this chapter, I will be dealing only with the finds made by Peppé at Piprahwa and not with the later but equally exciting discoveries made there by Srivastava in the 1970s.
2. William Claxton Peppé, "The Piprāhwā Stūpa Containing Relics of Buddha," *Journal of the Royal Asiatic Society of Great Britain and Ireland*, 1898, 575–576. Some of the gems were also found in the bottom of the coffer.
3. In this chapter, I will use "beads" as shorthand for all the ornaments, gems, and jewels that were found (many of which were perforated and so, literally, beads) and "bones" to indicate corporeal remains.

4. Alexander Cunningham, "Four Reports Made During the Years 1862–63–64–65," *Archaeological Survey of India* 1 (1871): 114–115.
5. Jonathan Duncan, "An Account of the Discovery of Two Urns in the Vicinity of Benares," *Asiatick Researches* 5 (1801): 131–132. It is interesting that Duncan described the finds as "a few human bones . . . some decayed pearls, gold leaves, and other jewels of no value." One wonders about the discrepancy between his depiction and the later one (given above) that Cunningham got from one of Jagat Singh's workers many years later.
6. Wannaporn Kay Rienjang, "Patronage along the Borderlands. The Case of the Apracas and Their Possible Connection with Nagarahara," paper presented to the European Association for South Asian Archaeology and Art (EASAA) Conference, Naples, 2018, p. 2.
7. On the British gifting of the Piprahwa relics to Siam, see Sraman Mukherjee, "Relics in Transition: Material Mediations in Changing Worlds," *Ars Orientalis* 48 (2018): 20–42.
8. Falk, "Ashes," 54.
9. Peppé, "The Piprāhwā Stūpa," 576.
10. It is important to distinguish these kinds of gems added to reliquaries from the naturally though somewhat mysteriously formed "hard glittering particles" or "crystalline beads," often found even today in the remains of great Buddhists' funeral pyres (on which see Francesca Tarocco's chapter in this volume). As we shall see, one possible way of interpreting the Piprahwa gems is as objects meant to replicate such relics.
11. See Sraman Mukherjee, "Transmissions, Translations, Reconstitutions: Revisiting Geographies of Buddha Relics in the Southern Asian Worlds," in *Imagining Asia(s): Networks, Actors, Sites*, edited by Andrea Acri, Kashshaf Ghani, Murari Jha, and Sraman Mukherjee (Singapore: ISEAS, forthcoming).
12. The coffer and the reliquary vases are still there, but the gems unfortunately "now seem to be untraceable" (Falk, "Ashes," 53).
13. This policy had not always been the case; when Alexander Cunningham and Frederick Maisey found relics of various disciples of the Buddha in the stupas in Sanchi in 1851, they and their reliquaries were all taken to museums in London (only to be returned to India almost a century later by the Victoria and Albert trustees). (See Torkel Brekke, "Bones of Contention: Buddhist Relics, Nationalism and the Politics of Archaeology," *Numen* 54 (2007): 270–303; see also, with regard to the Piprahwa case, Himanshu Prabha Ray, *The Return of the Buddha:*

Ancient Symbols for a New Nation (London: Routledge, 2014), 105–110.
14. For a picture, see Falk, "Ashes," 53.
15. Falk, "Ashes," 52, 67–68. Falk's argument, which cannot be gone into here, is complex but intriguing in its attempt to resolve a number of dilemmas surrounding the Piprahwa finds.
16. The note he sent to Smith has survived and is currently among the Peppé papers at the Royal Asiatic Society Archives in London (GB 891 WCP/1/5).
17. Royal Asiatic Society Archives, GB 891 WCP/1/6.
18. See Ray, *The Return of the Buddha,* 106–107, for a survey of global coverage in late nineteenth-century and early twentieth-century newspapers. For a recent example, see the 2013 documentary *Bones of the Buddha* (Icon Films), narrated by British freelance writer and popular historian Charles Allen. Available on line at http://www.pbs.org/wnet/secrets/bones-of-the-buddha-watch-the-full-episode/1073/.
19. See, e.g., Georg Bühler, "Preliminary Note on a Recently Discovered Śākya Inscription," *Journal of the Royal Asiatic Society,* 1898, 387–389; John F. Fleet, "The Inscription on the Piprawa Vase," *Journal of the Royal Asiatic Society,* 1906, 149–180; Sylvain Lévi, "L'Inde ancienne," *Journal des savants,* 1905, 540–541; Richard Pischel, "Die Inschrift von Piprāva," *Zeitschrift der deutschen morgenländischen Gesellschaft* 56 (1902): 157–158; Auguste Barth, "L'inscription du reliquaire de Piprava," *Journal des savants,* 1906, 541–554. For a discussion of the translation of the inscription, see Falk, "Ashes," 59–62.
20. Barth, "L'inscription," 554. See also Auguste Barth, "The Inscription on the Piprahwa Vase," translated by G. Tamson, *Indian Antiquary* 36 (1907): 117–124. The inscription itself reads: *sukitibhatinaṃ sabhagiṇikanaṃ saputadalanaṃ iyaṃ salilanidhane budhasa bhagavate saki[yanaṃ].*
21. See Charles Allen, *The Buddha and Dr. Führer: An Archaeological Scandal* (London: Haus Publishing, 2008); Falk, "Ashes," 44–45; Andrew Huxley, "Dr Führer's *Wanderjahre:* The Early Career of a Victorian Archaeologist," *Journal of the Royal Asiatic Society* 20 (2010): 489–502. For a copy of Vincent Smith's official report on his investigation of Führer, see Michael Willis, "Dhār, Bhoja and Sarasvatī: From Indology to Political Mythology and Back," *Journal of the Royal Asiatic Society,* 2012, 150–153.
22. Theodor Bloch, "Notes on the Exploration of Vaisali," *Annual Report, Bengal Circle, Archaeological Survey of India for the Year Ended*

April 1904 (Calcutta: Bengal Secretariat Press, 1904), 15. On other circumstances that accounted for these suspicions, see Falk, "Ashes," 62–63.

23. See Falk, "Ashes," 59–60, and Richard Salomon, "Observations on the Piprahwa Inscription and Its Epigraphic Context," paper presented at Harewood House, Yorkshire, July 9, 2006. I would like to thank Professor Salomon for sending me his article.
24. Terence A. Phelps, "The Piprahwa Deceptions: Set-Ups and Showdown." http://piprahwa.org.uk/ThePiprahwaDeceptions.htm. See also Michael Willis, "Review of Harry Falk, *Aśokan Sites and Artefacts,*" *Journal of the Royal Asiatic Society,* 2012, 188.
25. Andrew Huxley, "Who Should Pay for Indological Research? The Debate between 1884 and 1914," *Berliner Indologische Studien/ Berlin Indological Studies* 22 (2015), 49–86.
26. Royal Asiatic Society Archives GB 891 WCP/1/9.
27. Peppé appears to have allowed him not only to see the relics and the gems, but also to make a plaster cast of the inscription, which he then gave to Vincent Smith, who passed it on to T. W. Rhys Davids. See Vincent A. Smith, "The Piprāhwā Stūpa," *Journal of the Royal Asiatic Society,* 1898, 868.
28. On Subhuti, see Ananda Guruge, *From the Living Fountains of Buddhism* (Colombo: Department of Cultural Affairs, 1967), ch. 2.
29. For a biography of Jinavaravamsa, see Tamara Loos, *Bones around My Neck: The Life and Exile of a Prince Provocateur* (Ithaca, NY: Cornell University Press, 2016). For an account of his diplomatic career, see M. L. Manich Jumsai, *Prince Prisdang's Files on His Diplomatic Activities in Europe, 1880–1886* (Bangkok: Chalermnit, 1977).
30. *Foreign Records of the Bangkok Period up to A.D. 1932: Published on the Occasion of the Rattanakosin Bicentennial 1982* (Bangkok: Office of the Prime Minister, 1982), 175; see also S. Mukherjee, "Relics in Transition," 31–32.
31. *Foreign Records,* 171–172. A similar reason was later given when the British were trying to figure out what to do with the bones, also thought to be of the Buddha, found in the Kanishka Reliquary in Peshawar. See Frederick M. Asher, "Travels of a Reliquary, Its Contents Separated at Birth," *South Asian Studies* 28 (2012): 150.
32. S. Mukherjee, "Relics in Transition," 32–33.
33. *Foreign Records,* 181–182; see also S. Mukherjee, "Relics in Transition," 33.
34. *Foreign Records,* 181–182; see also Ray, *The Return of the Buddha,* 108.

35. The Golden Mount was built by Chulalongkorn so that the Piprahwa relics would remain high above the city (see Justin McDaniel, *The Lovelorn Ghost and the Magical Monk: Practicing Buddhism in Modern Thailand* [New York: Columbia University Press, 2011], 128).
36. On this see John S. Strong, "The Afterlives of Buddhist Relics," paper presented to the Lee and Won Buddhist Studies Workshop, Seoul, September 8, 2017.
37. T. Loos, *Bones,* 199n131.
38. Today, the Nagoya temple is called the Nittaiji (日泰寺 "Japan-Thailand" temple). On it, see Richard M. Jaffe, "Buddhist Material Culture, 'Indianism,' and the Construction of Pan-Asian Buddhism in Prewar Japan," *Material Religion* 2, no. 3 (2006): 266–292; Kawaguchi Kōfū 川口高風, "Kakuōzan no sōken ni tsuite 覚王山ノ創建について" [About the foundation of Kakuōzan (i.e., the Nittaiji)], *Journal of Aichi Gakuin University, Humanities and Sciences* 49 (2001): 3–26. During my visit there on November 17–18, 2017, to witness the veneration of the relics on the anniversary of the foundation of the temple, I noticed that a bronze statue of King Chulalongkorn in the courtyard had also received flower offerings.
39. Ronald Y. Nakasone and Heather Emi Nakasone, "The Diaspora of the Corporeal Remains of Lord Buddha," *Journal of Religion and Culture* 8 (2014): 169–178. I would like to thank Professor Nakasone for meeting with me in Berkeley on December 1, 2015, as well as the Reverend Ron Kobata for showing me the stupa on the roof of the Buddhist Church in San Francisco and for welcoming me the next day to his congregation's celebration of Bodhi Day, involving veneration of the relics.
40. Union Bouddhiste de France (UBF), "Les Reliques de l'Inde en France, via la Thaïlande." http://www.bouddhisme-france.org/reliques/article/le-contexte-historique.html.
41. I would like to thank M. Philippe Judenne of the UBF for facilitating my visit to the Grande Pagode on October 8, 2015, for answering many questions, and for showing me videos of the enshrinement of the relics. For an account of this place and the relics there, see Strong, "The Afterlives of Buddhist Relics." See also Olivier Reigen Wang-Genh, "L'Installation des reliques du Bouddha à la Pagode de Vincennes est une grande joie pour tous les bouddhistes de France"; http://www.bouddhisme-france.org/reliques/article/l-installation-des-reliques-du-bouddha-a-la-pagode-de-vincennes-est-une-grande-joie-pour-tous-les-bouddhistes-de-france-rev-olivier-reigen-wang-genh.html. Accessed March 27, 2019.

42. Royal Asiatic Society Archives, GB 891 WCP/1/38. Scans of the pages may now be found online at http://www.piprahwa.com/theletters. The list was sent to Dr. Bock, the director of the Indian Museum, August 3, 1898 (see GB 891 WCP/1/20). Smith published a summary of this list in his "Piprāhwā Stūpa," 869–870. See also Allen, *The Buddha and Dr. Führer,* 76–77.
43. Royal Asiatic Society Archives, GB 891 WCP/1/38.
44. Royal Asiatic Society Archives, GB 891 WCP/1/38. A gemological analysis commissioned recently by some of Peppé's descendants determined, more scientifically, that the materials used were "amethyst, aquamarine (blue beryl), carnelian (and etched carnelian and sardonyx), coral, citrine (yellow quartz), garnet, glass, green chalcedony, iolite, pearl, rock crystal and shell" and that though the pieces "could be described as 'beads' . . . for the sake of convenience . . . the group [also] contains objects that are small pendants, parts of what seem to be composite flowers, 'button' or appliqué ornaments, gold foil disks and unpierced stones, pearls and coral." See Jack Ogden, "Report on the Beads and Related Objects from the Piprahwa Stupa (2018)"; http://www.piprahwa.com/analysis, p. 1.
45. Royal Asiatic Society Archives, GB 891 WCP/1/38. This is according to my count, which differs somewhat from Allen's estimate that Peppé retained about one-sixth of the total (see Allen, *The Buddha and Dr. Führer,* 207).
46. Royal Asiatic Society Archives, GB 891 WCP/1/21.
47. Royal Asiatic Society Archives, GB 891/1/24. In his manifold career, Jinavaravaṃsa had once been director general of the Siamese Post and Telegraph Department and had facilitated its entry into the Universal Postal Union (T. Loos, *Bones,* 54–55).
48. Royal Asiatic Society Archives, GB 891 WCP/1/22 and WCP/1/25.
49. For pictures of many of these gems, see http://www.piprahwa.com/thejewels.
50. Around this time, one of the glass cases was broken, and Humphrey put its contents into a shoe box marked "relics." In time, other items—not from the original Piprahwa find—got mixed up with the gems in the shoe box. Eventually, two new glass cases were made for display purposes, but one of those contains extraneous items.
51. A scan may be found at http://www.piprahwa.com/the-dalai-lama-visits-birdpur.
52. I would like to thank Willie's great-grandson, Daniel Peppé, for showing me the collection at his home in London in October 2015.

53. Vicki Mackenzie, "Buried with the Buddha," *Sunday Times Magazine* (London), March 21, 2008. Reproduced at http://piprahwajewels.co.uk/page7.html.
54. I would like to thank Desmond Bidulph, president of the Buddhist Society, Eccleston Square, London, for showing me the box on October 5, 2015.
55. This has been contested by Stephen Hodge, who, in an email to H-Buddhism (posted April 7, 2004), declared: "Mr Seto is a new-comer at the Buddhist Society and was probably not aware that all the old staff, recently retired or displaced by his advent, knew for decades what was in the Society's display cabinet. All he has really done is to publicize their existence more widely—something that previous custodial staff had not done, so as to avoid attracting the wrong kind of interest. They will now probably be stolen as have other items in the past."
56. It later turned out that the handwriting on the Buddhist Society box was that of Willie Peppé himself, and it was supposed that it was the gift he had made to the Royal Asiatic Society when he had showed lantern slides there in 1903 and that either T. W. Rhys Davids or his wife Caroline had later given the gems to the Buddhist Society sometime after its establishment in 1924. See http://www.piprahwa.com/timeline.
57. Quoted in Mackenzie, "Buried with the Buddha."
58. Interview with Desmond Bidulph at the Buddhist Society, Eccleston Square, London, October 5, 2015.
59. For a list of sources describing reliquaries labeled as being of the Buddha, see John S. Strong, *Relics of the Buddha* (Princeton, NJ: Princeton University Press, 2004), 13n31.
60. Not all reliquaries were necessarily buried in stupas. Archaeological evidence in northwest India shows the existence of "relic shrines" in which reliquaries were brought out for veneration, on which occasions devotees could make more offerings. See Kurt Behrendt, *The Buddhist Architecture of Gandhāra* (Leiden: Brill, 2004), 239–253. Falk ("Ashes," 51) suggests something similar may have been the case with the Piprahwa stone coffer being out in the open when it was at Lumbinī, as he hypothesizes.
61. Wannaporn Kay Rienjang, "Honoring the Body: Relic Cult Practice in Eastern Afghanistan with Comparison to Dharmarajika Pakistan" (PhD diss., University of Cambridge, 2017), 159.
62. Even though monks may have been prohibited by their Vinaya rules from wearing jewelry, archaeologists have found gemstones and

beads in monks' cells. It is therefore "possible that the beads found in relic deposits may have belonged to the monks who may have received them from the laity and could as well have subsequently offered them to the relic assemblages." See Rienjang, "Honoring the Body," 144.

63. Wannaporn Kay Rienjang, Jonathan Mark Kenoyer, and Margaret Sax, "Stone Beads from the Relic Deposits: A Preliminary Morphological and Technological Analysis," in *Charles Masson and the Buddhist Sites of Afghanistan: Explorations, Excavations, Collections 1833–1835*, edited by Elizabeth Errington (London: British Museum, 2017), 56–57.
64. Ogden, "Report," 6.
65. Falk, "Ashes," 52–56.
66. See Naomi Appleton, *Many Buddhas, One Buddha: A Study and Translation of Avadāśataka 1-40* (Sheffield: Equinox, 2020), 72–74.
67. For a modern day offering that seems to parallel this, see Strong, *Relics of the Buddha,* 204. It should be said that Uesugi and Rienjang call into question such scenarios of spontaneous giving carried away by devotion. Based on the absence of the remains of string or thread in reliquary finds, they suggest that the perforated gems "were offered . . . not in the form of strung ornaments but in the form of individual beads from different original sources." See Uesugi Akinori and Wannaporn Kay Rienjang, "Stone Beads from Stupa Relic Deposits at the Dharmarajika Buddhist Complex, Taxila," *Gandhāran Studies* 11 (2018): 61. It is not clear that this was the case at Piprahwa.
68. Léon Feer, *Avadāna-çataka: cent légendes bouddhiques* (Paris: Ernest Leroux, 1891), 288–289.
69. Richard F. Gombrich, *Precept and Practice: Traditional Buddhism in the Rural Highlands of Ceylon* (Oxford: Clarendon Press, 1971), 114–116.
70. Rienjang, "Honoring the Body," 328.
71. Patrick J. Geary, *Furta Sacra: Thefts of Relics in the Central Middle Ages* (Princeton, NJ: Princeton University Press, 1978), 5. See also Robert H. Sharf, "On the Allure of Buddhist Relics," *Representations* 66 (1999): 81.
72. Rienjang, "Honoring the Body," 327.
73. Rienjang, Kenoyer, and Sax, "Stone Beads," 57.
74. See, on this, Gregory Schopen, *Bones, Stones, and Buddhist Monks: Collected Papers on the Archaeology, Epigraphy, and Texts of Monastic Buddhism in India* (Honolulu: University of Hawai'i Press, 1997, 114–147.
75. Rienjang, "Honoring the Body," 146.

76. Rienjang, "Honoring the Body," 331. See also Peter Skilling, "Relics: The Heart of Buddhist Veneration," in *Relics and Relic Worship in Early Buddhism,* edited by Janice Stargardt (London: British Museum Press, 2018), 3.
77. In some places today bits of bone from the bodies of great teachers are thought to crystallize or vitrify into bead-like relics through a process of metamorphosis over time (see J. L. Taylor, *Forest Monks and the Nation-State* [Singapore: ISEAS, 1993], 175–177). Somewhat similarly, in East Asia, bodily relics of the Buddha are sometimes thought to become precious wish-fulfilling jewels (*cintāmaṇi*), as though the relics themselves were evolving from bones to beads (see Brian D. Ruppert, *Jewels in the Ashes: Buddha Relics and Power in Early Medieval Japan* (Cambridge, MA: Harvard University Press, 2000; Harvard East Asian Monographs 188), 130–135.
78. Rienjang, "Honoring the Body," 331.
79. See Strong, *Relics of the Buddha,* 15, for multiple iterations of this view.
80. Johannes Bronkhorst, *Buddhism in the Shadow of Brahmanism* (Leiden: Brill, 2011), 193–246.
81. John S. Strong, "Relics and Images," *Oxford Handbook of Buddhist Practice,* edited by Paula Arai and Kevin Trainor (New York: Oxford University Press, forthcoming).
82. On this kind of relic, see the chapter by Francesca Tarocco in this volume.
83. See Strong, *Relics of the Buddha,* 10–12
84. *Sumangalavilāsinī: Buddhaghosa's Commentary on the Dīgha Nikāya,* 2nd ed., edited by William Stede (London: Pali Text Society, 1971) 2:603–604; English translation, An Yang-Gyu, *The Buddha's Last Days: Buddhaghosa's Commentary on the Mahāparinibbāna Sutta* (Oxford: Oxford University Press, 2003), 206.
85. Subhuti had been writing repeatedly to Peppé, asking him for Piprahwa bone relics, apparently thinking that he still possessed some of them. See http://www.piprahwa.com/letters-2; Royal Asiatic Society Archives, GB 891 WCP 1/18 and GB 891 WCP/1/22. That these were the gems is evidenced by the fact that in the same letter, he told Subhuti that he would see "how beautifully they are *made.*" See Anonymous, "Original Relics of the Buddha Sakyamuni," http://sharira.org/h_e.html, accessed September 20, 2015; italics added
86. *New Oxford American Dictionary,* online edition.
87. There is today considerable confusion in Waskaduwa, and more broadly in Sri Lanka, about Willie Peppé and the Piprahwa story. For

one illustration of this, see Rasika Nanayakkara, "Exposition of the Sacred Kapilavastu Relics at Sri Subhuti Maha Viharaya, Waskaduwa," *The Island* (Colombo), January 25, 2013. On the other hand, some of the Waskaduwe relics may actually be bones from Piprahwa sent to Sri Lanka by Chulalongkorn in 1900, in his first distribution. See T. Loos, *Bones*, 199n131.

88. Anonymous, "Original Relics." Jinavaravaṃsa had the gems enshrined in a new Bodhgaya-style dagoba he built there. There is some confusion, however, since in doing so, Jinavaravaṃsa also claimed that the relics he was enshrining were "tiny fragments of bone relics" he had brought back from Piprahwa. See Prisdang Chumsai Jinavaravaṃsa, "The Ratna Chetiya Dīpaduttamārāma, Colombo," edited by Sumet Jumsai, *Journal of the Royal Asiatic Society of Sri Lanka* 48 (2003): 214, 219.
89. Anonymous, "Original Relics."
90. Email from Chris Peppé to John Strong, September 3, 2015. Despite this realization, the gems have most recently been exhibited in museums: at the "Next Stop Nirvana—Approaches to Buddhism" exhibit (Museum Rietberg, Zurich, December 13, 2018–March 31, 2019) and at the Rubin Museum of Art in New York (June 2019–January 2020).

Chapter 9

Translating the Porcelain Pagoda of Nanjing

Ellen Huang

The grand Bao'en Si Ta 报恩寺塔 soars twenty-six stories high (roughly equivalent to a height of eighty meters). During the day, arrayed vectors of sunlight shine brightly by virtue of its eight-sided glass structure. At night, the towering structure offers an even more brilliant vision: an incandescent illumination resulting from its modern electric outfittings. The name "Bao'en Si Ta" translates loosely into English as the Temple Pagoda of Gratitude (fig. 4). Reincarnated as a heritage site and museum, it opened officially in December 2015 to great fanfare. Situated along the south bank of the Qinhuai 秦淮 River just outside present-day Nanjing's southern city gate (Zhonghuamen 中華門), the pagoda declares itself to be an unmistakable contemporary monument to the city of Nanjing's glorious past, built with steel girders and glossy tiers ornamented with colored designs. Lustrous glass casings highlight the reconstructed pagoda tower while equally transparent floors reveal the temple's preserved archaeological foundations. In 2010, a CEO promised funding of ten billion RMB to finance the first phases of a historical reconstruction project, constituting the largest single private philanthropic donation in twentieth- and twenty-first-century Chinese history at the time. The result of such a donation was a heritage site and architectural display touting Nanjing's significance in global and Chinese history. A visit will set one back 160 RMB (approximately $20 USD) for an adult admission ticket today.

The reconstructed tower ostensibly rings with newness, being made with light-mediating glass. Hologram-like figurines sitting on roof eaves hover in a diaphanous haze (fig. 5). Such a deployment of staining effects in the glass suggests the past through the vestigial

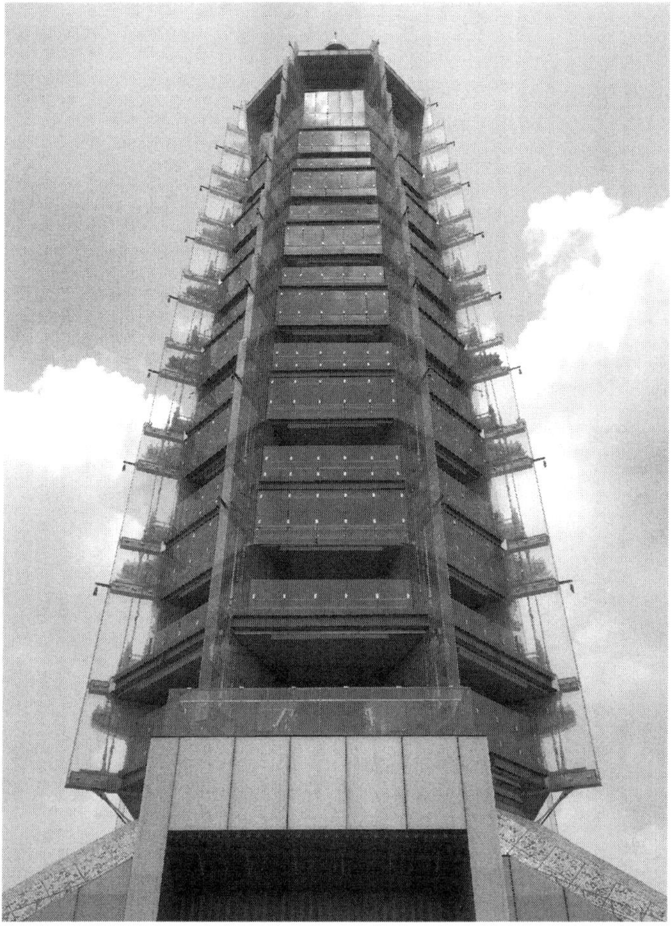

Fig. 4. Photo of reconstructed Nanjing Pagoda Temple of Gratitude. Photo credit: Ellen Huang.

markings that create faintly floating images. Their translucency alludes to apparitions on the verge of dissolving into air. The overall structure thus presents itself as a modern building whose material composition forgoes common expectations for historical authenticity and enduring monumentality.[1]

Paradoxically, for the last four hundred years, the Bao'en Si Ta was known precisely for a specific material composition. Rather than glass, the pagoda's worldwide reputation rested upon an admiration of its being made completely out of porcelain. The Bao'en Si Ta was a magnificent

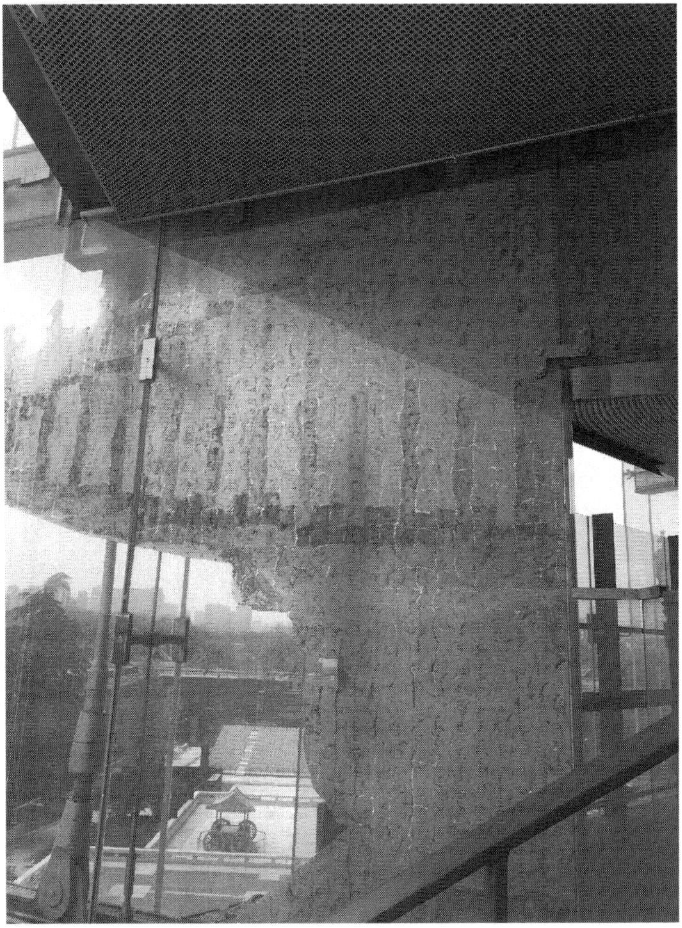

Fig. 5. Detail of glass showing historical tiles and roof tile figures of Nanjing Pagoda. Photo credit: Ellen Huang.

spectacle of shiny, glistening porcelain. Hence, it gained its eponymous name, with which its renown in Europe was mostly associated: the Porcelain Pagoda. During the seventeenth and eighteenth centuries, the pagoda captured the imagination of the European continent already enraptured in a reverie of China. The famous Swedish-English architect William Chambers (1723–1796) enthused about the Nanjing temple tower in emphatic terms: "The most considerable of [all the buildings of China] are the Porcelain Tower at Nanking and that of Tong Tchang Fou."[2]

Somewhat overshadowed by such seventeenth- and eighteenth-century European sources touting porcelain as the defining feature of the Nanjing Porcelain Pagoda (hereafter "Nanjing Pagoda") is the fact that the pagoda was variously connected to other types of extraordinary matter—most prominently, Buddhist relics.[3] Buddhist relics have been known as sacred objects that had some connection to the remains of the historical Buddha and other venerated Buddhist adepts.[4] Germane to the topic of this volume, scholars have noted a distinctively charming quality of Buddhist relics: frequently, remnants of the Buddha often appear as shimmering jewel-like things, including granulated ashes and bones. One Chinese-language source links such relic jewels to the Nanjing Pagoda itself. Transmitted as an English translation in the Hong Kong–based serial *Chinese Repository* (1844), the text identified porcelain as only one among many highly desired sparkly materials that made up the pagoda. The text begins by identifying the pagoda's monastic origins, first by noting the location of the Nanjing Pagoda as a site where the Buddha's relics were deposited in the fourth century. The text further describes the history after the fourth century, during which the pagoda underwent various cycles of disrepair and restoration. By the time an imperial renovation project executed by order of the Qing dynasty Jiaqing emperor (r. 1795–1810) was completed, the pagoda's topmost tiers consisted of a myriad of jewels, including five pearls; one ingot of gold; 133 pounds each of tea, silver, and medicine; a string of 1,000 coins; yellow silk; and sacred texts.[5] According to this text, the Nanjing Pagoda was both a landmark memorializing the location of sacred remains and a container for precious physical matter.

Was this nineteenth-century description merely an exaggeration of the power and prosperity of the imperial court's ability to sponsor construction projects? Research so far is inconclusive. However, it is not unthinkable that it was perhaps written by an official of the Jiaqing emperor's court. Whatever the nature of this nineteenth-century textual record was, it points to the ways in which the history of the Nanjing Pagoda brings together porcelain and Buddhist relics in a rich collage of bejeweled grandeur. Through the Nanjing Pagoda, Buddhist history, material culture, and the history of porcelain share a surprising point of contact, one that will be explored in this chapter.

The existing scholarship about the Nanjing Pagoda has neglected to consider the possible ways in which the porcelain qualities of the pagoda relate to the jewelness of Buddhist relics. One reason for this tendency is the overriding interest in porcelain as an object of consumption rather than as a material with a broad array of trajectories, functions, and effects.[6] Studied as an object and a collectible, porcelain's impact in scholarship is inextricably linked to connoisseurship studies. Furthermore, where histories of porcelain are written from a larger cultural context, the narrative reinforces the reception paradigm as traveling from China to the "West," often generalized to mean the rest of the world.[7] Such existing scholarship analyzes the reception of the Nanjing Pagoda in the context of *chinoiserie,* the artistic movement that fueled an obsession for things from China in Europe that played out over the seventeenth and eighteenth centuries.[8] As the scholarship demonstrates, *chinoiserie* ultimately engendered fantasies of a romantic East and produced representations of China that had as much to do with how the Europeans perceived and constructed a foreign "other" as much as how such imaginaries intersected with discursive constructions of race, class, and gender within early modern Europe.[9] Still, little is known about the Nanjing Pagoda in contexts other than its role in *chinoiserie* fantasy and illusions.

Another reason for this lack of attention to the significance of the pagoda's porcelain is due to the absence of any verifiable fragments that can be definitively associated with the historical pagoda itself. At present, the pagoda survives only in texts and in painted and printed images. These artifacts are dispersed across museums, archaeological institutes, and private collections worldwide.[10] Excavations of the Ming imperial ceramic kilns specializing in court-sponsored buildings during the Republican period (1927–1937) and in 1958 revealed architectural components such as tiles, beams, archways, and bricks. Scholars believe such fragments to have been made in the same kilns that produced tiles, finials, and ornaments for the pagoda, on the basis of their correspondence to descriptions in fifteenth-century Ming-era texts.[11] These extant fragments thus may have been produced in the same manufacturing center but have not definitively been identified as remains of the actual structure. In 1998, only portions of a stone bridge and stele from the 1430s architectural complex remained, surrounded by late twentieth-century buildings of Nanjing.[12] Experts surmise that the existing remains belonged to nearby buildings that made up the larger imperial monastic complex in which the pagoda stood during the Ming and Qing periods. Thus, no remnants have been positively and definitively associated with the pagoda structure itself. While historical records tell of its dismantling in the 1850s, the absence of any attributable pieces strikes one as puzzling. As a result, the tower's mystique intensifies, seemingly in accordance with the centuries-long European fantasies "reveling the pagoda."

In recent years, a separate narrative of the pagoda has emerged. Spurred by the discovery of underground crypts lying underneath historical pagoda foundations in Hangzhou and Shaanxi, the Nanjing Municipal Museum undertook a systematic excavation of the grounds on which the pagoda stood. In 2010, archaeologists excavating the site discovered that the pagoda had a less visible counterpart: an underground palace (*digong*) in which remnants of a reliquary and what is believed to be a piece of the Buddha's parietal bone 佛頂真骨 were found.[13] The historical anthropologist and scholar Jing Zhuge has analyzed the impact of the archaeological discovery of underground artifacts. As she notes, the excavation's findings of numinous Buddhist objects encouraged the municipal government to assign a Buddhist meaning to the historical reconstruction site rather than calling attention to its architectural composition of porcelain.[14] Indeed, while the contents of the relic deposit site have yet to be fully analyzed in terms of iconography and ritual function, the renovated pagoda and heritage center commits a large portion of its display to the excavated artifacts as demonstrative of Nanjing's role in the spread of Buddhism in Chinese history.

This chapter will attempt to bridge these two narratives of the pagoda's history—one about its underground contents and the other about its aboveground architecture. One narrative, adopted by the Nanjing municipal government and reflected in the renovated tourist site, posits the central role of archaeological evidence as indispensable to recovering a real history of the pagoda. The other narrative, as discussed above, privileges the discourse of porcelain from the perspective of scholars who primarily consider the pagoda through the lens of early modern sources written in European languages. Setting aside questions about which of the two discourses offers a more accurate history of the Nanjing Pagoda, I unravel the ways in which the pagoda as a material marvel and as a relic deposit site share surprising resonances. Building upon the growing body of recent scholarship that argues for the importance of material culture in Buddhist history, such as the research of John Kieschnick, Fabio Rambelli, John Strong, and Kevin Trainor, this chapter brings together the fields of ceramic studies and Buddhist art history, two fields that remain insular from one another.[15]

Focusing on the discourse about the pagoda's composition, the analysis presented here offers a material history of the Nanjing Pagoda. Bringing together the recent archaeological finds and early-modern textual sources, the chapter revisits the Nanjing Pagoda's history by focusing on the journeys and material reconstitution of the pagoda over the last three hundred years. Together, the sources reveal the changing concepts of materials associated with the pagoda that have significance across both religious and secular realms. Ultimately, I suggest that an examination of the Nanjing Pagoda through a focus on its material not only reveals the significance of porcelain beyond the history of global trade and connoisseurship. An examination of how the materials of the pagoda were received and produced also illuminates something about the logic of relics in Chinese Buddhist material culture. As Eugene Wang has shown for the case of the tenth-century Leifeng Pagoda on West Lake in Hangzhou, pagodas have been under the intense scrutiny of active myth making, imagination, and ideas about place.[16] In this vein, following the discourse and practice of the pagoda, I suggest that the material of the pagoda's namesake, porcelain, is best understood through the framework of the Buddhist concept of *śarīra* (Chinese: *sheli* 舍利 or relic deposits collected from the Buddha's body after cremation) as it was translated—physically and materially—into Southern Dynasties-era China (420–589).

I explore the history of the pagoda's material nature across two registers. First, by providing a brief overview of the pagoda as it was recorded in key Ming and Qing dynasty texts, I examine the many iterations of the pagoda in light of the European fascination with the pagoda as a product of cultural translation of highly desired materials. Second, I review the newly excavated archaeological finds in light of Buddhist textual records about the making of the sacred site and the way it reveals a different history of translation. Ultimately, the chapter illuminates not only the processes by which value is ascribed to precious materials, but also a view of porcelain from the perspective of Buddhist relics, much as Francesca Tarocco explores for the case of glass in Chinese Buddhism in this volume. The chapter thus avoids asserting the reality of a true porcelain by developing porcelain's contingent materiality within specific historical contexts. The result is a concept of porcelain whose authenticity lies not in a single definition but encompasses a range of concepts about materiality.

Monument or Miniature? Perceptions of the Nanjing Pagoda

The seventeenth-century compilation of historical records relating to Buddhist monasteries located around present-day Nanjing, entitled *Jinling fancha zhi* 金陵梵刹志, provides a nominal history of the

Nanjing Pagoda in an entry about its repair and restoration after it had been burned and destroyed sometime between 1407 and 1413.[17] The compilation also includes a woodblock print that shows the pagoda within a larger monastic complex (fig. 6). Protruding beyond the pictorial borders of the woodblock printed layout, the pagoda rises as a majestic tower among other devotional buildings, altars, and imperial halls. In the imperial record about its reconstruction, the Ming Yongle emperor provides motivations and reasons for the name that he gives to the renovated temple—"Bao'en Si," or the Temple of Gratitude. He records its history as follows:

> Built during the year *chiwu* 赤烏 [239] of King Wu [Sun Quan] [r. 238—251 CE] was a building, Tianxi Si 天禧寺, whose former name was Chang'gan Si 長干寺. Over many years spanning several generations, it [the building] experienced repeated periods of renewal and disrepair. During the Tianxi reign of the Song [dynasty] Emperor Zhenzong's (968–1022), [the temple] underwent restoration, after which the name was changed to Tianxi Si. [The temple] lasted as such until the present glorious dynasty and the reign of [the Emperor] Hongwu [1368–1398], at which point the temple exhibited some wear. So the Board of Works Deputy Vice Minister 工部侍郎 Huang Ligong called upon the people to raise funds for repairs. . . . Later, the temple . . . was destroyed completely by fire . . . and I, the imperial figure, reflected that there was nothing I had done to commemorate my mother, who had already passed away. So I committed military and civilian resources, etc. to expend much effort . . . to rebuild the temple. It is ten thousand times more magnificent. With this expanded and newly rebuilt temple complex, we can make offerings to my parents' spirit and request the blessings for all the people and land. . . . Thus the name of the temple will be known as the great Temple of Gratitude (報恩寺 Bao'en Si).[18]

As the imperial records outlining the plan for reconstructing the pagoda reveal, the project of purposefully renovating the pagoda served a broader aim to construct a large memorial complex in which the pagoda was one of many buildings. Also discernible from the imperial document is that the emperor built and expanded the temple site to remember his parents. By lavishing resources to increase the temple's grandiose quality, the emperor sought to memorialize and broadcast the effective rule of the imperial family and, by extension, the continued

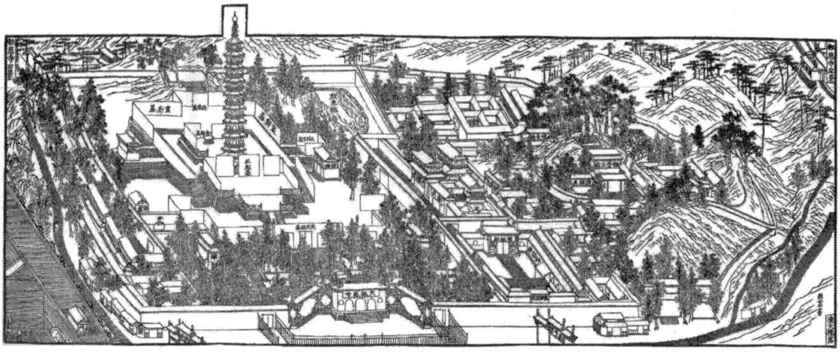

Fig. 6. Woodblock printed image of the Bao'en si from the 1607 *Jinling fanchazhi*. After Zhang Huiyi 張惠衣, *Jinling Da Bao'ensi ta zhi* 金陵大報恩寺塔志 (Beijing: Guoli Beiping yanjiu shi xue yan jiu hui, 1937), n.p. Public domain.

success of his own rulership over the Ming dynastic domain. The prevalence of the word *si* 寺 notwithstanding, the pagoda combined both religious and secular agendas. Moreover, the court's objectives for the monastery complex were to fulfill both commemorative symbolic aims and monumental functions, much as in the dual functions of the lavish reliquary stupa of the Fifth Dalai Lama (1617–1682), discussed in Nancy Lin's chapter in this volume.

By the late Ming and early Qing periods, late imperial texts in Chinese refer to the Nanjing tower as a *ta* 塔. Take, for instance, the seventeenth-century writer, historian, and member of the urban elite class Zhang Dai 張岱 (1597—d. after 1667), who referred to the temple in his memoirs simply as the "Bao'en Ta 報恩塔," replacing *si* with *ta*.[19] Over the course of the sixteenth century, the complex fell into disrepair, leaving only a couple of buildings standing, the Nanjing tower being one of the two.[20] Zhang Dai shares with the Yongle emperor a similar regard for the tower as a memorial and symbol but infuses an additional layer of rueful loss in his contextualization. Written around 1665, two decades after the defeat of the Ming dynasty in the north and just a few years after the defeat of Nanjing-based Ming loyalists in the south by the Manchu Qing forces, Zhang Dai's memoirs are replete with sentimental affect and recollection. Of the Nanjing structure, Zhang recalls, "China's great antique, a vessel produced from the kilns of the Yongle emperor, was the Bao'en Ta."[21] By referring to the tower as an antique, Zhang Dai's memoirs enact a museumification process. Using terms that evoke the object-centric language of a museum, his rhetoric seemingly transforms the tower from a monument of splendor to a symbol of the past. Further, rather than a monument whose definition often implies permanence and immobility, standing the test of time with site-specificity, the tower plays the role of a souvenir. Even the use of the binomial "*yaoqi* 窯器" (vessel from a kiln) implies a transition from colossal building to collectible—a transformation process consisting of miniaturization and objectification that effectively reduces the grandiose tower and its surrounding celebratory complex into a small token. For Zhang, the Bao'en Ta was a souvenir whose signification operated through nostalgia. As a reminder of a bygone epoch, the towering architecture was not simply a coherent structure celebrating and legitimating dynastic success, but also a fragmentary trace of a past no longer extant.[22]

Zhang's textual miniaturization anticipates the Nanjing Pagoda's nineteenth-century afterlife. Consider, for example, the multiple instances of the tower in diminutive form currently held in museum collections in the United Kingdom and France, to name just two locations. Research so far reveals ten model versions, eight of which are identical. The Victoria and Albert Museum maintains one such copy. Including its base, the Victoria and Albert copy is 276 centimeters tall and consists of multiple tiers of roofs marked by balustrades mounted by gilded dogs, glazed bells, and leaping fish (fig. 7). At almost 9 feet, its imposing height hardly makes it a miniature. At the same time, the scaled-down version, by implying monumentality as a smaller version, connotes its own status as a ruin defined by loss and absence. A paper label attached to its base section reinforces the centrality of loss, temporal ephemerality, and decay in a textual description from the late-nineteenth century: "The Porcelain Tower Nankin [Nanjing]. Built by the Emperor Yung Lo [Yongle, r. 1403–1424] in memory of his mother. . . . Destroyed by the sacking in 1853. Its name in Chinese was the Pao En [Bao'en] Jar or Pagoda of Gratitude."[23]

As these examples demonstrate, the Nanjing Pagoda's monumental nature operated on a variable scale. At times, the pagoda was gigantic; at others, it was miniature. Being polyscalar, the Nanjing Pagoda thus expands our idea of architecture to include materials and concepts beyond those of unchanging buildings. Rather, the pagoda's changing scale points to its ability to traverse physical dimensions and assume the form of a container, referred to as a "jar," or "kiln vessel." Spanning half a millennium, these passionate observers marshal a range of architectural terms to index various semantic concepts related to monument and memory to describe the landmark structure. Using the monastic

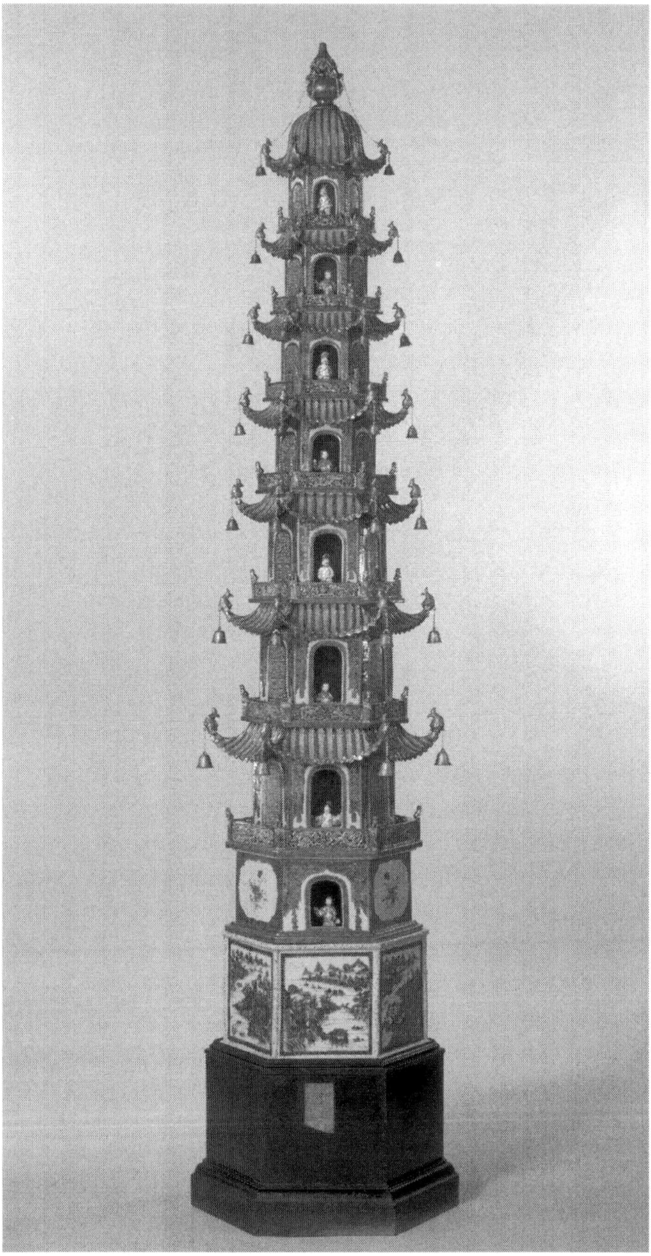

Fig. 7. Model of Nanjing Pagoda, porcelain, Victoria and Albert Museum, London, C.80–1954. Image © Victoria and Albert Museum, London.

architectural term *si,* the Yongle emperor not only celebrates his mother and father, but also proclaims the material wealth of the land over which he rules, legitimating his rulership and dynastic lineage all at once. For the late Ming writer Zhang Dai, who witnessed the fall of the very social order that the Yongle emperor upheld and experienced a social upheaval resulting in the establishment of a new dynastic state, the building memorializes not the present, but also a past already absent. Zhang Dai's Nanjing monument represents not wholeness but a remnant, a trace, and a fragment. Two modes of monumentality then aggregate into later perceptions of the object: over the span of the Qing dynasty to the cusp of its collapse in 1910, Chinese writers continued to refer to the tower as a *si-ta* (temple pagoda).[24]

Materializing the Pagoda

The Qing Chinese text by Zhang Dai suggests indirectly the material composition of the Nanjing building with the term "*yaoqi,*" generally meaning some object produced from a kiln. As a monument appearing in various physical sizes, shapes, and forms whose primary purpose was to exalt a glorious age or to reflect upon the passing of time, however, Zhang Dai's tower operated more as a dematerialized symbol rather than an object of matter. Whether using the character for temple, "*si,*" or pagoda, "*ta,*" or a phrase consisting of a composite of the two as in "*si ta*" to show their mutual reinforcement, Chinese-language records are suggestive of symbolism and meaning. In semiotic terms, the tower functioned as a signifier. By borrowing terms for sites and complexes connoting sacred contexts, their choice of words points more directly to such durational concerns as imperial immortality or imperial decay.[25]

In West European languages, the written record is consistent in its identification of the tower as an embodiment of great material value. *The Travels of Sir John Mandeville,* a mid-fourteenth-century text known as one of the world's first works of travel literature, is a case in point.[26] In a chapter about China, a passage about the emperor's palace includes a description praising an impressive pagoda "that is wrought of gold and of precious stones, and great pearls. At the four corners of the mountour [mound-shaped platform] be four serpents of gold. And all about there is made large nets of silk and gold and great pearls hanging all about the mountour."[27] While the spuriousness of the travelogue written by an author purportedly named John Mandeville is now widely acknowledged, such passages describing precious metals and sparkling gemstones demonstrate how writers even as early as the fourteenth century thematized the nature of a pagoda as a richly jeweled and dense surface.[28]

During the seventeenth and eighteenth centuries, the stylistic movement known as *chinoiserie* took hold of the European continent. From government institutions to gardens to music, nothing about China escaped its thrall, however fictive or real such concepts of China were.[29] In particular, one such material became the frenzied focus of the European fantasy with China: porcelain, the substance so precious and desired it was referred to as white gold.[30] Not only was there a desire for porcelain as an object—as evidenced by shipwreck goods and the spectacular expansion of princely collections—but there was also an ambition for an economy of material mimicry fueled by the scientific quest for its formula. The flourishing of this industry predicated upon simulation is best exemplified in the individual ceramic companies that adapted local raw clays and earth to look like a purely white and vitrified fired body that typified the best porcelain from China, including Meissen (Saxon), Sevres (France), Vincennes (France), and Delft (Netherlands).[31]

It is thus no surprise that porcelain came to dominate the European discourse on the Nanjing structure. Differentiation between a devotional *si* or glorious *ta* was largely absent; rather, texts often employed the respective terms for both buildings. Usually, tower and pagoda were used contemporaneously in the same sentence description. Most often, the *chinoiserie* writers fixated upon the word "pagoda," emptying out the memorial aspects of the Yongle monument and instead appreciating the pagoda as an architectural material marvel. The earliest description and visual images of the Nanjing structure reached Europe during this time period through the publication of the travel journal of Johan Nieuhoff, a Dutch official who served as secretary of the first Dutch East Indies trips to China between 1655 and 1657. He observed the pagoda as follows: "In the middle of the Plain stands a high Steeple or Tower made of *Porcelane,* which far exceeds all other Workmanship of the Chinese in cost and skill, by which the Chinese have declared to the world, the rare Ingenuity of their Artistry in former Ages."[32]

Clearly, the focus of Nieuhoff's admiration was the tower's material ontology as porcelain. For a continent enchanted by the luxurious material so representative that it became synonymous with the country of origin, an entire building composed of porcelain could only be a monument testifying to the country's wealth and magnificence. In the same text, Nieuhoff offers further reverence of the building's lavish features, highlighting details that enabled the pagoda's towering stature, visibility, and material value: "The outside is all Glaz'd over and Painted with several Colours, as Green, Red, and Yellow. . . . The Top of the tower was crown'd with Pine-Apple, which as they say was made of magic Gold. From the upper Gallery you may see not only over the whole City, but also over the adjacent Countries to the other side of the River Kiang, which is the most delightful Prospect, especially if you observe the vast circumference of the City, reaching with her Suburb to the River side."[33]

For Nieuhoff, the significance of the Nanjing tower lay in its material majesty and in its sheer technological mastery. His descriptions emphasize the tower's imposing architectural achievements, characterized by stunning monumental scale. As the earliest account in image and textual form of the Nanjing Pagoda to have been disseminated in Europe, Nieuhoff's eyewitness report enjoyed a broad audience, and his influence cannot be underestimated.[34] As seen in figure 8, almost all copperplate engravings printed after Nieuhoff's formative account stressed the pagoda's lofty height, marvelous monumentality, and material technology of porcelain.[35]

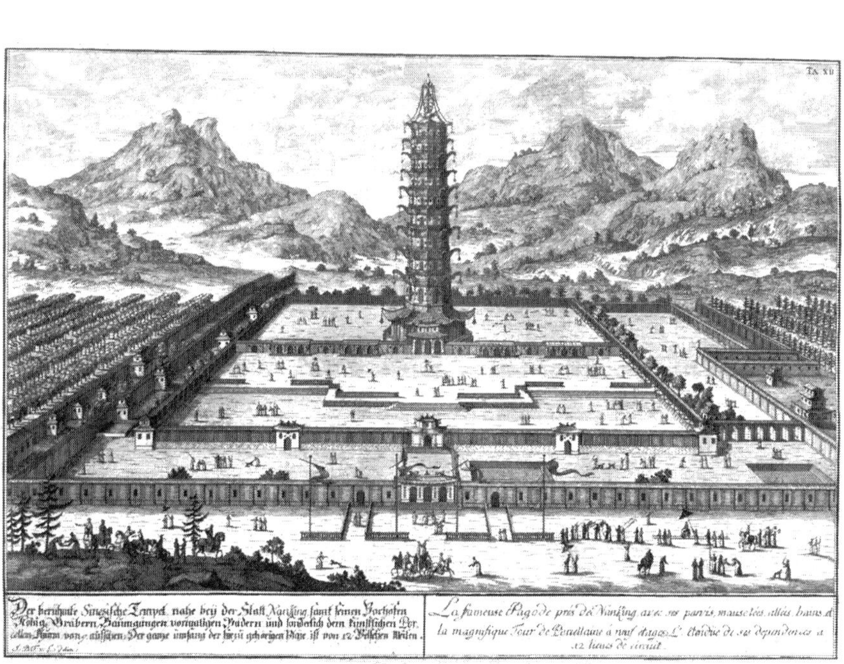

Fig. 8. Image of double folio engraved print of Nanjing Pagoda as towering monument. Johann Bernhard Fischer von Erlach, *A Plan of Civil and Historical Architecture* (London: Thomas Lediard, 1737 [first published 1715 in German]). Public domain.

Bound up with the fascination with the porcelain pagoda's architectural splendor were the related concepts of objectivity, authenticity, and singular, knowable truths. Take, for example, the comments of the French Jesuit Louis LeComte (1655–1728), who drew upon Nieuhoff's foundational images and writings. Sent by order of King Louis XIV to transmit mathematical knowledge to the imperial court of Qing China, LeComte visited Nanjing, where he confirmed that the pagoda was wholly made of porcelain. In his memoirs, he wrote of the great height of a building made entirely of a verifiable material, porcelain: "The Tower is nine stories high, each story being adorned with a cornice three feet wide. . . . The wall is at the bottom at least 12 feet thick and above eight and a half at the top, cased with Chinaware laid flat-wise; for though the weather has somewhat impaired its beauty, there is yet enough remaining to show that it is real Chinaware."[36] LeComte's epistolary account continues to discuss the visual sights offered by ascending the vertical rise of the porcelain pagoda, further tightening the relationship between architectural monument and material composition. What LeComte used as his standard of authenticating real Chinaware is unclear—he does not discuss the typical material traits of whiteness, translucence, and dense durability—but his assertion of "real" porcelain is suggestive that a "fake" or illusory porcelain awaits, ready to dissimulate.

In fact, only a few short decades later, the enchantment with the porcelain pagoda as a work of material and architectural technology soon became a disenchantment. In the sequel to the popular novel *Adventures of Robinson Crusoe,* the main character describes his disillusionment with the Nanjing Pagoda in an indignant harangue:

> Well, said I, are not the Materials of their Building the Product of their own country; and so it is all China Ware is not it? NO, no, said he, I mean it is a House all made of China Ware, such as you call it in England; or as it is calle'd in our Country, Porcellain. Well, said I, such a thing may be; how big is it? Can we carry it in a Box upon a Camel? If we can, we will buy it. Upon a camel! Said the old pilot, holding up both his Hands, why there is a Family of thirty People lives in it.
>
> I was then curious indeed to see it and when I came it see it, it was Nothing but this: it was a Timber-House, or a House-built, as we call it in England, with Lath and Plaister, but all the Plaistering was really China Ware, that is to say, it was plaistered with the Earth that makes China Ware. . . .

> The outside, which the Sun shone hot upon, was glazed, and look'd very well, perfect white, and painted with blue Figures, as the large China Ware in England is painted, and hard as if it had been burnt; as to the inside, all the Walls, instead of wainscot, were lined up with harden'd and painted Tiles, like the little square Tiles we call Gally-Tiles in England, but join'd so artificially with Mortar, being made of the same Earth, that it was very hard to see where the Tiles met.[37]

The character of Robinson Crusoe is of course fictional. Moreover, the novel's author, Daniel Defoe, did not himself visit the pagoda in Nanjing, adding another layer of cross-cultural invention to a story in which the adjudication of true or false (porcelain) was essential to the narrative. In a seminal article about the late Qing (1644–1911) Chinese translation of *Robinson Crusoe,* Lydia Liu has analyzed this episode in Robinson's travels as symptomatic of eighteenth-century epistemology and the production of colonialist knowledge frameworks predicated upon conceptual binaries such as West and non-West.[38] By contextualizing the linguistic translation of the term for porcelain within late nineteenth-century geopolitics, Liu shows the translingual aspects of translation and their role in reproducing static concepts of "self" and "other" within hierarchies of power. For the purposes of this discussion about the Nanjing Pagoda's material value, however, it is significant to note that Robinson's sentiments of disillusionment reveal assumptions about the criteria of the authenticity of porcelain. Denouncing the pagoda for being made of "Lath and Plaister [plaster]," Robinson Crusoe, and Daniel Defoe by extension, placed porcelain along a valuation framework in which "real" and "fake" are polar opposites. As historians of science and intellectual history of modernity have discussed, the eighteenth through nineteenth centuries saw shifts in the definition of objectivity, ultimately resulting in a scientific culture of seeking objectively real truths over false illusions. Thus, for Robinson, porcelain was a singular, identifiable entity whose objecthood was related to complex ideas about scientific objectivity ascendant in post-Enlightenment Europe.[39]

Relic Translations

Between 2007 and 2010, archaeologists from the Nanjing Municipal Institute of Archaeology began a comprehensive excavation of the areas and sites of the Ming dynasty buildings, including the Bao'en Si Ta. Archaeologists uncovered a lower crypt buried under the foundation of the pagoda temple. Within the lower crypt was a rectangular stone chest, the contents of which included containers and artifacts made up of precious materials, including gold, silver, copper, iron, porcelain, jade, agate, crystal, glass, and woven silk, to name just a few. Most significant, an inscription on the plank on the north side of the unearthed stone chest identified such materials found in the crypt as relics and their containers and accoutrements, dating to as early as the Jin dynasty (265–420).

The textual inscription adorning the unearthed stone crypt links the site of the Nanjing Pagoda to a miraculous history related to the transmission of the Dharma into the Nanjing region during the Eastern Jin dynasty (317–420), a history long transmitted in texts. The seminal text from 1607, *Jinling fancha zhi* (Gazetteer of monasteries in Jinling), compiled by Ge Yinliang (1570–1646), includes records of Ming imperial court projects to restore what were believed to be monastic stūpas that marked the divine location of the physical remains of the Buddha's body after parinirvāṇa.[40] The inscription on the underground stone chest begins as follows: "[The Buddha's] body was cremated near the river, the Hiraṇyavatī [Pali: Hiraññavatī] River. The Buddha's *śarīra* [*sheli*舍利] resembles a piece of gold. King Aśoka built stūpas to preserve them and redistributed the Buddha's *śarīra* widely, divided into 84,000 shares. Our land received 19 of them. Changgan Temple Pagoda in Jinling City held the second of these shares. Discovered during the Eastern Jin Dynasty, it was rebuilt by Emperor Wu of the Liang Dynasty."[41]

At the most basic level, then, the excavations provided archaeological verification of a perception of the pagoda's Buddhist past that had previously been documented only in texts. Whereas the locus of Western admiration since the seventeenth century had been the tower as an awe-inspiring architectural marvel, recent archaeological research traces a material history of the tower as a religious site and reliquary.

The unearthed inscription, dating to 1011 CE, connects the Nanjing Pagoda to another type of precious material in addition to porcelain. The inscription's description of the stone chest's contents focuses on its containment of relics. *Śarīra,* as explained in the inscription, refers to the physical remains of the Buddha's body after the Buddha's cremation. The excavated accoutrements—including the jeweled Aśoka Stūpa, made of sandalwood, silver, and gilt gold; the silver outer casket; and the inner gold casket—and devotee paraphernalia showcase materials that were not singular entities but physically part of an assemblage (fig. 9). For in their moment of relic enshrinement, as the inscription documents and in accordance with the analysis of the archaeological excavation, the relic pellets were encased within nested caskets inlaid with gems, the first being gold, then silver, a seven-jeweled stūpa reliquary, and finally an iron chest.[42] The final enshrinement was therefore a multi-compartment object, an accumulation of distinct individual objects. Moreover, the authenticity of the physical remains was assumed and left unquestioned.[43]

Indeed, the inscription references the fabled history of some of the earliest instances of relic devotion in Chinese Buddhist history. By referring to the physical division of Śākyamuni Buddha's remains after his death and cremation, the materials at the center of the pagoda take on an animate quality by indexing the movement of the Buddha's bodily remnants—from India to China.[44] The 2007–2010 archaeological discoveries also provide a twelfth-century connection to the third-century origins of relic veneration in Jinling, present-day Nanjing. Previously documented in texts, the records of relics highlight materials whose test of authenticity was their miraculous power and luminous agency. Consider, for example, the hagiography *Lives of Eminent Monks* (*Gao seng zhuan*), completed sometime between 519 and 530, in which the discussion of the Buddha's *śarīra* appears in Jinling. According to the hagiographic entry, in 248 Kang Senghui, a monk of Sogdian descent who grew up in Jiaozhi (present-day Vietnam), traveled to Jianye (present-day Nanjing), promising that he could produce relics of a crystalline nature, shining in infinite reflection. If relics appeared, then he was a medium of the Dharma. After praying for an extended number of days continuously, *śarīra* appeared in a vase (*ping* 瓶), rattling and emitting five colors. The King Sun Quan of the Wu kingdom thus established a stūpa at the site of where the relics appeared.[45]

Several concepts characterize the materials that make up the Nanjing Pagoda in such Buddhist writings. First, as a monastery built to signal the appearance of *śarīra* and its location, the pagoda did not function as a symbol or memorial of a bygone era but marked a presence of divinity. Second, the material, as *śarīra,* was fragmentary. It embodied a portion of the whole without establishing a hierarchy of the whole over the part. Further, more than representing a ruin that indicated decay and the passage of time, the *śarīra* was transtemporal. In the words of Kang Senghui, "The shifting traces of the Thus-come-one transcend a thousand years. The bone *śarīra* he left behind shines divinely and without measure."[46] Third and related, by revealing themselves to monks in Jinling, the relics themselves vocalized their miraculous agency. Rather than waiting to be discovered, described, and identified, the holy remains revealed themselves as agential forces rather than static objects. They

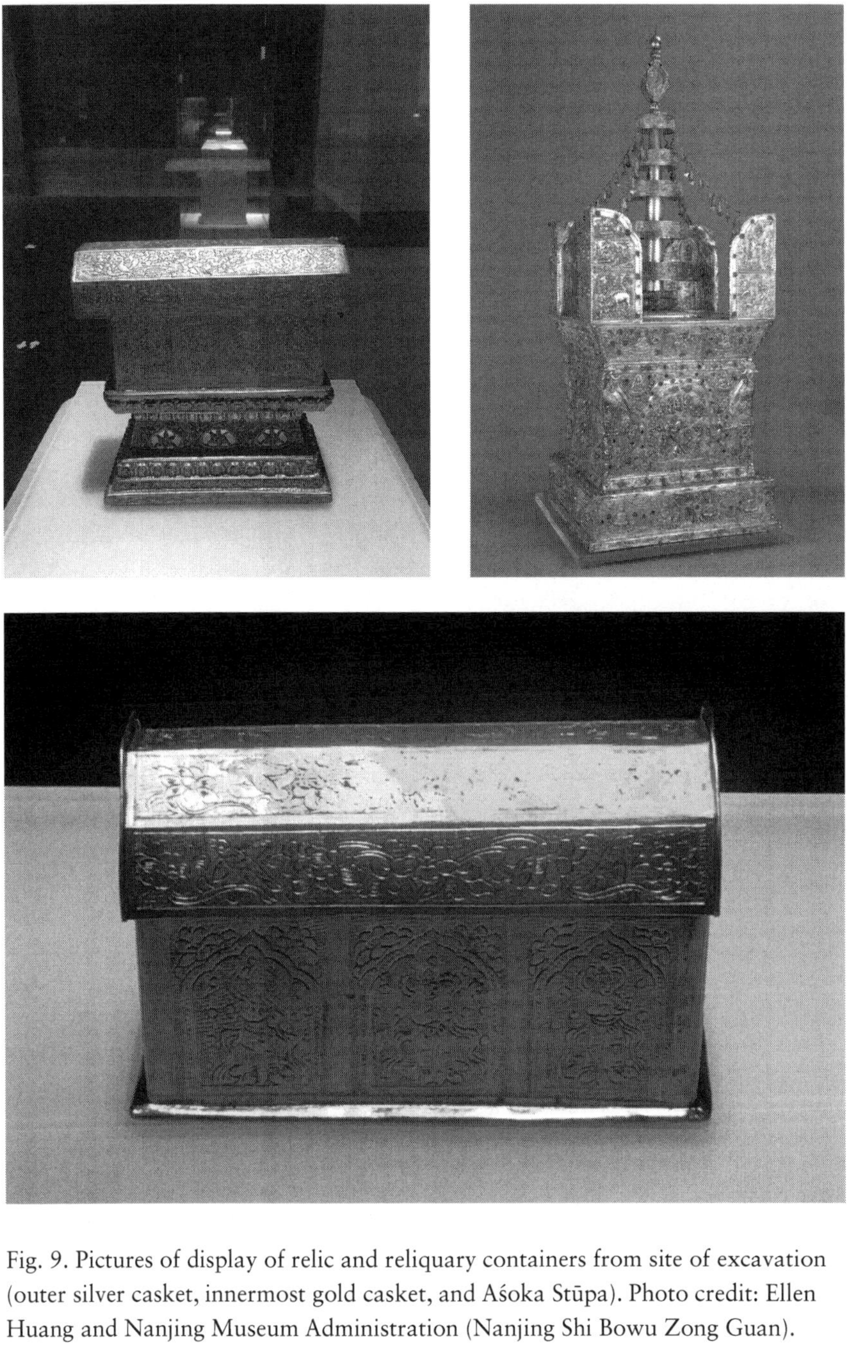

Fig. 9. Pictures of display of relic and reliquary containers from site of excavation (outer silver casket, innermost gold casket, and Aśoka Stūpa). Photo credit: Ellen Huang and Nanjing Museum Administration (Nanjing Shi Bowu Zong Guan).

moved, glowed, resisted decay, and made sounds. By rattling, the relics seemed sentient, almost as if they spoke through a language of material impact. In contrast to an object whose authenticity was determined by a knowing scientific subject, the relics were themselves animate and active.[47] They announced their own authenticity through manifesting brilliant and visual power, emitting five colors (*wucai*).[48]

In geometry, "translation" refers not to communication transfer, in which assumed equivalences between two linguistic terms are commensurable static entities.[49] Rather, geometric translation is a performance of movement. The newly excavated materials of the Nanjing Pagoda invite comparison with mathematical translation. In the context of Western observers' enchantment and disenchantment, the material value of the pagoda depended upon an achievable porcelain whose essence was true, definable, and measurable. As a bounded form, the pagoda was translatable as a commensurable object. The recovered relics and their inscribed historical references, however, speak of the diffusion of the Buddha's physical body, connoting their miraculous appearances and physical journeys. In their movement across political borders as part of the distribution of the Buddha's body, they translated as active agents, alive in death and across time.

Conclusion: Porcelain Homologies

When Robinson Crusoe declared the pagoda as a structure whose composition was not porcelain but timber and plaster, he may not have been entirely wrong in his critique of the building's illusion of porcelainness. Archaeological remnants of the pagoda structure itself remain difficult to ascertain and to authenticate. The whereabouts of the remains of the white cladding that gave rise to its reputation as the Porcelain Pagoda are for the most part not known.[50] Studies have shown that the several pieces of white ceramic bricks from the site were underfired and thus do not meet the criteria that Europeans held for porcelain. While Europeans defined porcelain as white, translucent, and highly vitrified, neither the white bricks nor the pieces of glazed archways were fired at the necessary temperature (above 1250 degrees C) to achieve the requisite fusion for material density and visual translucency.[51]

In historical Chinese texts until the late nineteenth century, however, porcelain belonged to an expanded category of ceramics. Instead of finished product features, including such qualities as whiteness and translucency, a shared process of manufacture guided the definition of high-fired glazed ceramics that included both porcelain and stoneware.[52] Importantly, the ceramic fragments recovered from the site now in collections worldwide are glazed and are thus reflective, glossy, and smooth to touch.[53] In this lustrous quality, the pagoda's structural traces suggest that the architecture emanated a brilliant sheen, sharing an important quality of Buddhist relics that have often taken the form of shiny bead-like gems.[54] In accounts about their extraordinary manifestation in third-century Nanjing, Buddhist texts characterize relics' miraculous brilliance as five-colored (*wuse*). Such descriptions of five-colored illuminations approximate the polychrome jewel-toned design schema that adorned porcelains, first introduced as part of the repertoire of Ming dynasty kiln productions when the pagoda was rebuilt and expanded in the 1430s (fig. 10). Indeed, as John Strong analyzes in his narrative of the history of Piprahwa relics (in this volume), beads are not inferior to the bones in relic finds; often, the beads of the gems replaced or substantiated the bones in relic finds as the crucial framing elements.[55]

Porcelain and relics also share similarities in terms of their physical production. Again, John Strong, in his investigation of the *śarīra-pūjā* in the *Mahāparinirvāṇa Sūtra,* illuminates a sequence of acts that he discusses as the funeral arrangements of the Buddha's body.[56] In the sequence, after the wrapping with shrouds, the body of the Buddha is encoffined in a sarcophagus denoted by the Sanskrit word *droṇi,* meaning vessel. Strong describes the importance of cremation, after which the fired burned so cleanly that it left no residues of ashes or soot. Even the skin, flesh, and sinews were consumed by the fire. Considering the use of the word *śarīrāni,* taken sometimes to mean bones but described as jasmine buds, pearls, and gold, Strong concludes that the *śarīrāni* relics resulting from this cremation step in the Buddha's funeral sequence were in fact materials that had undergone some transmutation, resulting in shiny jewel-like gems, to indicate the Buddha's own transformation to a final state.

Like the clean burning of the Buddha's body, porcelain is also known for its purity in its after-fired state. As a high-fired ceramic, porcelain is perhaps best known for its cleanliness (because of its fused surface, porcelain leaves no residual taste of last night's food), smooth, and unmarred appearance. Its whiteness, the quality so desired in Europe, enhanced this purity and lack of "residue." Chemically, it too is a product resulting from transformation by fire—like the resultant *śarīrāni* in the Buddha's funeral. Porcelain is also a material that is a result of firing,

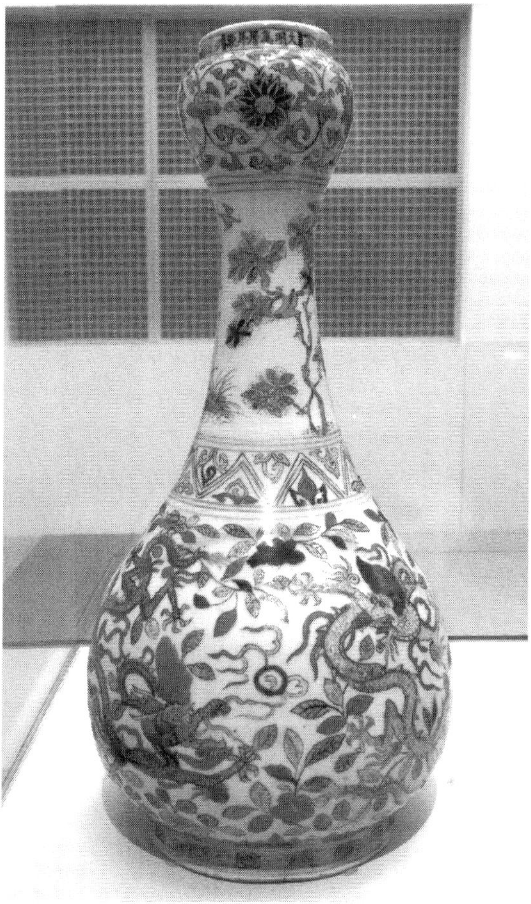

Fig. 10. Vase with mouth in the shape of a garlic bulb. China; Jiangxi Province, Ming dynasty (1368–1644), reign of the Wanli emperor (1573–1620). Porcelain with underglaze and overglaze polychrome decoration. Asian Art Museum San Francisco, Avery Brundage Collection, B60P56. Photograph © Asian Art Museum of San Francisco.

a process through which clay and minerals undergo chemical transformation, understood simply by scientists as "ceramic change."[57] Indeed, for the making of ceramics, the stages of transformation induced by fire can best be characterized as proceeding sequentially from a change from plastic clay to a dry, sintered clay body, followed by a molecular change during which a vitrified, or nearly vitrified, crystalline matter transpires.[58] Since the early eighteenth-century European reinvention of porcelain, chemists have defined porcelain to be a composite material. That is, porcelain is a combination of amorphous vitreous matter due to a rich silica content paired with crystalline material replete with mullite formations resulting from its constitution of the minerals kaolinite and quartz.[59] Firing without collapsing or cracking at above 1200 degrees Celsius, kaolin provided the structure, while the melted silica-rich quartz fused around its skeletal framework. In other words, the fused portion producing glistening translucency became known as the "flesh," while the crystalline structure became known as the white "bones" of porcelain.[60] Glassy, luminous, and brilliant, the jeweled nature of porcelain is an apt homology for a Buddhist relic—gemlike "beads and bones," to use Strong's terms.

The Nanjing Pagoda continues to pique the curiosity of scholars, whose primary interest has been focused upon recovering a true history of the tower. Because of the spate of archaeological discoveries that have transpired over the last fifty years and their impact on the study of Chinese history, an objectivist project that seeks to identify authentic remnants of the pagoda remains paramount. After all, the emphasis on reconstructing the true pagoda not only dovetails with heritage studies and development models that characterize post–World War II global humanities fields, as detailed by Lynn Meskell, but also seems to free the pagoda from the burden of the *chinoiserie* fantasy that has been part of the pagoda's European reception since the heyday of the European imitation of China.[61] One might remember the enthusiasm of the William Chambers, who situated a monumental pagoda inspired by the Nanjing Pagoda among other follies, including a replica of a mosque and the Alhambra in a portion of the renovated gardens at Kew entitled "the Wilderness" (fig. 11).[62]

This chapter has shifted the scholarly discussion away from the pagoda's authenticity by offering an alternative approach. A repeated interest in authenticity has obscured the ways in which the material culture of the pagoda—including its replicas and miniature instantiations—might be understood in terms of the physical logic of *śarīra*. Scholarship, most notably that of Gregory Schopen, has convincingly demonstrated the equivocal place of *śarīra* relics with textual objects in early Indian Buddhist practice. Further, scholars have rightly questioned the way in which Buddhist relics confound normative definitions of relics and reliquary containers when discussing figural sculptures that contain sacred

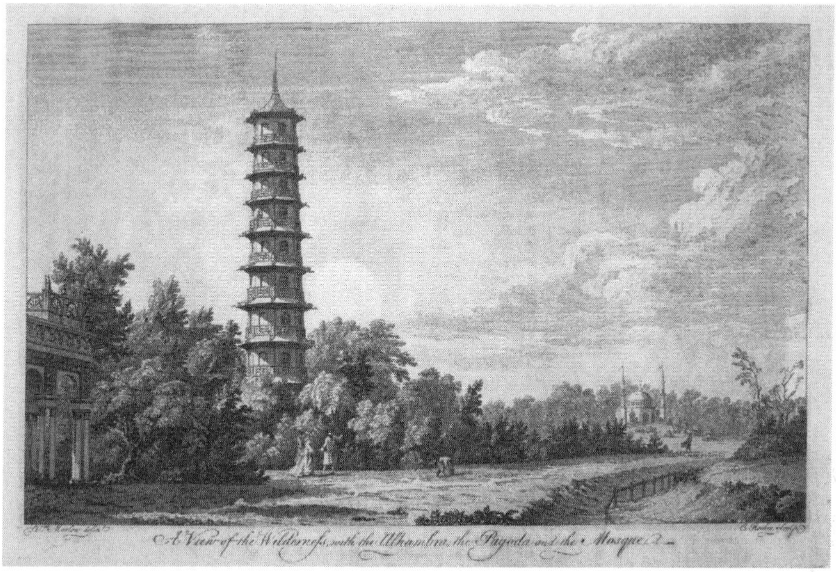

Fig. 11. Print of William Chambers's design for the "wilderness" at Kew Gardens, from folio volume published in 1763. Public domain.

relics. Sculptural images are at once containers, recipients, urns and stūpas.[63] In the case of the famed Nanjing Pagoda, even its replicated afterlife across scalar registers coheres with what Hsueh-man Shen shows for relic devotion in the dissemination of Buddhist worship across China: "Replication is an inherent practice of relic veneration."[64] By considering the shared material nature of a porcelain pagoda and its underground contents, in which the excavated relics held utmost importance, this essay demonstrates the significance of the porcelain material of the Nanjing Pagoda across the *chinoiserie* imagination of the pagoda, including its copies, and its ontology as a container-pagoda housing *śarīra* relics.

Tracing the changing concepts of materials related to the Nanjing Pagoda in different contexts illuminates a shared logic between porcelain and relics. Both resulting from fire, porcelain and relics, as well as related reliquary splendor and replication, exhibit the jeweled sheen in the concept of *śarīra*. As the eighth-century sutra text urged practitioners, in the absence of remains of the Buddha's posthumuous body, "take all sorts of precious materials, such as gold, silver, beryl, crystal, agate, and glass to be *śarīra*."[65] The production of relics as process of a transformed body, authenticity aside, captures the jeweled nature of the porcelain pagoda as landmark, trace, and appropriately, a five-colored numinous presence that made itself known to the Buddhist monk and evangelist Kang Senghui in third-century Nanjing. In this view, both Zhang Dai, our nostalgic writer of the late Ming and early Qing who used the term "kiln vessel," and the English researcher who labeled the diminutive porcelain pagoda in the Victoria and Albert Museum a miniature "Bao en Jar" drew upon yet another definition of porcelain, whose authenticity continues to escape us.

Perhaps there is a *śarīra* relic perspective on porcelain after all.

Appendix

From: *Jinling fancha zhi*, juan 31.

Imperial Decree for the Repair and Reconstruction of the Bao'en Si, Yongle, 11th year (1413)
重修报恩寺敕永乐十一年

天禧寺旧名长干寺，建于吴赤乌年间。缘及历代，屡兴屡废。宋真宗天禧年间，尝经修建，遂改名曰天禧寺。至我朝洪武年间，寺宇稍坏，工部侍郎黄立恭，奏请募众财略为修葺。朕即位之初，遂敕工部修理，比旧加新。比年有无籍僧本性，以其私愤，怀杀人之心，潜于僧室放火，将寺焚毁，崇殿修廊，寸木不存，黄金之地，悉为瓦砾，浮图煨烬，颓裂倾敝，周览顾望，丘墟草野。朕念皇考皇妣罔极之恩，无以报称，况此灵迹，岂可终废，乃用军民人等，勤劳其力，趋事赴工者，如水之流下，其势莫御，一新创建，充广殿宇，重作浮图，比之于旧，工力万倍。以此胜因，上荐父皇母后在天之灵，下为天下生民祈福，使雨旸时若，百谷丰登，家给人足，妖孽不兴，灾沴不作，乃名曰大报恩寺。表兹胜刹，垂耀无穷。告于有众，咸使知之。

Notes

I thank Vanessa Sasson, Nancy Lin, and two anonymous reviewers for their feedback, which helped shaped this chapter.

1. Joseph Koerner, "On Monuments," *Res: Anthropology and Aesthetics* 67 and 68 (2017): 5–20.
2. William Chambers, *Designs of Chinese Buildings, Furniture, Dresses* (London: Published by the author, 1757), 5. Tong Tchang Fou refers to a pagoda near Jinan in Shandong Province.

3. Chinese language historical sources, ranging from administrative gazetteers to colophons on paintings, frequently provide a history of the pagoda as being located on a site of Buddhist relic manifestation and devotion. For an example of such a narrative, one may consult an ink-and-color-on-silk painting sold by Christies on May 14, 2010, which bears a calligraphic colophon tracing a Buddhist site-specific history.
4. For a useful overview of relics in Buddhist history, see Brian Ruppert, "Relics and Relic Cults," in *Encyclopedia of Buddhism*, ed. Robert E. Buswell Jr. (New York: Macmillan 2003), 715–719.
5. *The Chinese Repository*, vol. 13 (Canton, China, 1832–1851; reprint, Vaduz: Kraus, 1844), 261–263.
6. This discussion about materials and their effects relies upon the recent scholarly turn toward exploring material and matter as "alive" in studies of artifacts and ecology. For instance, Jane Bennett coins the term "Active Matter," for her description of the material world, and Bruno Latour discusses the material world as "social agents" as examples of nonhuman agents. Jane Bennett, *Vibrant Matter: A Political Ecology of Things* (Durham, NC: Duke University Press, 2010); Bruno Latour, *Reassembling the Social* (Oxford: Oxford University Press, 2007).
7. Two excellent monographs that complicate the historical narrative of porcelain moving in a unidirectional trajectory by providing examples of nuanced appropriations that occurred are Robert Finlay, *The Pilgrim Art: Cultures of Porcelain in World History* (Berkeley: University of California Press, 2010), and Stacey Pierson, *From Object to Concept* (Hong Kong: Hong Kong University Press, 2013).
8. David Porter, *The Chinese Taste in Eighteenth-Century England* (Cambridge: Cambridge University Press, 2010); Christine Jones, *Shapely Bodies: The Image of Porcelain in Eighteenth-Century France* (Newark: University of Delaware Press, 2013), esp. ch. 1, 41–48. See Hugh Honour, *Chinoiserie* (New York: Dutton, 1962) for an overview.
9. See Christiane Hertel, *Siting China in Germany: Eighteenth-Century Chinoiserie and Its Modern Legacy* (University Park, PA: Pennsylvania State University Press, 2019); Elizabeth H. Chang, "'Eyes of the Proper Almond-Shape': Blue-and-White China in the British Imaginary, 1823–1883," *Nineteenth Century Studies* 19 (May 2005): 17–34. See also the fourth section of the edited volume by Petra Ten-Doesschate Chu and Ding Ning, *Qing Encounters: Artistic Exchanges between China and the West* (Los Angeles: Getty Research Institute, 2015), 216–264.
10. The remains of the pagoda are collected in the Nanjing Municipal Museum and Nanjing Museum. For Chinese-language prints and white

ceramic L-shaped beams excavated during the Republican period, see Zhang Huiyi 張惠衣, *Jinling Da Bao'ensi ta zhi* 金陵大報恩寺塔志 (Beijing: Guoli Beiping yanjiu shi xue yan jiu hui, 1937). For European and American accounts, see Zhao Juan, "Yiyu guankan: Jindai Ouren jizaizhong de Zhongguo baota—er, san, shi 异域观看:近代欧人记载中的 "中国宝塔" 二三事," *Zhongguo wenhua huabao* 中华文化画报 5 (2018): 90–95. For examples of ceramic portions, see the example from the British Museum, whose online database describes its collection into American and European museums circa 1870. https://www.britishmuseum.org/research/publications/online_research_catalogues/search_object_details.aspx?objectid=265225&partid=1&numpages=10&output=Terms%2F!!%2FOR%2F!!%2F15718%2F!%2F%2F!%2FMing+dynasty%2F!%2F%2F!!%2F%2F!!!%2F&orig=%2Fresearch%2Fonline_research_catalogues%2Frussian_icons%2Fcatalogue_of_russian_icons%2Fadvanced_search.aspx&currentPage=5. Accessed June 26, 2019.

11. Nanjing Municipal Museum 南京博物院, "Mingdai Nanjing Jubaoshan liuli yao 明代南京聚寶山琉璃窯," *Wenwu* 2 (1960): 41–48. Leng Mei 冷媚, "Mingdai Bao'en si liuli ta fenxi 明代报恩寺琉璃宝塔探析," *Wenwu jianding yu jianshang* 12 (2016): 56–57.
12. Li Zhu 李竹, "Jinlun song riyue fengduo hong qianli—Mingdai da Bao'en si ta wenwu shiyi 金輪聳日月風鐸鳴千里——明代大報恩寺塔文物拾遺," *Wenwu yanjiu* 3, no. 121 (1998): 1.
13. Nanjing Municipal Institute of Archaeology 南京市考古研究所, "The Excavation of the Pagoda Foundation and the Lower Crypt of the Grand Bao'en Temple in Nanjing City" 南京大報恩寺遺址塔基與地宮發掘簡報 *Wenwu* 5(2015): 4–5.
14. Jing Zhuge, "From Historical Monument to Urban Spectacle: Case Study on the Great Bao'en Pagoda Reconstruction Project," in *Architecture RePerformed: The Politics of Reconstruction,* edited by Tino Mager (Surrey: Ashgate, 2015), 117–136.
15. John Kieschnick, *The Impact of Buddhism on Chinese Material Culture* (Princeton, NJ: Princeton University Press, 2003); Kevin Trainor, *Relics, Ritual, and Representation in Buddhism: Rematerializing the Sri Lankan Theravāda Tradition* (Cambridge: Cambridge University Press, 1997); Fabio Rambelli, *Buddhist Materiality: A Cultural History of Objects in Japanese Buddhism* (Palo Alto, CA: Stanford University Press, 2007); John Strong, *Relics of the Buddha* (Princeton, NJ: Princeton University Press, 2004).
16. Wang, "Tope and Topos."

17. Ge Yinliang 葛寅亮 (1570–1646), *Jinling fancha zhi*, juan 31, 1607.
18. "重修報恩寺敕," Yongle 11th year, in Ge Yinliang, *Jinling fancha zhi* 金陵梵剎志, juan 31. Recorded in the *Xuxiu siku quanshu* (A continuation of the *Imperial Library of the Four Treasuries*), 718, p. 674. See Xia Weizhong 夏維中 et. al, "Nanjing Tianxi si de yange 南京天禧寺的沿革," *Jiangsu Social Sciences* 江苏社會科學 3 (2010): 229–236, appendix for Chinese text.
19. Philip Kalafas, *In Limpid Dream: Nostalgia in Zhang Dai's Reminiscences of the Ming* (Manchester: EastBridge Books, 2007), and Jonathan Spence, *Return to Dragon Mountain: Memories of a Late Ming Man* (New York: Viking, 2010).
20. Zhang Huiyi cites transmitted texts in the first chapter of his compilation, stating that by the Jiajing emperor reign (r.1521–1567), only the Bao'en tower and Chan temple (*chan dian* 禪殿) remained standing. Zhang Huiyi, *Jinling Da Bao'ensi ta zhi* 金陵大報恩寺塔志 (Beijing: Guoli Beiping yanjiu shi xue yan jiu hui, 1937), 7.
21. The Chinese text of Zhang Dai's description is as follows: "中国之大古董 永樂之大窰器 則報恩塔是也." Zhang Dai 張岱 *Taoan mengyi pingzhu* 陶庵夢憶 評註, annotated by Huai Min 淮茛 (Shanghai: Sanlian shudian, 2013), 6.
22. See Susan Stewart, *On Longing: Narratives of the Miniature, the Gigantic, the Souvenir, the Collection* (Durham, NC: Duke University Press, 1992).
23. Cited in Nick Pearce, "A Chinese Export Porcelain Pagoda," *Orientations* 18, no. 10 (1987): 38.
24. See, for example, the poetic inscriptions of the painter Xu Shangtian 徐上添, who published a set of landscape paintings in 1910 (金陵四十八景) and those of the late Qing painter Pu Hua 蒲华 (1832–1911), 金陵四十八景图, painted around 1901. See Xu Shangtian, *Jinling sishiba jing*金陵四十八景 (Nanjing: Nanjing chubanshe, 2012 [1910]), 43. The interplay of temple and tomb as either one and the same or distinct sites of political and religious practice is discussed for the periods from the Three Dynasties (Xia, Shang, Zhou) to the Eastern Han (25–220 CE) in "Temple, Palace, and Tomb," ch. 2, pp. 83–119, of Wu Hung, *Monumentality* (Palo Alto, CA: Stanford University Press, 1995).
25. Tracy Miller has shown cogently that the immediate association of *ta* with *stūpa* overlooks the historical nature of court-sponsored Buddhist devotional buildings and their translation from South Asia to China. See, for example, Tracy Miller: "Translating the *ta:* Pagoda, Tumulus, and Ritualized Mahāyāna in Seventh-Century China," *Tang*

Studies, 2018, 82–120, and "Perfecting the Mountain: On the Morphology of Towering Temples in East Asia," *Journal of Chinese Architecture History* 10 (2014): 419–449. Kevin Trainor, in *Relics, Ritual, and Representation in Buddhism,* 32–39, provides an etymology of the word *stūpa* and contrasts it with the term *caitya,* both of which scholars use interchangeably to mean built forms associated with Buddhist monastic buildings. Trainor specifies their divergent referents to either a container for relics or a memorial to the Buddha's journey.

26. A. W. Pollard, ed. *The Travels of Sir John Mandeville* (London: Macmillan, 1900).
27. Pollard, *The Travels of Sir John Mandeville,* 141. http://www.medievaltravel.amdigital.co.uk/collections/doc-detail.aspx?documentid=3599. For a definition of the term "mountour," an obsolete word meaning "platform," see the OED, http://www.oed.com/view/Entry/122933?rskey=jnr4Ur&result=1&isAdvanced=false#eid.
28. Ian Mcleod Higgins, *Writing East: The "Travels" of Sir John Mandeville* (Philadelphia: University of Pennsylvania Press, 1997), provides a useful analysis of the multi-authored text's history of versions since its first appearance during the latter half of the fourteenth century and continuing through the eighteenth century.
29. Honour, *Chinoiserie.* See also David Porter, "Chinoiserie and the Aesthetics of Illegitimacy," *Studies in Eighteenth-Century Culture* 28 (1999): 27–54, for an illuminating study of images and ideas about China from the perspective of British history.
30. Finlay, *The Pilgrim Art,* 62.
31. See Ellen Huang: "From the Imperial Court to the International Art Market: Jingdezhen Porcelain Production as Global Visual Culture," *Journal of World History* 23, no. 1 (2012): 115–145; "An Art of Transformation: Reproducing *Yaobian* Glazes in Qing-Dynasty Porcelain," *Archives of Asian Art* 68, no. 2 (2018): 133–156; and "Famille-Rose: Jingdezhen Porcelain as Meta-Chinoiserie," unpublished manuscript.
32. Johannes Nieuhoff, Pieter de Goyer, Jacob de Keizer, and John Ogilby, *An Embassy from the East-India Company of the United Provinces, to the Grand Tartar Cham, Emperor of China,* 2nd ed. (London: Printed by the author at his house in White-Friers, 1669), 78. http://gateway.proquest.com/openurl?ctx_ver=Z39.882003&res_id=xri:eebo&rft_id=xri:eebo:citation:12268734.
33. Nieuhoff, de Goyer, de Keizer, and Ogilby, *An Embassy from the East-India Company.*

34. The first edition of Nieuhoff's travel diary and drawings was published with engravings as *Het Gezantschap der Neerlandtsche Oost-Indische Compagnie, aan den grooten Tartarischen Cham* in Amsterdam by the bookseller and art dealer Jacob van Meurs in 1665. It was translated into French (*L'Ambassade de la Compagnie Orientale des Provinces Unies vers l'empereur de la Chine, ou grand cam de Tartarie,* 1665), German (*Die Gesantschaft der Ost-Indischen Geselschaft in den Vereinigten Niederländern an den tartarischen Cham und nunmehr auch sinischen Keiser,* 1666), Latin (*Legatio Batavica ad magnum Tartarae Chamun,* 1668), and English. For more about the book's status as a touchstone for books on China and the history of its being excerpted and reprinted through the early eighteenth century, see Marcia Reed and Paola Demattè, *China on Paper: European and Chinese Works from the Late Sixteenth to Early Nineteenth Century* (Los Angeles: Getty Research Institute, 2011).
35. Johann Bernhard Fischer von Erlach, *A Plan of Civil and Historical Architecture: In the Representation of the Most Noted Buildings of Foreign Nations, Both Ancient and Modern, Taken from the Most Approv'd Historians, Original Medals, Remarkable Ruins, and Curious Authentick Designs and Display'd in Eighty-Six Double Folio-Plates, Finely Engraven, at a very Great Expence, by the Most Eminent Hands, Divided into Five Books,* 2nd ed. (London: Published at the expence of the translator, and to be had only at his house in Smith's-Square, Westminster, 1737). Electronic reproduction: Farmington Hills, MI: Cengage Gale, 2009. (Eighteenth-Century Collections Online.) Available via the World Wide Web. Access limited by licensing agreements, pp. 23–24, and on pdf.
36. Louis Le Comte, *A Compleat History of the Empire of China: Being the Observations of Above Ten Years Travels Through That Country: Containing Memoirs and Remarks, Geographical, Historical, Topographical, Physical, Natural, Astronomical, Mechanical, Military, Mercantile, Political, and Ecclesiastical. Written by the learned Lewis Le Comte, Confessor to the Dutchess of Burgundy, and One of the French King's Mathematicians, Who Was a Missioner in China Near Twenty Years. A New Translation from the Best Paris Edition, and Adorn'd with Copper-Plates. The Second Edition Carefully Corrected* (London, 1739). Eighteenth-Century Collections Online.
37. Daniel Defoe, *The Farther Adventures of Robinson Crusoe; Being the Second and Last Part of His Life, and of the Strange Surprizing Accounts of His Travels Round Three Parts of the Globe. Written by*

Himself. To Which Is Added a Map of the World, in Which Is Delineated the Voyages of Robinson Crusoe (London, 1719). Eighteenth-Century Collections Online (Gale. Stanford Libraries. January 15, 2019), 310–311. http://find.galegroup.com/ecco/infomark.do?&source=gale&prodId=ECCO&userGroupName=stan90222&tabID=T001&docId=CB3329233599&type=multipage&contentSet=ECCOArticles&version=1.0&docLevel=FASCIMILE.

38. See Fa-ti Fan, *British Naturalists in Qing China: Science, Empire, and Cultural Encounter* (Cambridge, MA: Harvard University Press, 2004), and Lydia Liu, "Robinson Crusoe's Earthenware," *Critical Inquiry* 25, no. 4 (Summer 1999): 728–757.
39. J. S. Mill, *August Comte and Positivism* (London: Kegan Paul, Trench, Trubner, 1891 [1865]); Steven Shapin, *A Social History of Truth: Civility and Science in Seventeenth-Century England* (Chicago: University of Chicago Press, 1994). For how the culture of scientific empiricism systemized forms of dualism influencing categories of knowledge about the Orient, see Edward Said's foundational text, *Orientalism* (New York: Pantheon, 1979); also concisely described in Naoki Sakai, "Translation and the 'Figure of the Border': Toward the Apprehension of Translation as a Social Action," *Profession* (2010): 25–34.
40. Ge Yinliang was minister of rites for the Ming court during the Wanli reign (1572–1620). For records of the Ming court's interest in the pagoda site as monastic, see, for instance, Ge, *Jinling fancha zhi,* juan 31, "御製黃侍郎立恭塔記-洪武戊辰十二月日 [Yuzhi Huang silang li gong ta ji-Hongwu *wuchen* shi er yue ri]" (1388). http://tripitaka.cbeta.org/en/B29n0160_031.
41. The full inscription is reproduced in Nanjing Municipal Institute of Archaeology, "The Excavation of the Pagoda Foundation and Lower Crypt of the Grand Bao'en Temple in Nanjing City."
42. The citation of the text on the stone stele is as follows: 言告中貴，以事聞天，尋奉綸言，賜崇寺，塔。同將仕"郎，守滑州助教王文，共為導首。率彼眾緣，於先現光之地　，選彼名匠，載建磚塔，高二百尺，八角九層，又造寺宇。□□進呈感應舍利十顆，並佛頂真骨洎諸聖舍利，內用金棺，週以銀槨，並七寶造成阿育王塔，□"以鐵□□函安置。即以大中祥符四年太歲辛亥六月癸卯朔十八日庚申　，備禮式設闔郭大齋，於皋"際"，庶□名數，永鎮坤維.
43. For more on the assumed authenticity of relics, see Kieschnick, *The Impact of Buddhism on Chinese Material Culture,* 49.
44. The earliest account of the movement of the Buddha's body through the journey *sheli* appears in the *Wei shu* 魏書, compiled 551–554, a

historical text describing the history of the Northern Wei and Eastern Wei from 386 to 550 by Wei Shou 魏收 (507–572). See James Ware, "Wei Shou on Buddhism," *T'oung Pao* 30 (1933): 119; it is also cited and translated by Eugene Wang, "Of the True Body," in *Body and Face in Chinese Visual Culture,* edited by Wu Hung and Katherine Mino (Cambridge, MA: Harvard University Press, 2004), 79–118. By the seventh century, the monk Daoshi compiled in 688 the encyclopedic *Fayuan zhulin* 法苑珠林 (A grove of pearls in the garden of the dharma), no. 40, in which the dispersal of the Buddha's body is recounted in a section about *sheli* and its dissemination. T 2122, vol. 53, 599–600. http://cbetaonline.dila.edu.tw/zh/T2122_040.

45. Huijiao 慧皎 (497–554), *Gao seng zhuan* 高僧傳 1 no. 2059, vol. 50, p. 325 b (CBETA, T50, no. 2059, pp. 325a13–326a1).
46. The text as written by the monk Huijiao in the *Gao seng zhuan* reads: 如來遷迹忽逾千載。遺骨舍利神曜無方.
47. John S. Strong, *The Legend of King Aśoka: A Study and Translation of the Aśokāvadāna* (Princeton, NJ: Princeton University Press, 2014), 116, notes that in early Buddhist accounts relics move, arise, and have mobility, taking on an animated quality. See also Strong, *Relics of the Buddha* chs. 5–7, where relics are a figuration of the Buddha's life through performing the Buddha's biographical process.
48. Further demonstrating the power and agency of material *sheli* is the fact that their radiance is what attracted Liu Sahe to the location in the recorded story. See Wu Hung, "Rethinking Liu Sahe," *Orientations* 11 (1996): 32–33. Huijiao, *Gao seng zhuan* 13, no. 2059, vol. 50, p. 0410. (CBETA, T50, no. 2059, 409–410).
49. The assumption that translation simply transfers meaning is complexly analyzed in the case of constructing national identities in Lydia Liu, *Translingual Practice: Literature, Culture and Translated Modernity, China 1900–1937* (Palo Alto, CA: Stanford University Press, 1995) and for Buddhist cultural production during the Qing period (1644–1911) in Patricia Ann Berger, *Empire of Emptiness: Buddhist Art and Political Authority in Qing China* (Honolulu: University of Hawai'i Press, 2003), ch. 2, "When Words Collide."
50. Clarence Eng, *Colours and Contrast* (Leiden: Brill, 2015), 239. Eng has attempted to reconstruct the decorative program of the Bao'en Si Ta from its fragmentary remains. Also in this work, 320n24, Eng cites Jessica Harrison Hall, *Catalogue of Late Yuan and Ming Ceramics in the British Museum* (London: British Museum Press, 2001), 523–524, for

documentation of possible white bricks that may be extant portions of the architecture that made up the Nanjing pagoda.

51. The archaeological ceramic tiles and pieces extant were fired at approximately 940 degrees C. See Ding Yingzhong et al., “Nanjing Bao’en Si Ta liuli jiangou tai yuanliao de keji yanjiu南京报恩寺塔琉璃构建胎体原料的科技研究,” *Zhongguo Taoci China Ceramics* 47, no. 1 (2011): 70–75. For European definitions of porcelain, see A. M. Pollard “Letters from China: A History of the Origins of the Chemical Analysis of Ceramics,” *Ambix* 62, no. 1 (2015): 50–71. Martin Schonfeld, “Was There a Western Inventor of Porcelain?” *Technology and Culture* 39, no. 4 (October 1998): 716–727, esp. 725.
52. Julie Emerson, *Porcelain Stories* (Seattle: Seattle Art Museum in association with University of Washington Press, 2000), introduction and ch.1; the aporia between the technique of *ci* and the surface of “porcelain” is the main topic of exploration in my “Famille-Rose: Jingdezhen Porcelain as Meta-Chinoiserie.”
53. Examples of high-fired ceramic fragments found at the site of where the excavations have taken place and at the same strata of the imperial kilns in Jingdezhen reside in the collections of the British Museum, Acc. # AO+.151; PDF.703; PDF, A.458; and Franks.32; the Victoria and Albert Museum, #4696–1901; 4696a-1901; and 45–1883; and the Metropolitan Museum of Art, 79.2.790; 79.2.789; 89.7b; 89.7c; and 89.7d. The fragments from the Nanjing Municipal Museum and Nanjing Museum were analyzed with regard to chemical composition, firing temperature, microstructure, and physical properties and published in Ding Yingzhong et al., “Nanjing Bao’en Si Ta liuli jiangou tai yuanliao de keji yanjiu.”
54. Ruppert, “Relic and Relic Cults,” 2:714.
55. Hsueh-man Shen also notes the ways in which gems and shiny jewel-like objects accompanied *śarīra* matter in her book, *Authentic Replicas* (Honolulu: University of Hawai‘i Press, 2018), 173.
56. John S. Strong, “The Buddha’s Funeral,” in *The Buddhist Dead,* edited by Jacqueline Stone and Bryan Cuevas (Honolulu: University of Hawai‘i Press, 2007), 32–51. See also John S. Strong, *Relics of the Buddha* (2004), 10–11.
57. Linda Bloomfield, *Science for Potters* (Westerville, OH: American Ceramic Society, 2017), 113.
58. This composite of fused and non-fused crystalline matter that constitutes the nature of porcelain distinguishes it from glass, which is a non-crystalline material, the subject of Francesca Tarocco’s investigation in this volume.

59. Nicholas Zumbaulyadis, "Bottger's Eureka: New Insights into the European Reinvention of Porcelain," *Bulletin for the History of Chemistry* 35, no. 1 (2010): 24–32.
60. The Jesuit missionary Père d'Entrecolles recounts how a Chinese merchant explained the functions of the components of porcelain in terms of flesh and bones. François d'Entrecolles, "Lettre du père d'Entrecolles, missionnaire de la Compagnie de Jésus, *in Lettres édifiantes, et curieuses écrites de missions etrangères* (Lyon: Chez J. Vernarel, 1819), 131–176. Christine Jones also discusses the way in which European porcelain fans described the composition of porcelain in terms of the bones and flesh of the body in *Shapely Bodies*, 147.
61. Lynn Meskell has detailed the way in which archaeology and international organizations such as UNESCO have played a role in narratives of heritage, history, and reproducing institutional powers that are asymmetric with communities and marginal voices. See Meskell, *A Future in Ruins* (Oxford: Oxford University Press, 2018).
62. For the design by William Chambers of a towering building conceived as the Nanjing Porcelain Pagoda, see Chambers, *Plans, Elevations, Sections, and Perspective Views of the Gardens and Buildings at Kew in Surry* (Farnborough, Hants.: Gregg Press, 1966 [London: J. Haberkorn, 1763]), final plate.
63. Bernard Faure, "The Buddhist Icon and the Modern Gaze," *Critical Inquiry* 24, no. 3 (1998): 770. As Faure has discussed, sculptural figural images that house relics have a complex relationship between body and part that do not simply map onto an immaterial image/sign and material referent.
64. Shen, *Authentic Replicas,* 173.
65. See Tansen Sen, *Buddhism, Diplomacy, and Trade: The Realignment of Sino-Indian Relations, 600–1400* (Honolulu: University of Hawai'i Press, 2003), 75, who cites Rúyì bǎozhū zhuǎnlún mìmì xiànshēn chéngfó jīnlún zhòuwáng jīng 如意寶珠轉輪秘密現身成佛金輪咒王經, T.961, 19:332c.

Chapter 10

Luminous Remains

On Relics, Jewels, and Glass in Chinese Buddhism

Francesca Tarocco

The spread of Buddhism to China during the first centuries of the Common Era facilitated the diffusion of ritual practices centered on the numinous efficacy (*ling*靈) of special persons and the things associated with them. Likewise, the diffusion and worship of sacred objects—most crucially relics and images—was decisive for the growth of the religion. Like images, relics firmly belong to the same category of the Buddhist miraculous—their spectacular materiality prompted the Chinese to name Buddhism "the teaching of images" (*xiangjiao* 像教). In what follows, I will analyze the affinities and interactions among relics, jewels, and glass, a substance with unique characteristics and a long (if little studied) Buddhist lineage. Glass was not widely known in medieval China if not among Buddhists, who associated it with the West (India and beyond). It was cherished, among other things, for its transparency. Glass objects could be given as offerings; in particular, exquisitely decorated vessels imported from Persia and the eastern Mediterranean areas were highly prized exotica. In Dunhuang mural paintings we see representations of the bodhisattva Avalokiteśvara holding a glass flask in his hands.[1] Of course, not every glass object or every relic was transported to East Asia from elsewhere as the new Buddhist regions started to "produce" their own sacred things. This is important, as histories of Buddhist practices can usefully be understood as embedded in a wider network of connections with histories of trade, ritual, and iconography, as well as technology. Chinese Buddhists elaborated their own material assemblages and ritual protocols based on Indian models. Descriptions of *śarīra* relics, and their Chinese equivalent, *shelizi* (舍利子), as "pearl-like" substances point to many potential affinities with jewels and other gemlike substances and luminous materials including crystal and glass.[2] These materials could also stand in as relics. Conceived of as being produced by cremating the remains of an accomplished Buddhist, *shelizi* could actually be the result of more sophisticated processes. Buddhist practices, including funerary ones, I argue, may have facilitated the diffusion of glass in China from India, the Middle East, and Europe from medieval times down to the present day. The reverse may also be true—namely, that the use of glass or glass beads in funerary pyres gave origin to some of the language used to describe relics in both earlier and more recent eyewitness accounts. Such language alludes in fact to the vitreous appearance of the relics, which are often described as translucent, white, or multi-colored. Similar to jewels and precious stones in appearance, glass is made with fire, one of the governing forces of Buddhist funerals.

Relics

Buddhism, suggests Robert Sharf, is "among other things, a religion of relics."[3] In his study of the Buddha's finger bone relics at Famen Temple 法門寺—beautiful objects made of white jade encased in superbly crafted reliquaries—he reminds us that when we think about relics, we should be mindful of the actual materials that constitute Buddhist aesthetics and material culture. The English term "relic"—from the Latin *reliquiae,* or "remains," and *relinquere,* "to leave behind"—is somewhat inadequate to decode the broad semantic field and the variety of metaphoric associations of the Sanskrit *śarīra* and its Chinese equivalent *shelizi.*[4] The word indicates the variety of media through which a devotee can gain connection to a special figure after his or her death.[5] These can include various forms of bodily remains and personal articles.[6] Relics can be conceptualized as direct conduits to spiritual forces and serve as objects of devotion and veneration. The Roman Catholic Church recognizes as relics the bodily remains of saints, objects belonging to or used by saints, and items that came into contact with either of the other two types.[7] Studies of Buddhism now routinely acknowledge the important role relics played in ritual and devotional practices in the context of the religion's spread to Asia. Once one starts looking for them, relics are everywhere.[8] No relic exists without a reliquary. The *stūpa,* then, as a funerary structure, highlights the Buddha's absence because it reminds devotees of his death.

And yet, since the relic also enlivens its container, stūpas and other objects can suggest the presence of the soteriological power radiated by the physical remains.[9] Phyllis Granoff has argued that the widespread belief in the power of bodily remains should be seen as a pan-Indic phenomenon rather than a specifically Buddhist one. Reading of a wide range of Indian medieval texts, Granoff showed that "the belief that body parts can turn into precious substances worthy of being objects of worship or tools of worship is both ancient and fundamental in Indian religion."[10] The Pali text *Mahāparinibbāṇa Sutta* contains precise instructions on how to deal with the body of the Buddha after cremation: the corporeal remains are divided into eight shares and enshrined in the stūpa reliquaries. Worshippers who make offerings to them receive blessings and salvation.[11] A popular story (visualized in myriad ways) taken from the Lotus Sutra shows the Buddha's instructions to the Bodhisattva Medicine King to build eighty-four thousand reliquaries for the dissemination of his relics: "After my passage into extinction, whatever *śarīra* there may be I entrust to you also. You are to spread them about and broadly arrange for offerings to them. You are to erect several thousand *stūpa*."[12]

In China, the popularity of relics facilitated the appropriation of preexisting sacred sites by Buddhist monastic elites; the country was made into a sacred Buddhist land. Reliquaries attributed to Aśoka could "manifest" themselves there, appearing miraculously on their own. Relics occupied a central position in monastic compounds.[13] Sites where relics are present are inspiring destinations for Buddhist pilgrims seeking to benefit from divine power. The cult of Buddhist relics encompasses materiality, affect, and ritual behavior. In China, the minute *shelizi,* crystalline or vitreous in appearance, are conceived of as being the concentration of the remains of an enlightened person that occurs during the process of cremation. Ultimately, they function as a technology of embodied sacredness: once the human form has been destroyed in the funerary pyre, the corporeal materiality is understood as being distilled into a spiritual essence. Once placed inside an image—a statue or other support—the charisma of the relic infuses it with life and transforms it into a numinous icon. It is intriguing that Chinese Buddhists also worship "whole-body relics" (*quanshen sheli* 全身舍利), the mummified remains of eminent masters whose desiccated "flesh bodies" (*roushen* 肉身) are wrapped in layers of cloth, adorned with fine robes and other paraphernalia, and enshrined.[14]

Luminous Remains

> If this *sūtra* is installed inside a Buddha image, or a *stūpa,* this image should be fabricated from seven gems, or this stūpa should have a canopy of seven gems.[15]

Stories about the finding of relics and the incorruptibility of monks' bodies are used in China to illustrate the real existence of the Buddha in the world. Incorporated into Buddhist hagiographies, they are signs of faith attesting to the efficacy of the religion.[16] Not limited to cremation remains, relics can also be created through monastic ritual, prayer, and meditation, thus continually increasing in quantity.[17] By the tenth century, relics were understood as comprising two distinct types, those from the Buddha and those from eminent monks (and some nuns).[18] The deaths of charismatic monks could augment the supply whether their bodies were cremated or miraculously preserved intact. It is important, as John Kieschnick has pointed out, that before the introduction of Buddhism, China had no cult that focused on the physical remains of any great person; the numinous power attributed to Buddhist relics was a major factor in the religion's success.[19] In Buddhism, visions of divine light and radiance are often associated with any object taken to be sacred or spiritually potent. Often described as "jewels" or "pearls," relics are said to emit light.[20] The medieval hagiographies of monks and nuns contain numerous stories of relics that can work miracles and cause supernormal events. Numinous efficacy evokes a "miraculous response" (*ganying* 感應). Thus the hagiographies assimilate the well-established ideas of "resonance" (*gantong* 感通, *ganying* 感應) as signs of faith attesting to the efficacy of Buddhism. In fact, the two major collections of monastic life stories, compiled by Daoxuan 道宣 (596–667) and Zanning 贊寧 (919–1001), point to the production of relics as a measure of the saintliness of their protagonists. In the "Song Biographies of Eminent Monks" (*Song gaoseng zhuan* 宋高僧轉), the cremation of certain monks is reported to have produced hundreds, even thousands, of *śarīra* whose shape and color are construed as signs of spiritual attainment. Zanning tells us that after the cremation of the Chan monk Hui'an 慧安 "eighty *śarīra* grains, crystalline relics, were retrieved from among the ashes. Five of them emitted a purple light and were sent to the imperial palace."[21] Another eyewitness, Su E 蘇鶚 (fl. 876–886), recorded the portentous signs that accompanied the ceremonial display of relics: "Rays from the Buddha relic and auspicious clouds lighted up the roadside and this was regarded repeatedly as a supernatural sign by the happy people."[22] With similar enthusiasm, the Japanese pilgrim monk Ennin 圓仁 (794–864) records the story of the miraculous manifestation in China and discovery of three precious vessels—a golden one, a blue lapis lazuli one, and a white one—each containing relics whose radiance illuminated the whole room in which a monk was reciting the scriptures.[23] Juhyung Rhi has argued that jewels could be used in China to replace bone fragments and other corporeal remains. One among many examples of this practice is the gilded-bronze seated Buddha icon in the Sackler Museum at Harvard University. It is important that the hagiography of the scholar monk and gifted exegete Dao'an 道安 (314–385) tells us that "a bronze image from a foreign country emitted splendid light to fill the entire hall." In the story, a relic was discovered in the *uṣṇīṣa* (*ji* 髻) of the icon whose miraculous radiance was attributed to the relic itself.[24] When Dao'an tells us that the icon is efficacious because of its shimmering relic, it may well be that he is already looking at something that emits light because it is, in fact, a precious or semiprecious stone, a jewel. Rhi points out that the Chinese tradition of replacing bone fragments with shining jewels is well attested and dates back as early as the second century CE.[25]

Glass

The term "glass," from the Late Latin term *glesum,* designates a transparent, gleaming substance made by cooling molten ingredients such as silica sand.[26] Glass has been made into practical and decorative objects since ancient times in Egypt, Syria, and India, among other places. The oldest type of glass is silicate glass, based on the chemical compound silica, the primary constituent of sand. It can be colored by adding metallic salts. Many glass samples have been excavated in Chinese tombs dating from the fifth century BCE, and barium-rich glass was cast (but not blown) in China by the second century BCE. There is also much evidence that glass was regularly imported from abroad.[27] The earliest known glass objects, dating back to the mid-third-millennium BCE, are glass beads. In all probability these were created fortuitously as by-products of metal working or as a pre-glass vitreous material made by a process similar to glazing. In China, glass appears to have been used mostly for religious purposes. Examples of Roman glass have been found in India as well as China. The oldest glass-based forms of material culture found in China date to the late Spring and Autumn and early Warring States periods (ca. 500–400 BCE). Many scholars accept this as the earliest phase of glass making in China. Polychrome beads may have also entered China during this time and contributed to the creation of a local glass industry. The stylistic similarity between these beads and locally produced Chinese beads makes this argument compelling.[28] During the period of the Six Dynasties relatively few pieces were found in excavated tombs, and it is perhaps the rarity of glass that made it so valued to the Chinese.[29] We know that blue glass ingots were deliberately fabricated as a synthetic replacement of lapis lazuli, a naturally occurring blue-colored stone. A metamorphic rock only mined in northeast Afghanistan, it was used as a semiprecious stone and widely traded in Eurasia.[30]

Scholars have shown that Buddhism was crucial to the development of trade between India and China from the first centuries of the Common Era, demonstrating that the role of foreign luxury goods was inseparable from the growing popularity of the religion.[31] From the Han period onward, the influence of Buddhism on Chinese material culture is a critical factor to consider. The use of precious and luminous substances did change significantly as a result of the encounter with Buddhist doctrines and technologies. Doris Dohrenwend divides Chinese glass into two categories: *liuli* (琉璃) and *boli* (玻璃). Both terms have Sanskrit origins and enter usage after contact with western regions. For Xinru Liu, the origin of *liuli* is "*vaiḍūrya,* which means lapis lazuli, beryl or cat's eye gem."[32] In Buddhist texts translated into Chinese during the fourth and fifth centuries, *liuli* is of a sky-blue color and is associated with the hair of the Buddha, bodhisattvas, and other deities. The *liuli* traded with the Chinese, notes Liu, was in fact blue glass, not lapis lazuli or other types of precious stones. It is possible that Chinese craftsmen may also have learned to make this type of glass. *Boli* underwent a similar path. In the early Buddhist context, *boli* and crystal (*shuijing* 水晶) are synonymous. Eventually, the Chinese came to realize that so-called crystal and *boli* were not stones but artefacts made by humans.[33] By the Tang period (618–907), the Chinese had already been familiar with glasses for centuries. In his pioneering study of Tang exotica, Edward Shafer notes that *liuli* was sometimes confused with real blue-colored stones such as lapis lazuli, beryl, and turquoise. *Boli,* on the other hand, was transparent and either colorless, like rock crystal and compared with water and ice, or else palely tinted. By the Tang, *liuli* was regarded as an "old thing," but blown vessels of *boli* were still a novelty.[34]

Chinese Buddhists in all likelihood viewed glass as one of the "seven treasures" (*qibao* 七寶) of Buddhism. The list of Sanskrit terms and their Chinese equivalents incudes gold, silver, *vaiḍūrya,* pearl, a red coral, ammonite, agate or coral, and something else that may be transparent glass or rock crystal.[35] All these materials were regarded as suitable offerings for the Buddha. Some of them were brighter than others or easier to obtain or more rare, and so on. Glass enjoyed "a very high status within the hierarchy of materials" that could be used in the making of Buddhist reliquaries.[36] In the "Biography of the Eminent Monk Faxian" (*Gaoseng Faxian zhuan* 高僧法顯轉), we read that the Chinese pilgrim to India Faxian (法顯; ca. 336–ca. 423) saw *stūpas* covered in gold and decorated with the seven treasures. The monk described a relic covering in the shape of a bell as literally made of *liuli* and decorated with pearls and precious stones.[37] Relics and glass can be found in close proximity to one another in excavated sites.[38] For instance, in 1987, archaeologists discovered a crypt underneath the pagoda at Famen Temple that had been sealed and left untouched since 874 CE.[39] They found more than four hundred objects made of silver and gold metalwork, as well as rare Chinese and foreign glass.[40] This case is far from unique. In *Surviving Nirvana,* Sonya Lee lists the findings at various sites, including those at Jingzhi Temple, which, again, consisted of hundreds of pieces of jade, ceramicware, and glassware.[41]

Burning

In China, relics have charisma and can perform miracles. Eventually, Chinese Buddhists envisioned a nomenclature and taxonomy of relics—their radiance, colors, and size mattered the most to Buddhist practitioners of the past. In his pioneering study *The Practice of Chinese Buddhism* (1967), based on extensive fieldwork in monasteries in China and Hong Kong, Holmes Welch noted that *śarīras* are "crystalline morsels believed to be left in the ashes of any saintly monk" and added that several modern biographies (*nianpu* 年譜) of Buddhist monks included photographs of relics in "neat piles, graded by size and color."[42] Not only does the possession of relics inspire reverence, but relics also bring prestige and reputation to the temples that own them.[43] For practitioners, relics are empirical evidence of Buddhist cosmology. As they set out to fabricate and then "discover" the relics of their masters, Buddhists create sites of thaumaturgy and talismanic power. Relics recovered from the pyre can appear as brightly colored crystallized minerals or else as bits of opaque glass-like matter. One wonders what these objects are made of. Might glass be present in the funerary pyre? Or sand? Could the bodies of Buddhist clerics be burned together with rosaries made of glass? Is a batch of glass-producing raw materials also thrown in? As a rule, Buddhist clerics are cremated rather than buried. And from the Tang period down to the present day, funerals that have incorporated ideas and practices surrounding rebirth in the Pure Land and the cult of Amitābha have been prevalent among Buddhist death practices.[44]

The cult of Amitābha and of rebirth in his Land of Bliss can be traced back as far as the Eastern Jin period (317–420). By the seventh century, Vinaya formulations already emphasized "Pure Land aspirations in a more obvious and technical manner."[45] Beliefs in rebirth in the Pure Land were widespread. Robert Sharf points out that the Chan monastic code, *Chanyuan qinggui* (禪 苑 清 規; 1103), also "explicitly mentions the recitation of Amitābha's name ten times in conjunction with monastic funerals, and during the more elaborate rites for a deceased abbot, the invocations of Amitābha's name are followed by the distribution of money called *nien-fo ch'ien* 念佛錢."[46] During the medieval period, *ling* appeared often in Buddhist and non-Buddhist mortuary ritual contexts. The *lingzuo* (靈座 or "spirit seat") of Chan abbots was displayed together with objects that belonged to the deceased in Song-period funerals.[47] Around this time, an increasing number of texts described miracles associated with the ritual distribution of relics.[48] These, together with the odor of sanctity—a fragrance held to proceed from the person of a saint after death—were understood as residues of such "efficacy." It is important that to this day, in Pure Land Buddhist funerary practices, the specially prepared bodies of eminent clerics are cremated in sealed encasements. The body is placed in a sealed niche (*kan* 龕; also "shrine") and cremated (*fenhua* 焚化) or "transformed by fire." Almost always, the desired outcome of these funerary practices is the production of relics, a process, as noted above, already outlined in early medieval sources.

Not Ash, Not Bone

Chinese Buddhist practices always refer to relics of monks and nuns as sites of devotion and veneration. When recovered from the funerary pyres of saintly clerics, relics manifest themselves in various shapes yet must shimmer and gleam. Once the relics are made, the followers of eminent monks employ multiple media to disseminate their power and presence. In a recent example, the followers of the Pure Land charismatic monk Yinguang 印光 (1861–1940)—one of modern China's most prominent clerics—not only took photographs of the relics, but also decided to display them under a microscope. The disciples of other revered clerics took similar steps. In fact, one can see how the twentieth-century Buddhist shrine became not only the protective shell practitioners fashioned for themselves, but also the locus of optical devices and philosophical toys of all sorts—the camera, the microscope—that seem to open the viewer's gaze onto a different world under the dominion of the image and semblance. A modern optical apparatus is put to the service of the Buddhist miraculous to show the brightly colored *śarīra* as empirical evidence that the charismatic teacher has successfully entered the Pure Land.[49] What are Yinguang's relics actually made of? We know that, beginning in the late imperial period, the Qing court established its own glass workshop (1696). Under the patronage of the court, there was a renewed interest in the appearance and the technology connected with glass. Glass making entered a new phase in which Europe and European glass played an important role.[50] We also know that in the early twentieth century, rosaries could be present in the enclosure prepared for the funerary pyre. In fact, Walter Perceval Yetts (1878–1957), who witnessed and studied Buddhist mortuary practices in modern times, tells us that rosaries were placed in the hands of the monks when their bodies were being prepared for cremation.[51] He pointedly noted that bodies were carefully prepared for cremation with the precise intent to provide relics—relics that would not only attract the public to the temples, but also inspire "generous contributions:"[52]

> Generally less than a day is allowed to elapse between the demise and cremation of a monk, but sometimes, when an abbot or priest of conspicuous sanctity dies, the body is kept for a week or more while special masses are being celebrated. In such a case the corpse is quickly fitted either into a *kan,* or into a wooden box, and packed round with charcoal mixed with fragments of sandal-wood. The receptacle is made quite airtight. When the time for burning comes the bier and its contents are put on the pyre just as they are, except in the case of a *kan,* when the vent-hole in its lid is opened. After cremation a handful or two of relics 舍利 are collected from among the ashes and deposited in an urn or in a red calico bag, which is then consigned to a room set apart for the purpose.[53]

Many Chinese eyewitness accounts of the cremation of eminent monks in modern times—for instance, that of Chan master Xuyun 虛雲 (ca.1840–1959), who is also said to have died in *odor sanctitatis*—echo earlier accounts. When Xuyun's cremation site was opened, one hundred large, five-color relics were found and an incalculable number of smaller ones, prevalently white but clear and bright.[54] Stories of shimmering relics are continuously circulated. In 1897, Xuyun conducted a pilgrimage to the Ayuwang Temple (阿育王寺) in Ningbo, whose Buddha relic had been the object of pilgrimage and devotion for centuries.[55] While there, he decided to burn off the ring finger of his left hand as an offering to the Buddha and to repay his debt of gratitude to his mother. The self-mortification practice of finger burning (*ran zhi* 燃指) in front of the relic at Ayuwang is well documented and can be accompanied by visions of the relics as shining and emitting multi-colored light.[56] In a dharma lesson I witnessed in 2016, the abbot of a temple located near Ningbo told his disciples of his own experiences of worshiping that same relic: it glimmered in front of his eyes and emitted mesmerizing beams of radiant light.[57]

One can find striking evidence of the connections among fire, relics, and glass in *To the Land of Bliss* (2001), the thoughtful ethnographic film by Wen-jie Qin—herself a Pure Land practitioner—that trails closely the cremation of a revered elderly monk with a large following.[58] After his body is burned, his disciples wait for about twenty-four hours before opening the enclosure. Just before those in charge start returning to the cremation site, Wen is told that the deceased master had just manifested himself to a group of nuns: a "golden light came out of the chimney," says a young nun; "his whole body appeared in the sky," and then the master left, "radiating a golden light."[59] Eventually, the clerics gather to search the ashes. This is done matter of factly, with plastic chopsticks. "Ordinary people won't be able to produce relics," proclaims a monk; "Spiritual practices transform the body," notes another. They appear to say these things to one another in order to instruct the laypersons who are there with them. As the ashes are carefully examined, the clerics start picking up tiny objects with their chopsticks: "This must be glass," says one of the small group of clerics, both monks and nuns. "No, it isn't!" says another. "Yes, it is; I have seen a Buddha relic just like this one," a third person exclaims conclusively. A few round objects of vitreous appearance are placed in plastic containers.[60] According to one of my informants, Yu Lan 余蓝, a Shanghai-based laywoman in her early fifties, relics still play a key role within communities of Pure Land Buddhists. It is the discovery of relics in the ashes, their number, size, and color, that points to one's attainment and rebirth in the Pure Land. Yu Lan herself witnessed one such event in 2015, when she took part in a ritual *nianfo* 念佛 recitation period to "accompany a saintly woman," a member of her community. After the cremation, everyone searched through the ashes in the hopes of finding relics. Their hopes were realized: they found dozens of them. They were bright and "looked like glass, not ash, not bone" (*xiang gen boli yiyang, bu shi hui bu shi gutou* 像跟玻璃一样, 不是灰不是骨头).[61]

Affinities

In this chapter, I have explored the affinities Chinese Buddhists discovered between relics and jewels and among fire, relics, and glass, a shimmering material created with molten sand. First of all, the fact that glass can be transparent made it suitable to contain and enshrine relics. What if, given the metonymic slippages characteristic of many Buddhist replication processes, the material of the reliquary became that of the relic, and vice versa? Glass glimmers like a jewel and, exactly like a jewel, can be made into a relic. I suggest that since Chinese Buddhist relics are assemblages and multilayered fabrications, we must further explore the possibility that what emerges from the funerary pyre of saintly clerics is some form of vitreous matter. Also, as excavations of several Buddhist sites clearly attest, glass beads were scattered around *stūpas* and enshrined in reliquaries inside them because of their connection with relics. It is precisely in this context that they were exported from India to China.[62] For instance, over 150,000 glass beads have been excavated from the site of the Yongning Temple 永寧寺 in Loyang, an important temple built in the early sixth century.[63] For centuries, glass beads proliferated in China thanks to Buddhism. Indian glass beads, and maybe even the Venetian *conterie* at a later stage, became increasingly more widespread.[64] What was the holy light that led Dao'an to discover a relic in the *uṣṇīṣa* of an icon? Perhaps we should understand the radiance of the bejeweled relic as not merely symbolic. Technological affinities served the religio-aesthetic and practical needs of a particular group of people and therefore must be very carefully considered. Moreover, at any one time and as one of the materials accessible to the Buddhist ritual repertoire, glass may have deliberately been put to work in the process of making the luminous remains of eminent clerics. This possibility appears even more likely in modern times and in light of the expectation of the faithful to "discover" a large number of fine-looking relics among the ashes of their dead as evidence of their successful passage to the Pure Land.[65] For Buddhist communities in China, Taiwan, and elsewhere in the Chinese Buddhist world, the objects that materialize among the cremation ashes as vitreous smidgens are vibrant and alive. Making large numbers of *shelizi* through cremation is imperative.

Notes

I am grateful to Vanessa Sasson, Nancy Lin, and Aldo Mignucci for their helpful feedback at various stages of preparation of this chapter.

1. Susan Whitfield and Ursula Sims-Williams, *The Silk Road: Trade, Travel War and Faith* (London: British Library, 2004), 157; see also Hsueh-Man Shen, "Luxury or Necessity: Glassware in Sarīra Relic Pagodas of the Tang and Northern Song Periods," in *Chinese Glass: Archaeological Studies on the Uses and Social Context of Glass Artefacts from the Warring States to the Northern Song Period*, edited by Cecilia Braghin (Florence: Leo S. Olschki Editore, 2002); Albert E. Dien *Six Dynasties Civilization*, 288–292.
2. See also John Strong in this volume.
3. Robert H. Sharf "The Buddha's Finger Bones at Famensi and the Art of Chinese Esoteric Buddhism," *Art Bulletin* 93, no. 1 (2011): 38.
4. For the other term for relic, *dhatu*, meaning "constituent part," "ingredient," see Gregory Schopen, "Relic," in *Critical Terms for Religious Studies*, edited by Mark C. Taylor (Chicago: University of Chicago Press, 1998), 256.
5. On Christian relics see Martina Bagnoli, et al., eds., *Treasures of Heaven: Saints, Relics, and Devotion in Medieval Europe* (Cleveland, OH: Walters Art Museum, 2010).
6. See especially Brian D. Ruppert, *Jewel in the Ashes: Buddha Relics and Power in Early Medieval Japan* (Cambridge, MA: Harvard University Press, 2000; Harvard East Asian Monographs 188); Bernard Faure: "Dato," in fasc. 8 of *Hōbōgirin* (Paris: Adrien Maisonneuve, 2003), 1127–1158; *The Rhetoric of Immediacy: A Cultural Critique of Chan/Zen Buddhism* (Princeton, NJ: Princeton University Press, 1991), 132–147; "Relics and Flesh Bodies: The Creation of Ch'an Pilgrimage Sites," in *Pilgrims and Sacred Sites in China*, edited by Susan Naquin and Chün-fang Yü (Berkeley: University of California Press, 1992), 150–189; and "Les cloches de la terre: Un aspect du culte des reliques dans

le bouddhisme chinois," in *Bouddhisme et lettrés dans la Chine médiévale,* edited by Catherine Despeux (Paris: Peeters, 2002), 25–44. On the cult of relics in China, see, for instance, John Kieschnick, *The Impact of Buddhism on Chinese Material Culture* (Princeton, NJ: Princeton University Press, 2003), 29–52.

7. Martina Bagnoli et al., *Treasures of Heaven.*
8. On the cult of relics in Asia, see especially John Strong, *Relics of the Buddha* (Princeton, NJ: Princeton University Press, 2004); Gregory Schopen, *Bones, Stones, and Buddhist Monks: Collected Papers on the Archaeology, Epigraphy, and Texts of Monastic Buddhism in India* (Honolulu: University of Hawai'i Press, 1997); David Germano and Kevin Trainor, eds., *Embodying the Dharma: Buddhist Relic Veneration in Asia* (Albany: State University of New York Press, 2004). See also Kieschnick, *The Impact of Buddhism on Chinese Material Culture;* Sonya S. Lee, *Surviving Nirvana: Death of the Buddha in Chinese Visual Culture* (Hong Kong: Hong Kong University Press, 2010); Ruppert, *Jewel in the Ashes;* Schopen, "Relic"; Dan Martin, "Pearls from Bones: Relics, Chortens, Tertons and the Signs of Saintly Death in Tibet," *Numen* 41 (1994): 273–323. See also the chapters by Strong and Lin in this volume.
9. For further discussion, see Lin's chapter in this volume. See also Strong, *Relics of the Buddha.* For some of Gregory Schopen's works related to these issues, see the following: "The Stūpa Cult and the Extant Pali Vinaya," *Journal of the Pali Text Society* 13 (1989): 83–100; "Monks and the Relic Cult in the Mahaparinibbana-sutta: An Old Misunderstanding in Regard to Monastic Buddhism," in *From Benares to Beijing: Essays on Buddhism and Chinese Religion,* edited by Koichi Shinohara and Gregory Schopen (Oakville, Ontario: Mosaic Press, 1991), 187–201; and "Burial *Ad Sanctos* and the Physical Presence of the Buddha in Early Indian Buddhism: A Study in the Archaeology of Religions," *Religion* 17 (1987): 193–225.
10. Phyllis Granoff, "Relics, Rubies and Ritual: Some Comments on the Distinctiveness of the Buddhist Relic Cult," *Rivista degli studi orientali, Nuova Serie* 81, nos. 1–4 (2008): 70.
11. See T. W. Rhys Davids, *Dialogues of the Buddha,* 3 vols. (London: Pali Text Society, 1890–1924), 2:71–191.
12. Leon Hurvitz, *Scripture of the Lotus Blossom of the Fine Dharma,* 272; in T., no. 262, vol. 9, 53c14–15.
13. Huaiyu Chen, *The Revival of Buddhist Monasticism in Medieval China* (New York: Peter Lang, 2007), 62–64.

14. See, for example, Faure: *The Rhetoric of Immediacy,* and *The Will to Orthodoxy: A Critical Genealogy of Northern Chan Buddhism* (Palo Alto, CA: Stanford University Press, 1997); John Kieschnick, *The Eminent Monk: Buddhist Ideals in Medieval Chinese Hagiography* (Honolulu: University of Hawai'i Press, 1997); Lee, *Surviving Nirvana;* Sharf, "The Buddha's Finger Bones."
15. Translation of the *Baoqieyin Sūtra* (Sūtra of the Precious Jewel Mudrā) by Zhiru Shi, "From Bodily Relic to Dharma Relic Stūpa: Chinese Materialization of the Aśoka Legend in the Wuyue Period," in *India in the Chinese Imagination: Myth, Religion, and Thought,* edited by John Kieschnick and Meir Shahar (Philadelphia: University of Pennsylvania Press, 2014), 105.
16. Tiziana Lippiello has shown how auspicious omens played an important role in politics in the medieval period as they foretold the coming of an era of peace and prosperity or a new reign or dynasty or appeared in response to good government. See Tiziana Lippiello, *Auspicious Omens and Miracles in Ancient China: Han, Three Kingdoms and Six Dynasties* (Leiden: Brill, 1995).
17. Faure, "Relics and Flesh Bodies," 214.
18. Lee, *Surviving Nirvana,* 256.
19. Kieschnick, *The Impact of Buddhism on Chinese Material Culture,* 30–32.
20. See Brian D. Ruppert, "Pearl in the Shrine: A Genealogy of the Buddhist Jewel of the Japanese Sovereign," *Japanese Journal of Religious Studies* 29, nos. 1–2 (2002): 1–33.
21. See the passage in the *Taishō Tripitaka*大正新脩大藏經, T. 2061: 823b.
22. Kenneth K. S. Ch'en, *Buddhism in China: A Historical Survey* (Princeton, NJ: Princeton University Press, 1964), 281.
23. Edwin O. Reischauer, *Ennin's Diary: The Record of a Pilgrimage to China in Search of the Law* (New York: Ronald Press, 1955), 300–303. When the Shingon monk and polymath Kūkai 空海 (774–835) returned to Japan from China, he brought back ritual paraphernalia and objects, including a number of pearl-like relics.For the relation between the imperial jewel, the Wish-Fulfilling Jewel (*cintamaṇi*), and relics in Japan, see Richard Payne's chapter in this volume. See also Ruppert, "Pearl in the Shrine."
24. See the passage in the Taishō Tripitaka大正新脩大藏經, T. 2059: 352b: 有一外國銅像像，形製古異，時眾不甚恭重。安曰：「像形相致佳但髻形未稱。」令弟子爐治其髻，既而光焰煥炳，耀滿一堂。詳視髻中，見一舍利，眾咸愧服。安曰：「像既靈異，不煩復治。」乃止。識者咸謂安知有舍利，故出以示眾.

25. Juhyung Rhi, "Images, Relics, and Jewels: The Assimilation of Images in the Buddhist Relic Cult of Gandhāra: Or Vice Versa." *Artibus Asiae* 65, no. 2 (2005): 183, 184, 201.
26. The melting temperature for the batch, the mixture of raw materials (often silica, soda or potash, and lime) that is melted in a pot or tank to make glass, is quite high. The heating causes the sand to undergo a chemical transformation. A cross between a solid and a liquid, glass features some crystalline structures generally found in solids. Scholars are still asking some fundamental questions with regard to the initial invention (or, indeed, multiple inventions) of glasses and glass-making recipes and techniques and about the spread and long-distance trade of the material. See Thilo Rehren, and Ian C. Freestone. "Ancient Glass: From Kaleidoscope to Crystal Ball," *Journal of Archaeological Science* 56 (2015): 233–241. In glassmaking, one can use alkali, a soluble salt consisting mainly of potassium carbonate or sodium carbonate. It is one of the essential ingredients of glass, generally accounting for about 15–20 percent of the batch. The alkali is a flux, which reduces the melting point of the major constituent of glass, silica.
27. See Dien, *Six Dynasties Civilization,* and Rehren and Freestone, "Ancient Glass."
28. Doris Dohrenwend, "Glass in China: A Review Based on the Collection in the Royal Ontario Museum," *Oriental Art Richmond-Surrey* 26, no. 4 (1980): 426–446; Cecilia Braghin, "Polychrome and Monochrome Glass of the Warring States and Han Periods" in Braghin, *Chinese Glass,* 3–43.
29. Dien, *Six Dynasties Civilization,* 286–290.
30. Andrew J. Shortland, *Lapis Lazuli from the Kiln: Glass and Glassmaking in the Late Bronze Age* (Leuven: Leuven University Press, 2012).
31. Xinru Liu, *Ancient India and Ancient China: Trade and Religious Exchanges AD 1–600* (Delhi: Oxford University Press, 1988); Shen, "Luxury or Necessity."
32. X. Liu, *Ancient India and Ancient China,* 59.
33. X. Liu, *Ancient India and Ancient China,* 59.
34. Edward H. Schafer, *The Golden Peaches of Samarkand: A Study of T'ang Exotica* (Berkeley: University of California Press, 1963), 236.
35. Shen, "Luxury or Necessity," 73n8.
36. Shen, "Luxury or Necessity," 73.
37. See *Taishō Tripitaka* 大正新脩大藏經T. 2085.
38. Relics are frequently preserved and displayed in glass containers and reliquaries. In Venice, in the Treasury of St. Mark's Basilica, gold and

enameled gold-work reliquaries sit side by side with striking late-antique vases of glass.

39. "Pagodas" are the tower-like architectural reliquaries housing the relics of the Buddha in East Asia and are rather different form the reliquarial mounds of India. Smaller portable reliquaries are also extremely popular.
40. Sharf, "The Buddha's Finger Bones," 38.
41. Lee, *Surviving Nirvana,* 212–220.
42. See Holmes Welch, *The Practice of Chinese Buddhism: 1900–1950* (Cambridge, MA: Harvard University Press, 1967), 345.
43. Kieschnick, *The Impact of Buddhism on Chinese Material Culture,* 36–50.
44. The corpus of so-called Pure Land scriptures comprises two Indian texts: the Larger and Smaller Sukhāvatīvyūha sūtra (Scriptures on the Land of Bliss), which exist in various Chinese translations, as well as the *Guan Wuliangshoufo jing* 觀無量壽佛經 (Scripture on the contemplation on the Buddha of Immeasurable Life), which is likely of Central Asian origin. These were interpreted and commented upon by eminent medieval monks and Pure Land patriarchs, notably Tanluan 曇鸞 (476–542), Daocho 道綽 (562–645), and Shandao 善導 (613–681). On Pure Land funerary practices, see, for instance, Daniel B. Stevenston, "Death-Bed Testimonials of the Pure Land Faithful," in *Buddhism in Practice,* edited by Donald S. Lopez (Princeton, NJ: Princeton University Press, 1995), 592–602. For a translation, see Luis Gómez, *The Land of Bliss* (Honolulu: University of Hawai'i Press, 1997).
45. Alan Cole, "Upside Down/Right Side Up: A Revisionist History of Funerals in China," *History of Religions* 35, no. 4 (1996): 322.
46. See Sharf, "On Pure Land Buddhism," 310.
47. See Sharf, "On Pure Land Buddhism," 319.
48. See Faure: "Relics and Flesh Bodies" and "Les cloches de la terre."
49. See Jan Kiely, "The Charismatic Monk and the Chanting Masses: Master Yinguang and His Pure Land Revival Movement," in *Making Saints in Modern China,* edited by by David Ownby, Vincent Goossaert, and Ji Zhe (Oxford: Oxford University Press, 2016), 70.
50. See Jiayao An, "Glass Beads Found at the Yongningsi Temple," *Journal of Glass Studies* 42 (2000): 81–84; Dohrenwend, "Glass in China"; and Braghin, "Polychrome and Monochrome Glass of the Warring States and Han Periods."
51. W. Perceval Yetts, "Notes on the Disposal of the Buddhist Dead in China," *Journal of the Royal Asiatic Society of Great Britain and Ireland,* July 1911, 703.

52. Yetts, "Notes on the Disposal of the Buddhist Dead in China," 712.
53. Yetts, "Notes on the Disposal of the Buddhist Dead in China," 706. In 1930, Yetts became the first lecturer in Chinese art and archaeology at the School of Oriental Studies at the University of London. In 1932, he became Professor of Chinese Art and Archaeology at London University until his retirement in 1946.
54. See Cen Xuelü 岑學呂, *Xuyun fashi nianpu* 虛云法师年谱 (Beijing: Zongjiao wenhua chubanshe, 1995). For Xuyun, see also Daniela Campo, *La construction de la sainteté dans la Chine moderne: La vie du maître bouddhiste Xuyun* (Paris: Les Belles Lettres, 2013). See also Xuyun, *Empty Cloud: The Autobiography of the Chinese Zen Master,* translated by Charles Luk (Longmead: Element Books, 1988).
55. Erik Zürcher, *The Buddhist Conquest of China: The Spread and Adaptation of Buddhism in Early Medieval China* (Leiden: Brill, 1959), 277–280.
56. See Welch, *The Practice of Chinese Buddhism,* 324–325, and Johannes Prip-Møller, *Chinese Buddhist Monasteries: Their Plan and Function as a Setting for Buddhist Monastic Life* (Hong Kong: Hong Kong University Press, 1967).
57. Francesca Tarocco, "Charismatic Communications: The Intimate Publics of Chinese Buddhism," in *Concepts and Methods for the Study of Chinese Religions III: Key Concepts in Practice,* edited by S. Trevagnin and P. Katz (Berlin: De Gruyter, 2019), 113–132.
58. Wen-jie Qin, *To the Land of Bliss,* 2001. Distributed by Documentary Educational Resources, Watertown, MA. docued@der.org.
59. Qin, *To the Land of Bliss,* min. 32.23.
60. Qin, *To the Land of Bliss,* min. 37.10.
61. Personal communication to author, Shanghai, November 22, 2018.
62. X. Liu, *Ancient India and Ancient China,* 63.
63. An, "Glass Beads Found at the Yongningsi Temple." The temple was built in 516 and destroyed by lightning in 534. The site was excavated in 1994. Its "magnificent nine storey pagoda" is mentioned in the famous record of Luoyang's Buddhist temples, the *Luoyang qielan ji* 洛陽伽藍級, compiled by Yan Xuanzhi 楊衒之. See W. J. F. Jenner, *Memories of Loyang: Yang Hsüan-chih and the Lost Capital (493–534)* (Oxford: Clarendon Press, 1981), and Yi-t'ung Wang, *Record of the Buddhist Monasteries in Loyang* (Princeton, NJ: Princeton University Press, 1984).
64. On Venetian glass and the *conterie* see Francesca Trivellato, *Fondamenta dei Vetrai: Lavoro, tecnologia e mercato a Venezia tra sei e settecento* (Roma: Donzelli, 2000).

65. For a recent example of the continuing relevance of Xuyun relics in contemporary China, see the blog of the prominent Buddhist nun Shengong, available at http://www.skamrta.com/contents/1175/12309.html (accessed December 18, 2019).

Chapter 11

Offerings for Prosperity to Wish-Fulfilling Jewel Cakra Avalokiteśvara

Richard K. Payne

The figure of Wish-Fulfilling Jewel Cakra Avalokiteśvara brings together two systems of symbols prominent in the Buddhism of the subcontinent and takes on a particular inflection in East Asia and Japan. The symbol of the Bodhisattva of Compassion, Avalokiteśvara, is combined with the symbol of the wish-fulfilling jewel, *cintāmaṇi*. The jewel is also represented as a discus that can destroy any dangers that may threaten devotees of the bodhisattva. The combination of bodhisattva and wish-fulfilling jewel in the figure of Wish-Fulfilling Jewel Cakra Avalokiteśvara creates a network of themes and then assimilates additional symbolic themes in East Asia.[1] This combination is not simply a kind of literary flourish or decorative metaphor, but it rather involves an identity of the bodhisattva and the jewel. There is an active process of creating new meanings by the interactions between different symbol systems—that is, intersemiosis.[2] Although masculine in South Asia, Avalokiteśvara becomes increasingly feminine in Sinitic representations through association with a number of local female deities in China. As a specific form of Avalokiteśvara, however, Wish-Fulfilling Jewel Cakra Avalokiteśvara only becomes a female figure in Japan. The dynamics of this change include a difference in conceptions of legitimation of sovereignty—conceptions that include sexual intercourse between the emperor and the living embodiment of the wish-fulfilling jewel, his consort.[3] The figure of Wish-Fulfilling Jewel Cakra Avalokiteśvara continues in the Shingon ritual corpus. And while her symbolic associations have been examined in the scholarly literature, little attention has been paid to cultic practices centering on her.[4] This chapter therefore contributes to the study of this bodhisattva who compassionately wields the wish-fulfilling jewel by examining the Shingon *homa* ritual devoted to Wish-Fulfilling Jewel Cakra Avalokiteśvara.

Contemporary Shingon praxis is a landscape lying atop a complex historical sedimentation of ideas, symbols, practices, texts, values, and so on, built up over more than a millennium and a half. The ritual examined here, the "Offerings for Prosperity to Wish-Fulfilling Jewel Cakra Avalokiteśvara," provides entrée by which we can go beneath the surface of present-day practices to explore two aspects of that sedimentation. One aspect is the *homa* rite itself, which reveals sediments laid down from early medieval India when tantric Buddhism was being formed.[5] The second aspect is the melding of the Chinese symbolism of the jewel woman with that of Avalokiteśvara, the Bodhisattva of Compassion. This melding produced the complex symbolism of Wish-Fulfilling Jewel Cakra Avalokiteśvara (Skt. *Cintamaṇicakra Avalokiteśvara;[6] Ch. Ruyilun Guanyin; Jpn. Nyoirin Kannon, 如意輪観音). Drawing these two aspects together allows us to see some dimensions of the cult of Wish-Fulfilling Jewel Cakra Avalokiteśvara. Cult as the dynamic interrelation of deity, practice, and ideology, together with the value of the category of cult for the study of Buddhism, will be discussed in the conclusion.

Homa

The *homa* (Jpn. goma, 護摩), a votive ritual in which offerings are made into a fire, was integrated into tantric Buddhism as part of the early medieval (ca. 500–1200) revision of Buddhism that took place after the end of the Gupta dynasty.[7] The ritual draws on Vedic, and probably Indo-Iranian, sources, though many of the steps of its development are subject to further research.[8] It is found throughout all forms of tantra, not only Buddhist, but also the Hindu and Jain forms as well. The use of the *homa* across all forms of tantra is so consistent that it can be taken as a marker for those traditions.

Its use in Buddhist tantra is found from the earliest records of the tradition. The *Vairocanābhisaṃbodhi tantra* is "one of the first fully developed expositions" of tantric Buddhism, composed sometime in the span from the mid-sixth to seventh centuries.[9] Thus, the integral role of the *homa* in the practices described in the text is evidence of the importance of the *homa* from early in the development of tantric Buddhism. One full chapter of the *Vairocanābhisaṃbodhi tantra* is, for example, devoted to distinguishing properly Buddhist forms of the *homa* from those that are not, and the ritual is mentioned repeatedly elsewhere in the text. One particularly important instance of the *homa* is as a key part of a practitioner's initiation "into the maṇḍala"—that is, into the practice of rituals evoking the deities of the womb world maṇḍala (Skt. **garbhadhātu maṇḍala;* Jpn. *taizokai mandara,* 胎蔵界曼荼羅).[10] The womb world maṇḍala, which shows the arrangement of Dharmakāya Mahāvairocana Buddha and his retinue, together with the *Vairocanābhisaṃbodhi tantra* itself, and the corpus of rituals prescribed in the text—including, a little self-referentially, the initiation into the maṇḍala—can be taken as the constitutive elements of one of the ritual lineages that informed the Shingon tradition in Japan. That tradition matches the womb world maṇḍala with the vajra world maṇḍala (Skt. **vajradhātu maṇḍala;* Jpn. *kongōkai mandara,* 金剛界曼荼羅), the former being understood as "the phenomenal world of the produced dharmas" (Skt. *saṃskṛta dharmas*) and the latter "the domain of the unproduced" (Skt. *asaṃskṛta dharmas*)[11]—that is, saṃsāra and nirvāṇa existing in a nondual relation.[12] The vajra world maṇḍala is associated with the other main text of the Shingon tradition, the **Vajraśekhara tantra*.[13]

While the history of the transmission of the *homa* rite to East Asia also remains a matter of some disagreement, in part based on definition of the rite, it was definitively part of the Zhenyan (Jpn. Shingon, 眞言; Skt. Mantranaya) form of tantric Buddhism propagated in the capital city of Chang'an during the Tang (618–907). The *Vairocanābhisaṃbodhi tantra* was translated into Chinese in 724–725 by two of the key figures in the establishment of tantric Buddhism in Tang, Śubhakarasiṃha (637–735) and his disciple Yixing (683–727), and the two also compiled an extensive commentary on the text.[14] The commentary includes an important exposition of the *homa* ritual in the context of medieval Tang Buddhism.[15]

Huiguo (746–805) was a master in the next generation after Śubhakarasiṃha and was a key figure in the spread of tantric Buddhism throughout East Asia. He was the holder of two lineages, each a compound of practice, maṇḍala, and text—that of the womb world maṇḍala and that of the vajra world maṇḍala. Kūkai, who established the foundations for the Shingon sect as it exists today, was one of the many monks who studied with Huiguo. Kūkai was initiated into both lineages and brought the teachings and practices of these lineages to Heian—including the *homa*. While the formation of the two-maṇḍala system is sometimes attributed to Kūkai, the history of its development is still an open question. For example, both the archaeological discoveries at Famensi and Borobudur in Java have been interpreted by reference to the two-maṇḍala system.

In the practice of the *homa* the fire is homologized with the transformative agency of Agni, the Vedic deity, who purifies offerings and transports them to the gods, with the transformative fires of digestion, and with the transformation of obscurations to awakening, by the fire of wisdom that comprehends that obscurations and awakening are fundamentally identical because both are empty. This is the three-way identification by which the *homa* ritual is effective—the mouth of the hearth is the mouth of the deity is the mouth of the practitioner; the offerings into the fire are offerings to the deity are the practitioner's own cognitive and emotional obscurations (Skt. *kleśāvaraṇa* and *jñeyāvaraṇa*); the fire in the altar hearth is the deity made present in the maṇḍala altar and is at the same time the transformative, purifying power of the practitioner's own already awakened consciousness.

Varieties of the *Homa*

Tantric practitioners have organized their ritual practices according to several different systems in which the purpose for the ritual is the main criterion. In the Shingon tradition one current category system identifies the following five kinds of rituals (*goshuhō,* 五種法):

stopping calamities, *sokusaihō* (息災法), *śāntika*
increasing merit and prosperity, *sōyakuhō* (增益法), *pauṣṭika*
summoning living beings, *kōchōhō* (鉤召法), *aṅkuśa*
creating love and respect, *keiaihō* (敬愛法), *vaśīkaraṇa*
subduing demons, *jōbukuhō* (調伏法), *ābhicāraka*

The Nyoirin Kannon Goma examined here is a *sōyakuhō*—that is a ritual for the increase of merit and prosperity.[16]

Structure of the Nyoirin Kannon Goma (*Cintamaṇicakra Avalokiteśvara Homa*)

Like many contemporary Shingon *homas,* this one has five sections or sets of offerings. Though the five sets of offerings take place within a larger frame ritual, they are usually the only part seen during a public performance. The preceding and following actions are frequently performed on the day before and the day after, respectively. This is not a matter of secrecy but rather because of the length of time involved in undertaking the full ritual. The five sets of offerings are the basic structure or format for the ritual, allowing for systematic changes by which rituals for different deities and different purposes can be created. Such changes include not only different deities, but also mantras and *mudrās,* visualizations, and traditionally the color of the clothing the practitioner wears, the shape of the hearth, the kinds of offerings made, and the time of day when the ritual is performed.

First section: Ka Ten (火天), Agni, the Vedic god of fire who burns away impurities from the offerings and then transmits the now-purified offerings to the deities.

Second section: "Lord of the Assembly": Kongōhō bosatsu (金剛宝菩薩), Vajraratna bodhisattva. Vajraratna is one of the Sixteen Great Protectors (Jyū roku dai gō; 十六大護), presumably chosen for this ritual because his name, Vajraratna, means "vajra jewel" and hence has a symbolic resonance with Wish-Fulfilling Jewel Cakra Avalokiteśvara.

Third section: Nyoirin Kannon (如意輪観音), Cintāmaṇicakra Avalokiteśvara is the chief deity (*honzon*, 本尊) of the third set of ritual offerings, evoked into the center of the hearth.[17]

Fourth section: various deities, including Dainichi (Mahāvairocana Buddha), Nyoirin, Seikannon (正観音, original Kannon), Tara (Tārā Bodhisattva), Seishi (Mahāsthāmaprāpta Bodhisattva), and Batō Kannon (Hayagrīva: Horse-Headed Avalokiteśvara).[18]

Fifth section: worldly deities, including Fudō Myōō (Acalanatha Vidyārāja) and the twelve devas. The twelve devas are classic Vedic deities such as Agni (Fire Deity, Katen), Surya (Sun Deity, Nichiten), and so on.

Visualization of Nyoirin Kannon in the *Homa*

The third and central section of the *homa* manual contains a visualization of Wish-Fulfilling Jewel Avalokiteśvara, the chief deity of this third section.

> Visualize the syllable HRIḤ [Jpn. *kiriku*] above the moon *cakra* located at one's heart.[19] On the left and right [of this syllable] are two TRAḤ [*taraku*] syllables. This changes becoming a vajra jeweled lotus [*kongō ho rin, vajra ratna padma*]. This changes becoming Nyoirin Kanjizai Bosatsu, with a gold-colored body. On top of his head is a

> magnificent jeweled crown. The body of this Buddha [*jizai-ō*] is seated, dwelling in the teaching posture. From his body a thousand bright lights [*kōmyō*] flow out. Behind his head is a circular light [*mandorla*]. His first right hand is pensive, his second holds a *cintāmaṇi* [*nyoishu*], his third holds a *mālā* [*nenju*], his first left hand rests on Mt. Potalaka (Kōmyōsan, 光明山), his second holds a lotus flower, and his third holds a wheel [eight-spoked wheel—i.e., *dharmacakra*].

This iconography is standard for the six-armed form of Nyoirin Kannon. The "teaching posture" is one in which the left leg rests on the ground horizontally, and the right leg is upright so that the elbow of the first right arm rests on the knee. This posture is also known as the "royal ease" *āsana* (Skt. *mahārājalīlāsana*). The order of hands indicated is in a circular order from top right to middle to lower, then to lower left and upward. The right-left designation is from the perspective of the visualized figure himself. That Nyoirin Kannon contemplates ways to bring all living beings to awakening is indicated by the pensive upper right hand, which is usually touching the right cheek.[20]

Commonly, the second—that is, middle—right hand, the one holding the wish-fulfilling jewel, is shown being held close to the bodhisattva's chest. The wish-fulfilling jewel (Skt. *cintāmaṇi;* Jpn. *nyoishu* 如意珠, or *nyoihōshu* 如意寶珠) is a precious stone or pearl to which is attributed the quality of granting wishes or fulfilling desires. E. Dale Saunders gives a number of mythic origin tales for the stone, as well as describing several symbolic associations and representations. For example, he cites the *Daichidoron* (*Dazhi du lun;* 大智度論, T. 1509, *Mahāprajñāpāramitā śāstra*) regarding the story that "the jewel came from the brain of a *nāga* and that, possessing it, one may escape from harm and poisons and entering into fire one will remain unburnt; possessing it, all earthly desires are fulfilled."[21] The unqualified beneficence of Kannon is matched by the unqualified beneficence of the wish-fulfilling jewel. The third, or lowest, right hand, holding a rosary (*nenju* 念珠; Skt. *mālā*), hangs down beside the bodhisattva's right hip. The number of beads, 108, is associated with the number of obscurations (*kleśa, bonnō,* 煩悩), providing a symbolic association to an adherent's liberation from those obscurations effected by the bodhisattva. According to Saunders, "the rosary carried by Kannon signifies that the divinity herself by her compassion assumes these passions [i.e., *kleśa*] which bind the worshiper to the world, and liberates him thus from the hindrance of desires."[22]

The first, or lowest, left hand rests on the original dwelling place of Avalokiteśvara in south India, Mt. Potalaka (Jpn. Kōmyōsan; also Fudarakusen 補陀落山). The symbolism of Mt. Potalaka comes from the *Gandhavyūha sūtra,* in which it is identified as the dwelling place of Avalokiteśvara. The *Gandhavyūha sūtra* recounts the travels of Sudhana in search of awakening, and the sutra describes his arrival at Mt. Potalaka:

> Then, the merchant's son Sudhana . . . arrived in due order at Mount Potalaka, and climbing Mount Potalaka he looked around and searched everywhere for the Bodhisattva Avalokiteśvara. Finally, he saw the Bodhisattva Avalokiteśvara on a plateau on the western side of a deeply forested mountain in a clearing, abundant with young grass, adorned with springs and waterfalls, and surrounded by various trees. He was sitting leisurely on a diamond rock surrounded by a multitude of Bodhisattvas firmly seated on rocks of various jewels. He was expounding the teaching called "the splendor of the door of great friendliness and great compassion" belonging to the sphere of caring for all sentient beings.[23]

Making reference to rocks that are jewels as seats for both Avalokiteśvara and his retinue suggests a kind of dual vision of the simultaneity of the ordinary and extraordinary, and it is resonant with the jewels that characterize many buddha-fields (*buddhakṣetra*). The imagery provides a clear association between Avalokiteśvara and precious jewels similar to other associations between jewels and buddhas and bodhisattvas made in Buddhist literature.

Like other important locales in Buddhist myth, Mt. Potalaka is identified with several well-known geographical sites, including the Potala in Lhasa, where the Dalai Lama as an incarnation of Avalokiteśvara dwelt, and with Putuoshan, an island off the coast of China. The association has facilitated Putuoshan's becoming a popular tourist destination in the last couple of decades.[24] In statuary when the figure of the bodhisattva is seated on a lotus throne, Mt. Potalaka is often represented as small rocklike pedestal beside the throne. In other cases, instead of on a lotus throne, the figure as a whole is seated on a rock-shaped base representing Mt. Potalaka.

While the first left hand rests on Mt. Potalaka, the second left hand, the one holding a lotus flower, is held over the left knee. The lotus is frequently associated with Avalokiteśvara. The final, third uppermost, left hand holds a *dharmacakra*.[25] One interpretation of the six arms of

Nyoirin Kannon is that they represent the bodhisattva's activity in each of the six realms of rebirth: hell, hungry ghost, animal, human, titan (*asura*), and god (*deva*) realms.[26]

This then is the figure that the practitioner is directed to visualize at the core of the *homa*.[27] This particular *homa* ritual is very consistent with other contemporary Shingon *homas,* particularly those in the extensive collection published by Soeda Takatoshi in 1982, from which the text discussed above is drawn. Starting as it does from a seed syllable above the practitioner's heart *cakra,* the visualization of Cintamaṇicakra Avalokiteśvara in this *homa* is quite normal for rituals of this kind. It is also visually quite consistent with other Japanese representations of the bodhisattva in his six-armed form. What is not revealed, however, is the complex symbolic associations between the bodhisattva and a variety of other figures, including jewel-women, which contributes to the feminization in Japan of a previously masculine deity, and the role of Nyoirin Kannon as a feminine figure in the legitimation of sovereignty.

From Avalokiteśvara to Kannon

Avalokiteśvara is well known as the Bodhisattva of Compassion and prominently associated with the bodhisattva vow to continue to be reborn in saṃsāra until all sentient beings attain liberation. In the version I have recounted to many undergraduate classes, the standard origin story has it as follows: standing on the verge of nirvāṇa, the bodhisattva hears cries of deep suffering of all of those who remain caught in saṃsāra. So boundless is the compassion of the bodhisattva that his head splits into eleven, and a thousand arms extend out from his body, each hand with an eye in the palm, so sensitive is the bodhisattva's awareness of suffering. Instead of entering nirvāṇa, the bodhisattva pledges to continue to be reborn so as to provide aid and comfort until all sentient beings—though countless in number—enter nirvāṇa. The eleven-headed, thousand-armed Avalokiteśvara is one representation of the bodhisattva's compassion. Many additional images of the compassion of Avalokiteśvara found in East Asia come from the *Lotus Sūtra* (Skt. *Saddharmapuṇḍarīka sūtra*).[28]

The twenty-fifth chapter of the Lotus Sutra gives a version in which Avalokiteśvara vows to manifest benefits in response to his devotees' needs. Thus, if a devotee is threatened with being pushed into a pit of fire; or off a mountain top; or threatened by robbers, bandits, poisonous dragons, demons, or evil animals, then contemplation of the power of

Avalokiteśvara will save the devotee.[29] The power of Avalokiteśvara in moments of crisis could be actualized through recitation of the bodhisattva's name, an action that Chün-fang Yü describes as "the most democratic method of religious supplication, since it was not restricted to any class, status, or gender."[30] To benefit from Avalokiteśvara's commitment, the "only requirement was to call his name with a sincere and believing heart."[31] The efficacy of calling Avalokiteśvara's name points to the power of reciting mantras, and *dhāraṇīs,* and *rakṣā* and *paritta* texts, which informs the use of the Jewel Sutta at the center of Maria Heim's chapter in this volume. Like the Jewel Sutta, Avalokiteśvara provides protection. This Indic concept was transmitted to China, and Christine Mollier points out that invocation of Avalokiteśvara's name is part of a broader pattern. "During the Six Dynasties period, the recitation of the names of buddhas and bodhisattvas, such as Amitābha, Maitreya, Kṣitigarbha, and Avalokiteśvara, became common practice among the Buddhist faithful, especially for adherents of the Pure Land currents."[32]

The *Lotus Sūtra* also describes the various forms that Avalokiteśvara takes in this Sahā world depending on what form sentient beings need in order to be rescued. Thus, "If there is any land where sentient beings are to be saved by the form of a buddha, Bodhisattva Avalokiteśvara teaches the Dharma by changing himself into the form of a buddha."[33] Particularly relevant to our inquiry here, after listing many additional forms, the sūtra asserts that "To those who are to be saved by the form of a wife of either a wealthy man, a householder, a state official, or a brahman, he teaches the Dharma by changing himself into the form of such a wife."[34] Similarly, there is "a group of thirty-three different incarnations of Kannon listed in the *Kannonkyō* 観音教, which obviously conveys the message that Kannon can manifest in numerous and appropriate guises as needed to alleviate the suffering of beings."[35] In Japan, this set of thirty-three forms of Avalokiteśvara served as an organizing principle for systems of temples connecting as pilgrimage routes, beginning as early as the Heian era (794–1185). Mark MacWilliams indicates the importance of these routes, noting that such "pilgrimage routes to thirty-three temples were a major feature of Kannon devotionalism in Japan."[36]

In the context of Indian Buddhism, the role of Avalokiteśvara as a beneficent savior continues across the next several centuries, being found, for example, in Buddhist sculpture from the Pāla Empire (750–1174). In several cases bodhisattvas, including a form of Avalokiteśvara identified as Pretasaṃtarpita Lokeśvara or "*Preta*-Satisfying Lokeśvara," are shown as "[a] standing, male bodhisattva figure with his left hand raised in the boon-granting gesture (*varada mudrā*)" and his right hand extended downward and turned open toward "small, malformed figures begging at the bodhisattvas' feet [who] seem to be the recipients of this generosity."[37] *Preta* are "hungry ghosts," described as "unfortunate beings [who] are said to be in a perpetual state of intense hunger because they have huge bellies, with proportional appetites, and tiny pinhole-sized mouths."[38] One finds this motif frequently in East Asian representations of the standing, two-armed form of Avalokiteśvara, though the hungry ghost figure is often replaced by a child.

While the six-armed form described in the visualization above is common in Japan, it seems to be much rarer in China and largely unknown in India or Nepal.[39] The variety of different forms of Avalokiteśvara was a relatively popular theme in Chinese Buddhist art, being found, for example, in Dunhuang paintings from the seventh century forward, and this variety includes Wish-Fulfilling Jewel Cakra Avalokiteśvara.[40] Scriptures describing other esoteric/tantric forms of Avalokiteśvara were already introduced during the Northern Zhou dynasty (557–581); however, Cintāmaṇicakra (Ch. Ruyilun) per se does not seem to have been introduced until the Tang dynasty.[41] In contrast to the six-armed form, more commonly found is a related figure, that of Cintāmaṇi Lokeśvararāja, who is most frequently represented as a standing, two-armed bodhisattva, like the sculptures of *Preta*-Satisfying Lokesvara from the Pāla Empire discussed above.

In Chinese Avalokiteśvara is known as Guanyin (觀音, also Guanshiyin 観世音), meaning the one who "looks and hears" the sounds of suffering (and the one who "looks and hears [the suffering of] the world").[42] According to both Chün-fang Yü and Sarah Fremerman, it is in China that Avalokiteśvara is transformed from a male into a female savior figure. In contrast, the specific figure of Wish-Fulfilling Jewel Avalokiteśvara remains male in China, becoming female in Japan.

Avalokiteśvara Gendered

Yü summarizes the idea of Guanyin as "a compassionate universal savior who responds to anyone's cry for help regardless of class, gender, or even moral qualifications."[43] Yü argues that the transformation from Avalokiteśvara as a male bodhisattva into Guanyin as a female one took place as a part of the adaptation of Buddhism to Chinese religious needs. Yü sees the development of feminine figures in both Yuan-era Daoism and Buddhism as a response to lacunae in the dominant religious traditions.[44] "The feminization of Kuan-yin and new developments in religious Taoism could be seen as responses to the partiarchal stance of institutional Buddhism and Neo-Confucianism. . . . If Neo-Confucianism and organized Buddhism had not lacked feminine symbols and female practitioners, Kuan-yin may not have undergone a sexual transformation."[45] Christine Mollier calls attention to the role of Avalokiteśvara as "the prototype of a number of 'new' Chinese divinities over the centuries . . . who are providers of fertility and protectors of children. All of them flourished following Guanyin's initial feminization—that is, from the time of the Five Dynasties or the Song dynasty on—and they became particularly prominent during the Ming dynasty, by which time the bodhisattva was a completely sinicized goddess."[46]

In attempting to explain the feminization of Avalokiteśvara, Yü points to the role in the ideology of kingship that Avalokiteśvara plays in other Asian countries. In Yü's view, such a role in legitimating sovereignty necessarily required Avalokiteśvara as a masculine figure, inheritance of royal status running through the male line. The transformation of Guanyin into a feminine figure in China was possible because Avaolokiteśvara could not be integrated into the Chinese ideology of kingship. Such a role "was preempted in China by the Confucian belief in the Mandate of Heaven, which was firmly in place long before the introduction of Buddhism."[47] The niche of royal legitimation that Avalokiteśvara filled elsewhere in the Buddhist cosmopolis was already filled in China.

This transformation did not, however, extend to the full variety of different forms of Avalokiteśvara. Fremerman writes that "In the Tang (618–907) Chinese texts devoted to Nyoirin Kannon, there is no precedent for her feminization, or for her appearance as the 'jewel woman.' "[48] According to Fremerman, the transformation of Cintamaṇicakra Avalokiteśvara from masculine to feminine, together with several other associations with the imagery of jewels and jewel-women, takes place in Japan. We noted above Yü's suggestion that Guanyin was transformed into a feminine figure in part because of a felt need for feminine figures otherwise absent from institutional Buddhism and Daoism, made possible because Guanyin could not play any part in the legitimation of sovereign power. Inversely, what we find in Japan is that it is specifically as a feminine figure that Nyoirin Kannon played a part in the legitimation of sovereign power. This role was facilitated by a complex identification between Nyoirin Kannon, jewel-women, the imperial jewel (*magatama*), the wish-fulfilling jewel, and relics (*śarīra, shari*) as jewels.[49] In contrast to the situation in China, where, because Avalokiteśvara could not play a role in legitimating sovereignty and could therefore be transformed into a feminine figure filling a different religio-cultural niche, in Japan it was because Nyoirin Kannon was considered feminine that she could play a part in legitimating sovereignty.

Jewel and Jewel-Women in Japanese Buddhism

The figure of Nyoirin Kannon draws together a variety of different symbolic themes from a variety of Buddhist and East Asian sources. According to Brian Ruppert, "the worship of Nyoirin Kannon was a feature of Shingon practice since at least the tenth century."[50] Given the associations between Nyoirin Kannon and other Buddhist and Daoist deities in India and China, she is already a complex figure, but even more meanings accrue to her in the symbolic network of Japanese religious culture. As mentioned by John Strong in this volume, one of the seven "jewels" possessed by a "wheel-turning emperor" (*cakravartin*) is a precious queen. Maria Heim explains that the seven jewels of the *cakravartin* are so precious that they cannot be owned by ordinary people, no matter how much wealth they might accrue.

Wish-Fulfilling Jewel Cakra Avalokiteśvara became identified with other jewel-women (also sometimes rendered as "jade-women" and "jade maidens"). Jewel-women originate in the religious culture of Daoism, broadly defined. The "Jade Maiden" (Yu nu, 玉女) is a goddess known in the literature of the early part of the Han Dynasty (206 BCE–220 CE), in which "she is a secondary figure and . . . her role is rather vague, but at the same time she has definite associations with immortality either by her proximity to others such as the Queen Mother of the West or by her own possession of drugs capable of creating the state of deathlessness."[51] By the Tang (618–907), Jade Maidens, in the plural, make their appearance in poetry, dispersing the elixir of immortality or dancing in a style similar to that of a shamaness.[52] They "are celestial attendants, minor goddesses who carry the Queen Mother's messages, serve the peaches of immortality at transcendent feasts, and entertain guests with performances of sacred dance, song and instrumental music."[53] It was probably during this period that such jewel-women were integrated into Buddhist practice in China.[54] As with so many other supernatural figures, jewel-women are not unambiguously positive in Daoist thought. Michel Strickmann notes that they can also cause disease, being "beautiful celestial women who cause the dreamer to lose precious vital-essence."[55] A similar ambivalence is reflected in the "eleventh century esoteric Buddhist rituals [that] identified Nyoirin as the formerly demonic, flesh-eating goddess Dakiniten."[56]

This complex of intersemiotic connections is revealed in the dreams of two important medieval Japanese monks, Myōe (明慧, 1173–1232) and Jien (慈圓, 1155–1225). In the dreams of both, a jewel-woman appears "as a metaphor for the *cintāmaṇi,* or wish-fulfilling jewel."[57] Additionally, the wish-fulfilling jewel was identified with one of the three insignia of imperial legitimacy, the "curved jewel" (*yasakani no magatama*), which, along with a sword and mirror, is still employed in Japan's enthronement ceremonies.[58] The status of the *magatama* as one of the three imperial insignia recalls the importance of jewels as markers of royal status, discussed by Vanessa R. Sasson in this volume, as well as the political role of relics such as those given to King Chulalongkorn of Siam, who "decided to use them for his own diplomatic and political purposes," as discussed by John Strong in this volume. Sasson notes that the possession of jewels is important for royalty; the abandonment of attachment, including to precious jewels, is marked by bodhisattvas giving away such treasures. The emperor of Japan, however, is not a renunciant, and the three imperial insignia are retained as part of the symbolism of legitimacy.

This semiotic complexity of interconnections in Japan was facilitated by the doctrine of *honji suijaku* (本地垂迹), the idea that local deities (*kami* 神), guardian deities, and other figures were manifestations (avatars) of more exalted and more powerful buddhas and bodhisattvas.[59] Bernard Faure has identified five ways in which symbolic associations among figures were established.[60] First is a similarity of name. Thus, for example, the nun "Nyoi" is considered to be an avatar of "Nyoirin Kannon."[61] Second, there is a shared symbol. Faure notes as an instance that the *cintāmaṇi* jewel was not only identified with Nyoirin Kannon, but also with Benzaiten (弁財天; Skt. Sarasvatī), Dakiniten (荼枳尼天; Skt. Ḍakinī), Aizen Myōō (愛染明王; Skt. Rāga vidyārāja), and Daikokuten (大黒天; Skt. Mahākāla). Third is a numerical matching, such as pairs or trinities. Although not an instance in which different figures are associated, this is the kind of association being made between the six arms of the form of Nyoirin Kannon visualized in the *homa* and the six realms of rebirth. Similarly, this same association also provided a rationale for the group of Six Kannon. Sharing a *mudrā* or a seed syllable mantra (*bīja mantra*) was the fourth vehicle for asserting an association. The final way is the association of similar themes.

Nyoirin Kannon provides not only the kind of protection offered by Avalokiteśvara generally, but more specifically is also a source of wealth and prosperity. Avalokiteśvara is also considered to manifest as Jambhala, the god of wealth, who carries a mongoose that spits out jewels.[62] Similarly, the offering of a jewel by the daughter of the nāga king to the Buddha, as recounted in the *Lotus Sūtra,* is part of the complex of symbolic links between Nyoirin and nāgas generally, as well as to other oceanic and riverine deities.[63]

The various strands connecting Nyoirin Kannon to other figures have been explored by several scholars already.[64] We can therefore focus here on issues related to the role of Nyoirin Kannon in the legitimation of sovereignty and the complex identification that facilitated that role.

Understandings of the legitimation of sovereignty are based in sources much earlier than the medieval period when Buddhist ideologies were prevalent. Allan Grapard has discussed how in the earliest mythologies of Japan, female deities establish the barriers between the ordinary and extraordinary realms as a self-defense against intrusive sexualized male curiosity. Being driven back from the extraordinary realms marked by birth, death, and decay, male deities undergo purification in the process of which cultural order is created. This gendering of space—the "realms beyond" being feminine and the ordinary world being masculine[65]—not only divides space, but also explains why most shamans in Japan are women.[66] This opposition between the natural processes of birth, death, and decay, on one hand, and culture, on the other, actualized as an opposition between women and men, sheds light on the import of a female bodhisattva in legitimating the dominion of a male emperor. The juxtaposition between the two thus involves more than simply the symbolism of the imperial regalia, but also the female bodhisattva instantiating the feminine extraordinary worlds in contrast to the male emperor instantiating the masculine ordinary world of social order.

Jien's Dream

When the priest Jien (1155–1225) was in attendance at the court, he was tasked as a "protector-monk" (*gojisō,* 護持僧) to maintain the monarch's health during the night through the performance of a Kannon ritual. Jien records a dream that he had on one such night:

> In the year Kennin 3 (1203) at dawn on the 22nd day of the 6th month I had a dream of the two royal treasures, the divine seal (*jinji* 神璽) and the treasure sword (*hōken* 璽劔), the divine seal was the jewel woman 玉女, and this jewel woman was the body of the sovereign's wife, the queen. When the king enters the body of the jewel woman, who is pure in and of herself, and they have intercourse, both actor and recipient are free from fault![67]

In his discussion of Jien's dream, Faure explains it as follows:

> According to his *Jichin oshō musōki,* in 1203 Jien dreamt of a jade woman in relation to the royal regalia and to the imperial consecration ritual (*sokui kanjō*). Jien interprets his dream allegorically, seeing this jade woman as the *shindama* (divine jewel), or *cintāmaṇi* (wish-fulfilling jewel). Thus, in this way the sexual union between the jade woman and the *cakravartin* seen by Jien in his dream expresses the procreative principle sustaining imperial power.[68]

Faure has pointed to this and similar instances as evidencing not only that "the power of women seems to have served to legitimize and protect imperial power," but also as a religious trope in which "monks obtain salvation by having sex with a woman who is an avatar of a bodhisattva."[69] Although this is less common than the trope of "women attaining buddhahood by changing into men," Faure notes that "jade women" provide "a positive image of women as initiators."[70] This sexual initiatory function adds to the complex identification of the sovereign's wife with the curved jewel signifying royal authority, the wish-fulfilling jewel, relics of both buddhas and *kami*, and Cintāmaṇicakra Avalokiteśvara.[71] Allan Grapard explains these associations and Jien's tantric interpretation of the dream. Jien interprets the dream by reference to the sword and sheath *mudrā* of Fudō Myōō (Acalanātha Vidyārāja) as symbolizing sexual union. Thus,

> the intercourse between the emperor and his consort . . . as the full realization of . . . the "sword-and-sheath" *mudrā* [rkp: ritual manual gesture associated with the Immoveable Wisdom-King, Fudō Myōō]. . . . Jien associates the sword half of the *mudrā* with the body [penis] of the emperor and the sword of the regalia, the sheath half of the *mudrā* with the body [vagina] of his consort and the *magatama* [rkp: curved jewel regalia], and he understands their union to be the completion of

> the sword-in-sheath *mudrā* as the emblem of Fudō Myōō . . . in its role as primary icon . . . of the emperor.[72]

Additionally, identification was also made in Ryōbu Shintō texts "between the wish-fulfilling jewel, royal authority, and Amaterasu," the imperial ancestress.[73] Instead of Nyoirin Kannon, however, in some cases Amaterasu is identified with a different manifestation of Avalokiteśvara, Jūichimen Kannon, the Eleven-Headed Kannon.

Cult as a Theoretical Category

Above we have examined a *homa* ritual for prosperity devoted to Wish-Fulfilling Jewel Cakra Avalokiteśvara and the historical and symbolic background of that deity. Understanding the two requires seeing them as linked together—that is, as comprising a cult—the deity and the practice each informing the other. Protestant conceptions regarding the salvific role of belief have been sublated into presumptions regarding the nature of religion that continue to raise belief and doctrine to a place of primacy. Frits Staal has pointed out that this prioritization of belief and doctrine does not apply to Buddhism. "Like the other so-called religions of Asia, Buddhism is characterized by the fact that ritual (in which all the monks engage) is more important than mystical experience (which only a few attain), which is in turn more important than belief or doctrine (a matter confined to philosophers, scholarly monks or reserved for Western converts, anthropologists, and tourists)."[74] Borrowing a phrase from Cynthea Bogel, we can see that an almost exclusive focus on doctrine means that "Esotericism is held firmly to its singularized status as an abstruse belief system."[75] While much of Buddhist studies has focused on doctrine, a complementary understanding of the lived religion of people over the course of Buddhist history is also needed. Ritual practice is central to understanding that lived religion.

The failure to study ritual practices in close detail, the kind of detail one would expect of an art historical work or a philological one, does more than simply leave a large lacuna in our understanding of the history of Buddhism. By failing to acknowledge the value that Buddhist practitioners gave to ritual, the intense study and effort that was put into ritual performance, the representation of Buddhism is necessarily profoundly distorted. That distortion results from the dialectic between the conception of Buddhism as an object of study—that is, as a doctrinal system—and the methods employed in the study of Buddhism—that is, methods designed to uncover or explicate Buddhism as a doctrinal system. Focusing on the category of cult, however, leads to the dissolution of the apparent object of study—that is, Buddhism as a system of doctrinal claims.

Critical reflection has increasingly led to an awareness of the constructed, and therefore artificial, character of Buddhism as an object of study.[76] This in turn raises questions about both the representations of Buddhism that have been created over the last century and a half and the methodologies employed—in other words, both content and process. Commenting on the work of European Indologists such as Rhys Davids and Oldenberg, H. L. Seneviratne has described both the representation of Buddhism created and its methodology:

> For these early Western interpreters of Buddhism, there was no question or ambiguity as to the object and focus of their study, which was a select corpus of Buddhist texts. To them any material that did not conform to the imagined Buddhism of this Euro-Buddhist canon was outside Buddhism. Such material were labelled and classified away as pagan cults, animism, folk supernaturalism, idolatry and so forth. By the process of biblification in the form of printed translations into Western languages, they fixed and placed boundaries on this canon, paving the way for a new Buddhist scripturalism. . . . Living Buddhism constituted a picture different from the essentialized, sanitized, cleansed, scripturalized, and objectified Buddhism of these texts.[77]

Like textual studies, studies of specific buddhas and bodhisattvas continue to be produced. However, the solidity of such figures is itself also problematic. What are we talking about when we say things like "a buddha"? This question has annoyed me for decades. It is not merely a philosophical quibble over the concept of identity, as some might dismissively presume, but also rather an issue critical to the kinds of methodological presumptions that are brought to bear in the study of Buddhism.

The question initially occurred to me when I was trying to understand the relation between Amida in Japan and the two figures of Amitābha and Amitāyus in India. The answer one repeatedly encounters is that there is a single buddha, known in Japanese as Amida, who has two different epithets: "unlimited light" Amitābha and "unlimited life" Amitāyus. This is certainly how Amida is treated in contemporary Japanese Pure Land. Having a perverse twist of mind, however, I continued to wonder: Was that in fact the case in India? Did Mahāyāna Buddhists in India think that there was one buddha with two names or two buddhas with different specializations?

My confusion was only increased when I discovered that there is a small corpus of texts devoted to a figure named Aryāparimitāyus, who, like Amitāyus, specialized in longevity. Although hardly known today, Aryāparimitāyus was one of the most popular buddhas in the Dunhuang community.[78] Is this yet another epithet of "the same" buddha or a third buddha?

In her study of Nyoirin Kannon, Sarah Fremerman is one of the few people to express a similar sensibility about the malleability of buddhas and bodhisattvas. As discussed above, the issue she raised is that of gender identity: What does it mean to say that when Avalokiteśvara is introduced to China, at some point he becomes she? More specifically, while one particular form of Avalokiteśvara, Cintāmaṇicakra Avalokiteśvara, apparently continues to be understood as male in China, he becomes she in Japan. Thus, Fremerman notes that "no single, fixed entity inhabits the name Ruyilin/Nyoirin, so we cannot speak of even a mythological 'individual' changing from one gender to another."[79] One approach to addressing, if not entirely resolving, these questions is to focus on cult as complexes of practices, ideologies, and deities that take particular form at a particular time and place—in a sense, a crystallization of elements that over time drop into the sediment of a religious landscape. Though it may be invisible, such sedimentation still effects not only the lay of the land, but also its fertility and productivity. Unlike several other ways of conceptualizing the Buddhist tradition, cult is more closely a "natural kind" than simply an academic artifact.

While other objects of inquiry have proven to be academic constructs, cult is a natural object, one not determined by our study of it but rather preexisting that study.[80] Examining this Nyoirin Kannon Goma has, however, led me to wonder what the concept of a cult of Nyoirin Kannon means today. As a category in a broader theory about how to study Buddhism as a lived religion and conceptualize the history of Buddhism as a history of praxis, cult appears to serve a useful function.

One useful characterization of cult has been given by Erhard S. Gerstenberger. In an attempt to give focus to the study of the psalms, Gerstenberger considers their relation with the cults of ancient Israel.[81] Strategically, this attempts to avoid what he describes as the "constant flux" in the ways in which research on the psalms has been organized and categorized. At the same time he wishes to avoid "fixed traditional theories."[82] He turns therefore to the concept of cult and identifies five "main dimensions" of cult. Four of these have been employed previously—place, time, act, and person—and he adds a fifth, social setting. Arguing for the integral character of this fifth as a main dimension of cult, he states:

> After all, different groups of people bring forth religious rituals, including supplications and hymns, meditations and teachings. Neither words nor rituals generate themselves, nor are they the exclusive property of individuals. Rather, they are the creation of people in communication and interaction, given a determined social structure, even if a gifted person should shape and transmit established discourses. And within any particular community, most certainly in regard to its religious ceremonialism, certain idiosyncratic patterns of speech and ritual inevitably develop.[83]

While one might reasonably question the need to ascribe inevitability to "certain idiosyncratic patterns of speech and ritual," the set of five main dimensions suggests that this kind of analysis can move us closer to an understanding of the lived religion of people over the course of Buddhist history. Subsisting as they do in lived religion, cults are not static. They are instead fluid.

At a simplified level of analysis, cult may be conceptualized as the co-construction of three major elements: deity, practice, and ideology. Each of these three is fluid, and although co-constructed, each is semi-autonomous from the others. For example, as a practice, *homa* can be used for a variety of deities, but at the same time the deities evoked in the ritual also change. Practices both change over time and are subject to being displaced by other practices.[84] And ideologies are revised in interaction—sometimes active appropriation, sometimes contestation—with other cults.

In the case of Nyoirin Kannon, we find a great deal of fluidity in the cult—both in the sense that the figure of Nyoirin Kannon has multiple intersemiotic relations, as discussed above, and in the sense that the practices involved are dependent on place, can vary over time, require different kinds of ritual actions, have different persons as agents, and are located in different social settings.

In her discussion of the cult of Six Kannon, Sherry Fowler notes that "Buddhist icons are often identified closely with the specific place where they are housed, yet we find that they are not always fixed permanently in a single location and can travel."[85] That deities can be relocated is indicative of the more general fluidity of the cult, which as a theoretical concept provides a way of organizing our methodological toolkits.

Describing her own work on deathbed practices, Jacqueline I. Stone has critiqued the "longstanding scholarly models of religious traditions as bounded, unified, and internally cohesive entities or systems."[86] The model of religions as unified entities "works to reify traditions, obscuring complexity and internal dissonance and reducing them to core essences. This way of understanding traditions proves inadequate to make sense of the general messiness and inconsistencies of religion on the ground."[87] In Western academic discourse, what is generally taken to make a tradition a "unified entity" is a set of key doctrinal teachings.

Instead of presuming a defining essence of Japanese Buddhism, Stone adopts a theoretical orientation that "sees religious traditions as toolkits or repertoires of resources, including symbols, discourses, practices, schemas, normative claims, tropes, idioms, narratives, and other elements."[88] This way of conceptualizing the Buddhist tradition is of particular value as it "helps us to understand how, together with local variation, remarkable thematic continuity is to be found across Asia" in Buddhist praxis.[89] She places particular importance for this continuity on Buddhist practitioners' "conceptual capacity to encompass disparate elements within a compelling, if not always internally consistent, ritual program."[90]

This "compelling, if not always internally consistent, ritual program" indicates that it would be a mistake to think that Stone is suggesting that Buddhism is nothing more than an unorganized jumble of tools crowded together in a catch-all bag. While the tools can be brought to bear in differing combinations as needed, they are organized into cultic praxes.

Conclusion

The cult of Wish-Fulfilling Jewel Avalokiteśvara spans a historical and cultural arc from India through China to Japan. The symbolic associations of jewels established connections between one manifestation of the Bodhisattva of Compassion with nāgas as the source of jewels, the god of wealth and his jewel-spitting mongoose, jewel-women, the curved jewel of the Japanese imperial regalia, and royal legitimation by means of the emperor's sexual union with a feminine form of Wish-Fulfilling

Jewel Avalokiteśvara, who is at the same time the emperor's consort, and the sheath to the emperor's sword. These connections between symbol systems, intersemiosis, created new meanings. Neither Wish-Fulfilling Jewel Avalokiteśvara nor the cult associated with him/her remained static but continued to adapt and change over the centuries. The *homa* ritual at the core of this study provides one instance of the cult of Wish-Fulfilling Jewel Avalokiteśvara, bringing together the deity with the ritual function of prosperity.

Notes

1. Bernard Faure has called this process "metonymic drift." Sarah Alizah Fremerman, "Divine Impersonations: Nyoirin Kannon in Medieval Japan" (PhD diss., Stanford University, 2008), 14, citing Bernard Faure, "A Jewel of a Woman: Medieval Ideology and Wishful Thinking," paper presented at Yale University, April 1999, 19. Cf. Bernard Faure, "Une perle rare: La 'nonne' Nyoi et l'idéologie médiévale," *Cahiers d'Extrême-Asie* 13 (2002): 187. See also Sarah Fremerman Aptilon, "Goddess Genealogy: Nyoirin Kannon in the Ono Shingon Tradition," in *Esoteric Buddhism and the Tantras in East Asia,* edited by Charles Orzech, Henrik Sørensen and Richard K. Payne (Leiden: Brill, 2011), 893–903.
2. We prefer intersemiosis to metonymic drift as allowing for a greater sense of agency on the part of practitioners, rather than an abstract historical process. The idea of intersemiosis can be traced to Roman Jakobson, "On Linguistic Aspects of Translation," in *On Translation,* edited by R. A. Brower (Cambridge, MA: Harvard University Press, 1959), 232–239. According to Susan Bassnett, Jakobson distinguishes among "three types of translation, which he defined as intralingual, or rewording within the same language, interlingual, or what he saw as translation proper, and intersemiotic translation or transmutation." See her article, "The Translator as Cross-Cultural Mediator," in *The Oxford Handbook of Translation Studies,* edited by Kirsten Malmkjær and Kevin Windle (New York: Oxford University Press, 2011), 96; online: DOI: 10.1093/oxfordhb/9780199239306.013.0008.
3. The idea that benefits follow from the sovereign mating with a divine female also appears to be found in early China. Discussing the poems attributed to Song Yu (fl. 298–263 BCE), Edward H. Schafer has asserted that "the Divine Woman of Shamanka Mountain was an ancient fertility goddess whose ritual mating with a shaman-king was

necessary to the well-being of the land." See Schafer, *The Divine Woman: Dragon Ladies and Rain Maidens* (San Francisco: North Point Press, 1980), 46.

4. For example, Fremerman, "Divine Impersonations," 3n5.
5. Wish-fulfilling Jewel Cakra Avalokiteśvara was also the subject of two visualization rituals written by Amoghavajra (705–774) in China. Koichi Shinohara, *Spells, Images, and Maṇḍalas: Tracing the Evolution of Esoteric Buddhist Rituals* (New York: Columbia University Press, 2014), 168–193.
6. There is no clear Sanskrit equivalent; for convenience, however, we will henceforth not add the asterisk indicating reconstruction as this is now the conventionally accepted form. This reconstruction is suggested by Fremerman, "Divine Impersonations," 3. Fremerman also suggests, as an alternate rendering, Cakravarti cintāmaṇi Avalokiteśvara. See also Bernard Faure, *Gods of Medieval Japan,* vol. 1: *Fluid Pantheon* (Honolulu: University of Hawai'i Press, 2016), 286.
7. Ronald M. Davidson, *Indian Esoteric Buddhism: A Social History of the Tantric Movement* (New York: Columbia University Press, 2002), 26, 65, 142–143.
8. Holly Grether: "Tantric Homa Rites in the Indo-Iranian Ritual Paradigm," *Journal of Ritual Studies* 21, no. 1 (2007): 16–32, and "Burning Demons and Sprinkling Mantras: A History of Fire Sacrifice in South and Central Asia" (PhD diss., University of California at Santa Barbara, 2010). Richard K. Payne, "Homa: Tantric Fire Ritual," *Oxford Research Encyclopedias, Religion* (New York: Oxford University Press, 2016); online: DOI:10.1093/acrefore/9780199340378.013.82). Aaron Ullrey has argued that contrary to the standard picture of continuity between Vedic and tantric forms of magic, there is a marked rupture, references in the latter to Vedic practices being more of an attempt at legitimation than historically accurate expressions of continuity. Aaron Michael Ullrey, "Grim Grimoires: Practical Ritual in the Magic Tantras" (PhD dissertation, University of California at Santa Barbara, 2016).
9. "Mahāvairocanābhisaṃbodhisūtra," in *The Princeton Dictionary of Buddhism,* edited by Robert E. Buswell Jr., and Donald S. Lopez Jr. (Princeton, NJ: Princeton University Press, 2014), 511.
10. Rolf W. Giebel, trans., *The Vairocanābhisaṃbodhi Sutra* (Berkeley: Numata Center for Buddhist Translation and Research, 2005), 54–56.
11. Adrian Snodgrass, *The Matrix and Diamond World Mandalas in Shingon Buddhism,* 2 vols. (New Delhi: Aditya Prakashan, 1988), 1:124.

12. This nondual relation can be approached negatively, as emptiness (*śūnyatā*)—described in Madhyamaka thought—or positively, as co-emergent (*sahaja*)—described in Yogācāra thought.
13. The name derives from the Tang dynasty Chinese translations of just the first chapter of the *Sarvatathāgatatattvasaṃgraha tantra*.
14. Giebel, *The Vairocanābhisaṃbodhi Sutra,* xvi–xvii.
15. Michel Strickmann, "Homa in East Asia," in *Agni: The Vedic Ritual of the Fire Altar,* edited by Fritz Staal (Berkeley: Asian Humanities Press, 1983), 2:418–455.
16. The specific manual being examined here is Soeda Takatoshi, "Nyoirin Kannon soyaku goma shiki shidai," in vol. 24 of *Goma Zenshū,* 66 vols. (Osaka: Tōhō Shuppan, 1982).
17. In the frame ritual within which the five sets of offerings are made, the ritual practitioner identifies with the chief deity of that ritual, becoming awakened in this body (*sokushin jōbutsu*, 即身成仏)—a prominent theme of tantric Buddhist praxis, which is characterized by teaching that its practices are powerful enough that through their use one can become awakened in this lifetime instead of over "countless aeons" as in other forms of Buddhist praxis. The five sets of offerings are made by the identity of practitioner and chief deity of the frame ritual, usually Fudō Myōō.
18. Although this is a set of six, these do not correspond directly to the set of six Kannon known from medieval Japan. See Sherry D. Fowler, *Accounts and Images of Six Kannon in Japan* (Honolulu: University of Hawai'i Press, 2016), 29.
19. In the six-syllable mantra associated with the set of six Kannon, HRIḤ (rendered in Japanese as *kiriku*) is the syllable identified with Nyoirin Kannon. Fowler, *Accounts and Images of Six Kannon in Japan,* 67.
20. Cf. E. Dale Saunders, *Mudrā: A Study of Symbolic Gestures in Japanese Buddhist Sculpture* (Princeton, NJ: Princeton University Press, 1960), 130–131.
21. Saunders, *Mudrā,* 155.
22. Saunders, *Mudrā,* 176.
23. Marcus Bingenheimer, *Island of Guanyin: Mount Putuo and Its Gazetteers* (Oxford and New York: Oxford University Press, 2016), 80.
24. Courtney Bruntz, "Commodifying Mount Putuo: State Nationalism, Religious Tourism, and Buddhist Revival" (PhD diss, Graduate Theological Union, 2014).
25. For discussion of the iconography, see Sherry Fowler, "Nyoirin Kannon," *Orientations* 19, no. 6 (June 1988): 62–65. See also Pratapaditya

Pal, "The Iconography of Cintāmaṇi Cakra Avalokiteśvara," *Journal of the Indian Society of Oriental Art* 2 (1967–68): 39–48, and Helen B. Chapin, "A Study in Buddhist Iconography," *Ostasiatische Zeitschrift:* vol. 8 (1932), nos. 1–2, pp. 29–43; no. 3, pp. 111–129; vol. 11 (1935), nos. 3–4, pp. 125–134; no. 5, pp. 195–210.

26. This interpretation appears to be unique to Japan. Similarly, the six realms of rebirth are associated with the six members of the cult of Six Kannon. Sherry Fowler notes that "the most well-known function of the Six Kannon was to help beings navigate the six paths"—that is, the six realms of rebirth (Fowler, *Accounts and Images of Six Kannon in Japan,* 128).

27. Robert Sharf makes two arguments for claiming that visualization of deities in the maṇḍala does not form part of the practice of tantric rituals in Japan ("Visualization and Mandala in Shingon Buddhism," in *Living Images: Japanese Buddhist Icons in Context,* edited by Robert Sharf and Elizabeth Horton Sharf [Palo Alto, CA: Stanford University Press, 2001], 151–197). One is philological, asserting that *kan* (觀) does not actually mean "visualize." The other is "ethnographic," which apparently is a reference to Sharf's own experience in a Hosso training temple. Regarding the latter point, it is a fallacy to have generalized from his own personal experience to making a universal claim. Speaking from my own experience training in a Shingon temple, visualization is very much a part of ritual practice. This is also the report of experienced Shingon masters (Nathan Michon, personal communication to author via email, April 19, 2018). One of the limitations of training temples is that practitioners there are often rushed and wind up being perfunctory in their performance. This is equally true of Shingon training temples, as I was told by another trainee who was on Mt. Kōya training at the same time I was but in a different temple.

28. This sutra originates in about the third century, its earliest translation into Chinese by Dharmarakṣa dating from 286. The Lotus Sutra, however, comprises at least three different textual strata, the earliest of which may be even earlier. See Andrew Rawlinson, "Studies in the Lotus Sutra (Saddharmapuṇḍarīka)" (PhD diss., University of Lancaster, 1972).

29. Tsugunari Kubo and Akira Yuyama, trans., *The Lotus Sutra* (*Taishō,* vol. 9, no. 262), rev. 2nd ed. (Berkeley: Numata Center for Buddhist Translation and Research, 2007), 299–301.

30. Chün-fan Yü, *Kuan-yin: the Chinese Transformation of Avalokiteśvara* (New York: Columbia University Press, 2001), 91.

31. Yü, *Kuan-yin,* 489–490. Belief in the efficacy of invoking the name of a deity enters East Asia as part of the philosophy of language originating in the tantric milieu of India in the sixth to eighth centuries. It is that tantric philosophy of language that structures both explicitly tantric practices and more popular usages such as those found in Pure Land traditions. See Richard K. Payne, *Language in the Buddhist Tantra of Japan: Indic Roots of Mantra* (London: Bloomsbury, 2018).
32. Christine Mollier, *Buddhism and Taoism Face to Face: Scripture, Ritual, and Iconographic Exchange in Medieval China* (Honolulu: University of Hawai'i Press, 2008), 190.
33. *The Lotus Sutra,* 297.
34. *The Lotus Sutra,* 298.
35. James L. Ford, "Jōkei and Kannon: Defending Buddhist Pluralism in Medieval Japan," *The Eastern Buddhist* 39, no. 1 (2008): 14.
36. Mark W. MacWilliams, "Temple Myths and the Popularization of Kannon Pilgrimage in Japan: A Case Study of Ōya-ji on the Bandō Route," *Japanese Journal of Religious Studies* 24, nos. 3–4 (1997): 376.
37. Robert DeCaroli, *Haunting the Buddha: Indian Popular Religions and the Formation of Buddhism* (New York: Oxford University Press, 2004), 175.
38. DeCaroli, *Haunting the Buddha,* 179.
39. Stephen Little, *Visions of Dharma: Japanese Buddhist Paintings and Prints in the Honolulu Academy of Arts* (Honolulu: Honolulu Academy of Arts, 1991), 60.
40. Patricia Berger, "Preserving the Nation: The Political Uses of Tantric Art in China," in *Latter Days of the Law: Images of Chinese Buddhism 850–1850,* edited by Marsha Weidner (Honolulu: University of Hawai'i Press, 1994), 98.
41. Chün-fang Yü, "Guanyin: The Chinese Transformation of Avalokiteshvara," in Weidner, *Latter Days of the Law,* 155.
42. "Guanyin," in Buswell and Lopez, *The Princeton Dictionary of Buddhism,* 332–333.
43. Yü, *Kuan-yin,* 5.
44. This is better thought of as a niche that could be filled, rather than as a religious need of some kind.
45. Yü, *Kuan-yin,* 21.
46. Mollier, *Buddhism and Taoism Face to Face,* 177.
47. Yü, *Kuan-yin,* 489.
48. Fremerman, "Divine Impersonations," 3.

49. Brian D. Ruppert, "Pearl in the Shrine: A Genealogy of the Buddhist Jewel of the Japanese Sovereign," *Japanese Journal of Religious Studies* 29, nos. 1–2 (2002): 1–33.
50. Ruppert, "Pearl in the Shrine," 9.
51. Susan N. Erickson, "'Twirling Their Long Sleeves, They Dance Again and Again . . . ': Jade Plaque Sleeve Dancers of the Western Han Dynasty," *Ars Orientalis* 24 (1994):39–63: 55.
52. Erickson, "'Twirling Their Long Sleeves, They Dance Again and Again . . . ,'" 56.
53. Susan B. Cahill, "Performers and Female Taoist Adepts: Hsi Wang Mu as a Patron Deity of Women in Medieval China," *Journal of the American Oriental Society* 106, no. 1 (January–March 1986): 157.
54. Faure, "Une perle rare," 188. See also Livia Kohn and Russell Kirkland, "Daoism in the Tang (618–907)," in *Daoism Handbook,* edited by Livia Kohn (Leiden: Brill, 2000), 357; Michel Strickmann, *Chinese Magical Medicine,* edited by Bernard Faure (Palo Alto, CA: Stanford University Press, 2002), 107.
55. Strickmann, *Chinese Magical Medicine,* 209.
56. Fremerman, "Divine Impersonations," 14.
57. Bernard Faure, *The Red Thread: Buddhist Approaches to Sexuality* (Princeton, NJ: Princeton University Press, 1998), 123.
58. Cf. Fabio Rambelli, "The Emperor's New Robes: Processes of Resignification in Shingon Imperial Rituals," *Cahiers d'Extrême-Asie* 13 (2002–2003), 427–453.
59. As indicated by Max Moerman's reference to *honji suijaku* as "militant syncretism," establishment of this relationship implies not simply an ordering by means of a power imbalance, but also acts of subjugation. D. Max Moerman, *Localizing Paradise: Kumano Pilgrimage and the Religious Landscape of Premodern Japan* (Cambridge, MA: Harvard University Press, 2005), 236.
60. Faure, "Une perle rare," 179. For more examples, see also Bernard Faure, "The Impact of Tantrism on Japanese Religious Traditions: The Cult of the Three Devas," in *Transformations and Transfer of Tantra in Asia and Beyond,* edited by Istvan Keul (Berlin: DeGruyter, 2012), 399–410.
61. Faure, "Une perle rare," 177.
62. Regarding Jambhala (also Dzambhala) practice in the modern era, see Tam Wai Lun, "The Tantric Teachings and Rituals of the True Buddha School: The Chinese Transformation of Vajrayāna Buddhism," in *Tantric Traditions in Transmission and Translation,* edited by David B. Gray

and Ryan Richard Overbey (New York: Oxford University Press, 2016), 318.

63. Faure, *Gods of Medieval Japan,* 1:302–304.
64. Faure, *Gods of Medieval Japan,* 1:285–316. Fremerman, "Divine Impersonations." See also Fowler, "Nyoirin Kannon," and Cynthea J. Bogel, "Canonizing Kannon: The Ninth-Century Esoteric Buddhist Altar at Kanshinji," *The Art Bulletin* 84, no. 1 (March 2002): 30–64. On the relation between Avalokiteśvara and Cundī (Ch. Zhunti; Jpn. Juntei), see the valuable comments by Robert Gimello, "Icon and Incantation: The Goddess Zhunti and the Role of Images in the Occult Buddhism of China," in *Images in Asian Religions: Texts and Contexts,* edited by Phyllis Granoff and Koichi Shinohara (Vancouver: UBC Press, 2004), 249–250 n. 1.
65. Allan G. Grapard emphasizes that in Japanese myths there are three different "realms beyond." Rather than conflating these into a single realm, as has been done by other scholars, he notes that each has its own name and characteristics ("Visions of Excess and Excesses of Vision: Women and Transgression in Japanese Myth," *Japanese Journal of Religious Studies* 18, no. 1 [1991]: 3).
66. Grapard, "Visions of Excess and Excesses of Vision," 22. Grapard's essay is also important for understanding both that there is a complexity to the notion of the "realms beyond" and that the male-female opposition in Japanese mythology has a distinct structure giving rise to the predominance of women shamans.
67. Richard Bowring, *The Religious Traditions of Japan: 500–1600* (Cambridge: Cambridge University Press, 2005), 281.
68. Bernard Faure, *The Power of Denial: Buddhism, Purity, and Gender* (Princeton, NJ: Princeton University Press, 2003), 206.
69. Faure, *The Power of Denial,* 207.
70. Faure, *The Power of Denial,* 207, 205.
71. Ruppert, "Pearl in the Shrine," 11. Sexual initiation relates our discussion here to two topics that fall outside the scope of this chapter. One is the interpretation of Shinran's famous dream, sometimes being taken as (simply) serving to justify the breach of monastic rules in the Shin tradition. For discussions of this, see Faure, *The Red Thread,* 122–123, and Galen Amstutz, "Sexual Transgression in Shinran's Dream," *The Eastern Buddhist* 43, nos. 1–2 (2012): 225–269. The second topic is the association between such sexual initiation and tantra. Tantra is often characterized in the scholarly, and not so scholarly, literature as valorizing sexual transgression as both initiatory and liberative. On

this aspect in Japan, see Faure, *The Red Thread,* 124–129. For background, cf. David Gordon White, *Kiss of the Yoginī: "Tantric Sex" in its South Asian Contexts* (Chicago : University of Chicago Press, 2003), and more directly relevant to the Buddhist context, David B. Gray, *The Cakrasamvara Tantra (The Discourse of Śrī Heruka)* (New York: American Institute of Buddhist Studies, 2007), 103–131.

72. Allan G. Grapard, "Of Emperors and Foxy Ladies," *Cahiers d'Extrême-Asie* 13 (2002): 138. Two emendations by this author are marked as "rkp," while the other two are in the original.
73. Ruppert, "Pearl in the Shrine," 20.
74. Frits Staal, *Rules without Meaning: Ritual, Mantras and the Human Sciences* (New York: Peter Lang, 1989), 400.
75. Bogel, "Canonizing Kannon," 36.
76. Tomoko Masuzawa, *The Invention of World Religions: Or, How European Universalism Was Preserved in the Language of Pluralism* (Chicago: University of Chicago Press, 2005), 121–146.
77. H. L. Seneviratne, *The Work of Kings: The New Buddhism in Sri Lanka* (Chicago: University of Chicago Press, 1999), 2–3.
78. Richard K. Payne, "Aparimitāyus: 'Tantra' *and* 'Pure Land' in Medieval Indian Buddhism?" *Pacific World,* 3rd series, no. 9 (2007): 273–308.
79. Fremerman, "Divine Impersonations, 5.
80. As institutional categories in the sociology of religion, church, sect, and cult are defined in relation to one another, forming an apparently coherent and comprehensive typology of religious institutions. Since that three-part system is constructed almost entirely on the basis of instances in the history of Christianity, we should be wary of applying that system outside that field of study. Attempting to adapt that categorical scheme to Buddhism would necessarily entail the hazard of adapting Buddhism to that categorical scheme. Instead, I have been employing the category of cult as such, pointing as it does back to pre-Christian Meditteranean religious practices. See Lorne L. Dawson, "Church–Sect–Cult: Constructing Typologies of Religious Groups," *The Oxford Handbook of the Sociology of Religion,* edited Peter B. Clarke (Oxford: Oxford University Press, 2011); online: DOI: 10.1093/oxfordhb/9780199588961.013.0030.
81. Erhard S. Gerstenberger, "Non-Temple Psalms: The Cultic Setting Revisited," in *The Oxford Handbook of the Psalms,* edited by William P. Brown (Oxford: Oxford University Press, 2014); online: DOI: 10.1093/oxfordhb/9780199783335.013.022.
82. Gerstenberger, "Non-Temple Psalms," 338.

83. Gerstenberger, "Non-Temple Psalms," 338.
84. A contemporary example might be the displacement of Zen in popular religious culture by mindfulness.
85. Fowler, *Accounts and Images of Six Kannon in Japan,* 120.
86. Jacqueline I. Stone, *Right Thoughts at the Last Moment: Buddhism and Deathbed Practices in Early Medieval Japan* (Honolulu: University of Hawai'i Press, 2016), 4.
87. J. Stone, *Right Thoughts at the Last Moment,* 4.
88. J. Stone, *Right Thoughts at the Last Moment,* 4.
89. J. Stone, *Right Thoughts at the Last Moment,* 5.
90. J. Stone, *Right Thoughts at the Last Moment,* 5.

Chapter 12

Hidden Treasures

Wish-Fulfilling Jewels in Japanese Esoteric Buddhism

Casey Collins

On June 9, 2011, as part of a years-long renovation of its headquarters in Tokyo, the Buddhist lay community called Shinnyo-en 真如苑 rededicated a small stone statue of the bodhisattva Jizō 地蔵 (Skt. Kṣitigarbha) that had been at the site since 1942. In the run-up to the service itself, Shinnyo-en's current leader, Shinsō Itō 真聰 伊藤, announced that every attendee of the rededication ceremony would receive a commemorative gift: a small ceramic Jizō figure (fig. 12). This kindly bodhisattva is well known in Japan as the guardian of travelers, children, and the dead and is recognizable by his monkish appearance.[1] Compared to other bodhisattvas, who wear crowns, silks, and lavish jewelry, Jizō is bald, wears a simple robe, and usually carries a ringed staff called a *shakujō* 錫杖 and a spherical or onion-shaped wish-fulfilling jewel. The commemorative bauble conformed to Jizō's familiar iconography, but there was something special about the jewel proffered in his hand. Ceramic blue-green against the ash-colored earthenware of the rest of the image, the jewel was made with *homa* ashes and spring water from the Shinnyo-en headquarters.[2] To the Shinnyo-en member, this specific wish-fulfilling jewel was thus imbued with special associations particular to Shinnyo-en, layered on top of, or hidden within, a Buddhist symbol ubiquitous in Japanese visual and material culture. As a Buddhist symbol, the wish-fulfilling jewel has one set of historical, textual, and ritual associations. In Shinnyo-en, Buddhist texts, rituals, and symbols—such as the wish-fulfilling jewel—are given new meanings that are all in some way associated with Shinnyo-en's founders.

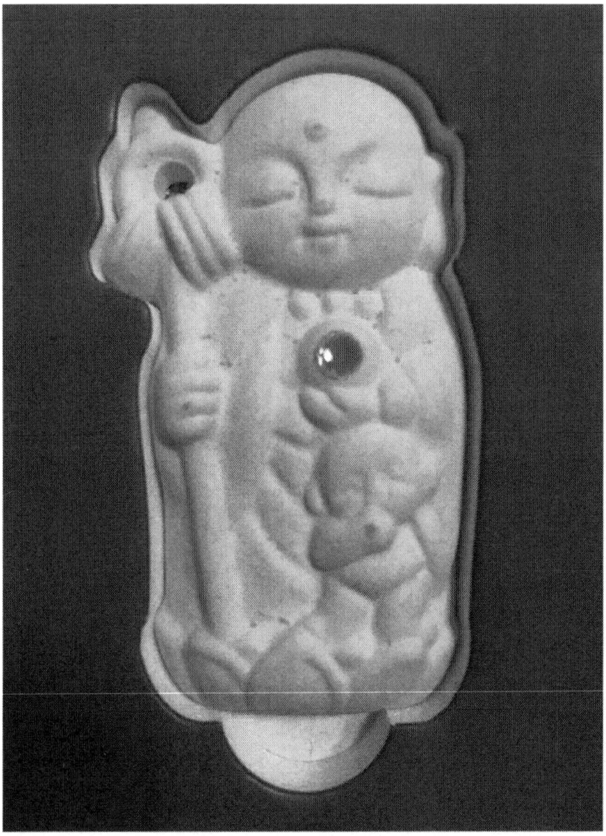

Fig.12. Ceramic Jizō distributed to Shinnyo-en members in commemoration of June 9, 2011, on the occasion of a special service officially titled "Enhancement of Oyasono: Re-Enshrinement of the Bodhisattva Jizō in the Oyasono Courtyard with Gratitude to Kyodoin Sama, the Foundation of Our Belief" 教導院様定心感謝聖地親苑荘厳地蔵尊安座法要. Photo credit: Casey Collins.

Although many Japanese Buddhist lay organizations of the twentieth century adopt and use Buddhist themes, the newness of their doctrines and practices—centered on devotion to charismatic founders—cannot be fully understood solely with reference to their use of Buddhist texts, but also through their use of Buddhist material culture. Recognizably Buddhist images and objects can be overlaid—or inlaid, in the case of Jizō's special ceramic jewel—with narratives and symbolic associations that assert a charismatic leader's power and soteriological significance. In examining how the founders and members of large, lay-oriented Buddhist organizations understand and use Buddhist objects, we discover modern articulations of Buddhism based on devotion to charismatic founders that are often concealed within Buddhist stories, objects, and images. These stories lend coherence to the novel practices, relationships, and identities cultivated by members who use the founders' exemplary lives as "the means by which the individual [is] able to dramatically resolve his or her own crisis."[3] The founders of Shinnyo-en presented themselves as connected to Buddhist tradition by foregrounding Buddhist texts and the meanings ascribed to objects in those texts. Their lives and innovations, treasured by their followers, are thus hidden within Buddhist *things* and covertly represented by a common set of symbols and objects imbued with unique and novel meanings.

This chapter introduces wish-fulfilling jewels as a material and visual motif in Japanese Buddhist contexts. First, we take up the case of Japan's esoteric Shingon 真言 tradition, from which Shinnyo-en and several other lay organizations emerged in the twentieth century.[4] Then I offer Shinnyo-en's use of wish-fulfilling jewels to highlight the changing meanings of Buddhist texts and objects. As Richard Payne notes in his chapter in this volume, symbols are subject to "metonymic drift," a process of linking, confusing, and overlapping symbolic referents whereby new associations are introduced into an existing network of meanings.[5] I hope to build on this by exploring the wish-fulfilling jewel's unique associations in Shinnyo-en, which, like other Buddhist symbols and objects, refer members to the sacred biography of Shinnyo-en's founders. This narrative is crystalized in symbols adopted from Shingon Buddhism, such as the wish-fulfilling jewel, and then dramatized, internalized, and performed by members whose identities and relationships are produced and reinforced through the lens of the charismatic founders' actions, ideals, and bodies.[6]

Wish-Fulfilling Jewels in Shingon

The type of jewel covered in this chapter is the "wish-fulfilling jewel"—*cintāmaṇi* in Sanskrit and *nyoihōju* 如意宝珠 in Japanese. This precious object appears in many South and East Asian stories, Buddhist and otherwise. *Cintā* refers to a "thought" or "wish," and the corresponding Japanese term, *nyoi* 如意, means "as one wishes."[7] The character 寶 or 宝, meaning treasure, is usually pronounced as *takara* or *hō*.[8] *Ju* 珠 means pearl. Together, *hōju* 宝珠 or *maṇi* (Jpn. *mani* 摩尼) refers to a precious gem. A wish-fulfilling jewel is thus a gem or treasure said to grant wishes, to heal diseases, or to purify muddy water. Usually shaped like a ball or tapered bulb (reminiscent of an onion), wish-fulfilling jewels are said to be found under the sea, guarded by or inside the brains of dragons, or may appear among the ashes of a cremated buddha or sage.[9] The likenesses of wish-fulfilling jewels frequently appear as decorative carvings or caps called *giboshi* 擬宝珠 (lit. "psedo-treasure" or "pretend treasure") on bridge posts, fences, and railings. They also appear in a number of other architectural decorations, including on top of "finials" (*sōrin* 相輪) that cap the roofs of many temple buildings and stupas. They are omnipresent ornamental motifs. For centuries, wish-fulfilling jewels have appeared on Japanese textiles, tea ceremony utensils, lacquerware, the titles of aristocratic poetry collections (e.g., Fujiwara no Kintō's *Nyoi hōshū* 如意宝集), the names of mountain tops and people, in esoteric Buddhist rituals, and a multitude of other things. In Shingon and other forms of Japanese Buddhism, the wish-fulfilling jewel is associated with and evokes a number of mythic tropes—mineral, bodily, and ritual.

Shingon Buddhism is a twelve-hundred-year-old esoteric, or tantric, Buddhist tradition in Japan. It was established by a monk named Kūkai 空海 (a.k.a. Kōbō Daishi 弘法大師; 774–835) around 812 CE at the beginning of the Heian period (794–1195). Kūkai traveled to Tang China in 804 and while there received esoteric teachings from a figure named Huiguo 惠果, one of two masters residing at Qinglong Temple 青龍寺. Kūkai returned to Japan with these teachings and a collection of texts, ritual paraphernalia, and various other objects, including a number of pearl-like relics.[10] Relics (Skt. *śarīra;* Jpn. *shari* 舎利) of buddhas or saintly Buddhists are bodily remains, such as bones, ash, hair, or teeth, that are often enshrined within monuments called stūpas throughout the Buddhist world. As we will see below, relics have long been associated with wish-fulfilling jewels.

On certain Shingon altar arrangements, there is often an encasement that looks like a miniature stūpa. In fact, this object is called a jewel tower (*tahōtō* 多宝塔). Inside there may be relics or, more often, a statue of Mahāvairocana, Samantabhadra, or another deity.[11] Sometimes statues will themselves have gemstones, scriptures, and other objects hidden inside to represent their buddha nature and to empower them as objects of devotion. Jewels also appear in some of the maṇḍalas brought back by Kūkai and used in Shingon today, including the Vajra Realm (Jpn. *kongōkai* 金剛界) and Womb Realm (Jpn. *taizōkai* 胎蔵界) maṇḍalas. Many of the deities in these maṇḍalas are shown holding various objects, including wish-fulfilling jewels, which represent these deities' various attributes and faculties. In parts of some maṇḍalas, the deities are represented not anthropomorphically but by an object called their *samaya* form (Jpn. *sanmaya gyō* 三摩耶形), which is associated with the deity's essential qualities. For example, in the Samaya Assembly (Jpn. *sanmayakai* 三昧耶會), a section of the Vajra Realm maṇḍala, the buddha Ratnasambhāva (Jpn. Hōshō Nyorai 宝生如来) is represented by a wish-fulfilling jewel.[12]

As mentioned above, jewels also adorn the tops of buildings and a variety of ritual objects in Shingon and other East Asian Buddhist sects. For example, there are two very common kinds of stūpa that both have a wish-fulfilling jewel on top. One is called a five-element stūpa (Jpn. *gorintō* 五輪塔), and the other is a jewel-case seal stūpa (Jpn. *hōkyōin tō* 宝篋印塔). The five-element stūpa represents the body of Mahāvairocana, and the jewel-case seal stūpa contains a special scripture that represents the collective meritorious power of all the Buddhist teachings, itself representing a wish-fulfilling jewel.

The content of the Shingon teachings that Kūkai relayed to Japan was based on tantric texts that were likely composed in India in the seventh century. These teachings were believed to come not from Śākyamuni but from an ahistorical, ultimate buddha called Mahāvairocana (Jpn. Dainichi 大日). In Shingon, the universe is believed to be a manifestation of Mahāvairocana's body, all sounds are believed to be Mahāvairocana's speech and teachings, and consciousness is believed to be a manifestation of Mahāvairocana's mind. Through esoteric practices involving one's own body, speech, and mind, the Shingon adherent comes to understand the unity of him- or herself and Mahāvairocana, thereby becoming a buddha and being liberated from suffering in this very lifetime.[13] Shingon is called "esoteric Buddhism" (Jpn. *mikkyō* 密教; lit. "secret teachings") because the knowledge of Mahāvairocana's unity with all things, as well as the means for realizing that knowledge experientially or wielding it ritually, is considered a delicate matter that requires personalized instruction and transmission from a qualified teacher. The history of Shingon Buddhism is punctuated with the lives of charismatic adepts believed to possess miraculous powers, including the ability to interact with divinities and compel their powers through ritual.

Shingon has developed a rich material culture that is tied to its complex ritual praxis, of which relics and wish-fulfilling jewels are a part. As Brian Ruppert demonstrates, this material culture was a component of Shingon's appeal to Heian- and Kamakura- (1185–1333) period emperors and aristocrats who hoped to harness Shingon's power for a variety of ends.[14] Shingon ritual manuals developed during these periods call for elaborate altars, expensive and plentiful offerings, and exquisite ceremonial paraphernalia to "adorn" (Jpn. *sōgon* 荘厳) temples, rituals, ritual specialists, and images.

As Sara Fremerman demonstrates, the Ono 小野 lineage of Shingon mobilized jewel motifs in the medieval period. Citing the work of Brian Ruppert, Fremerman points out that "Ono monks' expertise in the production of *cintāmaṇi* and the practice of rituals surrounding them helped establish their position at court."[15] This lineage, associated with Daigoji 醍醐寺 just south of Kyoto, was founded by Shōbō Rigen Daishi 聖宝理源大師 (832–909; note that the name Shōbō itself means "sacred treasure"). Shōbō was a disciple of Kūkai's brother Shinga 真雅 and also a Shugendō practitioner.[16] In addition to being credited with expelling poisonous snakes from Mount Omine through performance of an outdoor fire rite called *saitō goma* 斎藤護摩, Shōbō founded Daigoji after experiencing visions of Nyoirin Kannon 如意輪観音 (Skt. Cintāmaṇicakra Avalokiteśvara) and Juntei Kannon 准胝観音 (Skt. approximations include Cuṇḍī, Cundā, Caṇḍī), esoteric forms of Avalokiteśvara. Nyoirin Kannon, as Richard Payne describes in his chapter in this volume, is associated with the wish-fulfilling jewel.

The uses of jewels are many. Ruppert shows that they were often equated with relics, which were enshrined and imagined to be wish-fulfilling jewels, such as in the Latter Seven-Day Rite (Jpn. *goshichinichi mishiho* 後七日御修法) or the Serpent Exorcism Rite (Jpn. *byakuja hō* 避蛇法).[17] Worshipping these relic-jewels with secret ritual procedures was believed to accomplish various material wishes, such as protection of the emperor and the realm or the expulsion of evil creatures.

In medieval Japan, the line between relics and wish-fulfilling jewels became so thin as to be nonexistent. As such, wish-fulfilling jewels became coveted and powerful objects of devotion, proof of the possessor's authority, whether the possessor was a monk or layperson. Jewels were part of an economy of power involving Buddhist institutions and the imperial family and sometimes even the locus of serious political or sectarian rivalry. Ruppert writes as follows:

> The development of competing traditions concerning the numbers and character of wish-fulfilling jewels suggests their intimate ties with the ritual prestige of the Shingon school as well as with the power of the court. The perceived powers of these jewels underscored their increased worship and their consequent increase in value. . . . The development of traditions concerning multiple jewels paralleled the crystallization of lineages that increasingly splintered Shingon and the court during the twelfth and thirteenth centuries. These valuable objects empowered lineages and mediated between social groups, adding to the contention over their powers and prestige. At the same time, as both the court and Shingon were dividing into a growing number of factions, the larger lay community was increasingly worshipping relics.[18]

Although the imperially sponsored medieval rites that center on wish-fulfilling jewels are no longer practiced, the symbol of the wish-fulfilling jewel is still used by organizations derived from Daigoji's Ono lineage, such as Shinnyo-en, to conceal and convey new meanings that exalt their founders. In the last century, a number of new religious organizations emerged from or were influenced by Shingon. The founder of each proposed that he was both an inheritor of the Shingon teachings and lineage while also reformulating old practices and institutions and introducing new ones that were believed to be better suited to the needs of modern people.[19] The twentieth-century lay organizations inherited or appropriated "classical" Buddhist meanings, often adding new self-referential associations that link the wish-fulfilling jewel to the particular, local, and idiosyncratic arenas where charismatic founders and their followers innovate new practices and identities.

Following the model of the thaumaturgic founders and adepts of Shingon and its many sects, the charismatic founders of these twentieth-century Shingon-derived lay organizations assert that they are returning to a truer, purer, more powerful form of Buddhism even as they introduce novel practices based on new ontological and soteriological claims. In the cases of Shinnyo-en, Gedatsukai, and Agonshū, these new beliefs are inextricably linked with the life and person of their founders—rare and treasured individuals considered modern-day buddhas by their followers. Shinnyo-en became institutionally independent of Shingon in 1946, tacitly claiming to supersede Shingon teachings through the adoption of the *Mahāyāna Mahāparinirvāṇa Sūtra* (*Daijō daihatsunehan kyō* 大乗大般涅槃経; hereafter simply the *Nirvāṇa Sūtra*) and through the powers of its own charismatic founders, both of which are likened to wish-fulfilling jewels. Comparative analysis of wish-fulfilling jewels in mainstream Shingon and Shinnyo-en illustrates continuities and divergences of belief. Wish-fulfilling jewels are one example of Shinnyo-en's appropriation of a symbol that aligns Shinnyo-en with Buddhism while simultaneously concealing Shinnyo-en's distinction from Shingon within that same symbol. In Shinnyo-en, the concealed distinctiveness—the "hidden treasure"—is devotion to Shinnyo-en's founders as the means and goal of salvation.

Wish-Fulfilling Jewels in Shinnyo-en

Wish-fulfilling jewels appear in Shinnyo-en's textual, oral, and material culture and are used in many of the same ways as they are in Shingon. They have been imbued, however, with new associations that foreground the founders and privilege their importance and power. Before comparing the uses and meanings of wish-fulfilling jewels in Shingon and Shinnyo-en, I will briefly summarize Shinnyo-en's origin story and its gradual emergence from Shingon.[20]

In the early 1930s, a recently married couple originally from a village in the mountains of Yamanashi moved to Tachikawa in western Tokyo prefecture. The husband, Fumiaki Itō 文明 伊藤 (1906–1989), was employed as an aircraft engineer at the local military base, and the wife, Tomoji Itō 友司 伊藤 (1912–1967), stayed at home to take care of their two children. Fumiaki and Tomoji's families had both passed down to them a variety of religious traditions, consisting of Sōtō Zen, Tenrikyō 天理教, a divination technique called *byōzeishō* 病筮鈔, devotion to various buddhas and *kami,* and mediumistic practices. In Tokyo, Fumiaki became interested in the study of psychic abilities, palmistry, physiognomy, Pure Land Buddhism, Protestant Christianity, and eventually Shingon through the introduction of a friend and monk named Shukō Ōbori 修弘 大堀, whom he met in a meeting of a group devoted to the study of psychic phenomena. Fumiaki began offering divination consultation services to his neighbors and coworkers at the Tachikawa air base where he worked.

Around this time Tomoji also began to express mediumistic abilities that she would later fully inherit from her aunt. Eventually people began gathering in the Itōs' home in Tachikawa, where the Itōs led their followers in a variety of spiritual practices centered on their own spiritual power, including divination, chanting, healings, and exorcisms. These activities inevitably attracted the attention of the special police, who regarded any private religious meetings as punishable and traitorous state crimes—especially ones that involved unauthorized religious activities officially regarded at the time as superstitious and dangerous to the nation. After neighbors began to complain and after a couple of run-ins with the police, the Itōs decided that it would be necessary and expedient to become affiliated with an established Buddhist institution recognized by the imperial government.

First, they purchased a Buddhist statue. On December 28, 1935, after the group attracted to the Itōs' spiritual powers had begun to expand, Fumiaki went to the shop of Buddhist sculptor Ōdō Nakamaru 奥堂 仲丸 to pick up an image of the Buddhist deity Acala *vidyārāja* (Jpn. Fudō Myō-ō 不動明王), which he had previously secured. This statue became the new object of devotion for the Itōs and their followers, who saw the Itōs as a connection to the power contained in the statue, which was believed to be eight hundred years old and sculpted by the master sculptor Unkei 運慶 (1150–1223). Through the introduction of his friend Shukō Ōbori, Fumiaki came under the tutelage of Hōkai Urano 法海 浦野, a Shingon monk who mentored Fumiaki, helped organize his followers, and secured ordination for Fumikai through Daigoji in Kyoto.

In May 1936, the Itōs registered their group, then called Risshō Kaku 立照閣, as a confraternity (called a *kō* 講 in Japanese) that periodically visited a Shingon temple called Naritasan Shinshōji 成田山新勝寺, located in Chiba and home to a famous Acala image.[21] As the Itōs' following continued to grow, Urano felt that it would be necessary for Fumiaki to obtain monastic credentials and convinced Fumiaki to do so. Urano felt that Daigoji (his own "mother temple") would be most amenable to the Itōs' activities given Daigoji's historical association with Shugendō, which includes elements of esoteric Buddhism. Shugendō practice allows monks and laymen to pursue the cultivation of spiritual abilities in the mountains. These abilities are meant to then be used for the material benefit of common people. Fumiaki's own diaries convey that he saw himself as a *shugenja* and his religious activities as altruistic attempts to first improve the lives of his followers through the Buddha's compassionate power and then guide them to practice the Buddhist teachings as he understood them. The following is from a diary entry from early 1936:

> In the preface of a book I bought in January this year at a secondhand bookstore, it says: "The word shugen means to master the Dharma and manifest the divine power it holds and to do so for the sake of others

> through conducting Buddhist rituals.[22] A practitioner of shugen [*shugenja*] is a person who applies the esoteric Dharma as a lay Buddhist. [A *shugenja*] is also called [a] yamabushi, which means a Buddhist who practices mountain asceticism. Practitioners of esoteric Buddhism pursue the way of the bodhisattva in two ways. One is to become a monk, and the other is to live a bodhisattva life as a lay person. A practitioner of shugen is one who chooses the latter.[23]

Fumiaki went on to receive basic ordination and Shingon training in 1936 under Daigoji's ninety-sixth abbot, Egen Saeki 恵眼 佐伯 (1873–1951), as well as the Tōzan-ha 当山派 Shugendō training offered through Sanbōin 三宝院, called the Ein consecration (Jpn. *ein kanjō* 恵印灌頂) in 1939, and further Shingon initiations in 1943.[24] By this time Daigoji had officially appointed Fumiaki (now Shinjō) as the head priest of his group in Taichikawa and granted him permission to formally take on his own disciples, the first of whom was his wife, Tomoji. During this period Shinjō and Tomoji practiced severe austerities in order to convey spiritual powers to their followers and pave the way for their new community. Their ascetic practices included ablutions in ice water and waterfall training at Mount Takao. At the time, Shinjō also frequently prayed with candles burning on his arm.

It was during this period that the Itōs lost their two sons, Chibun 智文 (1934–1936) and Yūichi 友一 (1937–1952). The Itōs and their followers believed that both children had sacrificed their lives in their parents' place. It seemed that as Shinjō performed esoteric rites for those who came to him seeking healing and other worldly benefits, his own sons became more and more ill until they eventually passed away. Chibun passed away before he was two years old, only months after his parents had committed themselves full time to their training and to guiding their followers.[25] Yūichi died at age fifteen after suffering from a congenital bone condition that affected his hip and caused him to require crutches for most of his short life. Yūichi was born on April 8, the day on which the birth of the Buddha is celebrated in Japan. It had been hoped that Yūichi would become his parents' successor, and indeed he managed to become the youngest person (aside from Chibun) to cultivate his mother's spiritual faculty when he was ten years old.[26] The Itōs and those close to them struggled with the deaths of the two boys, who became known as the two "acolytes" (Jpn. *dōji* 童子, Skt. *kumāra*), similar to those who assist and accompany many Buddhist deities.[27] After their deaths, Tomoji and other members she had trained noticed that they were able to use their spiritual faculties more readily, and members reported all manner of miraculous resolutions to their spiritual and mundane problems. It seemed that the Two Dōjis' deaths had enabled miraculous wish-fulfilling spiritual powers to flow to the Itōs and their followers, who went on to create Shinnyo-en much as it is today. The Two Dōjis are now believed to extend a spiritual power called *bakku-daiju* 抜苦代受 ("shouldering and lifting of karmic suffering," similar to the compassionate activity of a bodhisattva) from a spiritual realm they created. *Bakku-daiju* is the subject of many testimonies and sermons that relate miraculous relief from accidents, illness, and misfortune.

The Jizō statue (mentioned above) was in fact originally dedicated on June 9, 1942, the day of Chibun's seventh memorial service. This was appropriate because Shinnyo-en followers had already been associating Chibun with Jizō and because Jizō is considered the special guardian of deceased children. Ahead of the stone Jizō's rededication in 2011, Shinsō Itō explained the following in reference to her deceased brothers:

> Jizo is a buddha that is able to take on the sufferings of both those in this world and in the next, and to soothe their pain. This power is equivalent to the bakku-daiju of the Two Dojis . . . The Jizo is also the very image of Kyodoin Sama [Chibun] and Shindoin Sama [Yūichi], in form and in spirit.[28] The bodhisattva holds a shakujo, a Buddhist staff, in his right hand, because he is constantly traveling, using the support of his staff. In his left hand he holds a mani gem, a treasure that is said to remove any calamity and fulfill all wishes.[29]

Thus, the commemorative item is explained as having a second set of meanings particular to the Itōs. Encouraged by Shinsō, adherents may now associate Jizō with the Two Dōjis and the wish-fulfilling jewel that he holds with the *Nirvana Sūtra,* Shinnyo-en, or the Itōs themselves.

When the Pacific War ended in 1945, the Allied Occupation administration abolished State Shintō, introduced freedom of religion into the new constitution, and lifted the restrictions on religious gatherings and activities. In the late 1940s, Shinnyo-en changed from being a subtemple of Daigoji to an association called Makoto Kyōdan and then to the completely independent Shinnyo-en in 1953. After the Allied Occupation, Shinnyo-en adopted the *Nirvāṇa Sūtra* as its scriptural locus. Śākyamuni became the main image of worship, and the group adopted a modern aesthetic that eschewed some measure of the disciplines, rituals, and robes of Shingon monasticism. Shinnyo-en grew and spread to other parts of Japan, and in the 1960s, it began to expand internationally as the Itōs embarked on trips abroad. Following the Itōs' 1965 trip to Thailand, Shinnyo-en received what they believed to be genuine relics from the body of Śākyamuni Buddha himself from a well-known Thai temple called Wat Paknam in 1966. This event seemed to confirm to the Itōs and their followers that Shinnyo-en was indeed the ultimate Buddhist teaching, endorsed by the physical remains of Śākyamuni being bestowed upon them. Tomoji and Shinjō passed away in 1967 and 1989, respectively, having entrusted the religion they created to their daughter Shinsō, who remains the head of Shinnyo-en to this day.[30]

Shinnyo-en has always centered on the Itōs—their unique lives, charisma, and powers. Shinnyo-en began as a local confraternity centered around a powerful Shingon monk/Shugendō adept and his mediumistic partner (not an uncommon type of community in early twentieth-century Japan).[31] Since then it has evolved into an international devotional community that is inflected by Buddhism and centered on the Itōs.

In Shinnyo-en, wish-fulfilling jewels retain traditional meanings but are also associated with the Itō family, as we see with the commemorative Jizō. Wish-fulfilling jewels and other Buddhist symbols are associated with the Itōs and then used to suggest their ontological and soteriological primacy. Wish-fulfilling jewels appear in all the familiar places in Shinnyo-en—on and within the jewel tower placed on altars, on top of buildings, in Buddhist iconography such as statues and maṇḍalas, and as parts of stūpas and ornaments on ritual paraphernalia, all inherited from Shingon.

To begin to understand the innovative deployment of jewels as symbols for the Itōs and their power, we first must contextualize the Itōs' doctrinal turn to the *Nirvāṇa Sūtra* during the late 1940s and early 1950s. Around that time, the Itōs' group was able to shift away from being directly affiliated with and constrained by Daigoji, a move made possible through the religious freedoms enshrined in Japan's new postwar constitution.[32] They applied to the Japanese government to become a religious corporation (*shūkyō dantai hōjin* 宗教団体法人).[33] The Itōs decided to officially—in their application—base their teachings not solely on the scriptures venerated in Shingon, but also on the *Nirvāṇa Sūtra*.

This sutra is said to contain the final, ultimate teachings Śākyamuni gave immediately before his death.[34] Along with the Lotus Sutra and other *tathāgatagarbha* texts, the *Nirvāṇa Sūtra* contains teachings on buddha nature (Jpn. *busshō* 仏性), the inherent potential of all living things to become buddhas. These sutras and the ideas they contain had a broad influence in East Asian Mahāyāna Buddhism, particularly through Tendai, and in Sōtō Zen, Nichiren, and Jōdō-Shin.[35] The *Nirvāṇa Sūtra* is also noteworthy because it contains several inversions of classic Buddhist beliefs. In the *Nirvāṇa Sūtra,* the world in which we live is not seen to be one of impermanence (Skt. *anitya*), suffering (Skt. *duḥkha*), non-self (Skt. *anātman*), and impurity (Skt. *kaṣāya*), but one of permanence, bliss, self, and purity.

The Itōs saw in these notions a corollary to the tantric worldview of Shingon, in which the phenomenal universe of saṃsāra is in realty not separate from the diamond-like maṇḍala realm of Mahāvairocana. As the *Nirvāṇa Sūtra* is not an esoteric tantric text, reserved for the study of a small number of literate specialists, the Itōs believed they could use the *Nirvāṇa Sūtra* to teach laypeople about the essence of Shingon Buddhism without violating its traditions of initiation and secrecy. They also believed that the *Nirvāṇa Sūtra* contains justifications for their mediumistic abilities, spiritual powers, and the miraculous experiences of their followers. Gradually, the Itōs came to regard Shinnyo-en and the *Nirvāṇa Sūtra* as virtually synonymous. To the Itōs and their followers, Shinnyo-en itself was the vehicle for the Buddha's final, ultimate teachings in the modern world. A verse composed by Shinjō says the following:

> How rare to come across the jewel that is the teaching,
> The treasure of all treasures in the world.[36]

But the text of the *Nirvāṇa Sūtra* is in fact *not* the primary focus of study or devotion in Shinnyo-en. Although the Itōs published short paraphrases of the sutra and incorporated several verses into the Shinnyo-en liturgy, members are not encouraged to study the text itself (in fact they are *discouraged* from doing so, lest they become "confused" by it).[37] Rather, the *Nirvāṇa Sūtra* serves to conceal and legitimize the Itōs' claims of miraculous and salvific abilities. The Itōs carefully selected and published edited passages from the *Nirvāṇa Sūtra* that serve to both connect their teachings to Buddhism and to situate it at the pinnacle of all religions. For example, the *Nirvāṇa Sūtra* refers to itself in the following ways in its sixth chapter:

> All the splendid teachings expounded until now and all profound esoteric teachings are included in mahaparinirvana. . . . Of all the

> footprints in the world, those of an elephant are the largest. This sutra is the same. It is the greatest of all. It allows the highest state of samadhi that can be attained through all the other sutras. . . . It is the best of all. It is like sarpirmanda [Jpn. *daigo* 醍醐] (the essence of milk), the most effective of all medicines, capable of curing even feverish anxiety and delusion. Great nirvana (mahaparinirvana) takes its rightful place at the zenith of all things.[38]

This kind of rhetorical hierarchy is of course found in nearly every form of Buddhism, including Shingon, which Kūkai placed at the pinnacle of all forms of Buddhism extant in his day. The Itōs employed a time-tested textual and material strategy for negotiating their teaching's relationship to the Buddhist establishment. But the Itōs' glorification of the *Nirvāṇa Sūtra* and the passages they hold forth as almost prophetic scriptural justifications for their teachings do not tell us what makes Shinnyo-en new or unique. This brings us back to the wish-fulfilling jewel. The following is a quote from a sermon given by Shinjō Itō in 1979:

> One who is grateful for coming across the last teaching
> Has found a mani gem.
> Once you have come across the teachings of the Nirvana Sutra and develop a heart of appreciation and gratitude, you will in due time attain the truth of *emptiness*. It will truly be like finding the rare, wish-fulfilling mani gem. Here is another sonouta verse I created:[39]
>
> Among the many paths in the world,
> In the end, one comes to the last teaching.[40]

The "last teaching" here refers to both the *Nirvāṇa Sūtra* and Shinnyo-en.

Repeated in Shinnyo-en on every possible occasion, this idea is also anchored to physical objects: Shinnyo-en is the modern articulation of the Buddha's ultimate teachings, which the Itō family has revealed to humanity through tremendous personal sacrifice, even giving up their lives in so doing. Coming across such a precious treasure should gradually come to fill one's life with gratitude, even to the point where one feels *enabled* to live—*ikaseteiru* 生かせている—thanks entirely to the merciful compassion and spiritual powers extended by the Itōs. Eventually, through meditative practices and various forms of "edification," the member will come to see that his or her life, and even those of their living relatives and ancestral spirits, have been immeasurably improved by the wish-fulfilling jewel-like power of the *Nirvāṇa Sūtra,* which, combined with the esoteric power of Shingon Buddhist rites and their own spiritual abilities, the Itōs unleashed and continue to bestow even after death as the "ever-present buddhas" of Shinnyo-en. Wish-fulfilling jewels are thus one of many metonymic moorings connecting Shinnyo-en to symbols anchored in Shingon Buddhism, drifting as meanings become "linked, confused, and overlapped" with tropes from the Itōs' sacred biography.

Although reverence for founders and teachers is common in Japanese Buddhism—and there are many instances in Japanese literature and folklore of humans becoming powerful spirits or deities after death, Shinnyo-en encourages members to go somewhat further in their reverence for the Itōs. Shinnyo-en is a Buddhist movement that centers upon the Itōs, who are believed to have ontologically altered the universe in creating Shinnyo-en. This is hinted at obliquely through carefully chosen passages from the *Nirvāṇa Sūtra,* where the Buddha is described as an ever-present Tathāgata (Jpn. *jōjū nyorai* 常住如来). In Shinnyo-en's English publications from roughly the last fifteen years, this concept has been pluralized and applied to "buddhas" generally, then extended to the Itōs, who are the buddhas of Shinnyo-en, and reinforced through oral tradition, ritual, and material culture.[41] The Itōs' many Buddhist associations—including those with wish-fulfilling jewels—transform them into the nexus of salvation within Shinnyo-en.

For members of Shinnyo-en, wish-fulfilling jewels are associated with the *Nirvāṇa Sūtra,* the Shinnyo-en community itself, or its charismatic founding family. Shinnyo-en sermons and publications frequently and purposefully reinforce these associations, adding "hidden" meanings to a recognizable Buddhist symbol. This deliberate manipulation of *maṇi* iconography places the Itōs at the center of devotion and hints that *they are the Three Jewels*—they are buddhas, their teachings are dharma, and their followers are a modern saṅgha that is linked to but transcends traditional Buddhism. When a member of Shinnyo-en makes a pilgrimage to Oyasono 親苑, the headquarters of Shinnyo-en, and visits, for example, the Shinnyo Stūpa (beneath which the relics of the Itōs are enshrined), he or she will see wish-fulfilling jewels there aplenty, which appear in close association with the Itōs or an event in their sacred biography. Jewels appear elsewhere at Oyasono, on buildings, in maṇḍalas, and on ritual objects. They are also mentioned in sermons and during *sesshin* 接心, Shinnyo-en's unique meditative practice wherein the trainee is quietly given advice and admonishments that focus on the Itōs and paraphrases of their teachings. Thus, while jewels are used in Shinnyo-en much as they are in Shingon, they are imbued with meaning and importance that both derive from and refer to the Itōs as possessing and extending salvation. And so members are taught to see the Itōs hidden within Buddhist objects: the story of Chibun and his parents' struggle with his death in the stone Jizō statue at Oyasono and again the Itōs or Shinnyo-en itself within the ceramic mini-Jizō holding his special wish-fulfilling jewel.

In Shinnyo-en, wish-fulfilling jewels are self-referential, even as they retain their inherited Buddhist meanings and associations. Shinnyo-en presents itself as a precious wish-fulfilling jewel, created by and made available through the sacrifices of the charismatic founding family. Shinnyo-en is a precious treasure for which adherents are taught they should feel eternal gratitude and which they should constantly strive to joyfully share with others. Thus, jewels are constant reminders of the Itōs' and Shinnyo-en's importance, as well as the need to proselytize and remain enthusiastically involved, ever motivated by gratitude for receiving such a precious treasure.

Conclusion

The Shingon-affiliated lay movements of the twentieth century stand out because scholarly models for understanding Buddhist modernity tend to portray them as aberrant social phenomena, "pressure chambers for the socially disadvantaged" or "deviant responses to abnormal conditions," that there is almost nothing new about them at all, or that such novelties are mere superficialities undeserving of serious scholarly consideration.[42] For example, James Coleman characterizes Sōka Gakkai 創価学会 (a lay organization that emerged from Nichiren Buddhism) as "perched somewhere between" what he sees as "old" and "new" forms of Buddhism.[43] This characterization is shortsighted. It fails to recognize the agency and intentions of charismatic founders who saw themselves as engaged in a modern reformation of Buddhism not entirely allied with monastic or academic institutions. Such characterizations that see Shinnyo-en and other lay movements as either old or new, traditional or modernist, overlook the phenomenology of how these movements may shape their members' identities and relationships. Shinnyo-en's use of wish-fulfilling jewels, adopted from Shingon and imbued with new meanings, teaches members to embody the sacred narrative of the Itōs. Repeated dramatization, internalization, and externalization of that narrative locates the Shinnyo-en member within "a religious culture that cannot be confined to a single national or spatial context."[44]

In comparing the meanings of wish-fulfilling jewels among various forms of contemporary Japanese esoteric Buddhism, we find that the relative "newness" of Shinnyo-en, for example, is not merely a matter of superficial innovations. Wish-fulfilling jewels in Shinnyo-en are, to paraphrase H. Byron Earhart, part of how what was old is becoming new.[45]

Shinnyo-en from its very beginnings centered on the Itōs and their unique powers. They associated with and adopted elements of Shingon Buddhism's visual and material culture to protect their community and conceal their teachings, which in the 1930s were considered illegal. At the same time, Shingon symbols and objects could be imbued with new associations that refer insiders' thoughts back to Shinnyo-en and to the Itōs, whose unique ontological status is now hidden in plain sight within and among Buddhist objects. The Itōs created a network of strategic linkages with wish-fulfilling jewels that have served to rhetorically and symbolically create their authority. Indeed, the wish-fulfilling jewel has proved to be exceedingly useful for Shinnyo-en, granting legitimacy, power, and value through its many associations with the *Nirvāṇa Sūtra*, relics, and the Three Jewels of Buddhism.

Notes

1. See William R. LaFleur *Liquid Life: Abortion and Buddhism in Japan* (Princeton, NJ: Princeton University Press, 1994); Milla Micka Moto-Sanchez. "Jizō, Healing Rituals, and Women in Japan." *Japanese Journal of Religious Studies* 43, no. 2 (2016): 307–331.
2. The ashes were purportedly taken from a "grand *homa*" (Jpn. *ōgoma* 大護摩) performed on December 28, 2010, the seventy-fifth anniversary of Shinnyo-en's founders' first enshrining of a Buddhist image on the same date in 1935. This date is sometimes considered the beginning of Shinnyo-en. The *homa* was dedicated to the successful "enhancement" or renovation of Shinnyo-en's headquarters (Shinsō Itō, "Untitled Sermon from the Spring Higan Service," unpublished manuscript, Tokyo, 2011.
3. H. Byron Earhart, *Gedatsu-Kai and Religion in Contemporary Japan: Returning to the Center* (Bloomington: Indiana University Press, 2000), 9.

4. For example, Agonshū 阿含宗 (see Ian Reader, "The Rise of a Japanese 'New New Religion': Themes in the Development of Agonshu," *Japanese Journal of Religious Studies* 15, no. 4 (1988): 235–261), and Gedatsukai 解脱会 (see H. Byron Earhart: "Toward a Theory of the Formation of the Japanese New Religions: A Case Study of Gedatsu-Kai," *History of Religions* 20, nos. 1–2 (1980): 175–197, and *Gedatsu-Kai and Religion in Contemporary Japan*). The causes and nature of these movements' emergence from "established" Japanese Buddhist institutions in the twentieth century are themselves highly contested subjects for scholars of religions in Japan. As such, I do not engage here with ongoing conversations about "new religious movements," Buddhism in a globalizing world, or the problematics inherent in scholarly attempts to locate pure or authentic Buddhisms.
5. See Sarah A. Fremerman, "Divine Impersonations: Nyoirin Kannon in Medieval Japan" (PhD diss., Stanford University, 2008), 13.
6. Here I am building on Simon Coleman's model for understanding the role of narrative—words, texts, testimonies, etc.—in the construction of charismatic Christian identities. See Simon Coleman, *The Globalization of Charismatic Christianity: Spreading the Gospel of Prosperity* (Cambridge: Cambridge University Press, 2000).
7. Charles Muller, "如意" (Jpn. *nyoi*), in *Digital Dictionary of Buddhism* (buddhism-dict.net, 2017).
8. The most common referent for "jewel" in Buddhism is *ratna,* a Sanskrit word that means jewel, gem, or treasure. It is used for the "three jewels" (Skt. *triratna;* Jpn. *sanbō* 三宝) of *buddha*, *dharma*, and *saṅgha*. Throughout the Buddhist world, these three are considered "treasures" because they are reliable sources of refuge—one can trust in the awakened one (*buddha*), his teachings (*dharma*), and the community of people devoted to upholding and transmitting those teachings (*saṅgha*) to help guide one out of cyclical suffering and toward some ideal of a better life. See Charles Muller, "三寶" (Jpn. *sanbō*), in *Digital Dictionary of Buddhism* (buddhism-dict.net, 2018b).
9. Charles Muller, "如意珠" (Jpn. *nyoiju*), in *Digital Dictionary of Buddhism* (buddhism-dict.net. 2009).
10. Kazuhiro Fujimaki, 藤巻 和宏. *Seinaru tama no monogatari: Kūkai, seichi, nyoihōju* 聖なる球の物語：空海•聖地•如意宝珠 [Stories of sacred treasures: Kūkai, sacred sites, and wish-fulfilling jewels] (Bukkuretto: Kakimono wo hiraku 10. Japan: Heibonsha 平凡社, 2017). Yoshito S. Hakeda, ed. *Kūkai: Major Works* (New York: Columbia

University Press, 1972; UNESCO Collection of Representative Works: Japanese Series, No. 87), 146.

11. Fujimaki, *Seinaru tama no monogatari,* 17–20; Steven Trenson, "Rice, Relics, and Jewels: The Network and Agency of Rice Grains in Medieval Japanese Esoteric Buddhism," *Japanese Journal of Religious Studies* 45, no. 2 (2018): 269–307.
12. It is also worth mentioning that the mantra of Ratnasambhāva is often chanted to venerate relics.
13. For more on Shingon, see Robert H. Sharf, "Visualization and Mandala in Shingon Buddhism," in *Living Images: Japanese Buddhist Icons in Context,* edited by Robert H. Sharf and Elizabeth Horton Sharf (Palo Alto, CA: Stanford University Press: 2001), 157–166; Minoru Kiyota, *Shingon Buddhism: Theory and Practice* (Los Angeles: Buddhist Books International, 1978); Taikō Yamasaki, *Shingon: Japanese Esoteric Buddhism,* 1st ed., edited by Yasuyoshi Morimoto and David Kidd, translated by Richard Peterson and Cynthia Peterson (Boston: Shambhala, 1988); Elizabeth Tinsley, "Kūkai and the Development of Shingon Buddhism," in *Esoteric Buddhism and the Tantras in East Asia,* edited by Charles D. Orzech, Henrik Hjort Sorensen, and Richard Karl Payne, (Leiden: Brill, 2011), Handbook of Oriental Studies, vol. 24, section 4, China, 691–708; Ryūichi Abe, *The Weaving of Mantra: Kūkai and the Construction of Esoteric Buddhist Discourse* (New York: Columbia University Press, 1999).
14. Ruppert's research elucidates how monks and monastic institutions used wish-fulfilling jewels to empower emperors, monks, monastic lineages, temples, and institutions. See Brian D. Ruppert, *Jewel in the Ashes: Buddha Relics and Power in Early Medieval Japan* (Cambridge, MA: Harvard University Asia Center, 2000; Harvard East Asian Monographs 188).
15. Fremerman, "Divine Impersonations," 36.
16. Shugendō 修験道 is a syncretic tradition indigenous to Japan, believed to have been started by the semi-mythical En-no-gyōja 役行者 (also known as the Great Bodhisattva Jinben 神辺大菩薩). Shugendō involves magico-ascetic practices conducted in sacred mountain ranges, and many Shugendō lineages have for at least several centuries been associated with Buddhist temples, including Daigoji.
17. Ruppert, *Jewel in the Ashes,* 119–121.
18. Ruppert, *Jewel in the Ashes,* 168–169.
19. In addition to Shinnyo-en, Gedatsukai 解脱会, Agonshū 阿含宗, and Bentenshū 辯天宗 also incorporate Shingon rituals and concepts.

Gedatsukai was founded in 1929 by Okano Seiken 岡野 聖憲, who, like Shinnyo-en's founder, received priestly ordinations through Daigoji. Agonshū was founded in 1954 by Kiriyama Seiyū 桐山 靖雄, and Bentenshū was founded in 1952 by Ōmori Chiben 大森 智辯.

20. These events are described in more detail in Shinnyo-en publications, such as "Pursuing the Way," the fifth section of *The Path of Oneness,* English rev. ed. (Tokyo: International Affairs Department of Shinnyo-en, 2009), 369–513, and Shinjō Itō, *The Light in Each Moment,* English rev. ed. (Tokyo: International Affairs Department of Shinnyo-en, 2010).
21. Shinnyo-en has changed its name several times. As of March 28, 1936 (several months after the Itōs began attracting followers), the group was registered with Shinshōji as the "Fellowship of Light" (Risshō Kō 立照講). The name was officially changed to "Tachikawa Fellowship of Achala" (Tachikawa Fudōson Kyōkai 立川不動尊教会, affiliated with Daigoji) on August 15, 1938. On February 28, 1946, the Tachikawa Fellowship of Achala became legally independent of Shingon Buddhism when the Shingon denomination that had been unified during World War II was dismantled. On January 23, 1948, the name was again changed to "Fellowship of Truth" (Makoto Kyōdan まこと教団). The group was officially renamed "Shinnyo-en" (真如苑; lit. "Borderless Garden of Thusness") on June 16, 1951, and Shinnyo-en's registration as a religious corporation was completed on May 20, 1953.
22. Readers may notice here and in other quotations from Shinnyo-en materials that non-English terms are not formatted according to the conventions used in my own writing. Shinnyo-en has for decades mostly eschewed italics, standard academic transliteration, and diacritical markings in its English publications, as these are regarded as too "difficult" for members to read or as being associated with an elitist academic presentation of Buddhism. Editors at Shinnyo-en justify their choice as a reflection of the Itōs' desire to simplify Buddhism and present its texts and practices as more accessible to laypeople. I have therefore preserved nonstandard spellings and formatting in order to faithfully represent Shinnyo-en's editorial choices that, remarkably, also refer to the Itōs.
23. *House of Resolve* (Tokyo: International Affairs Department of Shinnyo-en, 2001), 16.
24. Fumiaki began using his priestly name, Shinjō 真乗, in 1942.
25. *The Path of Oneness,* 432–433.
26. *The Path of Oneness,* 434–435.

27. A *dōji* is an acolyte, youth, son, or prince who serves and assists a buddha or Buddhist deity. *Dōji* may also be applied to novice monks, or even to bodhisattvas, who are regarded as sons of the Buddha. See Charles Muller, "童子" (Jpn. *dōji*), in *Digital Dictionary of Buddhism* (buddhism-dict.net, 2018a). Certain deities in Japan may be shown surrounded by anywhere from two to thirty-six *dōji*.
28. Chibun and Yūichi are more often referred to by their posthumous names, Kyōdōin 教導院 and Shindōin 真導院. The honorific *-sama* 様 is added to all of the Itōs' posthumous names or religious titles (e.g., Shinsō Itō is referred to as Keishū-sama 継主様).
29. Shinsō Itō, "Untitled Sermon from the Spring Higan Service." In this passage Shinsō tacitly draws parallels between Jizō and her brothers Yūichi and Chibun. "Using the support of his staff" would be a clear reference to Yūichi, who used crutches. A "treasure that is said to remove any calamity and fulfill all wishes" refers to Chibun, who began appearing to his mother and other members after his death, granting wishes and relieving members' spiritual and material burdens.
30. Not all members of the Itō family are felt to be as religiously or soteriologically significant as Shinjō, Tomoji, Chibun, Yūichi, and Shinsō. For example, the Itōs' two elder daughters, Eiko 映子 (b. 1933) and Atsuko 孜子 (b. 1940), left Shinnyo-en and now linger in infamy, remembered only for their perceived betrayals. Shinjō compared these two daughters to two of the Buddha's sons mentioned in the *Nirvāṇa Sūtra* (Upamana, Jpn. 優波摩那; and Sunakṣatra, Jpn. Zenshō 善星), who betrayed the Buddha and each became a deluded *icchantika* (Shinsō Itō, "Untitled Sermon from a Monthly Feast of Eternal Bliss," unpublished manuscript, Tokyo, 1977). Shinrei 真玲 (b. 1943), the Itōs' youngest daughter, has faded in importance since the mid-1990s. According to Shinjō's will (the *Teiki* 定記), Shinsō was to be the "front" (*omote* 表) while Shinrei the "back" (*ura* 裏) of a dual leadership structure. Nevertheless, Shinsō emerged as the unquestioned leader of Shinnyo-en after some initial years of "confusion" over each daughter's role following Shinjō's death in 1989. Shinrei was stripped of her religious responsibilities, largely removed from public view, and placed in charge of one of Shinnyo-en's philanthropic organizations in order to keep her occupied and unable to hamper Shinsō's activities.
31. See Carmen Blacker, *The Catalpa Bow: A Study of Shamanistic Practices in Japan,* 3rd ed. (London: Routledge, 1975); Ichirō Hori: *Folk Religion in Japan: Continuity and Change.* (Chicago: University of Chicago Press, 1968; Haskell Lectures on History of Religions 1), and

"Shamanism in Japan," *Japanese Journal of Religious Studies* 2, no. 4 (1975): 231–287; Hitoshi Miyake, *Shugendō: Essays on the Structure of Japanese Folk Religion,* edited by H. Byron Earhart (Ann Arbor: Center for Japanese Studies, University of Michigan, 2001; Michigan Monograph Series in Japanese Studies, no. 32).

32. The change may have also been necessary as part of the legal settlement of a case brought against Shinjō in 1950 by a former disciple who accused Shinjō of abuse and financial crimes (*The Path of Oneness,* 401–410). Shinjō was found guilty and given a suspended jail sentence. After this "dharma crisis" Shinnyo-en was reorganized with Tomoji as the official "head" of the order (Jpn. *enshū* 園主) and Shinjō the head priest (Jpn. *zasu* 座主) of their temple, founder (Jpn. *kaisō* 開祖), and master (Jpn. *kyōshū* 教主). Some of these roles were eventually recombined in the early 1990s, when the Itōs' daughter Shinsō emerged as the sole leader of Shinnyo-en.
33. *The Path of Oneness,* 410–413.
34. This type of doctrinal hierarchy is not at all uncommon in Buddhism. Many Mahāyāna doxographies are often comprehensive or inclusive but place one practice or school at the pinnacle—the best, most powerful, or easiest way to practice Buddhism in a given social or historical moment. The Itōs expressed the simultaneous inclusivity and superiority of the Shinnyo teachings using the language and metaphors of "embracement" (Jpn. *shōju* 摂受) found in the *Nirvāṇa Sūtra.* The Itōs adopted the five-part canonical classification system called *goji hakkyō setsu* 五時八教説, developed by the Tiantai monk Zhìyǐ 智顗, which places the *Lotus* and *Nirvāṇa Sūtras* at the pinnacle of the Buddha's teachings, only the Itōs asserted that the teachings of the *Nirvāṇa Sūtra* are superior to those of the Lotus Sutra (*The Path of Oneness,* 102–103). An interesting subtext here may be the suggestion that Shinnyo-en, being based on the *Nirvāṇa Sūtra,* is superior to competing Buddhist lay organizations based on the Lotus Sutra, such as Sōka Gakkai.
35. This fact is downplayed in Shinnyo-en. Many members are under the misapprehension that the Itōs "rediscovered" the *Nirvāṇa Sūtra* after it had been hidden for centuries. Shinnyo-en has done little to disabuse its members of this misunderstanding, instead pointing out that while the *Nirvāṇa Sūtra* is known in the Sōtō Zen sect, for example, only Shinnyo-en regards it as the prime canonical source for its teachings and actively teaches about it (*The Path of Oneness,* 102–103).
36. Shinjō Itō, "Untitled Sermon from a Monthly Feast of Bezaiten," unpublished manuscript, Tokyo, 1974.

37. Ian Reader has noted a similar use of text in Agonshū, another twentieth-century Shingon-derived lay movement: "There is actually very little emphasis on the Āgamas as texts, and virtually no systematic study of them in Agonshū" (Reader, "The Rise of a Japanese 'New New Religion,'" 250).
38. *The Path of Oneness*, 73–74.
39. *Sonoutas* 苑歌 (lit. "garden poems"), like the ones quoted above, are short poetic verses composed by Shinjō or Tomoji, meant to convey simplified, easy to remember Buddhist teachings.
40. Shinjō Itō, "Untitled Sermon from a Monthly Feast of Bezaiten," unpublished manuscript Tokyo, 1979.
41. Certain ambiguities in Japanese have allowed a similar transition from Shinjō's focus on a monistic "Buddha" to Shinsō's representation of the Itōs as ever-present Tathāgatas (Jpn. *jōjū nyorai* 常住如来). Shinjō variously referred to the former as *"hotoke-sama"* 仏様 or *"budda"* 仏陀 (lit. "buddha"), Mahāvairocana, Acala, or, starting in the late 1950s, as the Eternally Abiding Śākyamuni Tathāgata (Jpn. Kuon Shōchū Shakamuni Nyorai 久遠常住釈迦牟尼如来), represented in his "Nirvana Image" sculpture, which became Shinnyo-en's main object of devotion (Jpn. *honzon* 本尊) in 1957. Under Shinsō's leadership, statues of the Itōs have been combined with the Nirvana Image on Shinnyo-en altars to form what she calls a "shinnyo mandala" containing the buddhas of Shinnyo-en—Śākyamuni *and* the Itōs.
42. Earhart "Toward a Theory of the Formation of the Japanese New Religions," 178.
43. James William Coleman, *The New Buddhism: The Western Transformation of an Ancient Tradition* (New York: Oxford University Press, 2001), 9.
44. S. Coleman, *The Globalization of Charismatic Christianity,* 13.
45. Earhart *Gedatsu-Kai and Religion in Contemporary Japan,* 238.

Bibliography

Abe, Ryūichi. *The Weaving of Mantra: Kūkai and the Construction of Esoteric Buddhist Discourse.* New York: Columbia University Press, 1999.

Adamson Sijapati, Megan. *Islamic Revival in Nepal: Religion and a New Nation.* London: Routledge, 2011.

Agrawal, R. C. "Stupas and Monasteries: A Recent Discovery from Satdhara, India." In *South Asian Archaeology, 1995: Proceedings of the 13th International Conference of the European Association of South Asian Archaeologists,* edited by F. R. Allchin and B. Allchin, 403–415. New Delhi: Published for the Ancient India and Iran Trust, 1997.

Aktor, Mikael. "Five Stones—Four Rivers—One Town: The Hindu *Pañcāyatanapūjā.*" In Ferrari and Dähnhardt, *Soulless Matter, Seats of Energy,* 3–27.

Ali, Daud. *Courtly Culture and Political Life in Early Medieval India.* Cambridge Studies in Indian History and Society 10. New York: Cambridge University Press, 2004.

Allen, Charles. *The Buddha and Dr. Führer: An Archaeological Scandal.* London: Haus Publishing, 2008.

Amstutz, Galen. "Sexual Transgression in Shinran's Dream." *The Eastern Buddhist* 43, nos. 1–2 (2012): 225–269.

An, Jiayao. "Glass Beads Found at the Yongningsi Temple." *Journal of Glass Studies* 42 (2000): 81–84.

Anonymous. "Original Relics of the Buddha Sakyamuni." http://sharira.org/h_e.html. Accessed September 20, 2015.

Appleton, Naomi. "In the Footsteps of the Buddha? Women and the Bodhisatta Path in Theravāda Buddhism." *Journal of Feminist Studies in Religion* 27, no. 1 (2011): 33–51.

———. *Jātaka Stories in Theravāda Buddhism: Narrating the Bodhisatta Path.* Burlington: Ashgate, 1988.

———. *Many Buddhas, One Buddha: A Study and Translation of Avadānaśataka 1–40.* Sheffield, UK: Equinox, 2020.

Appleton, Naomi, and Sarah Shaw, trans. *The Ten Great Birth Stories of the Buddha: The Mahānipāta of the Jātakatthavaṇṇanā,* 2 vols. Chiang Mai: Silkworm, 2015.

Aptilon, Sarah Fremerman. "Goddess Genealogy: Nyoirin Kannon in the Ono Shingon Tradition." In *Esoteric Buddhism and the Tantras in East Asia,* edited by Charles Orzech, Henrik Sørensen, and Richard K. Payne, 893–903. Leiden: Brill, 2011.

Aris, Michael. *Hidden Treasures and Secret Lives: A Study of Pemalingpa (1450–1521) and the Sixth Dalai Lama (1683–1706).* London: Kegan Paul International, 1989.

Asher, Frederick M. "Travels of a Reliquary, Its Contents Separated at Birth." *South Asian Studies* 28 (2012): 147–156.

Bagnoli, Martina, et al., eds. *Treasures of Heaven: Saints, Relics, and Devotion in Medieval Europe.* Cleveland: Walters Art Museum, 2010.

Bailey, Greg, and Ian Mabbett. *The Sociology of Early Buddhism.* Cambridge: Cambridge University Press, 2003.

Bajpai, K. D. "Authority of Minting Coins in Ancient India." *Journal of the Numismatic Society of India* 25, no. 9 (1963): 17–21.

Bajrācārya, Barṇa Bajra. *Maṇiśaila Mahāvadāna.* Bhom̐ta: Sāgar Pres, N.S. 1119 (1998 CE). (1st ed. NS 1082 [1961 CE]), 30.

Barth, Auguste. "L'inscription du reliquaire de Piprava." *Journal des savants,* 1906, 541–554.

———. "The Inscription on the Piprahwa Vase." Translated by G. Tamson. *Indian Antiquary* 36 (1907): 117–124.

Barthes, Roland. "Des joyaux aux bijoux." In *Œuvres complètes,* edited by Éric Marty, 1089–1093, vol. 1: *Livres, textes, entretiens, 1942–1961.* Paris: Seuil, 2002.

Bassnett, Susan. "The Translator as Cross-Cultural Mediator." In *The Oxford Handbook of Translation Studies,* edited by Kirsten Malmkjær and Kevin Windle. New York: Oxford University Press, 2011), 96; online: DOI: 10.1093/oxfordhb/9780199239306.013.0008.

Bautze-Picron, Claudine. *The Bejewelled Buddha: From India to Burma, New Considerations.* New Delhi: Sanctum Books, 2010.

Bayly, C. A. *Rulers, Townsmen and Bazaars: North Indian Society in the Age of British Expansion, 1770–1870.* Cambridge: Cambridge University Press, 1983.

Bays, Gwendolyn, trans. *The Lalitavistara Sūtra, Voice of the Buddha: The Beauty of Compassion,* 2 vols. Berkeley: Dharma Publishing, 1983. Tibetan Translation Series.

Beck, Brenda E. F., et al., eds. *Folktales of India.* Chicago: University of Chicago Press, 1987.

Behrendt, Kurt. *The Buddhist Architecture of Gandhāra*. Leiden: Brill, 2004.

Benn, James. *Burning for the Buddha: Self-Immolation in Chinese Buddhism*. Honolulu: University of Hawai'i Press, 2007. Kuroda Institute Studies in East Asian Buddhism 19.

Bennett, Jane. *Vibrant Matter: A Political Ecology of Things*. Durham, NC: Duke University Press, 2010.

Berger, Patricia Ann. *Empire of Emptiness: Buddhist Art and Political Authority in Qing China*. Honolulu: University of Hawai'i Press, 2003.

———. "Preserving the Nation: The Political Uses of Tantric Art in China." In *Latter Days of the Law: Images of Chinese Buddhism 850–1850,* edited by Marsha Weidner, 89–123. Honolulu: University of Hawai'i Press, 1994.

Berkwitz, Stephen C. *The History of the Buddha's Relic Shrine: A Translation of the Sinhala Thūpavaṃsa*. New York: Oxford University Press, 2007.

Bernardi, A. "The Economic Problems of the Roman Empire at the Time of Its Decline." In *The Economic Decline of Empires,* edited by Carlo M. Cipolla, 16–83. London: Methuen, 1970.

Bhattacarya, V. A., ed. *Viṣṇu Purāṇa*. Calcutta, 1882.

Bhattacharyya Panda, Nandini. "Women in the Sastric Traditions: Colonialism, Law, and Violence." In *Blackwell Companion to Religion and Violence,* edited by Andrew R. Murphy, 389–405. Oxford: Wiley Blackwell, 2011.

Bhikkhu Bodhi, trans. *The Sutta Nipāta: An Ancient Collection of the Buddha's Discourses*. Somerville: Wisdom Publications, 2017.

Bhikkhu Ñāṇamoli, trans. *The Minor Readings and Illustrator.* London: Pali Text Society, 1978.

———, trans. *The Path of Purification* [*Visuddhimagga*]. Seattle: Pariyatti Editions, 1999.

Bingenheimer, Marcus. *Island of Guanyin: Mount Putuo and Its Gazetteers*. Oxford: Oxford University Press, 2016.

Blackburn, Stuart. *Moral Fictions: Tamil Folktales in Oral Tradition*. Helsinki: Suomalainen Tiedeakatemia, 2001. Folklore Fellows' Communication, no. 278.

Blacker, Carmen. *The Catalpa Bow: A Study of Shamanistic Practices in Japan,* 3rd ed. London: Routledge, 1975.

Bloch, Theodor. "Notes on the Exploration of Vaisali." *Annual Report, Bengal Circle, Archaeological Survey of India for the Year Ended April 1904*. Calcutta: Bengal Secretariat Press, 1904.

Bloomfield, Linda. *Science for Potters*. Westerville, OH: American Ceramic Society, 2017.

Bodiford, William. "Zen in the Art of Funerals: Ritual Salvation in Japanese Buddhism." *History of Religions* 32, no. 2 (1992): 146–164.

Bogel, Cynthea J. "Canonizing Kannon: The Ninth-Century Esoteric Buddhist Altar at Kanshinji." *The Art Bulletin* 84, no. 1 (March 2002): 30–64.

———. *With a Single Glance: Buddhist Icon and Early Mikkyo Vision.* Seattle: University of Washington Press, 2009.

Boulnois, Luce. "Gold, Wool and Musk: Trade in Lhasa in the Seventeenth Century." In *Lhasa in the Seventeenth Century: The Capital of the Dalai Lamas,* edited by Françoise Pommaret, 132–156. Leiden: Brill, 2003.

Bowring, Richard. *The Religious Traditions of Japan: 500–1600.* Cambridge: Cambridge University Press, 2005.

Boyer, A. M., E. J. Rapson, E. Senart, and P. S. Noble, eds. *Kharoṣṭhī Inscriptions Discovered by Sir Aurel Stein in Chinese Turkestan.* Oxford: Clarendon Press, 1920–1929.

Braghin, Cecilia, ed. *Chinese Glass: Archaeological Studies on the Uses and Social Context of Glass Artefacts from the Warring States to the Northern Song Period.* Florence: Leo S. Olschki Editore, 2002.

Braghin, Cecilia. "Polychrome and Monochrome Glass of the Warring States and Han Periods." In Braghin, *Chinese Glass,* 3–43.

Brekke, Torkel. "Bones of Contention: Buddhist Relics, Nationalism and the Politics of Archaeology." *Numen* 54 (2007): 270–303.

Brill, Robert H., and John H. Martin, eds. *Scientific Research in Early Chinese Glass: Proceedings of the Archaeometry of Glass Sessions of the 1984 International Symposium on Glass, Beijing, September 7, 1984, with Supplementary Papers.* Corning, NY: Corning Museum of Glass, 1991.

Bronkhorst, Johannes. *Buddhism in the Shadow of Brahmanism.* Leiden: Brill, 2011.

———. "Why Is There Philosophy in India?" *1998 [Sixth] Gonda Lecture.* Amsterdam: Royal Netherlands Academy of Arts and Sciences, 1999.

Brown, Claudia, and Donald Rubiner. *Clear as Crystal, Red as Flame: Later Chinese Glass.* Seattle: University of Washington Press, 1990.

Brown, Robert L. "Narrative as Icon: The Jātaka Stories in Ancient Indian and Southeast Asian Architecture." In *Sacred Biography in the Buddhist Traditions of South and Southeast Asia,* edited by Juliane Schober, 64–108. Honolulu: University of Hawai'i Press, 1997.

Brunnhölzl, Karl, trans. *When the Clouds Part: The Uttaratantra and Its Meditative Tradition as a Bridge between Sūtra and Tantra.* Ithaca, NY: Snow Lion, 2015.

Bruntz, Courtney. "Commodifying Mount Putuo: State Nationalism, Religious Tourism, and Buddhist Revival." PhD diss., Graduate Theological Union, 2014.

Bühler, Georg. "Preliminary Note on a Recently Discovered Śākya Inscription." *Journal of the Royal Asiatic Society,* 1898, 387–389.

Burgess, James, ed. *Epigraphia Indica: A Collection of Inscriptions Supplementary to the Corpus Inscriptionum Indicarum of the Archaeology Survey,* 2 vols. Calcutta: Superintendent of Government Printing, 1892–1894.

Burgess, James, and Bhagwanlal Indraji. *Inscriptions from the Cave-Temples of Western India.* Delhi: Indian India, 1976 (1881).

Burlingame, Eugene Watson. "The Act of Truth (*Saccakiriyā*): A Hindu Spell and Its Employment as a Psychic Motif in Hindu Fiction." *Journal of the Royal Asiatic Society of Great Britain and Ireland,* July 1917, 429–467.

Burrow, T. *A Translation of the Kharoṣṭhi Documents from Chinese Turkestan.* London: Royal Asiatic Society, 1940.

Buswell, Robert E., Jr., ed. *Encyclopedia of Buddhism.* New York: Macmillan, 2004.

Buswell, Robert E., Jr., and Donald S. Lopez Jr., eds. *The Princeton Dictionary of Buddhism.* Princeton, NJ: Princeton University Press, 2014.

Cahill, Susan B. "Performers and Female Taoist Adepts: Hsi Wang Mu as a Patron Deity of Women in Medieval China." *Journal of the American Oriental Society,* 106, no. 1 (January–March 1986): 155–168.

Campo, Daniela. *La construction de la sainteté dans la Chine moderne: La vie du maître bouddhiste Xuyun.* Paris: Les Belles Lettres, 2013.

Casey, Jane. "Ornaments of Faith: Himalayan Jewelry and Jeweled Objects." In *Vanishing Beauty: Asian Jewelry and Ritual Objects from the Barbara and David Kipper Collection,* edited by Madhuvanti Ghose, 26–124. Chicago: Art Institute of Chicago, 2016.

Cen Xuelü 岑學呂. *Xuyun fashi nianpu* 虚云法师年谱. Beijing: Zongjiao wenhua chubanshe, 1995.

Cerulli, Anthony, and Caterina Guenzi. "Mineral Healing: Gemstone Remedies in Astrological and Medical Traditions." In Ferrari and Dähnhardt, *Soulless Matter, Seats of Energy,* 73–93.

Chakraborti, Haripada. *Early Brāhmī Record in India (c. 300 B.C.–c. 300 A.D.).* Calcutta: Sanskrit Pustak Bhandar, 1974.

Chambers, William. *Designs of Chinese Buildings, Furniture, Dresses.* London: Published by the author, 1757.

———. *Plans, Elevations, Sections, and Perspective Views of the Gardens and Buildings at Kew, in Surry.* Farnborough, Hants.: Gregg Press, 1966. (London: J. Haberkorn, 1763.)

Chandra, Moti. *Trade and Trade Routes in Ancient India.* Delhi: Abhinav Publications, 1977.

Chandra, R. P. "Some Unpublished Amaravati Inscriptions." *Epigraphia Indica* 25 (1919–1920): 258–274.

Chang, Elizabeth H. "'Eyes of the Proper Almond-Shape': Blue-and-White China in the British Imaginary, 1823–1883." *Nineteenth Century Studies* 19 (May 2005): 17–34.

Chapin, Helen B. "A Study in Buddhist Iconography." *Ostasiatische Zeitschrift:* vol. 8 (1932), nos. 1–2, pp. 29–43; no. 3, pp. 111–129; vol. 11 (1935), nos. 3–4, pp. 125–134; no. 5, pp. 195–210.

Chavannes, Édouard. *Cinq cents contes et apologues extraits du Tripitaka Chinois,* 4 vols. Paris: E. Leroux, 1910.

Chen, Huaiyu. *The Revival of Buddhist Monasticism in Medieval China.* New York: Peter Lang, 2007.

The Chinese Repository, Canton, China. 1832–1851; reprint, Vaduz: Kraus, 1844.

Ch'en, Kenneth K. S. *Buddhism in China: A Historical Survey.* Princeton, NJ: Princeton University Press, 1964.

Chiu, Angela S. *The Buddha in Lanna: Art, Lineage, and Power in Northern Thailand.* Honolulu: University of Hawai'i Press, 2017.

Chou, Wen-shing, and Nancy G. Lin. "Karmic Affinities: Lives of Lamas and Emperors at the Qing Court." In *Water Moon Reflections: Essays in Honor of Patricia Berger,* edited by Ellen Huang, Nancy G. Lin, Michelle McCoy, and Michelle H. Wang. Berkeley: IEAS publications, forthcoming.

Choudhary, Radhakrishna. *Kautilya's Political Ideas and Institutions.* Varanasi: Chowkhamba Sanskrit Series Office, 1971.

Chu, Petra Ten-Doesschate, and Ding Ning. *Qing Encounters: Artistic Exchanges between China and the West.* Los Angeles: Getty Research Institute, 2015.

Clarke, John. *Jewellery of Tibet and the Himalayas.* New York: V&A Publications, 2004.

Clarke, Shayne. *Family Matters in Indian Buddhist Monasticisms.* Honolulu: University of Hawai'i Press, 2013.

Claus, Peter. "Playing *Cenne:* The Meanings of a Folk Game." In *Another Harmony: New Essays on the Folklore of India,* edited by Stuart Blackburn and A. K. Ramanujan, 265–293. Berkeley: University of California Press, 1986.

Coedès, Georges. "Documents sur l'histoire politique et religieuse du Laos occidental." *Bulletin de l'École Française d'Extrême-Orient* 25 (1925): 1–201.

———. "Notes sur les ouvrages Pālis composés en pays Thai." *Bulletin de l'École Française d'Extrême-Orient* 15 (1915): 39–46.

Cole, Alan. "Upside Down/Right Side Up: A Revisionist History of Funerals in China." *History of Religions* 35, no. 4 (1996): 307–338.

Colebrooke, Henry Thomas. *Essays in the Religion and Philosophy of the Hindus.* London: Williams and Norgate, 1858.

Coleman, James William. *The New Buddhism: The Western Transformation of an Ancient Tradition.* New York: Oxford University Press, 2001.

Coleman, Simon. *The Globalization of Charismatic Christianity: Spreading the Gospel of Prosperity.* Cambridge: Cambridge University Press, 2000.

Collins, Steven. *Nirvana and Other Buddhist Felicities.* Cambridge: Cambridge University Press, 2009.

———, ed. *Readings of the Vessantara Jātaka.* New York: Columbia University Press, 2016.

Coomaraswamy, A. K. "The Buddha's *Cūḍā,* Hair, Uṣṇīṣa, and Crown." *Journal of the Royal Asiatic Society,* 60, no. 4 (1928): 815–841.

———. "The Origin of the Buddha Image." *Art Bulletin* 9 (1927): 287–328.

———. "Ornament." *Art Bulletin* 21, no. 4 (1939): 375–382.

Cowell, E. B., ed. *The Jātaka or Stories of the Buddha's Former Births,* 6 vols. London: Pali Text Society, 1995.

Cowell, E. B., and R. A. Neil, eds. *Divyāvadāna.* Cambridge: Cambridge University Press, 1886.

Cowherds, The. *Moonshadows: Conventional Truth in Buddhist Philosophy.* New York: Oxford University Press, 2011.

Crooke, William. *The Tribes and Castes of the Western Provinces and Oudh,* vol. 4. Calcutta: Office of the Superintendent of Government Printing, 1896.

Cunningham, Alexander. "Four Reports Made during the Years 1862–63–64–65." *Archaeological Survey of India* 1 (1871): 114–115.

Cüppers, Christoph, Leonard van der Kuijp, and Ulrich Pagel, eds., *Handbook of Tibetan Iconometry.* Leiden: Brill, 2012.

Dalrymple, William, and Anita Anand. *Koh-i-Noor: The Story of the World's Most Famous Diamond.* New York: Bloomsbury, 2017.

Daṇḍin. *The Kávyádarśa of Śrí Daṇḍin.* Edited, with a commentary, by Paṇḍita Premachandra Tarkabágíśa. Calcutta: Asiatic Society of Bengal, 1863. Bibliotheca Indica 40.

Davidson, Ronald M. "Imperial Agency in the Gsar ma Treasure Texts during the Tibetan Renaissance: The *Rgyal po bla gter* and Related Literature." In *Tibetan Buddhist Literature and Praxis: Studies in Its Formative Period, 900–1400,* edited by Ronald M. Davidson and Christian K. Wedemeyer, 125–148. Leiden: Brill, 2006.

———. *Indian Esoteric Buddhism: A Social History of the Tantric Movement.* New York: Columbia University Press, 2002.

Davis, Donald. *The Spirit of Hindu Law.* Cambridge: Cambridge University Press, 2010.

Dawson, Lorne L. "Church–Sect–Cult: Constructing Typologies of Religious Groups." In *The Oxford Handbook of the Sociology of Religion,* edited by Peter B. Clarke. Oxford: Oxford University Press, 2011. DOI: 10.1093/oxfordhb/9780199588961.013.0030.

Dbyug pa can [Daṇḍin]. *Slob dpon dbyug pa can gyis mdzad pa'i snyan ngag me long ma zhes bya ba skad gnyis shan sbyar ba lde ba.* In *Tā'i si tu pa kun mkhyen chos kyi 'byung gnas bstan pa'i nyin byed kyi bka' 'bum,* vol. 6, 629–731=*cha* 1a–52a. Kangra, H. P., India: Sherab Gyaltsen, 1990.

DeCaroli, Robert. *Haunting the Buddha: Indian Popular Religions and the Formation of Buddhism.* New York: Oxford University Press, 2004.

———. *Image Problems: The Origin and Development of the Buddha's Image in Early South Asia.* Seattle: University of Washington Press, 2015.

Deeg, Max. *The Places Where Siddhārtha Trod: Lumbinī and Kapilavastu.* Lumbini: Lumbini International Research Institute, 2003.

Defoe, Daniel. *The Farther Adventures of Robinson Crusoe; Being the Second and Last Part of His Life, and of the Strange Surprizing Accounts of His Travels Round Three Parts of the Globe. Written by Himself. To Which Is Added a Map of the World, in Which Is Delineated the Voyages of Robinson Crusoe.* London, 1719.

Dehejia, Vidya. "Aniconism and the Multivalence of Symbols." *Ars Orientalis* 21 (1991): 45–66.

———. *The Body Adorned: Dissolving Boundaries between Sacred and Profane in India's Art.* New York: Columbia University Press, 2009.

de Jong, Willem. "Review of Lienhard *Maṇicūḍāvadānoddhṛta.*" *Indo-Iranian Journal* 9, no. 1 (1965): 74–75.

d'Entrecolles, François. "Lettre du père d'Entrecolles, missionnaire de la Compagnie de Jésus. In *Lettres édifiantes, et curieuses écrites de missions etrangères.* Lyon: Chez J. Vernarel, 1819.

De Romanis, F. "Aurei after Trade: Western Taxes and Eastern Gift." In *Dal denarius al dinar—L'oriente e la moneta Romana (Atti dell'incontro di studio, Roma 16–18 settembre 2004*), edited by F. De Romanis and S. Sorda, 54–82. Rome: Istituto Italiano di Numismatica, 2006.

Derris, Karen. "When the Buddha Was a Woman: Reimagining Tradition in the Theravāda." *Journal of Feminist Studies in Religion* 24, no. 2 (2008): 29–44.

de Silva, Lily. *Paritta: The Buddhist Ceremony for Peace and Prosperity in Sri Lanka.* Peradeniya: National Museums of Sri Lanka, 1980.

Desi Sangyé Gyatso. *Mirror of Beryl: A Historical Introduction to Tibetan Medicine*, translated by Gavin Kilty. Library of Tibetan Classics 28. Boston: Wisdom Publications, 2010.

Dharmacakra Translation Committee, *The Play in Full* [*Lalitavistara*], 2019. http://read.84000.co/translation/UT22084–046–001.html.

Dhavalikar, M. K. "Environment: Its Influence on History and Culture in Western India." *Indica: Journal of the Heras Institute of Indian History and Culture* 33, no. 2 (1996): 81–118.

Dien, Albert E. *Six Dynasties Civilization.* New Haven, CT: Yale University Press, 2007.

Ding Yingzhong, et al. "Nanjing Bao'en sita liuli jiangou tai yuanliao de keji yanjiu 南京报恩寺塔琉璃构建胎体原料的科技研究." *Zhongguo Taoci China Ceramics* 47, no. 1 (2011): 70–75.

Dohrenwend, Doris. "Glass in China: A Review Based on the Collection in the Royal Ontario Museum." *Oriental Art Richmond-Surrey* 26, no. 4 (1980): 426–446.

Doniger, Wendy. *The Bedtrick: Tales of Sex and Masquerade.* Chicago: University of Chicago Press, 2000.

———, trans. *The Lady of the Jewel Necklace and the Lady Who Shows Her Love.* New York: New York University Press, 2006. Clay Sanskrit Series.

———. *The Ring of Truth: And Other Myths of Sex and Jewelry.* New York: Oxford University Press, 2017.

———. *The Woman Who Pretended to Be Who She Was.* New York: Oxford University Press, 2005.

Doniger O'Flaherty, Wendy. *Textual Sources for the Study of Hinduism.* Chicago: University of Chicago Press, 1990.

Doniger O'Flaherty, Wendy, with Brian K. Smith, trans. *The Laws of Manu.* Harmondsworth: Penguin Books, 1991.

Dorjee, Pema. *Stupa and Its Technology: A Tibeto-Buddhist Perspective.* New Delhi: Indira Gandhi National Centre for the Arts, 1996.

Dumont, Louis. "The Conception of Kingship in Ancient India." *Contributions to Indian Sociology* 6 (1962): 48–77.

Duncan, Jonathan. "An Account of the Discovery of Two Urns in the Vicinity of Benares." *Asiatick Researches* 5 (1801): 131–132.

Earhart, H. Byron. *Gedatsu-Kai and Religion in Contemporary Japan: Returning to the Center.* Bloomington: Indiana University Press, 2000.

———. "Toward a Theory of the Formation of the Japanese New Religions: A Case Study of Gedatsu-Kai." *History of Religions* 20, nos. 1–2 (1980): 175–197.

Eaton, Richard. *The Rise of Islam and the Bengal Frontier 1204–1760*. Berkeley: University of California Press, 1993.

Edwards, Charles. *The History and Poetry of Finger Rings*. New York: John W. Lovell, 1855.

Ehrhard, Franz-Karl. "A Thousand-spoke Golden Wheel of Secular Law: The Preamble to the Law Code of the Kings of gTsang." In *Secular Law and Order in the Tibetan Highland: Contributions to a Workshop Organized by the Tibet Institute in Andiast (Switzerland) on the Occasion of the 65th Birthday of Christoph Cüppers*, edited by Dieter Schuh, 105–125. Andiast: Andiast International Institute for Tibetan and Buddhist Studies, 2016.

Emerson, Julie. *Porcelain Stories*. Seattle: Seattle Art Museum in association with University of Washington Press, 2000.

Emmrich, Christoph. "How Bisvaṃtara Got His Dharma Body: Story, Ritual and the Domestic in the Composition of a Newar Jātaka." *Journal of the American Oriental Society* 132, no. 4 (2012): 539–566.

Eng, Clarence. *Colours and Contrast*. Leiden: Brill, 2015.

Erickson, Susan N. "'Twirling Their Long Sleeves, They Dance Again and Again . . .': Jade Plaque Sleeve Dancers of the Western Han Dynasty." *Ars Orientalis* 24 (1994): 39–63.

Errington, Elizabeth, ed. *Charles Masson and the Buddhist Sites of Afghanistan: Explorations, Excavations, Collections 1833–1835*. London: British Museum, 2017.

Falk, Harry. "The Ashes of the Buddha." *Bulletin of the Asia Institute* 217 (2013; pub. 2017): 43–75.

———. "Money Can Buy Me Heaven: Religious Donations in Late and Post-Kushan India." *Archäologische Mitteilungen aus Iran und Turan* 40 (2008): 137–148.

Fan, Fa-ti. *British Naturalists in Qing China: Science, Empire, and Cultural Encounter*. Cambridge, MA: Harvard University Press, 2004.

Faure, Bernard. "The Buddhist Icon and the Modern Gaze." *Critical Inquiry* 24, no. 3 (1998).

———. "Les cloches de la terre: Un aspect du culte des reliques dans le bouddhisme chinois." In *Bouddhisme et lettrés dans la Chine médiévale*, edited by Catherine Despeux, 25–44. Paris: Peeters, 2002.

———. "Dato." In fasc. 8 of *Hōbōgirin*, 1127–1158. Paris: Adrien Maisonneuve, 2003.

———. *Gods of Medieval Japan*, vol. 1: *The Fluid Pantheon*. Honolulu: University of Hawai'i Press, 2016.

———. "The Impact of Tantrism on Japanese Religious Traditions: The Cult of the Three Devas." In *Transformations and Transfer of Tantra in Asia and Beyond*, edited by Istvan Keul, 399–410. Berlin: DeGruyter, 2012.

———. "A Jewel of a Woman: Medieval Ideology and Wishful Thinking." Paper presented at Yale University, April 1999.

———. "Une perle rare: La 'nonne' Nyoi et l'idéologie médiévale." *Cahiers d'Extrême-Asie* 13 (2002): 177–196.

———. *The Power of Denial: Buddhism, Purity, and Gender.* Princeton, NJ: Princeton University Press, 2003.

———. *The Red Thread: Buddhist Approaches to Sexuality.* Princeton, NJ: Princeton University Press, 1998.

———. "Relics and Flesh Bodies: The Creation of Ch'an Pilgrimage Sites." In *Pilgrims and Sacred Sites in China,* edited by Susan Naquin and Chün-fang Yü, 150–189. Berkeley: University of California Press, 1992.

———. *The Rhetoric of Immediacy: A Cultural Critique of Chan/Zen Buddhism.* Princeton, NJ: Princeton University Press, 1991.

———. *The Will to Orthodoxy: A Critical Genealogy of Northern Chan Buddhism,* Stanford, CA: Stanford University Press, 1997.

Feer, Léon. *Avadāna-çataka: Cent légendes bouddhiques.* Paris: Ernest Leroux, 1891.

Fergusson, James, and James Burgess. *The Cave Temples of India.* Delhi: Oriental Books Reprint Corporation, 1969.

Ferrari, Fabrizio M., and Thomas W. P. Dähnhardt, eds. *Soulless Matter, Seats of Energy: Metals, Gems and Minerals in South Asian Traditions.* Sheffield: Equinox, 2016.

Findly, Ellison Banks. *Dāna: Giving and Getting in Pali Buddhism.* Delhi: Motilal Banarsidass, 2003.

Finlay, Robert. *The Pilgrim Art: Cultures of Porcelain in World History.* Berkeley: University of California Press, 2010.

Finot, Louis. *Les lapidaires indiens.* Paris: Émile Bouillon, 1896.

———. "Recherches sur la littérature laotienne." *Bulletin de l'École Française d'Extrême-Orient* 17 (1917): 1–218.

Fiordalis, David. "Buddhist Miracles in Narrative and Doctrine." *Journal of the International Association of Buddhist Studies* 33 (2010): 381–408.

Fischer von Erlach, Johann Bernhard. *A Plan of Civil and Historical Architecture: In the Representation of the Most Noted Buildings of Foreign Nations, Both Ancient and Modern, Taken from the Most Approv'd Histori-*

ans, Original Medals, Remarkable Ruins, and Curious Authentick Designs and Display'd in Eighty-Six Double Folio-Plates, Finely Engraven, at a very Great Expence, by the Most Eminent Hands, Divided into Five Books, 2nd ed. London: Published at the expence of the translator, and to be had only at his house in Smith's-Square, Westminster, 1737. Electronic reproduction: Farmington Hills, MI: Cengage Gale, 2009.

Fleet, John F. "The Inscription on the Piprawa Vase." *Journal of the Royal Asiatic Society,* 1906, 149–180.

Ford, James L. "Jōkei and Kannon: Defending Buddhist Pluralism in Medieval Japan." *The Eastern Buddhist* 39, no. 1 (2008): 11–28.

Foreign Records of the Bangkok Period up to A.D. 1932: Published on the Occasion of the Rattanakosin Bicentennial 1982. Bangkok: Office of the Prime Minister, 1982.

Foucher, Alfred. *L'art greco-bouddhique du Gandhāra: Étude sur les origines de l'influence classique dans l'art bouddhique de l'Inde et de l'Extrême-Orient.* Paris: Imprimerie Nationale, 1922.

———. *The Beginnings of Buddhist Art, and Other Essays in Indian and Central Asian Archaeology.* Translated by L. A. Thomas and F. W. Thomas. Paris: Paul Geuthner, 1917.

Foulk, Griffith T., and Robert H. Sharf. "On the Ritual Use of Ch'an Portraiture in Medieval China." *Cahiers d'Extrême-Asie* 7 (1993–1994): 149–219.

Fowler, Sherry D. *Accounts and Images of Six Kannon in Japan.* Honolulu: University of Hawai'i Press, 2016.

———. "Nyoirin Kannon" *Orientations* 19, no. 6 (June 1988): 62–65.

Fremerman, Sarah A. 2008. "Divine Impersonations: Nyoirin Kannon in Medieval Japan." PhD diss., Stanford University, 2008.

Fujimaki, Kazuhiro 藤巻 和宏. *Seinaru tama no monogatari: Kūkai, seichi, nyoihōju* 聖なる球の物語：空海•聖地•如意宝珠 [Stories of sacred treasures: Kūkai, sacred sites, and wish-fulfilling jewels]. Bukkuretto: Kakimono wo hiraku 10. Japan: Heibonsha 平凡社, 2017.

Fynes, R. C. C. "The Religious Patronage of the Sātavāhana Dynasty." *South Asian Studies* 11 (1995): 43–50.

Gabriel, Hannelore. *The Jewelry of Nepal.* New York: Weatherhill, 1999.

Ge Yinliang 葛寅亮 (1570–1646). *Jinling fancha zhi* 金陵梵剎志. 1607.

Geary, Patrick J. *Furta Sacra: Thefts of Relics in the Central Middle Ages,* rev. ed. Princeton, NJ: Princeton University Press, 1978, 2011.

Geiger, Wilhelm, trans. *Cūḷavaṃsa,* part 1. London: Pali Text Society, 1973.

Gell, Alfred. *Art and Agency: An Anthropological Theory.* Oxford: Clarendon Press, 1998.

Gellner, David N. *Monk, Householder, and Tantric Priest: Newar Buddhism and Its Hierarchy of Ritual.* Cambridge: Cambridge University Press, 1992.

Gellner, David N., and Declan Quigley, eds. *Contested Hierarchies: A Collaborative Ethnography of Caste among the Newars of the Kathmandu Valley, Nepal.* Oxford: Oxford University Press, 1995.

Gentry, James Duncan. *Power Objects in Tibetan Buddhism: The Life, Writings, and Legacy of Sokdokpa Lodrö Gyeltsen.* Leiden: Brill, 2017.

Germano, David, and Kevin Trainor, eds. *Embodying the Dharma: Buddhist Relic Veneration in Asia.* New York: State University of New York Press, 2004.

Gerow, Edwin. *A Glossary of Indian Figures of Speech.* The Hague: Mouton, 1971.

Gerstenberger, Erhard S. "Non-Temple Psalms: The Cultic Setting Revisited." In *The Oxford Handbook of the Psalms,* edited by William P. Brown. Oxford: Oxford University Press, 2014. DOI: 10.1093/oxfordhb/9780199783335.013.022.

Ghosh, A. *The City in Early Historical India.* Simla: Indian Institute of Advanced Study, 1973.

Giebel, Rolf W., trans. *The Vairocanābhisaṃbodhi Sutra.* Berkeley: Numata Center for Buddhist Translation and Research, 2005.

Gimello, Robert. "Icon and Incantation: The Goddess Zhunti and the Role of Images in the Occult Buddhism of China." In *Images in Asian Religions: Texts and Contexts,* edited by Phyllis Granoff and Koichi Shinohara. Vancouver: UBC Press, 2004.

Gokhale, Balkrishna Govind. "The Merchant in Ancient India." *Journal of the American Oriental Society* 97, no. 2 (1977): 125–130.

Gombrich, E. H. *The Sense of Order: A Study in the Psychology of Decorative Art.* Ithaca, NY: Cornell University Press, 1979.

Gombrich, Richard F. *Precept and Practice: Traditional Buddhism in the Rural Highlands of Ceylon.* Oxford: Clarendon Press, 1971.

———. "The Vessantara Jātaka, the Rāmāyaṇa and the Dasaratha Jātaka." *Journal of the American Oriental Society* 105, no. 3 (1985): 427–437.

Gómez, Luis. *The Land of Bliss.* Honolulu: University of Hawai'i Press, 1997.

———. "Proto-Madhyāmika in the Pāli Canon." *Philosophy East and West* 26, no. 2 (1976): 137–165.

Gonda, Jan. "Ancient Indian Kingship from the Religious Point of View." *Numen* 3, no. 1 (1956): 36–71.

———. "Ancient Indian Kingship from the Religious Point of View (continued)." *Numen* 3, no. 2 (1956): 122–155.

———. "Ancient Indian Kingship from the Religious Point of View (continued and ended)." *Numen* 4, no. 2 (1957): 127–164.

———. "The Meaning of the Word *Alaṃkāra*." In *Selected Studies Presented to the Author by the Staff of the Oriental Institute, Utrecht University, on the Occasion of His 70th Birthday*, vol. 2: *Sanskrit Word Studies*, 257–274. Leiden: Brill, 1975.

Grabar, Oleg. *The Mediation of Ornament*. Princeton, NJ: Princeton University Press, 1992.

Granoff, Phyllis. "The Gift of the Two Merchants: Defining the Buddhist Community through Story." *East and West* 55, nos. 1–4 (2005): 129–138.

———. "Maitreya's Jewelled World: Some Remarks on Gems and Visions in Buddhist Texts." *Journal of Indian Philosophy* 26, no. 4 (1998): 347–371.

———. "Relics, Rubies and Ritual: Some Comments on the Distinctiveness of the Buddhist Relic Cult." *Rivista degli studi orientali, Nuova Serie* 81, nos. 1–4 (2008): 59–72.

———, trans. "The Story of Kuberadatta and Kuberadattā from the *Dharmābhyudāyamahākāvya*." In *Religions of India in Practice*, ed. Donald S. Lopez Jr., 415–417. Princeton, NJ: Princeton University Press, 1995. Princeton Readings in Religion.

Grapard, Allan G. "Of Emperors and Foxy Ladies." *Cahiers d'Extrême-Asie* 13 (2002): 127–149.

———. "Visions of Excess and Excesses of Vision: Women and Transgression in Japanese Myth." *Japanese Journal of Religious Studies* 18, no. 1 (1991): 3–22.

Gray, David B. *The Cakrasamvara Tantra (The Discourse of Śrī Heruka)*. New York: American Institute of Buddhist Studies, 2007.

Grether, Holly. "Burning Demons and Sprinkling Mantras: A History of Fire Sacrifice in South and Central Asia." PhD diss., University of California at Santa Barbara, 2010.

———. "Tantric Homa Rites in the Indo-Iranian Ritual Paradigm." *Journal of Ritual Studies* 21, no. 1 (2007): 16–32.

"Guanyin." In Buswell and Lopez, *The Princeton Dictionary of Buddhism*, 332–333.

Gunawardana, R. A. L. H. "Social Function and Political Power: A Case Study of State Formation in Irrigation Society." In *The Study of the State*, edited by Henri J. M. Claessen and Peter Skalnik, 133–145. The Hague: Mouton, 1981.

Guruge, Ananda. *From the Living Fountains of Buddhism*. Colombo: Department of Cultural Affairs, 1967.

Gutschow, Niels, and Axel Michaels. *Getting Married: Hindu and Buddhist Marriage Rituals among the Newars of Bhaktapur and Patan, Nepal.* Wiesbaden: Harrassowitz Verlag, 2012.

———. *Growing Up: Hindu and Buddhist Initiation Rituals among Newar Children in Bhaktapur, Nepal.* Wiesbaden: Harrassowitz Verlag, 2008.

———. *Handling Death: The Dynamics of Death and Ancestor Rituals among the Newars of Bhaktapur, Nepal.* Wiesbaden: Harrassowitz Verlag, 2005.

Hahn, Michael. *Candragomins Lokānandanāṭaka.* Wiesbaden: Otto Harrassowitz, 1974. Asiatische Forschungen 39.

———, ed. *Der große Legendenkranz (Mahajjātakamālā). Eine mittelalterliche buddhistische Legendensammlung aus Nepal.* Wiesbaden: Otto Harrassowitz, 1985.

Hakeda, Yoshito S., ed. *Kūkai: Major Works.* New York: Columbia University Press, 1972.

Hallisey, Charles. "Devotion in the Medieval Literature of Sri Lanka." PhD diss., University of Chicago, 1988.

Harrison Hall, Jessica. *Catalogue of Late Yuan and Ming Ceramics in the British Museum.* London: British Museum Press, 2001.

Harṣa. *Priyādarśikā.* Edited by V. D. Gadré. Bombay, 1884.

Harṣa. *Ratnāvalī.* Edited by Ashokanath Bhattacharya and Maheshwar Das. Calcutta: Modern Book Agency, 1967.

Hay, Jonathan. "The Passage of the Other: Elements for a Redefinition of Ornament." In Necipoğlu and Payne, *Histories of Ornament,* 62–69.

———. *Sensuous Surfaces: The Decorative Object in Early Modern China.* Honolulu: University of Hawai'i Press, 2010.

Heesterman, J. C. *The Ancient Indian Royal Consecration: The Rājasūya Described According to the Yasju Texts and Annotated.* The Hague: Mouton, 1957.

Heim, Maria. "The Aesthetics of Excess." *Journal of the American Academy of Religion* 71, no. 3 (2003): 531–554.

———. *The Voice of the Buddha: Buddhaghosa on the Immeasurable Words.* New York: Oxford University Press, 2018.

Heitzman, James. "Early Buddhism, Trade and Empire." In *Studies in the Archaeology and Palaeoanthropology of South Asia,* edited by Kenneth A. R. Kennedy and Gregory L. Possehl, 121–137. Oxford: IBH Publishing, 1984.

———. "The Urban Context of Early Buddhist Monuments in South Asia." In *Buddhist Stūpas in South Asia: Recent Archaeological, Art-Historical, and Historical Perspectives,* edited by Jason Hawkes and Akira Shimada, 192–215. Delhi: Oxford University Press, 2009.

Hertel, Christiane. *Siting China in Germany: Eighteenth-Century Chinoiserie and Its Modern Legacy.* University Park, PA: Pennsylvania State University Press, 2019.

Hiltebeitel, Alf, and Barbra D. Miller, eds. *Hair: Its Power and Meaning in Asian Cultures.* New York: SUNY, 1998.

Honour, Hugh. *Chinoiserie.* New York: Dutton, 1962.

Hori, Ichirō. *Folk Religion in Japan: Continuity and Change.* Chicago: University of Chicago Press, 1968. Haskell Lectures on History of Religions 1.

———. "Shamanism in Japan." *Japanese Journal of Religious Studies* 2, no. 4 (1975): 231–287.

House of Resolve. Tokyo: International Affairs Department of Shinnyo-en, 2001.

Huang, Ellen. "An Art of Transformation: Reproducing *Yaobian* Glazes in Qing-Dynasty Porcelain." *Archives of Asian Art* 68, no. 2 (2018): 133–156.

———. "From the Imperial Court to the International Art Market: Jingdezhen Porcelain Production as Global Visual Culture." *Journal of World History* 23, no. 1 (2012): 115–145.

Huang, Ellen, and Mary Lewine. "Ineffable Gloss: Qing Ornament on Porcelain." In *Water Moon Reflections: Essays in Honor of Patricia Berger,* edited by Ellen Huang, Nancy G. Lin, Michelle McCoy, and Michelle H. Wang. Berkeley: IEAS Publications, forthcoming.

Huijiao 慧皎. *Gao seng zhuan* 高僧傳. Beijing: Beijing Zhonghua shuju, 1991. UNESCO Collection of Representative Works: Japanese Series, No. 87.

Hung, Wu. *Monumentality.* Stanford, CA: Stanford University Press, 1995.

———. "Rethinking Liu Sahe." *Orientations* 11 (1996): 32–33.

Huntington, Susan L. "Aniconism and the Multivalence of Emblems: Another Look." *Ars Orientalis* 22 (1992): 111–156.

———. "Early Buddhist Art and the Theory of Aniconism." *Art Journal* 49 (1990): 401–408.

Hurvitz, Leon. *Scripture of the Lotus Blossom of the Fine Dharma,* 272; in T., no. 262, vol. 9, 53c14–15.

Huxley, Andrew. "Dr Führer's *Wanderjahre:* The Early Career of a Victorian Archaeologist." *Journal of the Royal Asiatic Society* 20 (2010): 489–502.

———. "Who Should Pay for Indological Research? The Debate between 1884 and 1914." *Berliner Indologische Studien/Berlin Indological Studies* 22 (2015): 49–86.

Ibrahim, M. *Merchant Capital and Islam.* Austin: University of Texas Press, 1990.

Inden, Ronald. "Ritual, Authority, and Cyclic Time in Hindu Kingship." In *Kingship and Authority in South Asia,* edited by J. F. Richards, 41–91. Delhi: Oxford University Press, 1998.

Ishihama, Yumiko. "The Dalai Lama as the *Cakravarti-rāja* as Manifested by the Bodhisattva Avalokiteśvara." *Cahiers d'Extrême-Asie* 24 (2015): 169–188.

———. "On the Dissemination of the Belief in the Dalai Lamas as a Manifestation of the Bodhisattva Avalokiteśvara." *Acta Asiatica* 64 (1993): 38–56.

Itō, Shinjō. *The Light in Each Moment,* English rev. ed. Tokyo: International Affairs Department of Shinnyo-en, 2010.

———. "Untitled Sermon from a Monthly Feast of Bezaiten." Unpublished manuscript. Tokyo, 1979.

———. "Untitled Sermon from a Monthly Feast of Eternal Bliss." Unpublished manuscript. Tokyo, 1977.

———. "Untitled Sermon from the Spring Higan Service." Unpublished manuscript. Tokyo, 2011.

Jacobson, Doranne. "Women and Jewelry in Rural India." In *Women in India: Two Perspectives,* edited by Doranne Jacobson and Susan S. Wasley, 171–223. New Delhi: Manohar, 1999 (1977).

Jaffe, Richard M. "Buddhist Material Culture, 'Indianism,' and the Construction of Pan-Asian Buddhism in Prewar Japan." *Material Religion* 2, no. 3 (2006): 266–292.

Jakobson, Roman. "On Linguistic Aspects of Translation." In *On Translation,* edited by R. A. Brower, 232–239. Cambridge, MA: Harvard University Press, 1959.

Jayawickrama, N. A., trans. *The Sheaf of Garlands of the Epochs of the Conqueror: Being a Translation of the Jīnakālamālīpakaraṇaṃ.* London: Pali Text Society, 1978.

———, trans. *The Story of Gotama Buddha* [*Jātaka-nidāna*]. Oxford: Pali Text Society, 1990.

Jenner, W. J. F. *Memories of Loyang: Yang Hsüan-chih and the Lost Capital (493–534).* Oxford: Clarendon Press, 1981.

Jinaratna. *The Epitome of Queen Lilávati,* 2 vols. Translated by Richard Fynes. New York: NYU Press, 2006. Clay Sanskrit Library.

Jinavaravaṃsa, Prisdang Chumsai. "The Ratna Chetiya Dīpaduttamārāma, Colombo." Edited by Sumet Jumsai. *Journal of the Royal Asiatic Society of Sri Lanka* 48 (2003): 213–236.

Jones, Christine. *Shapely Bodies: The Image of Porcelain in Eighteenth-Century France.* Newark: University of Delaware Press, 2013.

Jones, J. J., trans. *The Mahāvastu,* 3 vols. London: Pali Text Society, 1976, 1978, 1987. Sacred Books of the Buddhists.

Kalafas, Philip. *In Limpid Dream: Nostalgia in Zhang Dai's Reminiscences of the Ming*. Manchester: EastBridge Books, 2007.

Karma pa III Rang byung rdo rje. *The Tibetan Rendering of the Jātakamālā of Āryaśūra, Supplemented with Sixty-Seven Additional Jātaka Stories,* 2 vols. Darjeeling: Kargyud Sungrab Nyamso Khang, 1974.

Karmay, Samten G. "The Soul and the Turquoise: A Ritual for Recalling the *bla*." In *The Arrow and the Spindle: Studies in History, Myths, Rituals and Beliefs in Tibet,* 310–338. Kathmandu: Mandala Book Point, 1998.

Kathāsaritsāgara of Somadevabhaṭṭa [The ocean of the rivers of story]. Bombay: Nirnaya Sagara Press, 1930.

Kaushik, Garima. *Women and Monastic Buddhism in Early South Asia: Rediscovering the Invisible Believers.* Abington: Routledge, 2016.

Kawaguchi Kōfū 川口高風. "Kakuōzan no sōken ni tsuite 覚王山ノ創建について" [About the foundation of Kakuōzan (i.e., the Nittaiji)]. *Journal of Aichi Gakuin University, Humanities and Sciences* 49 (2001): 3–26.

Kenderdine, Sarah. "Pure Land: Inhabiting the Mogao Caves at Dunhuang." *Curator: The Museum Journal* 56, no. 2 (2013): 199–218.

Kiely, Jan. 2016. "The Charismatic Monk and the Chanting Masses: Master Yinguang and His Pure Land Revival Movement." In *Making Saints in Modern China,* edited by David Ownby, Vincent Goossaert, and Ji Zhe, 30–77. Oxford: Oxford University Press, 2016.

Kieschnick, John. *The Eminent Monk: Buddhist Ideals in Medieval Chinese Hagiography.* Honolulu: University of Hawai'i Press, 1997.

———. *The Impact of Buddhism on Chinese Material Culture.* Princeton, NJ: Princeton University Press, 2003.

Kieschnick, John, and Meir Shahar, eds. *India in the Chinese Imagination: Myth, Religion, and Thought,* 141–170. Philadelphia: University of Pennsylvania Press, 2014.

Kinsey, Danielle C. "Koh-i-Noor: Empire, Diamonds, and the Performance of British Material Culture." *Journal of British Studies* 48, no. 2 (2009): 391–419.

Kiyota, Minoru. *Shingon Buddhism: Theory and Practice.* Los Angeles: Buddhist Books International, 1978.

Koerner, Joseph. "On Monuments." *Res: Anthropology and Aesthetics* 67 and 68 (2017): 5–20.

Kohn, Livia, and Russell Kirkland. "Daoism in the Tang (618–907)." In *Daoism Handbook,* edited by Livia Kohn, 339–383. Leiden: Brill, 2000.

Kölver, Ulrike, and Iswarananda Shresthacarya, eds. *A Dictionary of Contemporary Newari. Newari—English* (with the assistance of Daya Ratna Sakya and Nirmal Man Tuladhar, edited by Bernhard Kölver and Siegfried Lienhard). Vol. 8: *Nepalica*. Sankt Augustin: VGH Wissenschaftsverlag, 1994.

Konow, Sten. *Kharoṣṭhī Inscriptions with the Exception of Those of Aśoka*. New Delhi: Director General, Archaeological Survey of India, 1991 (1929). Corpus Inscriptionum Indicarum, vol. 2, part 1.

Kosambi, D. D. *The Culture and Civilization of Ancient India in Historical Outline*. Delhi: Vikas Publishing, 1997.

Kubo, Tsugunari, and Akira Yuyama, trans. *The Lotus Sutra* (*Taishō*, vol. 9, no. 262). Revised 2nd ed. Berkeley: Numata Center for Buddhist Translation and Research, 2007.

LaFleur, William R. *Liquid Life: Abortion and Buddhism in Japan*. Princeton, NJ: Princeton University Press, 1994.

Laidlaw, James. *Riches and Renunciation: Religion, Economy, and Society among the Jains*. New York: Oxford University Press, 1995.

Lama Kunsang, et al. *History of the Karmapas: The Odyssey of the Tibetan Masters with the Black Crown*. Ithaca, NY: Snow Lion, 2012.

Lane, Kris. *Colour of Paradise: The Emerald in the Age of Gunpowder Empires*. New Haven: Yale University Press, 2010.

Latour, Bruno. *Reassembling the Social*. Oxford: Oxford University Press, 2007.

Laurent, Yannick. "An Important Documentary Tibetan Gilt-Inscribed Jade River Pebble 'Kapala' Box and Cover." In *Water, Pine and Stone Retreat Collection: Treasures*, 54–63. Hong Kong: Sotheby's, October 3, 2017.

The Laws of Manu [*Manusmṛti*]. Edited by Harikrishna Jayantakrishna Dave. Bombay: Bharatiya Vidya Bhavan, 1972–1985.

Le Comte, Louis. *A Compleat History of the Empire of China: Being the Observations of Above Ten Years Travels through That Country: Containing Memoirs and Remarks, Geographical, Historical, Topographical, Physical, Natural, Astronomical, Mechanical, Military, Mercantile, Political, and Ecclesiastical. Written by the Learned Lewis Le Comte, Confessor to the Dutchess of Burgundy, and One of the French King's Mathematicians, Who Was a Missioner in China Near Twenty Years. A New Translation from the Best Paris Edition, and Adorn'd with Copper-Plates. The Second Edition Carefully Corrected*. London, 1739. Eighteenth-Century Collections Online. Gale. Stanford Libraries.

Lee, Sonya S. *Surviving Nirvana: Death of the Buddha in Chinese Visual Culture*. Hong Kong: Hong Kong University Press, 2010.

Leng Mei 冷媚, "Mingdai Bao'en si liuli ta fenxi 明代报恩寺琉璃宝塔探析." *Wenwu jianding yu jianshang* 12 (2016): 56–57.

Lévi, Sylvain. "L'Inde ancienne." *Journal des savants,* 1905, 534–548.

Lévi-Strauss, Claude. *The Elementary Structures of Kinship.* Boston: Beacon Press, 1971.

———. *Structural Anthropology.* Translated by Claire Jacobson and Brooke Grundfest Schoepf. Harmondsworth: Penguin, 1963.

Lewis, Todd T., and Subarna Man Tuladhar, eds. and trans. *Sugata Saurabha: An Epic Poem from Nepal on the Life of the Buddha by Chittadhar Hṛdaya. Annotated Newari-English Translation and Introduction.* Cambridge, MA: Harvard University Press, 2007.

Lienhard, Siegfried. *Die Legende vom Prinzen Viśvantara. Eine nepalesische Bilderrolle aus der Sammlung des Museums für Indische Kunst Berlin.* Berlin: Museum für Indische Kunst Berlin, 1980. Veröffentlichungen des Museums für Indische Kunst Berlin, vol. 5.

———. *Maṇicūḍāvadānoddhṛta: A Buddhist Re-Birth Story in the Nevārī Language.* Stockholm: Almqvist and Wiksell, 1963.

———. "The Monastery and the Secular World: Saṅgha-Buddhism and Caste-Buddhism." *Journal of the American Oriental Society* 11 (1989): 593–596.

———. *Nevārīgītimañjarī: Religious and Secular Poetry of the Nevars of the Kathmandu Valley,* vol. 10. Acta Universitatis Stockholmiensis. Stockholm Oriental Series. Stockholm: Almqvist and Wiskell, 1974.

Lin, Nancy G. "Recounting the Fifth Dalai Lama's Rebirth Lineage." *Revue d'Études Tibétaines* 38 (February 2017): 119–156.

Lingat, Robert. "Le culte du Bouddha d'Émeraude." *Journal of the Siam Society* 27, no. 1 (1934): 9–38.

Lippiello, Tiziana. *Auspicious Omens and Miracles in Ancient China: Han, Three Kingdoms and Six Dynasties.* Leiden: Brill, 1995.

Little, Stephen. *Visions of Dharma: Japanese Buddhist Paintings and Prints in the Honolulu Academy of Arts.* Honolulu: Honolulu Academy of Arts, 1991.

Liu Changdong 劉長東. *Jin Tang Mitojing xingyang yenjiu* 晉唐彌陀淨土信仰研究 [Study of the belief in Amitābya in the Jin and Tang periods]. Chengdu: Bashu, 2000.

Liu Hongxiao 刘鸿孝. *Gsang ba kun 'dus pho brang po ta la / 布达拉宫秘宝/* [Gems of the Potala Palace]. Beijing: Krung go'i mi rigs par ris sgyu rtsal dpe skrun khang, 1999.

Liu, Lydia. "Robinson Crusoe's Earthenware." *Critical Inquiry* 25, no. 4 (Summer 1999): 728–757.

Liu Lizhong. *Buddhist Art of the Tibetan Plateau.* Hong Kong: Joint Publishing, 1988.

———. *Translingual Practice: Literature, Culture and Translated Modernity, China 1900–1937.* Stanford, CA: Stanford University Press, 1995.

Liu, Shufen. "Death and the Degeneration of Life: Exposure of the Corpse in Medieval Chinese Buddhism." *Journal of Chinese Religion* 28 (2000): 1–30.

Liu, Xinru. *Ancient India and Ancient China: Trade and Religious Exchanges AD 1–600.* Delhi: Oxford University Press, 1988.

Li Zhu 李竹. "Jinlun song riyue fengduo hong qianli—Mingdai da Bao'en sita wenwu shiyi 金輪聳日月風鐸鳴千里——明代大報恩寺塔文物拾遺." *Wenwu yanjiu* 3, no. 121 (1998): 122–125.

Locke, John K. *Buddhist Monasteries of Nepal: A Survey of the Bāhās and Bahīs of the Kathmandu Valley.* Kathmandu: Sahayogi Press, 1985.

Lokuliyana, Lionel, trans. *The Great Book of Protections.* Singapore: Singapore Buddhist Meditation Centre, 1975.

Long, Christopher. "The Origins and Context of Adolf Loos's 'Ornament and Crime.'" *Journal of the Society of Architectural Historians* 68, no. 2 (June 2009): 200–223.

Loos, Adolf. "Ornament and Crime." In *Ornament and Crime: Selected Essays,* translated by Michael Mitchell, 167–176. Riverside, CA: Ariadne Press, 1998.

Loos, Tamara. *Bones around My Neck: The Life and Exile of a Prince Provocateur.* Ithaca, NY: Cornell University Press, 2016.

Lopez, Donald S., Jr. *Prisoners of Shangri-La: Tibetan Buddhism and the West.* Chicago: University of Chicago Press, 1998.

Lüders, Heinrich. *List of Brahmi Inscriptions from the Earliest Times to about A.D. 400 with the Exception of Those of Aśoka.* Appendix to *Epigraphia Indica,* vol. 10. Edited by Sten Konow. Calcutta, 1912.

Lun, Tam Wai. "The Tantric Teachings and Rituals of the True Buddha School: The Chinese Transformation of Vajrayāna Buddhism." In *Tantric Traditions in Transmission and Translation,* edited by David B. Gray and Ryan Richard Overbey, 308–335. New York: Oxford University Press, 2016.

MacCormack, Ian. "Buddhism and State in Seventeenth-Century Tibet: Cosmology and Theology in the Works of Sangyé Gyatso." PhD diss., Harvard University, 2018.

Mackenzie, Vicki. "Buried with the Buddha." *Sunday Times Magazine* (London), March 21, 2008. Reproduced at http://piprahwajewels.co.uk/page7.html.

MacWilliams, Mark W. "Temple Myths and the Popularization of Kannon Pilgrimage in Japan: A Case Study of Ōya-ji on the Bandō Route." *Japanese Journal of Religious Studies* 24, nos. 3–4 (1997): 375–411.

Mahābhārata of Vyāsa. Poona: Bhandarkar Oriental Research Institute, 1933–1969.

"Mahāvairocanābhisaṃbodhisūtra." In Buswell and Lopez, *The Princeton Dictionary of Buddhism,* 511–512.

Maity, Pradyot Kumar. *Historical Studies in the Cult of the Goddess Manasa: A Socio-Cultural Study.* Calcutta: Punthi Pustak, 1966.

Maity, S. K. *Economic Life of Northern India.* Calcutta: World Press, 1957.

Malalasekera, G. P. *Dictionary of Pāli Proper Names,* 3 vols. Oxford: Pali Text Society, 1997.

———. *The Pāli Literature of Ceylon.* Kandy: Buddhist Publication Society, 1994.

Malamoud, Charles. "The Theology of Debt in Brahmanism." In *Debts and Debtors,* edited by Charles Malamoud, 21–40. London: Vices, 1983.

Māli, Indra, ed. *Nepālbhāṣā taḥkhaṁgvaḥdhukū* [Practical Nepal Bhasa dictionary]. Yeṁ: Nepālbhāṣā ākādemiyā niṃtiṃ, 1130 NS (2009/10 CE).

Malla, Kamal P., et al., eds. *A Dictionary of Classical Newari Compiled from Manuscript Sources.* Kathmandu: Nepal Bhasa Dictionary Committee, 2000.

Manandhar, Sushila. "Bijoux et parures traditionnels des Néwar au Népal: Une approche anthropologique et historique." PhD diss., Université de Paris X, 1998.

Manandhar, Thakur Lal, and Anne Vergati, eds. *Newari-English Dictionary: Modern Language of the Kathmandu Valley.* Delhi: Agam Kala Prakashan, 1986.

Manich Jumsai, M. L. *Prince Prisdang's Files on His Diplomatic Activities in Europe, 1880–1886.* Bangkok: Chalermnit, 1977.

Martin, Dan. "Pearls from Bones: Relics, Chortens, Tertons and the Signs of Saintly Death in Tibet." *Numen* 41 (1994): 273–323.

———. "Tables of Contents (*dKar chag*)." In *Tibetan Literature: Studies in Genre,* edited by José Ignacio Cabezón and Roger R. Jackson, 500–514. Ithaca, NY: Snow Lion, 1996.

Masuzawa, Tomoko. *The Invention of World Religions: Or, How European Universalism Was Preserved in the Language of Pluralism.* Chicago: University of Chicago Press, 2005.

Mayer, R. "Observations on the Tibetan Phur-ba and the Indian Kīla." In *The Buddhist Forum,* edited by Tadeusz Skorupski, 2:163–192. London: School of Oriental and African Studies, 1991.

McClintock, Sara. "Compassionate Trickster: The Buddha as a Literary Character in the Narratives of Early Indian Buddhism." *Journal of the American Academy of Religion* 79, no. 1 (2011): 90–112.

McCoy Owens, Bruce. "The Politics of Divinity in the Kathmandu Valley: The Festival of Bungadya/Matsyendranath." PhD diss., Columbia University, 1989.

McDaniel, Justin. *The Lovelorn Ghost and the Magical Monk: Practicing Buddhism in Modern Thailand.* New York: Columbia University Press, 2011.

———. "*Paritta* and *Rakṣā* Texts." In Buswell, *Encyclopedia of Buddhism,* 634–635.

Mcleod Higgins, Ian. *Writing East: The "Travels" of Sir John Mandeville.* Philadelphia: University of Pennsylvania Press, 1997.

Mehta, Suketu. *Maximum City: Bombay Lost and Found.* New York: Vintage, 2004.

Mengele, Irmgard. "The Artist's Life." In *The Black Hat Eccentric: Artistic Visions of the Tenth Karmapa,* edited by Karl Debreczeny, 33–63. New York: Rubin Museum of Art, 2012.

Meskell, Lynn. *A Future in Ruins.* Oxford: Oxford University Press, 2018.

Mill, J. S. *August Comte and Positivism.* London: Kegan Paul, Trench, Trubner, 1891 (1865).

Miller, Tracy. "Perfecting the Mountain: On the Morphology of Towering Temples in East Asia." *Journal of Chinese Architecture History* 10 (2014): 419–449.

———. "Translating the *ta:* Pagoda, Tumulus, and Ritualized Mahāyāna in Seventh-Century China." *Tang Studies,* 2018, 82–120.

Mirashi, Vasudev Vishnu. *The History and Inscriptions of the Sātavāhanas and the Western Kshatrapas.* Bombay: Maharashtra State Board for Literature and Culture, 1981.

Mitra, Debala. *Sanchi.* New Delhi: Archaeological Survey of India, 1992 (1957).

Mitra, R. L. trans. *The Lalita-Vistara: Memoirs of the Early Life of Sakya Sinha* (chs. 1–15). New Delhi: Sri Satguru, 1998.

Miyake, Hitoshi. *Shugendō: Essays on the Structure of Japanese Folk Religion,* edited by H. Byron Earhart. Ann Arbor: Center for Japanese Studies, University of Michigan, 2001. Michigan Monograph Series in Japanese Studies, no. 32.

Moerman, D. Max. *Localizing Paradise: Kumano Pilgrimage and the Religious Landscape of Premodern Japan.* Cambridge, MA: Harvard University Press, 2005.

Mollier, Christine. *Buddhism and Taoism Face to Face: Scripture, Ritual, and Iconographic Exchange in Medieval China.* Honolulu: University of Hawai'i Press, 2008.

Monier-Williams, M. *A Sanskrit-English Dictionary.* Delhi: Motilal Banarsidass, 1997.

Morrison, Kathleen. "Commerce and Culture in South Asia: Perspectives from Archaeology and History." *Annual Review of Anthropology* 26 (1997): 87–108.

———. "Trade, Urbanism, and Agricultural Expansion: Buddhist Monastic Institutions and the State in Early Historic Western Deccan." *World Archaeology* 27, no. 2 (1995): 203–221.

Moto-Sanchez, Milla Micka. "Jizō, Healing Rituals, and Women in Japan." *Japanese Journal of Religious Studies* 43, no. 2 (2016): 307–331.

Mrozik, Susanne. "Astonishment: A Study of an Ethically Valorized Emotion in Buddhist Narrative Literature." In *Embedded Languages: Studies of Sri Lankan and Buddhist Cultures, Essays in Honour of W. S. Karunatilllake,* edited by Carol S. Anderson et al., 261–288. Colombo: Godage International, 2012.

Mukherjee, B. N. *The Economic Factors in Kushana History.* Calcutta: Pilgrim Publishers, 1970.

Mukherjee, Sraman. "'Bones . . . Have No Value!': Evaluating Buddhist Relics in South and Mainland Southeast Asia." Unpublished manuscript, 2015.

———. "Relics in Transition: Material Mediations in Changing Worlds." *Ars Orientalis* 48 (2018): 20–42.

———. "Transmissions, Translations, Reconstitutions: Revisiting Geographies of Buddha Relics in the Southern Asian Worlds." In *Imagining Asia(s): Networks, Actors, Sites,* edited by Andrea Acri, Kashshaf Ghani, Murari Jha, and Sraman Mukherjee. Singapore: ISEAS, forthcoming.

Muller, Charles. "Nyoi 如意." In *Digital Dictionary of Buddhism.* buddhism-dict.net, 2017.

———. "Nyoiju 如意珠." In *Digital Dictionary of Buddhism.* buddhism-dict.net, 2009.

———. "Dōji 童子." In *Digital Dictionary of Buddhism.* buddhism-dict.net, 2018a.

———. "Sanbō 三寶." In *Digital Dictionary of Buddhism.* buddhism-dict.net, 2018b.

Murthy, S. R. N. *Gemmological Studies in Sanskrit Texts.* Bangalore: Sri N. Subbaiah Setty, 1990.

Mus, Paul. "Le Buddha paré, son origine indienne, Çākyamuni dans le Mahāyānisme moyen" *Bulletin de l'École Française d'Extrême-Orient* 28, no. 1 (1928): 153–278.

Nakasone, Ronald Y., and Heather Emi Nakasone. "The Diaspora of the Corporeal Remains of Lord Buddha." *Journal of Religion and Culture* 8 (2014): 169–178.

Nanayakkara, Rasika. "Exposition of the Sacred Kapilavastu Relics at Sri Subhuti Maha Viharaya, Waskaduwa." *The Island* (Colombo), January 25, 2013.

Nanjing Municipal Institute of Archaeology 南京市考古究所. "The Excavation of the Pagoda Foundation and Lower Crypt of the Grand Bao'en Temple in Nanjing City 南京大報恩寺遺址塔基與地宮發掘簡報." *Wenwu* 5 (2015): 4–52.

Nanjing Municipal Museum 南京博物院. "Mingdai Nanjing Jubaoshan liuli yao 明代南京聚寶山琉璃窯." *Wenwu* 2 (1960): 41–48.

Necipoğlu, Gülru, and Alina Payne, eds. *Histories of Ornament: From Global to Local.* Princeton, NJ: Princeton University Press, 2016.

Neelis, Jason. *Early Buddhist Transmission and Trade Networks: Mobility and Exchange within and beyond the Northwestern Borderlands of South Asia.* Leiden: Brill, 2011.

Ngag dbang blo bzang rgya mtsho, Tā la'i bla ma V. *Rgyal dbang lnga pa ngag dbang blo bzang rgya mtsho'i gsung 'bum* [Collected works of the fifth victorious Lord Ngawang Lobzang Gyatso], 28 vols. Beijing: Krung go'i bod rig pa dpe skrun khang, 2009.

Nicholson, Andrew. *Unifying Hinduism: Philosophy and Identity in Indian Intellectual History.* New York: Columbia University Press, 2010.

Nieuhoff, Johannes, Pieter de Goyer, Jacob de Keizer, and John Ogilby. *An Embassy from the East-India Company of the United Provinces, to the Grand Tartar Cham, Emperor of China,* 2nd ed. London: Printed by the author at his house in White-Friers, 1669.

Nornang, Ngawang L. "Monastic Organization and Economy at Dwags-po Bshad-grub-gling." In *Reflections on Tibetan Culture: Essays in Memory of Turrell V. Wylie,* edited by Lawrence Epstein and Richard F. Sherburne, 249–268. Lewiston, NY: Edwin Mellen Press, 1990. Studies in Asian Thought and Religion 12.

Ogden, Jack. "Report on the Beads and Related Objects from the Piprahwa Stupa" (2018). http://www.piprahwa.com/analysis.

Olivelle, Patrick. "Hair and Society: Social Significance of Hair in South Asian Traditions." In *Language, Texts, and Society: Explorations in Ancient Indian Culture and Religion,* edited by Patrick Olivelle, 321–350. Cambridge: Cambridge University Press, 2011.

———, trans. *Life of the Buddha by Ashvaghosha.* New York: New York University Press, 2008. Clay Sanskrit Library.

———, ed. and trans. *Manu's Code of Law: A Critical Edition and Translation of the Mānava-Dharmáśāstra.* New York: Oxford University Press, 2005.

Ollett, Andrew. *Language of Snakes: Prakrit, Sanskrit, and the Language Order of Premodern India.* Berkeley: University of California Press, 2017.

———. "Making It Nice: Kāvya in the Second Century." *Journal of Indian Philosophy* 47 (2019): 269–287.

Pakhoutova, Elena. "Reproducing the Sacred Places: The Eight Great Events of the Buddha's Life and Their Commemorative Stūpas in the Medieval Art of Tibet (10th–13th Century)." PhD diss., University of Virginia, 2009.

Pal, Pratapaditya. "The Iconography of Cintāmaṇi Cakra Avalokiteśvara." *Journal of the Indian Society of Oriental Art* 2 (1967–1968): 39–48.

Parthasarathy, R., trans. *The Tale of an Anklet: An Epic of South India (The Cilappatikaram of Ilanko Atikal)*. New York: Columbia University Press, 1993.

The Path of Oneness. English rev. ed. Tokyo: International Affairs Department of Shinnyo-en, 2009.

Payne, Richard K. "Aparimitāyus: 'Tantra' *and* 'Pure Land,' in Medieval Indian Buddhism?" *Pacific World*, 3rd series, no. 9 (2007): 273–308.

———. "Homa: Tantric Fire Ritual." In *Oxford Research Encyclopedias, Religion*. New York: Oxford University Press, 2016. DOI:10.1093/acrefore/9780199340378.013.82.

———. *Language in the Buddhist Tantra of Japan: Indic Roots of Mantra*. London: Bloomsbury, 2018.

Payutto, Prayudh. *Buddhist Economics: A Middle Way for the Market Place*, 2nd ed., revised and enlarged. Bangkok: Buddhadhamma Foundation, 1995.

Pearce, Nick. "A Chinese Export Porcelain Pagoda." *Orientations* 18, no. 10 (1987): 38.

Penzer, N. M., ed. *Kathāsaritsāgara of Somadevabhaṭṭa* [The ocean of the rivers of story], 10 vols. Translated C. W. Tawney. London: C. J. Sawyer, 1924–1928.

Peppé, William Claxton. "The Piprāhwā Stūpa Containing Relics of Buddha." *Journal of the Royal Asiatic Society of Great Britain and Ireland*, 1898: 573–588.

Petech, Luciano. *China and Tibet in the Early XVIIIth Century*, rev. ed. Leiden: Brill, 1972.

Phelps, Terence A. "The Piprahwa Deceptions: Set-Ups and Showdown." http://piprahwa.org.uk/ThePiprahwaDeceptions.htm.

Phuntsok Namgyal. *Splendor of Tibet: The Potala Palace*. Dumont, NJ: Homa and Sekey Books in association with Encyclopedia of China Publishing House, 2002.

Pierson, Stacey. *From Object to Concept: Global Consumption and Transformation of Ming Porcelain*. Hong Kong: Hong Kong University Press, 2013.

Pingcuo Cidan 平措次旦. "Bu da la gong nei de wu shi da lai ling ta 布达拉宫内的五世达赖灵塔." *Wenwu* 文物 9 (1985): 95–96.

Pischel, Richard. "Die Inschrift von Piprāva." *Zeitschrift der deutschen morgenländischen Gesellschaft* 56 (1902): 157–158.

Pollard, A. M. "Letters from China: A History of the Origins of the Chemical Analysis of Ceramics." *Ambix* 62, no. 1 (2015): 50–71.

Pollard, A. W., ed. *The Travels of Sir John Mandeville*. London: Macmillan, 1900.

Pollock, Sheldon. *The Language of the Gods in the World of Men: Sanskrit, Culture, and Power in Premodern India*. Berkeley: University of California Press, 2006.

Pollock, Sydney. "The Divine King in the Indian Epic." *Journal of the American Oriental Society* 104, no. 3 (1984): 505–528.

Porter, David. *The Chinese Taste in Eighteenth-Century England*. Cambridge: Cambridge University Press, 2010.

———. "Chinoiserie and the Aesthetics of Illegitimacy." *Studies in Eighteenth-Century Culture* 28 (1999): 27–54.

Prip-Møller, Johannes. *Chinese Buddhist Monasteries: Their Plan and Function as a Setting for Buddhist Monastic Life*. Hong Kong: Hong Kong University Press, 1967.

Puri, B. N. *India under the Kushanas*. Bombay: Bharatiya Vidya Bhavan, 1965.

Rackham, H., trans. *Natural History*, by Pliny, 10 vols. Cambridge, MA: Harvard University Press, 1956–1962.

Ramanujan, A. K. *A Flowering Tree, and Other Oral Tales from India*. Berkeley: University of California Press, 1997.

———. "Three Hundred Ramayanas: Five Examples and Three Thoughts on Translation." In *The Collected Essays of A. K. Ramanujan*, 131–160. New Delhi: Oxford University Press, 1999.

Rambelli, Fabio. *Buddhist Materiality: A Cultural History of Objects in Japanese Buddhism*. Stanford, CA: Stanford University Press, 2007.

———. "The Emperor's New Robes: Processes of Resignification in Shingon Imperial Rituals." *Cahiers d'Extrême-Asie* 13 (2002–2003): 427–453.

Rañjitkār, Junu Bāsukalā. *Bhaktapurko Pañcadān Parva (Saṃskṛtibāre Viśleṣaṇātmak Adhyayan)*. Kāṭhmāḍauṃ and Lalitpur: Nhūjaḥ guṭhī samāj; Bauddha adhyayan samāj Nepāl, 2007 (NS 1127, VS 2064).

Raschke, Manfred. "New Studies in Roman Commerce with the East." In *Aufstieg und Niedergang der römischen Welt: Geschichte und Kultur Roms im Spiegel der neueren Forschung*, vol. 2.9.2, 604–1361. New York: W. de Gruyter, 1978.

Ratnagotravibhāga Mahāyānottaratantraśāstra. Edited by E. H. Johnston. Patna: Bihar Research Society, 1950.

Rawlinson, Andrew. "Studies in the Lotus Sutra [Saddharmapuṇḍarīka]." PhD diss., University of Lancaster, 1972.

Ray, Himanshu Prabha. *Monastery and Guild: Commerce under the Sātavāhanas*. Delhi: Oxford University Press, 1986.

———. *The Return of the Buddha: Ancient Symbols for a New Nation*. London: Routledge, 2014.

Reader, Ian. "The Rise of a Japanese 'New New Religion': Themes in the Development of Agonshu." *Japanese Journal of Religious Studies* 15, no. 4 (1988): 235–261.

Reed, Marcia, and Paola Demattè. *China on Paper: European and Chinese Works from the Late Sixteenth to Early Nineteenth Century*. Los Angeles: Getty Research Institute, 2011.

Regmi, Dilli Ram. *Medieval Nepal*, vol. 2. New Delhi: Rupa, 2007 (1965).

Rehren, Thilo, and Ian C. Freestone. "Ancient Glass: From Kaleidoscope to Crystal Ball." *Journal of Archaeological Science* 56 (2015): 233–241.

Reid, A. "Islamization and Christianization in Southeast Asia: The Critical Phase, 1550–1650." In *Southeast Asia in the Early Modern Era: Trade, Power, and Belief*, edited by A. Reid, 151–179. Ithaca, NY: Cornell University Press, 1993.

Reischauer, Edwin O. *Ennin's Diary: The Record of a Pilgrimage to China in Search of the Law*. New York: Ronald Press, 1955.

Reynolds, Frank E. "The Holy Emerald Jewel: Some Aspects of Buddhist Symbolism and Political Legitimation in Thailand and Laos." In *Religion and Legitimation of Power in Thailand, Laos and Burma*, edited by Bardwell L. Smith, 175–193. Chambursburgh: Anima Books, 1978.

———. "The Many Lives of the Buddha." In *The Biographical Process: Studies in the History and Psychology of Religion*, edited by Frank E. Reynolds and Donald Capps, 37–62. The Hague: Mouton, 1970.

Reynolds Frank E., and Mani B. Reynolds, trans. *Three Worlds According to King Ruang: A Thai Buddhist Cosmology*. Berkeley: Asian Humanities Press, 1982.

Rhi, Juhyung. "Images, Relics, and Jewels: The Assimilation of Images in the Buddhist Relic Cult of Gandhāra: Or Vice Versa." *Artibus Asiae* 65, no. 2 (2005): 169–211.

Rhys Davids, T. W. *Dialogues of the Buddha*, 3 vols. London: Pali Text Society, 1890–1924.

Rhys Davids, T. W., and William Stede. *The Pali Text Society's Pali-English Dictionary*. Oxford: Pali Text Society, 1992 (1925).

Richardson, Sarah Aoife. "Painted Books for Plaster Walls: Visual Words in the Fourteenth-Century Murals at the Tibetan Buddhist Temple of Shalu." PhD diss., University of Toronto, 2016.

Rienjang, Wannaporn Kay. "Patronage along the Borderlands: The Case of the Apracas and Their Possible Connection with Nagarahara." Paper presented to the European Association for South Asian Archaeology and Art (EASAA) Conference, Naples, 2018.

———. "Honoring the Body: Relic Cult Practice in Eastern Afghanistan with Comparison to Dharmarajika Pakistan." PhD diss., University of Cambridge, 2017.

Rienjang, Wannaporn Kay, Jonathan Mark Kenoyer, and Margaret Sax. "Stone Beads from the Relic Deposits: A Preliminary Morphological and Technological Analysis." In *Charles Masson and the Buddhist Sites of Afghanistan: Explorations, Excavations, Collections 1833–1835,* edited by Elizabeth Errington, 52–57. London: British Museum, 2017.

Risso, P. *Merchants and Faith: Muslim Commerce and Culture in the Indian Ocean.* Boulder, CO: Westview, 1995.

Roeder, Eric. "The Origin and Significance of the Emerald Buddha." *Explorations in Southeast Asian Studies* 3 (1999): 1–24.

Rotman, Andy. *Divine Stories: The Divyāvadāna, part 1.* Boston: Wisdom Publications, 2008. Classics of Indian Buddhism, inaugural volume.

———. *Divine Stories: The Divyāvadāna, part 2.* Boston: Wisdom Publications, 2017.

———. "Marketing Morality: The Economy of Faith in Early Indian Buddhism." In *Śrīnidhiḥ: Professor Shrikant Shankar Bahulkar's Gratitude Volume,* edited by Shripad G. Bhat, Shilpa Sumant, and Ambarish Vasant Khare, 253–290. Pune: Saṁvidyā Institute of Cultural Studies, 2009.

———. *Thus Have I Seen: Visualizing Faith in Early Indian Buddhism.* New York: Oxford University Press, 2009.

Rubin, Gayle. "The Traffic in Women: Notes on the 'Political Economy' of Sex." In *Toward an Anthropology of Women,* edited by Rayna Reiter, 157–210. New York: Monthly Review Press, 1975.

Ruppert, Brian D. *Jewel in the Ashes: Buddha Relics and Power in Early Medieval Japan.* Cambridge, MA: Harvard University Press, 2000. Harvard East Asian Monographs 188.

———. "Pearl in the Shrine: A Genealogy of the Buddhist Jewel of the Japanese Sovereign." *Japanese Journal of Religious Studies* 29, nos. 1–2 (2002): 1–33.

———. "Relics and Relic Cults." In Buswell, *Encyclopedia of Buddhism,* 2:715–719. Sahgal, Smita. "Spread of Jinism in North India between circa 200 B.C. and circa A.D. 300." In *Jainism and Prakrit in Ancient and Medieval India,* edited by N. N. Bhattacharya, 205–232. Delhi: Manohar Publications, 1994.

Said, Edward. *Orientalism.* New York: Pantheon, 1979.

Sakai, Naoki. "Translation and the 'Figure of the Border: Toward the Apprehension of Translation as a Social Action." *Profession* (2010): 25–34.

Śākya, Hemrāj. *Mayūrvarṇa mahāvihāryā saṃkṣipta itihās.* Lalitpur: Bhiṃchem̐ bāhāyā sarvasaṃgha (2571 V.S.), 1973.

Śākya, Motilakṣmī. *Jhigu tisā, kāsā va bhvayghāsā (svanigaḥ nevāḥta madhyeyā svaṃgū jāti śākya, bajrācārya, udāsataygu)* [Our jewelry, games, and dishes (of three cases among the Newars of the Kathmandu Valley, the Śākyas, the Vajrācāryas, and the Urāys)]. Khvapa (Bhaktapur): Kutaḥ pikāk, 2016.

Salomon, Richard. "Observations on the Piprahwa Inscription and Its Epigraphic Context." Paper presented at Harewood House, Yorkshire, July 9, 2006.

Salvini, Mattia. "*Ratna:* A Buddhist World of Precious Things." In Ferrari and Dähnhardt, *Soulless Matter, Seats of Energy,* 219–254.

Sarcar, H., and B. N. Misra. *Nagarjunakonda.* Delhi: Archaeological Survey of India, 1972.

Sasson, Vanessa R. "The Buddha's 'Childhood': The Foundation for the Great Departure." In *Little Buddhas: Children and Childhoods in Buddhist Texts and Traditions,* edited by Vanessa R. Sasson, 75–96. New York: Oxford University Press, 2013.

———. "Stories of Excess: Abraham and Vessantara." In *To Fix Torah in Their Heart: Essays on Biblical Interpretation and Jewish Studies in Honor of B. Barry Levy,* edited by J. Du Toit et al., 171–198. Cincinnati: Hebrew Union College, 2018.

———. "Tales of the Emerald Buddha: Simplicity and Splendor." BuddhistDoor Global, June 18, 2019. https://www.buddhistdoor.net/features/tales-of-the-emerald-buddha-simplicity-and-splendor.

Sastri, Dwarikadas, ed. and trans. *Bodhicaryāvatāra of Ārya Śāntideva with the Commentary of Śri Prajñākarāmati.* Varanasi: Bauddha Bharati, 1988.

Saunders, E. Dale. *Mudrā: A Study of Symbolic Gestures in Japanese Buddhist Sculpture.* Princeton, NJ: Princeton University Press, 1960.

Sax, William. *Dancing the Self: Personhood and Performance in the Pandav Lila of Garhwal.* New York: Oxford University Press, 2002.

Schaeffer, Kurtis R. "The Fifth Dalai Lama Ngawang Lopsang Gyatso." In *The Dalai Lamas: A Visual History,* edited by Martin Brauen, 64–91. Chicago: Serindia Publications, 2005.

———. "The King's Canons." In *The Culture of the Book in Tibet,* 90–119. New York: Columbia University Press, 2009.

———. "Salt and the Sovereignty of the Dalai Lama." In *Images, Relics, and Legends: The Formation and Transformation of Buddhist Sacred Sites*, edited by James Benn, Jinhua Chen, and James Robson, 298–322. Oakville, Ontario: Mosaic Press, 2012.

Schafer, Edward H. *The Divine Woman: Dragon Ladies and Rain Maidens*. San Francisco: North Point Press, 1980.

———. *The Golden Peaches of Samarkand: A Study of T'ang Exotica*. Berkeley: University of California Press, 1963.

Schonfeld, Martin. "Was There a Western Inventor of Porcelain?" *Technology and Culture* 39, no. 4 (October 1998): 716–727.

Schopen, Gregory. "Archaeology and Protestant Presuppositions in the Study of Indian Buddhism." *History of Religions* 31, no. 1 (1991) :1–23.

———. *Bones, Stones, and Buddhist Monks: Collected Papers on the Archaeology, Epigraphy, and Texts of Monastic Buddhism in India*. Honolulu: University of Hawai'i Press, 1997.

———. "Burial *Ad Sanctos* and the Physical Presence of the Buddha in Early Indian Buddhism: A Study in the Archaeology of Religions." *Religion* 17 (1987): 193–225.

———. "Burial *Ad Sanctos* and the Physical Presence of the Buddha." In Schopen, *Bones, Stones, and Buddhist Monks*, 114–147.

———. "Dead Monks and Bad Debts: Some Provisions of a Buddhist Monastic Inheritance Law." *Indo-Iranian Journal* 44 (2001): 99–148.

———. "The Lay Ownership of Monasteries and the Role of the Monk in Mūlasārvāstivādin Monasticism." *Journal of the International Association of Buddhist Studies* 19, no. 1 (1996): 81–126.

———. "Monks and the Relic Cult in the Mahaparinibbana-sutta: An Old Misunderstanding in Regard to Monastic Buddhism." In *From Benares to Beijing: Essays on Buddhism and Chinese Religion*, edited by Koichi Shinohara and Gregory Schopen, 187–201. Oakville, Ontario: Mosaic Press, 1991.

———. "Relic." In *Critical Terms for Religious Studies*, edited by Mark C. Taylor, 256–268. Chicago: University of Chicago Press, 1998.

———. "The Stūpa Cult and the Extant Pali Vinaya." *Journal of the Pali Text Society* 13 (1989): 83–100.

Schur Narula, Karen. *Voyage of the Emerald Buddha*. Kuala Lumpur: Oxford University Press, 1994.

Schwieger, Peter. *The Dalai Lama and the Emperor of China: A Political History of the Tibetan Institution of Reincarnation*. New York: Columbia University Press, 2015.

Sde srid Sangs rgyas rgya mtsho. *Drin can rtsa ba'i bla ma ngag dbang blo bzang rgya mtsho'i thun mong gi rnam thar du kū la'i gos bzang glegs bam gsum pa'i pa'i 'phros*. Vols. 8–10 of Tā la'i bla ma V Ngag dbang blo bzang rgya mtsho, *Rgyal dbang lnga pa Ngag dbang blo bzang rgya mtsho'i gsung 'bum* [Collected works of the fifth victorious Lord Ngawang Lobzang Gyatso]. Beijing: Krung go'i bod rig pa dpe skrun khang, 2009.

———. *Life of the Fifth Dalai Lama*, vol. 4, part 1. Translated by Zahiruddin Ahmad. New Delhi: International Academy of Indian Culture, 1999. Śata-Piṭaka Series 392.

———. *Mchod sdong 'dzam gling rgyan gcig rten gtsug lag khang dang bcas pa'i dkar chag thar gling rgya mtshor bgrod pa'i gru rdzings byin rlabs kyi bang mdzod: A Detailed Account of the Funeral Ceremonies and Entombment Rites of the Fifth Dalai Lama Ṅag-dbaṅ-blo-bzaṅ-rgya-mtsho*. 2 vols. New Delhi: T. Tsepal Taikhang, 1973. TBRC W8223.

Seeger, Martin. *Gender and the Path to Awakening: Hidden Histories of Nuns in Modern Thailand*. Chiang Mai: Silkworm, 2018.

Sen, Tansen. *Buddhism, Diplomacy, and Trade: The Realignment of Sino-Indian Relations, 600–1400*. Honolulu: University of Hawai'i Press, 2003.

Seneviratne, H. L. *The Work of Kings: The New Buddhism in Sri Lanka*. Chicago: University of Chicago Press, 1999.

Shakabpa, Tsepon Wangchuk Deden. *One Hundred Thousand Moons: An Advanced Political History of Tibet*, 2 vols. Translated and annotated by Derek F. Maher. Leiden: Brill, 2010.

Shapin, Steven. *A Social History of Truth: Civility and Science in Seventeenth-Century England*. Chicago: University of Chicago Press, 1994.

Sharf, Robert H. "The Buddha's Finger Bones at Famensi and the Art of Chinese Esoteric Buddhism." *Art Bulletin* 93, no. 1 (2011): 38–59.

———. "On Pure Land Buddhism and Ch'an/Pure Land Syncretism in Medieval China," *T'oung Pao* 88, nos. 4–5 (2003): 282–331.

———. "On the Allure of Buddhist Relics." *Representations* 66 (1999): 75–99.

———. "Visualization and Mandala in Shingon Buddhism." In *Living Images: Japanese Buddhist Icons in Context*, edited by Robert H. Sharf and Elizabeth Horton Sharf, 157–166. Stanford, CA: Stanford University Press, 2001.

Sharma, Ram Sharan. *Aspects of Political Ideas and Institutions in Ancient India*, 4th rev. ed. Delhi: Motilal Banarsidass, 1996 (1959).

———. *Urban Decay in India (c. 300–c. 1000)*. Delhi: Munshiram Manoharlal, 1987.

Shastri, Lobsang. "Activities of Indian Paṇḍitas in Tibet from the 14th to the 17th Century." In *Tibet, Past and Present: Tibetan Studies I: PIATS 2000: Tibetan Studies: Proceedings of the Ninth Seminar of the International Association for Tibetan Studies, Leiden, 2000,* edited by Henk Blezer, 129–145. Leiden: Brill, 2002.

Shen, Hsueh-Man. Honolulu: University of Hawa'ii Press, 2018.

———. "Luxury or Necessity: Glassware in Sarīra Relic Pagodas of the Tang and Northern Song Periods." In Braghin, *Chinese Glass,* 71–110.

Shepard, Joyce W. "Symbolic Space in Newar Culture." PhD diss., University of Michigan, 1985.

Shi, Zhiru. "From Bodily Relic to Dharma Relic Stūpa: Chinese Materialization of the Aśoka Legend in the Wuyue Period." In Kieschnick and Shahar, *India in the Chinese Imagination,* 83–109.

Shimada, Akira. *Early Buddhist Architecture in Context: The Great Stūpa at Amarāvatī (ca. 300 BCE–300 CE).* Leiden: Brill, 2013.

Shinohara, Koichi. *Spells, Images, and Maṇḍalas: Tracing the Evolution of Esoteric Buddhist Rituals.* New York: Columbia University Press, 2014.

Shortland, Andrew J. *Lapis Lazuli from the Kiln: Glass and Glassmaking in the Late Bronze Age.* Leuven: Leuven University Press, 2012.

Shulman, David. *God Inside Out: Siva's Game of Dice.* New York: Oxford University Press, 1997.

Siderits, Mark, and Shoryu Katsura, trans. *Nāgārjuna's Middle Way* [*Mūlamadhyamakakārikā*]. Boston: Wisdom Publications, 2013.

Sircar, D. C. *Select Inscriptions Bearing on Indian History and Civilization,* vol. 1. Calcutta: University of Calcutta, 1942.

———. "Some Brahmi Inscriptions." *Epigraphia Indica* 34 (1961–1962): 207–212.

Sirhandi, Marcella. *Royal Nepal through the Lens of Richard Gordon Matzene.* Chicago: Serindia Publications, 2009.

Sizemore, Russell F., and Donald K. Swearer, eds. *Ethics, Wealth and Salvation: A Study in Buddhist Social Ethics.* Columbia: University of South Carolina Press, 1992.

Skilling, Peter. "The Rakṣā Literature of the Śrāvakayāna." *Journal of the Pali Text Society* 16 (1992): 109–182.

———. "Relics: The Heart of Buddhist Veneration." In *Relics and Relic Worship in Early Buddhism,* edited by Janice Stargardt, 1–11. London: British Museum Press, 2018.

Smith, Vincent A. *The Jain Stupa and Other Antiquaries of Mathura.* Varanasi: Indological Book House, 1969 (1901). Archaeological Survey of India Reports.

———. "The Piprāhwā Stūpa." *Journal of the Royal Asiatic Society,* 1898, 868–870.

Snodgrass, Adrian. *The Matrix and Diamond World Mandalas in Shingon Buddhism,* 2 vols. New Delhi: Aditya Prakashan, 1988.

Sørensen, Per K. "Restless Relic: The Ārya Lokeśvara Icon in Tibet: Symbol of Power, Legitimacy and Pawn for Patronage." In *Pramāṇakīrtiḥ: Papers Dedicated to Ernst Steinkellner on the Occasion of His 70th Birthday,* edited by Birgit Kellner et al., 2:857–885. Vienna: Arbeitskreis für Tibetische und Buddhistische Studien, Universität Wien, 2007.

Spence, Jonathan. *Return to Dragon Mountain: Memories of a Late Ming Man.* New York: Viking, 2010.

Srivastava, K. M. *Buddha's Relics from Kapilavastu.* Delhi: Agam Kala Prakashan, 1986.

Staal, Frits. *Rules without Meaning: Ritual, Mantras and the Human Sciences.* New York: Peter Lang, 1989.

Stevenston, Daniel B. "Death-Bed Testimonials of the Pure Land Faithful." In *Buddhism in Practice,* edited by Donald S. Lopez, 592–602. Princeton, NJ: Princeton University Press, 1995.

Stewart, Susan. *On Longing: Narratives of the Miniature, the Gigantic, the Souvenir, the Collection.* Durham, NC: Duke University Press, 1992.

Stone, Elizabeth Rosen. *The Buddhist Art of Nāgārjunakoṇḍa.* Delhi: Motilal Banarsidass, 1994.

Stone, Jacqueline I. *Right Thoughts at the Last Moment: Buddhism and Deathbed Practices in Early Medieval Japan.* Honolulu: University of Hawai'i Press, 2016.

Strickmann, Michel. *Chinese Magical Medicine.* Edited by Bernard Faure. Stanford, CA: Stanford University Press, 2002.

———. "Homa in East Asia." In *Agni: The Vedic Ritual of the Fire Altar,* edited by Fritz Staal, 2:418–455. Berkeley: Asian Humanities Press, 1983.

Strong, John S. "The Afterlives of Buddhist Relics." Paper presented to the Lee and Won Buddhist Studies Workshop, Seoul, September 8, 2017.

———. *The Buddha: A Short Biography.* New York: Oneworld, 2001.

———. "The Buddha's Funeral." In *The Buddhist Dead,* edited by Jacqueline Stone and Bryan Cuevas, 32–51. Honolulu: University of Hawai'i Press, 2007.

———. *The Legend of King Aśoka: A Study and Translation of the Aśokāvadāna.* Princeton, NJ: Princeton University Press, 2014.

———. "Relics and Images." In *Oxford Handbook of Buddhist Practice,* edited by Paula Arai and Kevin Trainor. New York: Oxford University Press, forthcoming.

———. *Relics of the Buddha.* Princeton, NJ: Princeton University Press, 2004.

Sumangalavilāsinī: Buddhaghosa's Commentary on the Dīgha Nikāya, 2nd ed. Edited by William Stede. London: Pali Text Society, 1971.

Swearer, Donald K. *Becoming the Buddha: The Ritual of Image Consecration in Thailand.* Princeton, NJ: Princeton University Press, 2004.

———. "Hypostasizing the Buddha: Buddha Image Consecration in Northern Thailand." *History of Religions* 34, no. 3 (1995): 263–280.

Takakusu, J., trans. *A Record of the Buddhist Religion as Practiced in India and the Malay Archipelago (A.D. 671–695),* by Yijing (635–713). Oxford: Clarendon Press, 1896.

Takatoshi, Soeda. "Nyoirin Kannon soyaku goma shiki shidai." In vol. 24 of *Goma Zenshū,* 66 vols. Osaka: Tōhō Shuppan, 1982.

Tarocco, Francesca. "Charismatic Communications: The Intimate Publics of Chinese Buddhism." In *Concepts and Methods for the Study of Chinese Religions III: Key Concepts in Practice,* edited by S. Trevagnin and P. Katz, 113–132. Berlin: De Gruyter, 2019.

Taylor, J. L. *Forest Monks and the Nation-State.* Singapore: ISEAS, 1993.

Teiser, Stephen. "Ornamenting the Departed: Notes on the Language of Chinese Buddhist Ritual Texts." *Asia Major,* 3rd series, vol. 22, no. 1 (2009): 201–237.

Thakur, Vijay Kumar. *Urbanisation in Ancient India.* New Delhi: Abhinav Publications, 1981.

Thapar, Romila. *Sakuntala: Texts, Readings, Histories.* New Delhi: Kali for Women, 1999.

Theg pa chen po rgyud bla ma'i bstan bcos rnam par bshad pa (Mahāyānottaratantraśāstra-vyākhyā). Tōh. 4025. In *Sde dge bstan 'gyur,* vol. 123 (phi), 148–257=74b–129a. Delhi: Delhi Karmapae Choedhey, 1986.

Thompson, Stith. *Motif-Index of Folk Literature,* 6 vols. Bloomington: Indiana University Press, 1955–1958.

Tibetan Administrative Office of the Potala, ed. *The Potala: Holy Palace in the Snow Land.* Beijing: China Travel and Tourism Press, 1996.

Tinsley, Elizabeth. "Kūkai and the Development of Shingon Buddhism." In *Esoteric Buddhism and the Tantras in East Asia,* edited by Charles D. Orzech, Henrik Hjort Sørensen, and Richard Karl Payne, 691–708. Leiden: Brill, 2011. Handbook of Oriental Studies, vol. 24, section 4, China.

Townsend, Dominique. "Materials of Buddhist Culture: Aesthetics and Cosmopolitanism at Mindroling Monastery." PhD diss., Columbia University, 2012.

Trainor, Kevin. *Relics, Ritual, and Representation in Buddhism: Rematerializing the Sri Lankan Theravāda Tradition*. Cambridge: Cambridge University Press, 1997.

Trenson, Steven. "Rice, Relics, and Jewels: The Network and Agency of Rice Grains in Medieval Japanese Esoteric Buddhism." *Japanese Journal of Religious Studies* 45, no. 2 (2018): 269–307.

Trilling, James. *Ornament: A Modern Perspective*. Seattle: University of Washington Press, 2003.

Trivedi, Sushma. "Impact of Trade on Early Art of India (circa 200 B.C.–300 A.D.)." *Journal of the Asiatic Society of Bombay* 70 (1995): 151–158.

Trivellato, Francesca. *Fondamenta dei Vetrai: Lavoro, tecnologia e mercato a Venezia tra sei e Settecento*. Rome: Donzelli, 2000.

Tulādhar, Premśānti. *Nepalbhāṣā sahityayā itihāsa* (The history of Nepalbhasa literature). Yem̐ (Kathmandu): Nepālbhāṣā ekedami, 2000.

Tuladhar-Douglas, Will. *Remaking Buddhism for Medieval Nepal: The Fifteenth-Century Reformation of Newar Buddhism*. Abingdon: Routledge, 2006.

Uesugi Akinori, and Wannaporn Kay Rienjang. "Stone Beads from Stupa Relic Deposits at the Dharmarajika Buddhist Complex, Taxila." *Gandhāran Studies* 11 (2018): 53–83.

Ullrey, Aaron Michael. "Grim Grimoires: Practical Ritual in the Magic Tantras." PhD diss., University of California, Santa Barbara, 2016.

Union Bouddhiste de France. "Les Reliques de l'Inde en France, via la Thaïlande." http://www.bouddhisme-france.org/reliques/article/le-contexte-historique.html. 2009.

Vaidya, Janak Lāl, and Prem Bahādur Kaṃsakar, eds. *Āśā saphū kuthiyā abhilekh granthayā varṇātmak dhalaḥ* (A descriptive catalogue of selected manuscripts preserved at the Āśā Saphū Kuthi [Āśā Archives]). Kathmandu: Cvasāpāsā, 1991.

Vaidya, P. L., ed. *Avadānakalpalatā*. Darbhanga, Bihar: Mithila Institute, 1959.

———. *Lalitavistara*. Darbhanga, Bihar: Mithila Institute, 1958.

van Buitenen, J. A. B. *Tales of Ancient India*. Chicago: University of Chicago Press, 1959.

Vatsyayana. *Kamasutra*. Translated by Wendy Doniger and Sudhir Kakar. Oxford: Oxford University Press, 2002. Oxford's World Classics.

Vātsyāyana. *Kāmasūtra*. With the commentary of Śrī Yaśodhara. Bombay: Laksmivenkatesvara Steam Press, 1856.

Veyne, Paul. *Bread and Circuses: Historical Sociology and Political Pluralism*. Translated by Brian Pearce. London: Penguin Books, 1990.

Viśakhadatta, *Mudrārākṣasa*. Translated by M. R. Kale. Delhi: Motilal Banarsidass, 2011.

Waddell, L. Austine. *Lhasa and Its Mysteries: A Record of the Expedition of 1903–1904*. New York: E. P. Dutton, 1905.

Walshe, Maurice, trans. *Thus Have I Heard: The Long Discourses of the Buddha [Digha-nikāya]*. Boston: Wisdom Publications, 1987.

Walters, Jonathan S. "Stūpa, Story, and Empire: Constructions of the Buddha Biography in Early Post-Aśokan India." In *Sacred Biography in the Buddhist Traditions of South and Southeast Asia*, edited by Juliane Schober, 160–192. Honolulu: University of Hawai'i Press, 1997.

Wang, Eugene. "Of the True Body." In *Body and Face in Chinese Visual Culture*, edited by Wu Hung and Katherine Mino, 79–118. Cambridge, MA: Harvard University Press, 2004.

———. "Tope and Topos: The Leifeng Pagoda and the Discourse of the Demonic." In *Writing and Materiality in China*, ed. Judith Zeitlin and Lydia Liu, 488–552. Cambridge, MA: Harvard University Press.

Wang, Yi-t'ung. *Record of the Buddhist Monasteries in Loyang*. Princeton, NJ: Princeton University Press, 1984.

Wang-Genh, Olivier Reigen. "L'installation des reliques du Bouddha à la Pagode de Vincennes est une grande joie pour tous les bouddhistes de France." http://www.bouddhisme-france.org/reliques/article/l-installation-des-reliques-du-bouddha-a-la-pagode-de-vincennes-est-une-grande-joie-pour-tous-les-bouddhistes-de-france-rev-olivier-reigen-wang-genh.html.

Ware, James. "Wei Shou on Buddhism." *T'oung Pao* 30 (1933): 100–181.

Warmington, E. H. *The Commerce between the Roman Empire and India*. London: Curzon Press, 1974.

Welch, Holmes. *The Practice of Chinese Buddhism: 1900–1950*. Cambridge, MA: Harvard University Press, 1967.

Wheeler, Mortimer. *Rome beyond the Imperial Frontiers*. London: Bell, 1954.

White, David Gordon. *Kiss of the Yoginī: "Tantric Sex" in Its South Asian Contexts*. Chicago: University of Chicago Press, 2003.

Whitfield, S., and Ursula Sims-Williams. *The Silk Road: Trade, Travel War and Faith*. London: British Library, 2004.

Willis, Michael. "Dhār, Bhoja and Sarasvatī: From Indology to Political Mythology and Back." *Journal of the Royal Asiatic Society*, 2012, 129–153.

———. "Review of Harry Falk, *Aśokan Sites and Artefacts*." *Journal of the Royal Asiatic Society*, 2012, 187–188.

Wojtilla, Gyula. "Indian Precious Stones in the Ancient East and West." *Acta Orientalia Academiae Scientiarum Hungaricae* 27, no. 2 (1973): 211–224.

———. "Ratnaśāstra in Kauṭilya's *Arthaśāstra.*" *Acta Orientalia Academiae Scientiarum Hungaricae* 62, no. 1 (2009): 37–44.

Wood, Ernst, and S. V. Subrahmanyam, trans. *Garuḍa Purāṇa (Sāroddhāra).* Allahabad: Sudhindra Nath Vasu, 1911.

Wu, Hung. "Buddhist Elements in Early Chinese Art (2nd and 3rd Centuries A.D.)." *Artibus Asiae* 47, nos. 3–4 (1986): 263–303, 305–352.

Xia Weizhong 夏維中, et al. "Nanjing Tianxi si de yange 南京天禧寺的沿革." *Jiangsu Social Sciences* 江苏社會科學 3 (2010): 229–236.

Xu Shangtian. *Jinling sishiba jing* 金陵四十八景. Nanjing: Nanjing chubanshe, 2012 (1910).

Xuxiu Siku quanshu [A continuation of the *Imperial Library of the Four Treasuries*]. Shanghai: Shanghai guji chubanshe, 1995–2002.

Xuyun. *Empty Cloud: The Autobiography of the Chinese Zen Master.* Translated by Charles Luk. Longmead: Element Books, 1988.

Yamasaki, Taikō. *Shingon: Japanese Esoteric Buddhism,* 1st ed. Edited by Yasuyoshi Morimoto and David Kidd. Translated by Richard Peterson and Cynthia Peterson. Boston: Shambhala, 1988.

Yang-Gyu, An. *The Buddha's Last Days: Buddhaghosa's Commentary on the Mahāparinibbāna Sutta.* Oxford: Oxford University Press, 2003.

Yetts, W. Perceval. "Notes on the Disposal of the Buddhist Dead in China." *Journal of the Royal Asiatic Society of Great Britain and Ireland,* July 1911, 699–725.

Yü, Chün-fang. *Kuan-yin: The Chinese Transformation of Avalokiteśvara.* New York: Columbia University Press, 2001.

———. "Guanyin: The Chinese Transformation of Avalokiteshvara." In *Latter Days of the Law: Images of Chinese Buddhism 850–1850,* edited by Marsha Weidner, 151–181. Honolulu: University of Hawai'i Press, 1994.

Zhang Dai 張岱. *Taoan mengyi pingzhu* 陶庵夢憶 評註. Annotated by Huai Min 淮茛 Shanghai: Sanlian shudian, 2013.

Zhang Huiyi 張惠衣. *Jinling Da Bao'ensi ta zhi* 金陵大報恩寺塔志. Beijing: Guoli Beiping yanjiu shi xue yan jiu hui, 1937.

Zhao Juan. "Yiyu guankan: Jindai Ouren jizaizhong de Zhongguo baota—er, san, shi 异域观看:近代欧人记载中的 "中国宝塔" 二三事." *Zhongguo wenhua huabao* 中华文化画报 5 (2018): 90–95.

Zhuge, Jing. "From Historical Monument to Urban Spectacle: Case Study on the Great Bao'en Pagoda Reconstruction Project." In *Architecture RePerformed: The Politics of Reconstruction,* edited by Tino Mager, 117–136. Surrey: Ashgate, 2015.

Zimmer, Heinrich R. *Myths and Symbols in Indian Art and Civilization.* New York: Pantheon, 1946.

Zin, Monika. *The Kanaganahalli Stūpa: An Analysis of the 60 Massive Slabs Covering the Dome.* New Delhi: Aryan Books International, 2018.

Zubrzycki, John. *The Mysterious Mr. Jacob: Diamond Merchant, Magician, and Spy.* Gurgaon: Penguin India, 2012.

Zumbaulyadis, Nicholas. "Bottger's Eureka: New Insights into the European Reinvention of Porcelain." *Bulletin for the History of Chemistry* 35, no. 1 (2010): 24–32.

Zürcher, Erik. *The Buddhist Conquest of China: The Spread and Adaptation of Buddhism in Early Medieval China.* Leiden: Brill, 1959.

Contributors

Casey Collins is currently a PhD candidate in Asian studies at the University of British Columbia, focusing on modern Japanese Buddhism and Japanese new religious movements. Collins's work engages with the history of Shingon Buddhism during the interwar years, including the appearance of charismatic religious leaders who went on to found independent lay movements.

Wendy Doniger [O'Flaherty] is the Mircea Eliade Distinguished Service Professor Emerita of the History of Religions at the University of Chicago and the author of over forty books, most recently *The Hindus: An Alternative History* (2010); *Hinduism,* in the Norton Anthology of World Religions (2014); *The Ring of Truth: Tales of Sex and Jewelry* (2017); *Against Dharma* (2018); and *The Donigers of Great Neck: A Mythologized Memoir* (2019).

Christoph Emmrich is a Newarologist, Burmologist, Indologist, and associate professor of Buddhist Studies at the University of Toronto, where he has been teaching Newar, Burmese, Pali, Buddhist, and Jain Studies since 2006. When he does not teach, he divides his time between Lalitpur among the Newar Buddhists, Mawlamyine and Mandalay among the Mons and Burmese Brahmins, and Pondicherry among the Tamil Jains, conducting research on rites and ritual literature, shopkeeping, and list making. His monograph *Writing Rites for Newar Girls* is forthcoming with Brill.

Maria Heim is the George Lyman Crosby 1896 and Stanley Warfield Crosby Professor in Religion at Amherst College. She works on Pali and Sanskrit texts and has published numerous articles and four books, the most recent of which are *Voice of the Buddha: Buddhaghosa on the Immeasurable Words* (2018) and *Buddhist Ethics* (2020). She received a

Guggenheim Foundation Fellowship in 2005. Her current interests focus on emotions in classical Indian texts.

Ellen Huang is assistant professor of Material Culture, Art, and Technology at the Art Center College of Design (Pasadena, CA). She is also a curator, having organized exhibitions for the Ackland Art Museum at UNC Chapel Hill, Stanford University's Center for East Asian Studies, Cantor Arts Center, and the University of San Francisco. Her publications include essays about ink painting, technical illustrations, and ceramic production. She is finishing a manuscript about Jingdezhen porcelain as material in late imperial Chinese and global history.

Nancy G. Lin is a visiting scholar at the Center for Buddhist Studies, University of California at Berkeley. She has published essays on the cultural history of Tibetan Buddhism, literature, and art. Her current book project is a study of worldly Buddhists and courtly cultures of early modern Tibet. She previously taught at Dartmouth College and Vanderbilt University.

Richard K. Payne is Yehan Numata Professor of Japanese Buddhist Studies at the Institute of Buddhist Studies, Berkeley. His area of research is tantric Buddhist ritual, with particular focus on the *homa* both in the Shingon tradition of Japan and across the Buddhist cosmopolis. His research has also included the use of mantra in Shingon and the interface of tantric Buddhism and Pure Land. He has published in each of these areas and is editor-in-chief of the Oxford Bibliographies/Buddhism (online, ongoing), and co-editor-in-chief, along with Georgios Halkias, of the *Oxford Encyclopedia of Buddhism* (online, ongoing, and in print, forthcoming).

Andy Rotman is professor of religion, Buddhism, and South Asian Studies at Smith College. His publications include *Divine Stories: Translations from the Divyāvadāna*, part 1 and part 2 (2008, 2017), *Thus Have I Seen: Visualizing Faith in Early Indian Buddhism* (2009), and a coauthored volume, *Amar Akbar Anthony: Bollywood, Brotherhood, and the Nation* (2015). He has been engaged in textual and ethnographic work on religious and social life in South Asia for more than twenty-five years.

Vanessa R. Sasson is a professor of religious studies in the Liberal Arts Department of Marianopolis College, where she has been teaching since 1999. She is also a research fellow at the University of the Free State and research member at CERIAS for UQAM. She is the author and/or editor of a number of books. Most recently, she launched a novel entitled *Yasodhara and the Buddha* (Bloomsbury, 2021). Her research interests are focused on women, children, and hagiography.

John S. Strong is Charles A. Dana Emeritus Professor of Religious Studies at Bates College in Lewiston, Maine. During his time at Bates, he held visiting professorships at the University of Peradeniya (1987), the University of Chicago (1995), Princeton University (1997), Harvard University (2002), and Stanford University (2003). He is the author of a number of books, including *The Legend and Cult of Upagupta* (1992), *Relics of the Buddha* (2004), *Buddhisms: An Introduction* (2015), and *The Buddha's Tooth* (2021).

Francesca Tarocco is associate professor of Chinese religion and Buddhist Studies at Ca' Foscari University of Venice and visiting professor of Buddhist Cultures at New York University, Shanghai. Her area of research is Buddhist cultural and intellectual history, with particular focus on late imperial and modern China. This research has led to the publication of *The Cultural Practices of Modern Chinese Buddhism* (2008), the forthcoming *Altar Modern: Buddhism and Technology in China,* and several articles and book chapters. She is associate editor for China of the *Oxford Encyclopedia of Buddhism.*

Index

Page numbers in **boldface** type refer to figures.